D1729147

INTRODUCTION TO SWISS LAW

Third Edition

General Editors of the Series: Tuğrul Ansay and Don Wallace, Jr.

Introduction to Greek Law (second edition 1993)
Introduction to the Law of Israel (1995)
Introduction to German Law (1996)
Introduction to Turkish Law (fourth edition 1996)
Introduction to Hungarian Law (1998)
Introduction to Belgian Law (2001)
Introduction to the Law of the United States (second edition 2002)
Introduction to Italian Law (2002)
Introduction to the Law of South Africa (2004)
Introduction to Swiss Law (third edition 2004)

Introduction to Swiss Law

Third Edition

Edited by
F. Dessemontet
and
T. Ansay

KLUWER LAW INTERNATIONAL

GENERAL EDITORS OF THE SERIES

Tuğrul Ansay,
Professor of Law, Koç University, İstanbul
and

Don Wallace, Jr.
Professor of Law, Georgetown University, Director
International Law Institute, Washington, D.C.

Published by:
Kluwer Law International
P.O. Box 85889
2508 CN The Hague
The Netherlands

Sold and distributed in Switzerland by:
Schulthess Juristische Medien AG
Zwingliplatz 2
CH-8022 Zürich
Switzerland

Sold and distributed in North,
Central and South America by:
Aspen Publishers, Inc.
7201 McKinney Circle
Frederick, MD 21704
USA

Sold and distributed in all other countries by:
Extenza-Turpin Distribution Services
Stratton Business Park
Pegasus Drive
Biggleswade
Bedfordshire SG18 8QB
United Kingdom

Library of Congress Cataloging-in-Publication Data

Introduction to Swiss law / edited by F. Dessemontet and T. Ansay. -- 3rd ed.
   p. cm.
   Includes bibliographical references and index.
   ISBN 90-411-2260-5 (alk. paper)
    1. Law -- Switzerland. I. Dessemontet, François. II. Ansay, Tugrul.

KKW68.I58 2004

349.494 -- dc22   2004048408

Printed on acid-free paper

ISBN 90 411 22605 (Kluwer)
ISBN 3-7255-4739-4 (Schulthess: for distribution in Switzerland only)

© 2004 Kluwer Law International

Table of Contents

Chapter 13. Labor Law 233
Rémy Wyler

GENERAL INTRODUCTION

It is the intention that the following work is to be a part of the series of introductory books to the laws of various countries. The whole project is intended to prepare books which follow basically the same plan for each country. The books in the series are not designed to be definitive texts of the law of any country. Rather, they will attempt to provide academics, lawyers, businessmen, administrators, government officials, students and others with the basic knowledge of legal concepts of the country in broader terms, with special emphasis on practical issues, so that the interested persons will be able to understand the system and pursue research on special legal problems by knowing the proper questions to ask and the proper place to find the answer.

General Editors:

Tugrul Ansay,
Dr. jur., M.C.L., LL.M.,
Professor of Law
Dean of the Law School,
Koç University, İstanbul

Don Wallace, Jr.,
Professor of Law and Director,
International Law Institute,
Georgetown University

ACKNOWLEDGEMENTS

As a part of the series of 'Introduction' books this volume intends to give a general background on Swiss law to English-speaking lawyers and other interested readers.

During the preparation of the book we found encouraging the support of various persons and institutions. We should like to express a particular gratitude to the authors of the various chapters, who were willing to present vast fields of the Swiss law in a few pages, which was a difficult task, and who accepted the adjustments that were required by editors working on the basis of principles laid down for the entire series, which entailed even more work for the authors, especially for this third edition. The texts of this edition were partly prepared before 30 September 2002. New developments occurring after that date could not, therefore, be taken into account in a systematic way, although some of them are mentioned. However, this new edition includes all the substantial changes in various legal fields resulting from the new Swiss Federal Constitution enacted on 18 April 1999.

We express again our thankfulness to Mr. Peter B. Whitten, Director of Publishing of the International Law Institute of the Georgetown University Law Center in Washington, D.C., who has helped us in editing the first edition.

Alan Ragueneau and Raphael Gani, assistants at the Faculty of Law of Lausanne University, have been utmost helpful in the revision of the final texts.

Tuğrul Ansay
Dean of the Law School, Koç University
İstanbul

François Dessemontet
University of Lausanne

ABBREVIATIONS

Am.J.Comp.L.	American Journal of Comparative Law, Berkeley, California
APLA Q.J.	APLA Quarterly Journal, Arlington, Virginia
Art.	Article
AS	Official compilation of Federal Laws and Decrees
ATF	Official compilation of Judgments of the Federal Tribunal
Austl.Tax Rev.	Australian Tax Review, Sydney, Australia
BB	Bundesblatt/Feuille Fédérale
BG	Bundesgesetz (Federal Law)
BGE	Official compilation of Judgments of the Federal Tribunal
CC	Civil Code
CCP	Code of Civil Procedure
CCrP	Code of Criminal Procedure
Cf.	Compare
CO	Code of Obligations
Comp.	Compare
Cons.	Constitution
CPS	Swiss Penal Code
ECHR	European Convention on Human Rights.
FC	Federal Constitution
FF	Bundesblatt/Feuille Fédérale
Ind.& Lab.Rel.Rev.	Industrial and Labor Relations Review, Cornell Univ., Ithaca, New York
Int'l Bus.Law.	International Business Lawyer, Deventer, The Netherlands
Int'l Org.	International Organization, Madison, Wiconsin
JAAC	Jurisprudence des autorités administratives de la Confédération/Verwaltungspraxis der Bundesbehörden
JT	Journal des tribunaux
J. World Trade L.	Journal of World Trade Law, Twickenham, England
LCD	Fed. Law on Unfair Competition
LCR	Law on Road Traffic
La.L.Rev.	Louisiana Law Review, Baton Rouge, Louisiana
LEA	Law on Pacific Use of Atomic Energy
NRS	Systematic compilation of Federal Laws and Decrees
OR	Code of Obligations
Par.	Paragraph
PC	Swiss Penal Code
PILS	Federal Statute on Private International Law
RDS	Revue de droit suisse
RJB	Revue de la Société des juristes bernois
ROLF	Official compilation of Federal Laws and Decrees
RPS	Revue pénale suisse
RSJ	Revue suisse de jurisprudence

RS	Systematic compilation of Federal Laws and Decrees
RSPI	Revue suisse de la propriété intellectuelle
SJZ	Schweizerische Juristen-Zeitung
SPC	Swiss Penal Code
SR	Systematic compilation of Federal Laws and Decrees
SVG	Law on Road Traffic
VPB	Jurisprudence des autorités administrative de la Confédération/Verwaltungspraxis der Bundesbehörden
ZBJV	Zeitschrift des Bernischen Juristenvereins
ZBL	Zentralblatt für Staats- und Gemeindeverwaltung
ZGB	Civil Code
ZSR	Zeitschrift für schweizerisches Recht
ZStrR	Schweizerische Zeitschrift für Strafrecht

Chapter 1
Introduction[1]

*Joseph Voyame**

I. OVERVIEW OF SWISS HISTORY AND POLITICAL INSTITUTIONS

A. *Birth, Growing Pains*

The Swiss Confederation dates back to a diplomatic act – the freely negotiated 'everlasting' alliance (*Charte federale/Bundes brief*) signed on 1 August 1291, by three small communities: Uri, Schwyz and Nidwalden.

It is interesting to speculate on the nature of the society and the legal institutions revealed by this document. There are suggestions of communal democracy: the parties are 'the men of Uri, the corporate body (*universitas*) of Schwyz, the community or commune (*communitas hominum*) of Nidwalden'. It is a mutual assistance agreement aimed at protecting life and property against internal or external aggression. It contains confederate criminal provisions, the death penalty for murder, banishment and confiscation for other offenses, by virtue, we would say today, of federal law to be applied by the local courts of the valleys. It declares that 'we have unanimously decreed that we will accept no judge in our valleys who shall have obtained his office for a price, or who is not a native and resident among us.'[2] Respect for the law is the main feature of this treaty. While determined to organize their social order themselves, feuds and vengeance were abandoned in favor of the process of justice.

This alliance was confirmed and somewhat elaborated in 1315 by the Brunnen Alliance *(Pacte de Brunnen/Morgartenbrief)*.

The nucleus of allies soon grew from the original three to eight through military, arbitration and mutual assistance treaties with Lucerne (1332), Zurich (1351), Glarus (1352) Zug (1352) and Berne (1353). It was not until one-and-a-half centuries later that five new members were admitted, one by one, into this Confederation: Fribourg and Solothurn (1481), Basle and Schaffhausen (1501) and Appenzell (1513).

Although the number of cantons remained stable for nearly three centuries, the Confederation continued to grow. There were the 'outside allies' (*Verbündete,*

---

* Former Director, Federal Office of Justice, Berne, Switzerland.
1. I am indebted to Ms. Arlene Weingart, my assistant at the Federal Office of Justice, for the important part she played in the writing of this introduction.
2. M. Salamin, *Documents d'histoire suisse 1240–1516*, Sierre 1942, p. 16.

F. Dessemontet and T. Ansay (eds), Introduction to Swiss Law, 1–13.

Zugewandte) composed of a variety of adjacent territories, for example the City of Geneva, that of Biel/Bienne, St. Gallen and Mulhouse. There was a third category, the 'subject territories' (*bailliages/Herrschaften*) – today we would call them colonies – that included 'free Bailiwicks'; those having one canton as master. Western Aargau and Vaud for example, belonged to Berne; and 'common Bailiwicks', such as Ticino, administered by several cantons.

The fourteenth and fifteenth centuries saw the development of Switzerland as a great military power. During the first years of the sixteenth century it came very close to becoming a great political power as well, until an important military defeat in 1515. The crisis of the Reformation rendered impossible all joint policy by the cantons and from there on, the Swiss took literally the famous advice of Nicholas von der Fitie: 'Don't meddle in foreign wars'.[3] Ulrich Zwingli, following the former's footsteps, preached that the Swiss should stop trying to play a role in Europe, namely by way of mercenary service, and stay at home to lead simple, healthy lives. This doctrine reflects the basis of Swiss neutrality.

The Confederation continued to be attached to the Holy Roman Empire, in law if not in practice, until the peace of Westphalia, in 1648, ending the Thirty Years War. The independence of the Swiss Confederation was thereby finally and formally recognized by the international society.

B. Ancient Historical Institutions: The Diet and Confederal Arbitration

One of the peculiarities of the development of Switzerland before 1848 is that the dealings of the various constituent members with one another must be labeled as foreign relations. The Diet, the principal institution of authority in the old Confederation, was provided for in neither the Alliance of 1291 nor the Brunnen Alliance. It obtained a customary and moral authority from successive situations when the Confederates were called upon to mediate or decide, and in later years, when they come to rule conquered territories in common. The Diet was neither a central government nor a parliament. Similar to the American Congress before 1787, it was a council of ambassadors of the confederated republics, with representatives from each canton casting a single cantonal vote and acting under strict instructions from their respective government.

The cantons realized at the earliest stages of their association the benefits of negotiated peaceful solutions, and one of the great institutions that followed the early alliances was confederal arbitration. Although arbitration failed to completely eliminate internal or external conflicts, it did become one of the main forces that saved the Confederation from disruption. In most conflicts there were some cantons that were not directly involved and could thus offer their services as mediators to their quarrelling brethren.

This early period in history tells us of important occasions when Swiss citizens acted as arbitrators in international disputes which had nothing to do with them, but where experience in such matters and the permanently neutral status of Switzerland

---

3. W. Martin, *Switzerland from Roman Times to the Present*, London 1971, p. 74.

made them mediators of unrivalled moral authority. To cite only a few recent examples, Switzerland collaborated in the Armistice Commission in Korea, and played a role in the settlement of the Algerian War. Since the end of the Second World War and still now, Switzerland has been taking an important part acting as a protecting power in representing diplomatic and '*consularian*' national interests in other countries.[4]

C. Modern Times

The History of Switzerland from the late eighteenth century to the present of interest to jurists is essentially the history of the birth and development of the Federal Constitution and of contemporary political institutions. Although this subject is treated in detail in Chapter 2, we deem it useful to make some introductory remarks.

1. Federal Political Institutions

a. The Legislative Branch

The Federal Assembly *(Assemblée fédérale/Bundesversammlung)* was created along the lines of the American bi-cameral Congress. It is composed of the National Council and the Council of States *(Conseil des Etats/Staenderat)*. The 200 members of the National Council represent the Swiss population. The Council of States, which has 46 members, consists of two representatives from each canton and one representative from each of the six half-cantons.

The Swiss parliament is often referred to as a 'militia parliament'. It is to this day an assembly whose members exercise an ordinary occupation.

The Federal Assembly elects the Federal Council the members of which it cannot vote out before the end of their term. It also elects the justices that serve on the Federal Tribunal.

b. The Executive Branch

The Federal Council (*Conseil fédéral/Bundesrat*) is a collegial body of government consisting of seven members, each elected for a period of four years and eligible for re-election for an unlimited number of terms. Each member of this governmental body is at the same time a head administrator of one of the seven administrative departments. This second function may well be compared to that of Minister in other countries. Switzerland's multi-party system is well reflected in the political profile of this governing body: its members represent four different political parties. Its decisions emanate from the body as a whole, and it is badly considered for an individual member of the Federal Council to voice his dissenting opinion publicly.

There is no Prime Minister. The President of the Swiss Confederation, chosen each year from among the members of the Federal Council, serves as chairman of

---

4. See below, b.

this collegial body. The same Federal Councilor may not serve as President during two consecutive years.

c. The Judiciary

In contrast to the dual system of parallel federal and state courts practiced in the USA, the Swiss court system may best be imagined as a pyramid. The civil, criminal or administrative courts of first and second instance are cantonal, with the Federal Tribunal *(Tribunal fédérale/Bundesgericht)* as a court of last instance at the top of the pyramid. The cantons being responsible for the execution and implementation of federal legislation, also organize the courts that apply federal law, the Federal Tribunal has the power to decide on appeals from cantonal courts. The High Court also rules on appeals lodged against decisions emanating from federal agencies. The Federal Tribunal may not however declare a federal law unconstitutional. Article 191 of the Federal Constitution precludes the judicial control of the constitutionality of federal laws and international treaties ratified by the Federal Assembly. The Organization of the Federal Courts is currently under general revision. The proposed Bill foresees the creation of a new first level of federal courts competent for the federal administrative and criminal law in order to hand back to the Federal Tribunal its primary role of Supreme Court.

d. The Electorate

The direct democracy first developed within the Swiss governmental system during the latter part of the nineteenth century. The compulsory constitutional referendum, whereby the adoption of a constitutional measure requires a majority of cantons and a majority of the popular vote, and the optional referendum, whereby the adoption of a federal law may be put to the vote of the electorate upon the demand of 50,000 eligible voters, were introduced in 1874 when the Federal Constitution of 1848 underwent a total revision. The legislative initiative does not exist on the federal level. The constitutional initiative was introduced at the federal level in 1891. It presently requires a petition of at least 100,000 eligible voters.

2. The Cantons

The 26 Swiss cantons and half-cantons, although equally autonomous in law, vary considerably in size, population, and per capita income. Each one has a republican form of government with separate legislative, executive, and judicial branches.

Cantonal parliaments are uni-cameral and count from 46 to 200 members. In a few cantons, they take second place to the still existing People's Assemblies *(Landsgemeinden)*, where the voters meet to decide on various questions and for elections, the voters play an even greater role in the cantons than in the Confederation. Indeed, all laws may or have to be submitted to them, even the appropriation bill, depending on whether the referendum is obligatory or optional. The legislative initiative is extensively used in the cantons.

The executive branch is headed by a collegial government, and as at the federal level, coalitions and annual change of presidency are the rule.

As mentioned earlier each canton has a complete judicial system. The cantonal courts have jurisdiction over both federal and cantonal law, notwithstanding some special federal competences.[5] Judges are elected by either the Parliament or the people and must stand periodically for re-election.

Federal laws and programs are as a rule administered by the cantons, federal authorities being responsible for supervision. An obvious advantage of this system is better coordination by delivery agencies.

Each village, town, and city is organized as a 'commune' *(Gemeinde)*. The 'communes' differ greatly in size and in autonomy according to the canton; they all have their own executive and legislative authorities.

One of the most important criteria of a Confederation is the financial autonomy of its member states. In Switzerland, the cantons and communes have the right to levy their own income tax, corporation and wealth taxes. The Federal Government may only levy a tax provided for expressly by the Constitution.

II. SOURCES OF LAW

A. *Enacted Law*

In Switzerland as in other romano-germanic legal systems, enacted or written law is by far the most important source of law. Different forms of enacted law have different values; in order of priority they are the Federal Constitution, codes and other federal statutes, administrative regulations. The order of priority between the different forms of enacted law is largely governed by the following rules:

  (a) federal law takes precedence over cantonal law;[6]
  (b) constitutional rules prevail over ordinary statutes;[7] and
  (c) legislative statutes take priority over regulations promulgated by the government or administrative authorities.

The scope of federal legislative authority is subject to well-defined limitations; namely, the Federal Constitution leaves all law-making power to the cantons except as expressly delegated to the federal authorities by the Constitution itself.[8] In addition, even where the federal authorities have the power to enact a law, this power may be limited to the enactment of guiding principles, leaving the detailed regulation to the cantons.[9] Although constitutional provisions take precedence over ordinary statutes, the supremacy of federal law requires that all forms of federal statutes prevail over cantonal constitutions.

---

5. E.g. Article 340 of the Penal Code.
6. Art. 49 para. 1, Federal Constitution.
7. With the qualification that federal laws are not subject to judicial control of their constitutionality (see above I C 1 c).
8. Art. 3, Federal Constitution.
9. Art. 164 II, Federal Constitution; e.g. Arts. 38 II, 77, 79, Federal Constitution.

The priority of statutory law over administrative regulations results from the subordinate position of the administrative agencies in respect to the parliament. The Executive may enact legal rules only on the basis of a formal statutory delegation of power which specifies the content, purpose, and scope of the authority so granted.

Two basic rules govern the relationship between two legal rules otherwise having the same priority:

- recent law prevails over prior law,
- specific provisions or statutes prevail over general ones.

As for international treaties, as soon as they are approved by the parliament and the instruments of ratification have been deposited, they become, by that very fact, an integral part of the federal legal order. They have the force of federal law.

Federal statutes are published in two official collections, the 'Official Collection of Federal Laws' *(Recueil officiel des lois et ordonnances de la Confédération Suisse, RO/Amtliche Sammlung der eidgenössischen Gesetze, AS)* in chronological order of their entry into force, and in the 'Systematic Collection of Federal Law' *(Recueil systématique du droit fédéral, RS/Systematische Sammlung des Bundesrechts, SR)* classed according to content. The 'Official Newsletter' *(Feuille federate, FF/Bundesblatt, BB)* contains, among other texts, minor federal enactments that are not included in the 'Official Collection' cited above.[10] Each canton has a similar system of publication for its legislation.

The most important federal laws are:

- The Federal Constitution *(Constitution fédérale de la Confédération suisse/ Bundesverfassung der schweizerischen Eidgenossenschaft)*, of 18 April 1999.
- The Civil Code *(Code civil, CC/Zivilgesetzbuch, ZGB)*, of 10 December 1907,
- The Code of Obligations *(Code des obligations, CO/Obligationenrecht, OR)*, of 30 March 1911,
- The Code of Execution and Bankruptcy *(Loi fédérale sur la poursuite pour dettes et la faillite/Bundesgesetz über Schuldbetreibung und Konkurs)*, of 11 April 1889, completely revised by the Federal Law of 16 December 1994.
- The Penal Code *(Code pénal suisse, CPS/Schweizerisches Strafgesetzbuch, StGB)*, of 21 December 1937,
- Organization of the Federal Courts *(Loi fédérale d'organisation judiciaire/ Bundesgesetz über die Organisation der Bundesrechtspflege)*, of 16 December 1943, under revision.

B. Customary Law

Custom constitutes a source of legal rules only in the limited areas of non-codified law. But, like enacted law, custom is considered a primary source of law in the Swiss legal system.

---

10. All the Federal statutes are available on the internet, on the website of the Confederation at the following address: <www.admin.ch>.

Article 1 of the Swiss Civil Code opens the door to custom as a source of law in that it instructs the judge to apply customary law *(le droit coutumier/ Gewohnheitsrecht)*, if an applicable legislative provision is not to be found: 'In the absence of an applicable legal provision, the judge decides according to customary law.' The custom that applies must be recognized as valuable in all parts of Switzerland. A rule that starts out as customary law may be integrated into the legislation. This was the case for example of the 'banking secret', which is now protected by the Federal Banking Law.[11]

C. *Judicial Decisions*

Unlike precedents in Common Law systems, judicial decisions – even those of the Federal Tribunal – are only binding upon the court whose decision has been attacked. They are not binding upon other courts, even those at the trial or lower cantonal appellate levels. Although intentional deviations from a constant line of decisions are not infrequent, judicial precedents play a very significant role despite their nonbonding nature. The judge must examine a provision, often expressed in extremely general terms, or a general principle of law in order to give it a content and apply it to a particular case. Confronted with a new set of circumstances which the legislator could not have foreseen, the judge may indulge in the kind of free scientific research recommended by Article 1, III of the Civil Code. This article recognizes the creative role of the judge, in that it instructs him to decide 'as if he were himself acting as legislator' when both legal rule and custom are lacking. This was the case, for example, when the Federal Tribunal declared that public corporations are subject to Civil Code provisions on the owner's liability as owners of the public domain.

Since 1874, the most important decisions of the Swiss Federal Tribunal are published in the 'Official collection of the Decisions of the Federal Tribunal' *(Recueil Officiel des Arrêts du Tribunal Fédéral Suisse, ATF/Amtliche Sammlung der Entscheidungen des schweizerischen Bundesgerichts, BGE)*. One volume divided into five parts is published each year: I a) Constitutional Law; I b) Administrative and International Public Law; II. Civil Law; III. Seizure and Bankruptcy; IV. Criminal Law; V. Social Insurance.[12]

The Federal Tribunal publishes only its most important decisions and those that are considered to be leading cases. Many officially unpublished decisions appear however in professional journals.[13]

---

11. C. Du Pasquier, *Introduction à la théorie générale et à la philosophie du droit*, 6th edn., Lausanne/Paris 1988, p. 52.
12. Judicial opinions are cited by reference to the title, volume, section and page of the collection, e.g. ATF (BGE) 101 III 25 indicates the decision appearing on p. 25 of the section 'Seizure and Bankruptcy, 101st volume of the Decisions of the Federal Tribunal'. See III, below, for a discussion of the meaning of these divisions. Since 2000, all the Federal Tribunal's jurisprudence (case law) is also available on the internet, even if it is not published in the Official Collection of the Decisions, on the following website: <www.bger.ch>.
13. See below, D.

The decisions of the administrative authorities of the Confederation – the Federal Council, Departments and Offices – may be found in the 'Decisions of the Administrative Authorities of the Confederation' *(Jurisprudence des autorites administratives de la Confédération, JAAC/Verwaltungsentscheide der Bundesbehördén, VEB).*

Cantons sometimes publish cantonal judicial decisions.

D. *Works of Legal Scholars*

The judge often bases his opinion on the works of legal scholars. The opinions of certain writers exercise a profound influence on those responsible for making decisions. Criticism made by particularly influential legal scholars often leads to the abandonment of solutions that have been well established in decided cases. In perusing the decisions of the Federal Tribunal, the reader will often spot the works of legal writers cited by name. By operating in this manner, the judge is following the instructions laid down in Article 1, III of the Civil Code whereby the judge 'shall be inspired by the solutions ... contained in the writing of legal scholars'. The judge remains of course free to choose a different solution, but in making a decision in contradiction with a 'well-known' opinion of an eminent legal scholar, the judge believes that he must first of all rebut this opinion.

In Switzerland, the most important works of legal scholars are considered to be the 'Commentaries' *(Commentaires/Kommentare)*, annotated versions of the Codes and most important laws, and Treatises. Manuals, monographs and articles published in professional journals also serve to inspire the legislator and the judge. The following is a list of some of the most important periodicals:

- *Zentralblatt für Staats- und Gemeindeverwaltung, ZBL*
- *Revue de droit suisse RDS/Zeitschrift für schweizerisches Recht, ZSR*
- *Revue suisse de jurisprudence, RSJ/Schweizerische Juristenzeitung, SJZ*
- *Revue de la Société des juristes bernois, RJB/Zeitschrift des bemischen Juristenvereins, ZBJV*
- *Journal des tribunaux, JT*[14]
- *Praxis des Bundesgerichts*

III. DIVISIONS OF THE LAW (PUBLIC LAW AND PRIVATE LAW)

The division of the law into public law and private law is practiced in Switzerland as in all Civil Law systems. This classification of rules according to their subject-matter may be very puzzling to lawyers in other legal systems, but is serves three important purposes: didactic, jurisdictional and legislative.

---

14. The *Journal des tribunaux* contains, *inter alia*, decisions originally rendered in German or Italian that are translated into French. The *Praxis des Bundesgerichts* contains, *inter alia*, the German translation of decisions rendered in French or Italian (see section V below, concerning the problem of trilingualism in the application of law).

The arrangement of the law into more or less logical categories is a useful teaching and learning tool. It divides the law faculties into groups of 'privatists' and 'publicists'. The division of law is practical in that it eases the assignment of certain matters to the jurisdiction of various courts[15] and it aids in the apportioning of legislative powers between the Confederation and the cantons.

Public law (*droit public/öffentliches Recht or Staatsrecht*) is that part of the law that deals with the organization of the State and other public bodies, and their relations as holders of public authority, among themselves and with individuals. It also includes, for example, the area of basic human rights. Its major branches are constitutional law (*droit constitutionnel/Verfassungsrecht*), administrative law (*droit administratif/Verwaltungsrecht*), tax law (*droit fiscal/ Steuerrecht*), criminal law (*droit pénale VStrafrecht*), criminal procedure (*procedure pénale/Strafprozessrecht*), public international law (*droit international public/Völkerrecht*). Civil procedure (*procédure civile/Zivilprozessrecht*), including the law of seizure (*droit des poursuites/ Zwangs-vollstreckungsrecht*) and bankruptcy (*droit de faillite/Konkursrecht*) also come under the classification of public law in Switzerland.

Private law comprises civil law proper (*droit civil/bürgerliches Recht*), which is contained in the Civil Code and its supplementary laws and is arranged into four sections: I. Law of Persons; II. Family Law; III. Inheritance Law; and IV. Law of Property. Under the heading of private law, the following subjects are treated in the fifth section of the Civil Code (*code des obligations/Obligationenrecht*): contracts, torts (*responsabilité civile Haftpflichtrecht*), commercial law (*droit commercial/ Handelsrecht*), including the law of companies (*droit des societes/ Gesellschaftsrecht*) and the law of negotiable instruments (*droit des papiers-valeurs/ Wertpapierrecht*). Industrial property law (*droit de la propriété industrielle/ gewerbliches Eigentum*) and copyright (*droit d'auteur/Urheberrecht*) are parts of private law. Labor law (*droit du travail/Arbeitsrecht*) is made up of rules from both public and private law.

Article 6, paragraph 1 of the Civil Code states: 'The civil laws of the Confederation allow the legislative powers of the cantons to subsist in the area of public law'. This article underlines the practical importance of the distinction. The judge may be obliged to examine provisions that are formally labeled cantonal public law in order to decide if their content are in contradiction with certain guarantees of federal private law.

One other important difference between public law and private law is that while the major part of private law is codified, the major part of public law remains uncodified, that is, scattered in special enactments and not systematized in one code.

It should be noted here that the introductory articles of the Civil Code lay down certain general principles that are also applicable, by analogy, to public law: rules of interpretation,[16] of good faith (*bonne foi/Treu und Glauben*) and the prohibition of an abusive use of the rights (*abus de droit/Rechtsmissbrauch*).

The criterion of the interest involved is most often used to determine if a particular rule of law or legal relationship belongs to public or private law. Thus a provision

---

15. See, for example, Federal Constitution: Arts. 30 II, 122 I, 189 I lit. d, 190; CC Arts. 5, 6, 52, I, 87, 702, 784 I; CO Arts. 33 I, 59, 61, 73 II, 125, no. 3, 342; etc.
16. See above, II B, C, and D.

enacted chiefly in view of the general welfare constitutes public law. The function of a rule of law is also used as a distinguishing tool. Rules and relationships aimed at the performance of public tasks are thereby classified as public law.

IV. THE 'RULE OF LAW'

A. In Theory

In the Swiss legal system, the 'rule of law' *(règle de droit/Rechtsnorm)* may be defined as a rule of a general and abstract nature, applying to an unlimited number of persons in an unlimited number of cases. It is a rule of conduct that may either prescribe a certain activity, prohibit an activity, or lay down that an activity or state of things must be tolerated.

The judge and the lawyer consult the 'rule of law' as a foundation in solving individual cases. Contrary to the notion of the 'legal rule' found in Common Law systems, the 'rule of law' is not extracted by the judge from a particular case; it is the legislator – the Parliament and the electorate – influenced in part by legal science that formulates the 'rules of law' in general and abstract terms. The judge has a secondary role in that he applies the 'rule of law' to individual cases; he does not, in general, create it.

The law therefore consists of a body of substantive rule – 'rules of law' – that serve to inform people of their rights and obligations and the manner in which they should behave. The rationale behind the primacy of the 'rule of law', as laid down by the legislator, is the desirability of foreseeable solutions which are the guarantee of individual liberty. It satisfies the need for certainty in legal relations.

The 'rule of law' concept is the basis of the system of codification. A code, from the Swiss point of view, should not attempt to resolve all the concrete questions that may come before the courts. Its role is rather to prescribe a series of rules that are general enough and well-ordered so that the judges and the citizens shall be able to easily deduce the manner in which a particular problem must be resolved.

B. In Practice

The 'rule of law' usually leaves wide discretionary powers to the judge precisely because of its general nature and purposely laconic formulation in statutes. Faced with a 'rule of law' such as Article 8 I of the Federal Constitution ('All human beings are equal before the law'), the judge will necessarily have to clarify and complete the scope of the rule before he can apply it to a particular case. The 'rule of law' as expressed by the legislator is only the nucleus around which a whole body of secondary rules has been established by the judiciary.

Thus in practice, 'rules of law' are not only created by the legislative process but also by the interpretation that the judges give to scanty legislative provisions. This process may seem, *prima facie*, to closely resemble the 'judge-made law' known in Common Law systems. But the 'rules of law' developed by way of judicial decisions in Switzerland still retain a higher degree of generality than those developed by judges that are not guided by the legislator. The Swiss legal system remains thereby relatively simple and clear, unencumbered by the immense body of legal rules found in case law systems.

C. Jus et Equitas

Article 4 of the Civil Code declares: 'The judge applies the rules of law and of equity where the law reserves his power of discretion,[17] or where it instructs him to take into account either the circumstances[18] or the justified motives.'[19] The notion of 'equity' in the Swiss legal system is not to be confused with 'equity' found in Common Law systems. The latter is unknown in Swiss law.

This article refers to a category of rules in which the legislator has purposely omitted to define all the factors that may play a role in deciding a particular case. With Article 4 of the Civil Code, he has instructed the judge to do it in his place, leaving him the latitude to consider all the circumstances involved.[20]

This large power of discretion, however, does not permit the judge to decide according to his fancy or to ignore the general legal framework. He must decide objectively, taking into account only the significant circumstances that may be generalized into reference points for future decisions.

Article 4 of the Civil Code does not permit the judge to correct the law. This latter possibility exists in the case where the law is used in an abusive manner. The judge will then apply Article 2, II of the Civil Code which states: 'The law does not sanction the evident abuse of a person's rights'.

V. THREE OFFICIAL LANGUAGES

Article 70 of the Federal Constitution states that German, French, and Italian are the official languages of the Confederation. The use of the word 'official' means that all legal texts are published in these three languages and that all three are considered equally authoritative. According to Article 4, Romanche, besides German, French, and Italian, is a 'national language', which is not the same as an 'official language'. This means Romanche will be used by the Confederation in its relations with Romanche natural persons.[21] The quadrilinguism is an important peculiarity of the *Confederatio* since it represents one of its pillars.[22]

The fact that all three versions have the same legal value causes some problems of interpretation, because a term used in one language may not contain exactly the

---

17. Examples: 156 CC; Art. 50 para. 2, 100 para. 2 CO.
18. Examples: Art. 3 para., 333 para. 2 CC; Arts. 43 para. 1, 47 CO.
19. Examples: Arts. 30 para. 1, 72 para. 3, 92 CC; Arts. 269 para. 1, 337 para. 1 CO.
20. Examples: Arts. 30 para. 1, 151, 152, 256c para. 3, 260c para. 3 CC ; Arts. 44 para. 2, 47 para. 2, 52, 54 para. 1, 269 para. 1, etc. CO.
21. See Art. 70 para. 1, 2nd sentence.
22. D. Thürer, J.-F. Aubert and J.P. Müller (eds.), *Droit constitutionnel suisse*, Zurich 2001, p. 595.

same shades of meaning in one or the other language. The judge must therefore decide which of the three versions best expresses the intention of the legislator. The 'true version' is not always the one in which the text was originally devised.[23]

Article 70 of the Federal Constitution contains far more than an expression of confederal sympathy: It details the general Freedom of Language specified in Article 18 Federal Constitution, and completed it, presenting some accurate consequences of the Swiss peculiarities on Freedom of Language. This freedom, like all others for that matter, has its boundaries. It is governed by two basic principles:

- the Territorial Principle: in a German speaking canton or commune, the official language of the cantonal administration, schools included, is German. The same applies for a French speaking or Italian speaking canton. Each canton is determining its official language. To preserve harmony between the different linguistic communities, the cantons are attuned to the traditional apportionment of the languages by territory;[24]
- the Personal Principle: Whereby everyone may speak his national mother tongue in communicating with the Federal Administration and with its decentralized agencies.

The Territorial Principle takes generally priority over the Personal Principle in case of conflict. The practical consequences of this last fact are far-reaching, especially in certain cantons where two or more languages are officially recognized and where a shift in the population occurs. The implications of the Personal Principle are best seen within the federal civil service and within the administrations of bilingual or multilingual cantons. Much care is taken to respect, in the hiring and elections process, the proper proportions of the language balance in the Swiss national population.[25] For example, the Federal Council has nearly always been occupied by at least two members of the French or Italian speaking community. In the election of federal judges, a very watchful eye is kept on the language balance of the Federal Tribunal. As for the recruitment of federal civil servants, the mother tongue of the candidate constitutes an important factor in the selection process. This is due, however, more to practical considerations than to theoretical ones.

VI. CONCLUSION

What makes the Swiss legal system essentially different from other democratic nations having federalist structures?

The first and most striking factor is undoubtedly the politics of coalition and compromise. The political calm so characteristic of contemporary Switzerland does not depend on the cohesion of temporary coalitions formed for the sake of electoral convenience. The coalition in the Swiss Federal Council depends rather on continuing cooperation among the different parties in the cause both of national stability

---

23. See for example ATF 117 V 287, 291.
24. Art. 70 para. 2 Federal Constitution.
25. Germanophone 73.5%; Francophone 20.1%; Italophone 4.5%; others 1.9%.

and of harmony between the Confederation and the cantons. Under this system, the government is permanent representative of the major political forces which have developed from the diversity of life in the Confederation. It is a coalition above all of political interests and shifting cleavages. These shifting alliances and the consensus thereby required according to the particular problem at hand, lead to a certain continuity in political life and, consequently, in legislative programs. At the beginning of each four-year legislative period, the Federal Council proposes a comprehensive program of legislation to the Federal Assembly. Even if one or more members of the government change during the course of the legislature, the program to be accomplished remains unchanged. Thus, no single political tendency has left its lasting mark on contemporary Swiss legislation. It is rather the product of compromize between different political interests.

The numerous stages involved in the legislative process constitute a second distinguishing factor. In most cases, the drafting of new laws and the amendment of old ones is first handled by the Federal Council and its administrative services. The preliminary draft is then submitted to the cantons, political parties, and interest groups for their written opinion. The legislative proposals are next presented, separately, one after the other, to each Council of the Federal Assembly. The National Council and the Council of States have exactly the same legislative powers. No draft proposal can become law unless both Houses reach an agreement. The law does not enter into force until the deadline for filing a popular referendum has passed, or, if the referendum is requested,[26] after approval of the law by the electorate. This lengthy process, slowing the drafting and enactment of laws, contributes to and reinforces the necessity for solutions of compromise and precludes measures excessively influenced by current events.

A third important factor characteristic of Swiss law is its relative simplicity. The best evidence of this fact is the Swiss Civil Code which, in its original state,[27] contained no provision having more than three paragraphs, and no paragraph longer than one complete sentence. This marvel of legislation style has in part given way to more technical provisions necessitated by a more complicated society. However, largely owing to the fact that the voters have the last say in the enactment of laws by way of the popular referendum, new legal provisions have remained relatively understandable for the majority of the electorate. This is both the condition and the result of a political system that requires everyone to bear a share of responsibility for the running of the country.

26. See above, I C 1d.
27. The Swiss Civil Code entered into force in 1912.

Chapter 2
The Swiss Federal Constitution

J.-F. Aubert*
E. Grisel**

I. A BRIEF DESCRIPTION OF THE CONSTITUTION

A. The Nature of the Constitution

The Federal Constitution of the Swiss Confederation came into force on 1 January 2000, and since then has undergone three partial revisions: the civil and criminal procedure has been transferred to the Confederation, the consent of the Confederation for new dioceses to be set up has been suppressed, and new financial rules have been introduced in order to force the Confederation to keep its expenditure and receipts in balance. As a Constitution, its legal force is above that of ordinary laws and it may be modified only in accordance with a specific procedure. While ordinary laws are only subject to the facultative referendum, in which only the citizens' votes are counted, amendments to the Constitution are subject to the compulsory referendum and must be passed not only by the majority of citizens taking part in the voting but also by a majority of votes in a majority of cantons.

B. The Style of the Constitution

In its present version, the Federal Constitution consists of more than 190 articles and some 19,000 words. It is more than twice longer than the Constitution of the United States but one-sixth longer than that of the State of California. Some of its articles consist of only a few words, especially those which guarantee personal freedoms. Other articles use more than 250 words, especially those which state a legislative program.

The style is not uniform: sometimes the language is compact, sometimes it is diffuse. In general, the most recent texts are the most detailed, but there are so many exceptions to that rule that it is impossible to indicate a definite tendency. Also, we should guard against assuming that the shortest provisions are always the most important ones and that the lengthier ones contain useless ballast. The revised

* Former member of the Federal Senate (Council of State), and Professor at the University of Neuchâtel.
** Professor, University of Lausanne (updated the chapter for the new edition).

F. Dessemontet and T. Ansay (eds), Introduction to Swiss Law, 15–26.
© 2004 Kluwer Law International. Printed in The Netherlands.

version of 1999 has only marginally cured the defects of the former Constitution of 1874.

II. HISTORY OF THE CONSTITUTION

A. Until 1848

During more than half a millennium, from the end of the thirteenth century to the middle of the nineteenth, the Swiss cantons formed a Federation of States, as the term is understood by lawyers; that is, they were a group of States linked by international treaties (rather like the American States in 1781 at the time of the Articles of Confederation, or the German States before 1867). A real Swiss Constitution did not exist then; only certain contracts existed. This long period was interrupted for a few years from 1798 to 1803 when the French, who had invaded Switzerland, imposed the status of a unified republic. But, while that Constitution (called the 'Helvetic Constitution') was an interesting document, it did not penetrate Swiss consciousness and was contested from all sides. After a very short time, by a sort of arbitration called the 'Act of Mediation', Bonaparte again turned Switzerland into a Federation of States.

After Bonaparte's downfall, the cantons, under the supervision of the Allies, negotiated a new treaty among themselves, the Pact of 1815. However, the idea of a Swiss nation was taking hold progressively: the industrialists wanted a larger market, while the radical politicians demanded a stronger union. As some conservative, agricultural and catholic cantons opposed it in a separate League, or Sonderbund, the decision was made by force of arms, in a short civil war in the autumn of 1847 (the Sonderbund War).

B. The Constitution of 1848

The Federal Diet, which was then the principal authority of the Federation of States – and which resembled the American Congress before 1787 – created a committee in charge of the revision of the Pact. This committee, which was in session from February to April 1848, proposed to transform the Federation of States into a Federal State and to replace the Pact by a Constitution, for which it submitted a proposed text. The following June, the Diet approved the project. After that, the text was submitted to a popular referendum in the cantons. The referendum was positive in a majority of the cantons and, in the course of its last session, the Diet promulgated the Constitution (12 September 1848). It was no doubt not quite logical that a treaty, i.e. the Pact of 1815, should have been abolished against the will of certain treaty States, but the latter resigned themselves to the fact and finally accepted the new form of government, which, moreover, was not to their disadvantage.

The Constitution of 12 September 1848 was arranged in three chapters. It turned Switzerland into a national State, divided into nineteen cantons and six half-cantons. It assured, with some restrictions, the free circulation of persons, goods and services among the cantons. It endowed the central State with its own authorities, notably a bicameral parliament (the Federal Assembly) copied from the American Congress of 1787, and a Federal Council of seven members. It introduced universal suffrage for men and the compulsory referendum for later amendments of the Constitution.

C. The Constitution of 1874

Twenty years later, the Radical Party, supported on the left by a Democratic Party, demanded a total revision of the Constitution. The purpose was to give the federal authorities more powers and to grant the voters more rights. The first draft was considered too centralist and was rejected both by popular vote and by the cantons in 1872. A second draft, with the necessary amendments taking into account the objections raised against the first one, was accepted on 19 April 1874, and came into force on 29 May of that year.

The new Constitution granted additional powers to the central State regarding the armed forces, currency, and commercial and industrial legislation. On the other hand, it made each federal law subject to a facultative referendum, if requested by 30,000 citizens (50,000 since 1977) or eight cantons.

D. The Partial Revisions between 1874 and 1999

Up to 31 December 1976, the Federal Constitution of 1874 had been partially revised by 88 amendments. 81 of them were the result of an initiative by Parliament and the Federal Council, and only seven resulted from a popular initiative. During the same period, 83 proposed amendments had been rejected, including a proposed total revision which, in 1935, sought to turn Switzerland into an authoritarian State. Of those 83 amendements, 27 were proposed by the political authority and 56 by the citizens. Of course these figures give no indication of the relative importance of these amendments and proposals. There have been very important and relatively insignificant amendments: popular vote has decided, by incidental procedure, on economic systems and gambling halls.

From 1 January 1977 to 31 October 1983, the Federal Constitution had been the object of sixteen other partial revisions which emanated, all but one, from Parliamentary initiatives. These revisions were concerned in particular with the dependence of some international treaties on the referendum, the attribution of new competences to the Confederation in matters of economic policy and finance, the creation of a twenty-sixth canton (see IV below) and equality of man and woman.

During the same period, twenty-one proposed amendments were rejected. Fifteen came from popular initiatives and six were elaborated by Parliament. They had reference in particular to the protection of the environment, the status of foreigners, the financial reform, the introduction of a civil service for conscientious objectors, the protection of lessees, and the impunity of procured abortions.

From November 1983 through 1999, fourty-four revisions were adopted, notably regarding the Swiss nationality, the State monopoly over radio and television, the protection of tenants, the regulation of energy and the status of conscientious objectors. Among them, four came from popular initiatives. During this period, fifty-six proposals were rejected, among them articles on the right to life, extension of paid holidays, subsidies for cultural activities, reduction of work time, suppression of the army, adhesion of Switzerland to the European Economic Area, and facilitation of the young foreigners' naturalization. Forty-six among these fifty-six rejected proposals had a popular origin.

Most of the amendments since 1874 have granted the Confederation additional powers. This was notably the case in the fields of civil and penal law (1898), economic law (1908, 1947, 1981 and 1982), social security, transportation, energy, town and country planning (1969), protection of the environment (1971), culture, and taxation, and protection of tenants (1986). Several amendments concerned political institutions, such as women's suffrage (1971), the principle of proportional representation in electing the National Council, which is the Swiss counterpart of the American House of Representatives (1918), development of the popular initiative and of the referendum (1891, 1921, 1949, 1977). Some amendments concerned the personal freedoms and rights of the individual (guarantee of ownership; freedom of settlement; creation of a federal administrative jurisdiction).

Of the amendments which were turned down at first, many were eventually accepted after a second attempt. Those which, at least up to now, have not been passed were mostly the result of popular initiatives. This is quite natural. Such proposals come from minority groups, which appeal directly to the nation because they do not have the support of sufficient representation in Parliament, but rarely does a popular vote approve a request which has received only feeble support in Parliament. Thus, several demands for social legislation (right to work; right to housing; forty-hour work week; codetermination by employees in management of the enterprise) have met with a refusal. The same may be said of certain proposed further developments of direct democracy (popular initiative for ordinary laws; referendum on the appropriation of credits).

The popular initiative was often considered one of the main reasons that the Swiss Constitution of 1874 had become so cumbersome. This was partially so. As the citizens do not have the initiative for ordinary laws, they may propose a legislative revision only through use of the constitutional initiative, and many of these constitutional initiatives are verbose. Still, as we have mentioned above, experience has shown that they are almost always rejected. The eleven which did succeed were among the most concise. Finally, the popular initiatives have led to the adoption of such detailed texts only indirectly by instigating counter-formulations.

The Federal Constitution of 1874 has contained, in addition, several provisions which have addressed transitory concerns or anxieties. These have been contingent on, and explained by, the time when they were introduced. Here we think, for instance, of the very complex separation of powers in the military realm, of the prohibition (rescinded in 1973) of Jesuit activities and of new religious orders and convents and of the precautionary measures to keep the Presidents of both Houses from becoming personally too powerful. Here again, and contrary to widespread belief, these outdated measures do not go back to popular initiatives, with the exception of that (abolished in 1999) on absinthe, but rather to proposals from the Federal Council or Members of Parliament.

E. The Long Way to a Totally Revised Constitution

The cumbersomeness, the gaps, and the insufficiencies of the Swiss Federal Constitution of 1874 had troubled some lawyers and politicians so much that thirty-seven years ago they requested that steps be taken toward a total revision and motions to that effect were presented to both Houses. Since they were sufficiently vague and did not anticipate either the contents of an eventual formulation or even the principle of a revision, these motions were carried in 1966 without debate.

The first draft of a new Constitution was achieved in November 1977, and published in February 1978. The cantonal governments, the political parties, and many interested organizations were invited to present their observations until the end of 1979. In general, the reception has been rather mitigated: it has been relatively positive on the left, frankly negative on the right. The draft is criticized for not being sufficiently detailed and for allowing the legislators too much latitude. In particular, the attribution of a subsidiary competence to the Confederation in all jurisdictions is severely judged.

In November 1985, the Federal Council submitted its report to the Federal Assembly. After a debate of two years, the Parliament gave a new mandate to the government, namely to prepare a draft that should solely improve the formal wording of the Constitution without, however, altering its substance: the text was to be renewed and the language had to be adapted to modern times, but the system as a whole was meant to remain the same. This led to the present Constitution, which was debated by the Federal Assembly in 1998 and adopted by the referendum of 18 April 1999.

III. MODES OF REVISION

The rules on the revision of the Constitution are stated in the Constitution itself, in Title 4, Chapter 2 and in Title 6, and are detailed in two laws, on parliamentary procedure and on political rights, dated 1962 and 1976 respectively. The initiative for the revision can come from the Federal Assembly and Federal Council or from 100,000 citizens.

If the initiative comes from the political authorities, it is handled according to the procedure for ordinary legislation. Both Houses must accept the text in identical terms, but no specific majority is stipulated. However, unlike ordinary legislation, a proposal for revision or amendment of the Constitution must be submitted to a referendum, as already stated above. And it is accepted only if both a majority of the popular vote and of the cantons approve (see I, A above). If the initiative comes from the citizens, one distinguishes between an initiative for total revision and an initiative for a partial revision or amendment (according to a reform of 1891). If the request is for total revision, the citizens are consulted in a prior vote on the principle. If it is accepted, the two Houses are dissolved and a new Parliament starts working on the revision (no example so far). If the popular vote is negative, the proposal is dropped as in 1935, which has been the sole case so far (see II, D above).

When the citizens demand an amendment on a specific point, they do so usually in the form of an already formulated text. The two Houses may not change it, but they may propose a counter-formulation. The initiative and, where this is the case, the counter-formulation are then submitted to public vote and ballot by the cantons. Until recently, it was forbidden to vote yes for both proposals; therefore, one could only accept one or the other or reject both. In April 1988 a new, more complicated system was introduced (now Article 139, former Article 121bis): the voters are now allowed to say yes to both texts, and they are asked to choose simultaneously the one they want adopted, in case both receive a majority of the votes.

The citizens may also propose a partial revision in general terms. This happens rarely, but when it does, and if the two Houses accept the proposal, they must prepare an amendment which meets the terms of the proposal and submit it to the final vote of the people and the cantons. If the two Houses refuse the proposal, a preliminary public vote decides whether Parliament must work out an amendment.

IV. GENERAL CONTENTS OF THE CONSTITUTION

The Federal Constitution is a composite work, made up of texts which are rather different in essence.

A. *Fundamental Rules*

Like any Constitution worthy of the name, the Swiss Federal Constitution contains fundamental rules on the State, its structure, its organization, its relations with - society as a whole, and with the individual. We may even say that, despite the heterogeneity for which it is often reproached, these rules predominate.

1. Article 1 enumerates the 26 cantons,[1] which signifies, first of all, that Switzerland is a federative structure. No doubt the term 'federative State' is rather general and vague and applies to various formations. Swiss federalism is, for instance, not identical with the federalism of Germany, or of Austria. Nevertheless, the division of Switzerland into cantons does indicate that this national collectivity covers smaller collectivities, which in turn have their own powers and political bodies (see also Arts. 3, 42 *et seq.*).

But in addition, Article 1 indicates that no canton will be created or eliminated. In other words, this enumeration will not change without a formal revision of the Constitution, i.e. without the approval of the majority of the people and of the cantons (see Art. 53). This procedure, which is more complicated than that stipulated by the Constitution of the United States (in Sect. 3 of Art. IV), indicates an intentional conservatism.

Each canton has its institutions and authorities which it organizes freely in order to make use of the competence that belongs to it by the terms of the Federal Constitution. The citizens of the canton elect their parliament and government as

---

1. The first Article of the Constitution was revised on 24 September 1978. The revised text includes the name of a new canton, Jura, detached from the canton of Bern at the end of a long procedure. In other terms, the citizens and the Swiss cantons accepted that day by referendum that a twenty-sixth canton should belong to the Swiss Confederation.

well as their deputies to the Council of States. They have more extended rights of referendum and initiative than in federal matters.

Article 3 (following the example of the Tenth Amendment to the Constitution of the USA) specifies that the cantons exercise all the sovereign rights which the Constitution has not explicitly or implicitly assigned to the Confederation and which it does not forbid them to exercise by a specific rule (e.g. the guarantee of personal freedom). The rights assigned to the Confederation and the rather numerous checks on the sovereign exercise of cantonal rights are mostly defined in the remaining articles of Title 3 (Art. 54 *et seq.*).

Cantons have the right to conclude treaties among themselves in those domains where they have remained sovereign, provided the do not violated the rights and interests of the Confederation or third cantons (Art. 48). They are exceptionally authorized to conclude some international treaties with foreign States (Art. 56).

Citizens of each canton are granted the right of settlement and equal treatment in all other cantons (Arts. 24 and 37). Judgments pronounced by a civil court in any canton are binding for the whole territory of Switzerland (cf. Art. IV, Sect. I of the Constitution of the USA).

2. At the Federal level there are three authorities: the Federal Assembly (Parliament), the Federal Council (government), and the Federal Tribunals.

a. The Federal Assembly consists of two chambers (Art. 148 *et seq.*): the *National Council* which has two hundred members, allotted between the twenty-six cantons and in proportion to their population and elected for four-year terms by universal suffrage and by the system of proportional representation; the *Council of States*, which has 46 members, elected, generally by majority vote, in each canton at the rate of two per canton and one by each of the six cantons which were historically considered as half-cantons in the former constitutions of 1848 and 1874. The Assembly includes thirteen parties, four of them of great current importance: the Radical (Liberal) Party, the Social-Democratic Party, the Agrarian Party and the Christian-Democratic Party. The Constitution confers on the Federal Assembly the 'supreme authority' of the Confederation (Art. 148), including authority to prepare the laws, under reserve of referendum, to vote appropriations and to supervise the executive. It enumerates the most important competence of both chambers (Art. 163 *et seq.*), confers identical powers on them (Art. 148 para. 2), and orders them to meet separately with some exceptions (Arts. 156 and 157).

b. The *Federal Council* (Art. 174 *et seq.*) comprises seven members, elected for four-year terms by both chambers of Parliament voting together. The seven members are equal; there is neither a Prime Minister nor a Chancellor. Since 1960, the collegial body has been formed by a coalition of the four parties mentioned before. The Federal Council proposes the drafts of constitutional revisions and of laws. It passes legislative regulations where it is competent by the terms of the Constitution or a relevant law. It concludes international treaties and ratifies them after approbation by the Federal Assembly. Generally, it leads the country's foreign and domestic policy so far as allowed by the Constitution, the laws and the appropriations, under supervision of the Federal Assembly.

The Federal Assembly is not able to constrain the Federal Council to resign its office. The Federal Council, for its part, is not able to dissolve the Assembly.

c. The two *Federal Tribunals* (Art. 188 *et seq.*), which have forty-one members elected for six-year terms by both chambers of Parliament, watch over the application of federal laws and regulations. They verify whether cantonal laws and regulations are in accordance with the federal law and whether regulations issued from the Federal Council are in accordance with the federal laws; but they are not able to control if federal statutes themselves are in accordance with the Federal Constitution.

d. Swiss citizens eighteen years old and over (more than four million persons, among a population of 7.2 million) may elect the members of the National Council and take a decision on referendum over constitutional revisions (compulsory vote), laws and some international treaties; one hundred thousand citizens are required to propose a constitutional revision, which will be submitted to referendum; fifty thousand citizens are required to introduce referenda against laws and treaties which are submitted to it.

3. Article 8 guarantees equality before the law. Laws, both federal and cantonal, must be equal and must be equally applied. Of all the phrases of the Constitution, this is the one which is most often invoked during trials. By way of interpretation, the Federal Tribunal has long ago based many important consequences on this phrasing, such as the principle of the legality of acts of State, the prohibition of arbitrary and retroactive laws, the principle of good faith in the relations between the State and the individual, and guarantees of due process of law for all citizens. The Constitution of 1999 protected these rights explicitly (see Arts. 9 and 29 *et seq.*).

B. *Injunctions upon the Legislator*

What makes the Swiss Constitution somewhat unwieldy is the fact that it not only creates authorities, distributes powers, lays down procedures, and protects individual freedoms, but that in many instances it tries to predetermine the content of legislation. This phenomenon occurs especially in those texts which confer a given power upon the Confederation. Instead of simply saying that the Confederation will legislate on such and such a point, the constitutional text often goes on to define the specific goal which the federal legislators are to pursue and sometimes even the means which they must employ. Of course not all these attributions of authority are as detailed, but there are sufficient examples.

Article 111 *et seq* offer a typical example. First, they charge the federal legislators with the task of guaranteeing an adequate pension to the old and invalid, which is to cover basic living expenses appropriately. Then, the legislators are to make membership in company or association pension funds compulsory; those funds are to be constituted on the basis of capital reserves, i.e. the workers set aside capital reserves for their old age. Third (and this is what the popular political term 'three pillars doctrine' refers to), the legislators should favor individual savings. Prescriptions regarding the evolution of the amounts of the pensions, the participation of the employers in the premium payments, the State contribution, tax exemptions, and others complete the whole.[2]

---

2. Other examples will be found in Articles 116 (protection of the family) and 108 (encouragement for the construction of lodgings).

The method which we have described above is understandable for two main reasons. On the one hand, the Federal Assembly, in drafting an article of the Constitution, must take into consideration that its success will depend on the compulsory referendum to which it will be submitted. In order to win the voters' favor the Assembly introduces as many promises and compromises as possible. It guarantees what has already been achieved; it states in advance to what extent certain demands will be met. In short, the drafting of a text offers the occasion for a first reconciliation between divergent interests, i.e. a first political debate on the content of future laws.

The second reason, intermingled somewhat with the first, is that the groups which will be affected by a given constitutional amendment are highly aware of the consequences which the legislators will draw from it. And since the ordinary laws are submitted only to a facultative referendum and, in addition, a majority vote of the cantons is not necessary for their adoption, those who are particularly eager for a given innovation prefer to have it in the Constitution. Thus they get around the trouble of demanding a referendum against a certain law, and what they have obtained will be better protected against later changes.

V. UNWRITTEN RULES IMPLIED IN THE CONSTITUTION

It remains to be seen if the Federal Tribunal will infer unwritten rules from the new Constitution or not, and to what extent it will do so. Until 1999, it had given recognition to constitutional principles and unwritten rights, almost all of which are now explicitly mentioned in the new Constitution.

VI. MEASURES OF CONTROL OVER THE APPLICATION OF THE CONSTITUTION

The Federal Constitution is binding for all State authorities – the Federal Assembly, the Federal Council, the Administration, the Federal Tribunal, and the cantonal authorities. This is an uncontested proposition of difficult application; therefore, certain measures of control must be provided.

A. Political Controls

First of all let us state that the federal legislators, in preparing a law, take pains to make it constitutional. Arguments concerning constitutionality crop up frequently in the debates, and when the Federal Council elaborates a project, it often seeks the advice of experts. It also happens that the request for a referendum is based, at least in part, on the unconstitutionality of a law and that legalistic objections are used in support of the campaign which precedes the popular vote. Thus, in June 1976, those who opposed a federal law on town and country planning reproached Parliament, among other things, with having overstepped its competences: the bill was finally rejected by 650,000 against 620,000 votes. No doubt the refusal was mostly for political reasons, but the legal point may have convinced some of the voters.

B. *Judicial Controls*

Appeal may be made to the Federal Tribunal against decisions of cantonal authorities and of authorities at a lower level in the Confederation which violate the
Constitution. However, decisions of the Federal Council, with very rare exceptions,
are not subject to judicial control; they depend solely on the purely political
supervision of the Federal Assembly.

The fact that the cantonal constitutions must conform to federal law is assured by
a preliminary examination by the Federal Assembly in what is called a 'guaranteeing'
procedure (Art. 51). The findings of the Assembly are final and may not be questioned later before any court, unless the federal law changes in the meantime. Other
legislative acts of the cantons may be attacked before the Federal Tribunal, either
directly within a certain period of time, or indirectly at any time in connection with
a case where the law in question is applied.

Legislative acts of the Federal Council (ordinances, regulation) cannot be challenged directly, but only in connection with a case of application. For instance, if a
taxpayer is subject to a federal tax by an ordinance of the Federal Council, he may
refer the decision to the Federal Tribunal and plead that the ordinance violates the
principle of equality or of freedom of trade. The most remarkable characteristic of
the Swiss system, however, is that the legislative acts of the Federal Assembly, and
in particular the federal laws, are not subject to any judicial control, directly or
indirectly. This lack of control was intentional; in the regulation on the Federal
Tribunal, the constituent assembly of 1874 formally repudiated the solution adopted
by the Supreme Court of the United States for this problem in its Marbury decision
of 1803. The framers of the Swiss Constitution did not want judges to be in a
position to substitute their interpretation of the Constitution for that of Parliament.
And most of all, they did not want to grant to those judges the power to invalidate a
law which the people had previously adopted by way of a referendum. In short,
having the choice between the principle of democracy and that of the supremacy of
the Constitution over the laws, they gave preference to the former (Art. 190). In
1999, the Federal Council proposed the introduction of judicial review on federal
statutes, but the Parliament rejected this innovation, which would have been both
significant and necessary.

VII. THE CONSTITUTION AND POLITICAL REALITY

Persons only reading the Federal Constitution and making themselves familiar with
the conventions and other unwritten rules which have been added would not get an
accurate idea of Swiss political reality. There is always a certain latitude between a
code of law – especially at the highest level – and the matter in which it is actually
applied. Certainly it is not in Switzerland that we find this latitude most marked; but
it exists nevertheless. Its full extent is impossible to indicate in this brief chapter. We
shall therefore merely cite some illustrative examples.

Some provisions, though of ancient origin, are stillborn: for example, the right of
the cantons to a referendum (Art. 141) has never been made use of. Other provisions
indicate their real scope only very partially: trade associations, for instance, play a

much more important role than the Constitution would indicate; one meets them at every crossroad of Swiss political life. Then there are provisions which have changed their intended purpose in the course of application. Thus for example, the referendum tends to become a means of pressure; when it is applied, it serves less merely to decide on a law than to express, in a very broad manner, the voters' feelings about their authorities. On the day of voting many citizens refuse such a law without even having read it, simply in order to show that they are disgruntled. Also, on voting day many citizens do not participate at all. Here again is a point which the framers of the Constitution could not foresee; namely, how poor the participation in a vote might turn out to be!

Nothing is said in the Constitution about political parties nor – and this is quite natural – about the political composition of the two Houses, nor on the arrangements which are made prior to the choice of a Federal Councillor. Elections of the legislators have an almost insignificant effect on the government's programme, a fact that remains unmentioned in the Constitution. Finally Swiss society, which is relatively egalitarian, nevertheless does not prevent certain differences. There are persons and groups which are more powerful than others and, therefore, also freer; their influence in public matters has greater weight.

Taken together, the text of the Constitution contains no regulations which political reality belies radically. But it ignores phenomena of all kinds and someone who would want to study Swiss political life might easily say: 'Do not rely on the Constitution, but at least start by reading it.'

SELECTED BIBLIOGRAPHY

Aubert, J.-F., *Traité de droit constitutionnel suisse*, 2 vols., Neuchâtel 1967 and Supplement, Neuchâtel 1982.

Auer, A., G. Malinverni and M. Hottelier, *Droit constitutionnel suisse*, 2 vols., Berne 2000.

Grisel, E., *Initiative et referendum populaires, Traité de la democratie semi-directe en Suisse*, 2nd edn., Berne 1997.

Häfelin, U. and W. Haller, *Schweizerisches Bundesstaatsrecht*, 4th edn., Zurich 1998.

Hangartner, Y., *Grundzüge des schweizerischen Staatsrechts*, 2 vols., Zurich 1980 and 1982.

Müller, J.P., *Grundrechte in der Schweiz im Rahmen der Bundesverfassung von 1999, der UNO – Pakte und der EMRK*, 3rd edn., Berne 1999.

Thürer, D., Aubert, J.-F. and J.P. Müller (eds.), *Droit constitutionnel suisse*, Zurich 2001.

Chapter 3
Cantonal and Federal Administrative Law of Switzerland

*Thomas Fleiner**

I. INTRODUCTION

The administration has to have means available in order to fulfill its tasks. It needs financial resources and real estate as well as manpower at its disposal to implement its legal obligations, to balance different interests of the society and to pursue public interests for the future. However, administrative possibilities of obtaining such means are limited by the constitutional protection of ownership of property by individuals. Except for issues of individual property, the concept of administration with regard to its relationship to civil servants as well as to other resources necessary to fulfill public tasks the Swiss administrative law has developed considerably in the last forty years. Administration has become an important if not the important actor in economic life. But the traditional tools of income and expenditures of administrative agencies limited to the annual budget prevent administrative agencies as well as civil servants to act as credible partners of the private sector. In addition, the private citizen is more and more exposed to the whim of non-transparent administrative procedures and administrative authorities not really accountable to an efficient judiciary or to a parliament able to control all activities of its administration. These are some of the reasons which led to important changes and developments of administrative law in Switzerland in the last couple of years. They can be summed up as follows:

- Increasing control of administrative activities with a more powerful judiciary.
- New Public Management within the administration.
- Privatization or semi-privatization of some public service sectors.
- Introducing of public mediators in some cantons and in some federal agencies.

Finally one should not underestimate the influence of international law and international developments, which had direct or indirect effects on Swiss administrative law. This is mainly due to the monistic concept of Swiss municipal law with regard to international law of treaties. Thus the European Human Rights Convention did become an integral part of Swiss administrative law, the WTO treaty and in particular the bilateral treaties with the European Union have now to be considered

* Prof. Dr., Director of the Institute of Federalism at the University of Fribourg, Switzerland.

F. Dessemontet and T. Ansay (eds), Introduction to Swiss Law, 27–46.
© 2004 Kluwer Law International. Printed in The Netherlands.

also as an integral part of Swiss municipal law. Unlike the United States which were the model for the adoption of the monistic system in Switzerland the parliament has no power by approving international conventions to decide what parts of the treaty should be self-executing or not self-executing. Thus it remains the power of the judge to decide which provisions of international treaties should be self executing.

In the following remarks we shall be able only partially to explain those developments, as with regard to the basics of administrative Swiss law, they did not change fundamentally although within the new developments they have to be weighed out of the new developed context.

II. CONSTITUTIONAL INFLUENCES ON SWISS ADMINISTRATIVE LAW

The administrative law of every country is guided by the rule of law, the constitutional principles (Art. 5 of the new Federal Constitution), and the organization of its State. Swiss administrative law for instance, is integrated into the concepts of Swiss federalism, direct democracy and organization of civil and administrative courts. Therefore, this chapter will first explain the influence of basic constitutional principles on Swiss administrative law and then establish the main guidelines of administrative law in Switzerland.

A. *Federalism*

What is the impact of federalism on administrative law? Switzerland has on the cantonal and federal level the three different governmental branches: legislative and executive branch and the judiciary. On the local municipal level there is only a legislative and executive branch but no judiciary. Each canton decides by itself, within the framework of the Federal Constitution, how it will be organized, which political rights its citizens can exercise and how it shall empower and organize the special administrative court. It also regulates the checks and balances of the three governmental branches. In doing so, it has to respect the historical prerogatives of the local municipalities and to distribute in accordance therewith the cantonal and local responsibilities.

Administrative law therefore differs from canton to canton. Cantons have different court systems, different administrative procedures, different local authorities with different powers and jurisdiction and different administrative concepts such as: regulations of public lakes and rivers, relationship between municipalities and cantonal authorities. The diversity of Switzerland with four languages and two major religions requires an open concept of administrative law, which allows each community to develop its specific identity according to its own cultural tradition.

Federal and cantonal laws are mainly implemented by cantonal administrative authorities and according to the cantons also by local municipal authorities. In many cantons these authorities have important executive powers. They are responsible for cultural activities, local zoning and environment, police power, primary schools, traffic regulations, and in some cases even for public health. The municipalities have also a limited taxing power which permits them to finance their public services.

B. *Cantonal and Federal Administration*

The local authorities are elected by the voters of the municipalities. They can be controlled by the cantonal administration; however they are politically responsible to their constituency, to the parliament or assembly, and only up to a limited extent to the cantonal government.

Municipalities have a constitutional right to exercise their vested autonomous rights according to their own will. They dispose of the residual power. Cantonal or federal administrative authorities cannot infringe the autonomy of towns or villages without a legal basis. According to Article 50 of the Federal Constitution the autonomy of *communes* is guaranteed within the limits of the cantonal constitution. However, local authorities are bound by the principles of cantonal and federal administrative law. Their decisions may be reviewed on the grounds of these principles by the administrative court or administrative authorities of the canton, or even by the Federal Tribunal.

C. *Democracy*

The system of direct democracy has a great impact on administrative law. Laws are democratically voted on the federal, cantonal and local level. Unlike the Westminster system of parliamentary democracy, Switzerland has no single party in government. The Swiss executive (Federal Council) is worldwide the only executive branch, which has its roots in the Directory of the First Republic in France (1795). The government is composed of seven Federal Councilors each elected individually and each belonging to different regions of Switzerland and to one of the four different parties represented in the executive branch. Each member is elected for a fixed term, that is a four-year period, by the parliament. The executive has to propose laws, which may be rejected or accepted by parliament as well as the majority of the citizens (facultative referendum). Therefore laws have to take into account all important interests of different groups of the population. The consensus-driven Swiss democracy influences already the decision making process of the seven members of the executive branch.

To get informed of the different interests, the federal council must submit legislative drafts to the different interest groups, and the groups may respond by proposing the abolition of certain articles or amendments to the draft. The procedure is not regulated in the Federal Administrative Procedure Act as in the United States. On the federal level, different constitutional articles impose on the Federal Council the obligation to hear interest groups before it proposes a law to parliament.

Switzerland has no prime minister. The Federal Council as well as the cantonal governments is composed of seven, five or even nine members who have equal voting power and can decide only when they have reached a certain quorum on a majority basis. In most executive bodies every important party is represented with at least one member. Therefore not only the parliament but also the government reflects the different political opinions of the people.

The fact that all important economic and political opinions of the people are represented in the government gives parliament the possibility to delegate significant legislative powers to the government. The statutes accepted in parliament are therefore usually very general and vague. They have to be supplemented by governmental ordinances.

If the Confederation is enacting laws which are to be executed on the cantonal or local level, it usually conveys important legislative powers to specify the law by cantonal legislation. Cantons, which have local communities with important legislative powers themselves, delegate some rule-making functions to their local communities. So the legal process of a federal statute, as in the case of environmental laws, starts on the federal level and goes down to the cantonal and local levels. On each level it is submitted to a process of direct democracy which means that it has to be adopted mandatory or based on a facultative referendum by the people.

The fact that statutes have to be approved by the people either by the facultative or obligatory referendum gives to every bill a legitimacy permitting the administration to execute it without many law enforcement servants. The citizens obey the law because they believe it is democratically justified and therefore fair. The decision making process may take a lot of time, but the efficiency of the federal system has to be seen in the implementation of general federal statutes within a multicultural and very diverse society.

Compared with other countries, the number of civil servants employed by the Swiss administration is fairly low. Quite a few public acts are prepared or even decided by commissions and boards which are composed of private citizens. This is specially the case in the towns and villages where schools, urban planning, public health and welfare are controlled by committees elected by the people only paid by low honorariums.

Democracy has also influenced the civil service system. Unlike the civil servants of the neighbor States of Switzerland, the employees of the administration are not employed for life. They are usually in office for an unlimited time and may be fired based on reasons and procedures provided by the respective statute. If the administration seeks candidates for higher jobs, every Swiss who has the professional qualifications may get the job. The Swiss bill of employees of the administration does not exclude, as in other countries, all non-civil servants who are not integrated in the civil service career structure.

The Swiss democratic system is based on the idea that the nucleus of democracy resides in the small corporative community. It differs therefore from the concept of 'individual democracy' in Anglo-Saxon countries. Although individual rights are protected by the Constitution, it is according to its multiculturality much more the autonomy of the cantonal and communal community which is politically and legally protected. The Federal Council has, according to the law of the organization of Swiss government, an obligation to inform the citizens about governmental policies. However it is the executive which in principle decides what is fit to print.

Democracy has also influenced the way of organizing public administration. Unlike all other countries, the executive, which is the Federal Council, does not have the unlimited right to organize its administration according to its own concept of public management. The organization of the public administration is mainly decided by the constitution and the legislature. Specially, the parliament has an interest to distribute power and functions between the seven members of the Federal Council in order to avoid a 'super' minister. Within the framework of the law, however, the Federal Council can reorganize its administration according to its needs and possibilities.

D. Court System

In Switzerland, as in other countries on the Continent, in the last centuries, only the civil courts decided private law cases between private parties. Penalties were imposed by special authorities such as the *Landsgemeinde*, elected councils or even the government. In the past, the public authority was sovereign and immune from civil law courts and could not therefore be sued by an individual. There was one important exception to this rule, in the area of private property. The public authority was considered to be bound by private law in all cases concerning private property. When the private property of an individual was damaged, the private individual could sue the public authority, and the private law court could decide the case. So the courts tried to extend the private law as much as possible and to impose it on the public authority in order to protect individuals as much as they could. The part of the State Administration bound by private law was called 'Fiscus'.

With the 'Fiscus Theory' courts could protect individual property, but no other individual rights, against State action. To fill this gap, the legislature developed a system of better individual protection against governmental acts in general. First, it developed a procedure which gave individuals the right to appeal administrative decisions to the higher administrative authorities in order to get them reviewed. However, these procedures did not help very much towards making the administrative decisions fair and reasonable in the public opinion. Higher administrative authorities were not supposed to be independent enough to abolish unlawful decisions of their subordinate authorities. Thus the legislature introduced special administrative tribunals able to review cases of special statutes such as taxation and import regulations. These tribunals developed new fundamental administrative principles which permitted them to decide their cases on a generally accepted basis. These principles are even today important sources for the development of new administrative law.

If it is a case dominated by the *fiscus* he has to initiate a private law suit before the civil court. He may also have a case to sue the administration before the civil court according to public law, if it deals with expropriation.

If the case is based on administrative law and if the authority has issued an administrative order, he may ask the higher administrative authority to review the unlawful order. If the law permits an action against a specific authority before the administrative court, he can sue the administration in such a court. If he cannot sue the authority before the general administrative court, he may have the right to take the case to a special administrative court. However, according to the continental system of administrative law he can only ask a court to review an administrative order. He has no remedy against simple state activities such as prohibition, injunction or a mandamus to order an administration to fulfill a certain activity.

The system of specialized different administrative tribunals was very complicated and did not fill the gap between protected property rights and unprotected individual rights. Therefore lawyers and politicians asked that administrative courts be given a general competence to review administrative orders. This general competence was introduced on the federal level in 1968. However the statute regulating the rights of individuals to appeal against the federal administration contains various exceptions. If the administrative order is of political importance or if the administration has a large discretionary power the individual can only appeal to the Federal Council which can review the decisions of the administrative authorities as a last resort. Decisions of the Federal Council are in general not subject to any kind of court review.

The process to introduce independent administrative courts took even more time to be implemented within the cantons than within the Confederation. The fact that cantonal administrations are integrated in a small democratic community gives individuals a democratic possibility to defend themselves against arbitrary decisions of their administration. The executive who is politically responsible to the people does not want to surrender its authority to an administrative court, which is composed of lawyers and not of politicians elected by the people. These were the main reasons why it was difficult to establish administrative courts within the cantonal court system. However the great majority of the cantons followed the federal example and introduced administrative courts, which differ very much from each other because of their different competences.

The immunity of public administration before the private law courts except for the 'fiscal part' of the administration and the growing necessity for a better protection of individuals against unlawful State orders are the main reasons why public administration was forced to develop its own public law system. This public law regulates the relationship between the State and individuals or between public corporations.

These different courts systems are the reason for the complicated administrative law. If a right of a citizen is violated by an unlawful administrative activity, he may have the following possibilities to appeal against the administration:

In an important case of the 1980s the European Court of Human Rights decided that Article 6 of the European Human Rights Convention had to be fully respected by all federal and cantonal administrative authorities, although the federal government ratifying the convention reserved the applicability of Article 6 with regard to federal and cantonal administrative law. This decision had far reaching consequences on the entire administrative procedure on the federal and cantonal level. All cantons were obliged to provide a final court procedure in all cases protected by Article 6 EHRC. Thus, directly or indirectly the rule of law principle and in particular the right to access to justice developed by the European Human Rights Court has influenced to a great extent the Swiss administrative law system in the last few years.

If the individual has been injured by an administrative order he can sue the State on the basis of a special procedure, in order to get his damage compensated, if this is provided by a special statute, otherwise he has only a civil action against the civil servant. This right is not explicitly guaranteed on federal level by the Federal Constitution (Art. 146).

Actions against the authority within the social welfare system are all different from those against normal administrative orders. They have to be taken to the special Administrative Court of Insurance (*Versicherungsgericht/Tribunal des assurances*). The federal social welfare system is an insurance system. The risks of age, death, invalidity and unemployment are insured by a general public insurance, of which every citizen is a member. On the other hand, only a part of the population was obliged to insure the risks of illness and accident. Insurances for illness are nowadays compulsory.

III. GENERAL PRINCIPLES OF SWISS ADMINISTRATIVE LAW

As has been made clear in the first part of this chapter, it is almost impossible to give a reliable picture of the complexity of the Swiss administrative law. One can only explain its most important principles.

Those principles have been developed by the Federal Tribunal in several cases, some going back almost fifty years ago. It was specifically due to Article 4 of the old Federal Constitution, which guaranteed equal rights to every individual, that permitted the court to develop such different principles as 'natural justice', 'due process', administrative 'estoppel', the 'principle of legality', and of 'proportionality'. These principles are now almost entirely part of the new Federal Constitution. The rule of law is provided in Article 5 of the Constitution, which guarantees that the State is bound, limited and can only be empowered by law. State activities and decisions must be guided by public interest and have to be proportional. The trust of citizens in state authorities must be protected (no estoppel) and all authorities have to respect international law. In addition basic principles of due process, natural justice and access to justice are not guaranteed in Articles 29, 29a and 30 of the Constitution. Particularly worth mentioning is Article 29a, which guarantees everybody access to an independent court in controversies with the administration.

This article will come into force in the next years with the new statute on administrative justice and procedure.

Before taking a look at these principles it is necessary to show how and when these principles can be applied.

Administration can infringe peoples' rights with an administrative order, such as the prohibition of a public demonstration, or by administrative negligence, such as a damaging operation in a public hospital.

If the administration promulgates an administrative order obliging an individual to do something or to refrain from doing something, this administrative order has to be enacted by a specific procedure regulated by a statute. Further it can be reviewed according to the respective administrative procedure. In cases of administrative actions without issuance of an administrative order, the individual has no case against the administration unless he is injured by the administrator acting negligently.

As in most cases administrative courts examine administrative orders, I shall first deal with these acts and will then explain the most important administrative principles. The problem of tort and State responsibility shall only be taken up at the end of the chapter.

A. *The Administrative Order* (Verfügung/Acte administratif)

Unlike common law, which guarantees access to justice by specific writs such as injunction, prohibitive injunction, mandamus, certiorari etc. the Swiss system of administrative law is part of the civil law system, which was introduced by Napoleon. Since then it has mainly been developed by the French council of state and in this century by the German administrative law science. Napoleon introduced the public law independent from private law in order to protect the administration from the 'conservative' judges of the ordinary judiciary. Thus he created 'immunity' of the administration only controlled by public law from private law courts by introducing the new legal branch of public law. In order to have nonetheless a limited protection with regard to the abuse of discretionary power of the administration even within the new public law system, the French Council of State introduced and developed within its jurisdiction in the 19th century the notion and the function of the administrative order, which can be examined with regard to its lawfulness in a special procedure by independent courts (*recours pour excès de pouvoir*).

Thus, when the administration imposes on the individual, for instance the obligation to pay a certain amount of taxes, this decision is called 'administrative order' (*Verfügung/acte administratif*). As administrative order, the decision can be brought before an administrative court. The court can review the order and control whether it is lawful.

Every administrative order has to be prepared in accordance with the cantonal or federal administrative procedure with some guarantees of due process in particular with regard to the fact-finding, which is within the jurisdiction of the administration (right of be informed on all reproaches and right to defense, formal hearings are not provided). It has to be in conformity with the statutes and the governmental ordinances. The individual has to be informed in due form about the order binding him. The facts have to be established by the administrative authority, which is obliged to consider opinions of the concerned party. If the party does not appeal against the order to higher authorities, it can be enforced like a judgment after the elapsing of a certain period of time. Thus unlawful elements of the order will be healed.

The administrative activity, which imposes rights and duties on individuals, has four stages: the procedure preparing the order, the administrative order itself, the procedure of appeal, and the enforcement of the order. On the federal level the entire process is regulated by the Administrative Procedure Act (*Verwaltungsverfahrensgesetz/ Loi sur la procédure administrative*) and the Bill Concerning the Organization and the Procedure Before the Federal Administrative Court (*Verwaltungsrechtspflege durch das Bundesgericht, Organisationsgesetz, jurisdiction administrative du Tribunal Fédéral, loi sur l'organisation judiciaire* – in a short time new statutes will come into force). These federal acts will soon be considerably amended according to the new Article 29a of the Constitution guaranteeing a general and individual access to court in all controversies with the public authority. On the cantonal level there exist cantonal statutes and ordinances regulating the administrative procedure, within the administration and before the administrative court, in a way similar to the Confederation.

In most cases, an individual may request the higher authorities to review the administrative order only after it has been issued; he or she may also claim the unlawfulness of the procedure at this time. During the procedure preparing the order, appeals by individuals are usually excluded. Nor can they have the order reviewed after it has been issued and the time limit for appellants' procedure has elapsed. Therefore an order may even be enforced although the order itself or the procedure to prepare it was unlawful. The citizen has only a very limited right to ask for the revision of the order. He or she has to give evidence that the administration did not take into account important facts, that it violated the fundamental right of the individual to be heard (natural justice) or that the authority that formulated the order was composed of members who had a direct personal interest.

What kind of decision is to be considered as an administrative order? An administrative order is every license which gives e.g. the permission to build a house, to drive a car, to use public places for a demonstration, to import a certain amount of goods under import regulations, and to use the water power of a river for electric energy or to broadcast a radio program. Administrative orders which impose individual obligations are the obligation to pay a certain amount of taxes, to serve in the army, to go to school or to refrain from further water pollution. Administrative orders of the social welfare system concern the rights of aged people to get a certain amount of welfare insurance, the right of students to state scholarships or the right of farmers to receive state subsidies. In civil law countries administrative orders can be executed by force. They have similar legal validity as judgments of the ordinary court. Administrative orders should therefore be enacted with similar diligence as traditional court decisions.

The administrative order is to be distinguished from a public law (or private law) contract. With the administrative order the administration imposes a 'one-sided' obligation on the citizen, decides on his or her vested rights or delivers him or her with new vested rights. When the administration concludes a contract, rights and obligations depend on the agreement of the parties, while administrative orders are decided by the administration alone. Therefore administrative law must protect citizens against arbitrary administrative orders and ensure that administrative orders are only issued within the limits provided by the law.

B. *The Principle of Legality* (Prinzip der Gesetzmässigkeit/principe de légalité)

Private law obligations can only be imposed upon an individual through a contract, which depends on the agreement of the parties involved. If he or she is a member of a corporation he or she can be obliged to obey the will of the majority. However the majority can only impose its will on the minority in accordance with the articles of the public entity. In any case, the individual decides by his or her free will whether he or she will enter into the territory controlled by this legal system. If the articles are modified, he or she has the possibility to withdraw from the territory.

Every individual is on the other side obliged to accept the administrative regulations notwithstanding his or her consent. Everybody has a duty to observe obligations issued by the administration. However, administration can only impose duties if they are justified. This jurisdiction is based on the ground that every administrative order is deduced from a statute adopted by parliament or by the people. The statute gets its legitimacy from the consent of the people. With this democratic legitimacy the administration can impose rights and obligations on citizens. Therefore, administrative activity or an administrative order which has an external effect is only justified if they have a statutory basis, a law somehow regulating this activity. In order to be lawful an administrative activity must not violate existing laws (*ultra vires*), and must also be derived from an existing law. The Federal Tribunal has authority to invalidate even administrative orders issued by parliament if they have no legal ground. The legislature, however, has a large competence of delegation of legislative powers. It can delegate to the government the competence to elaborate and issue ordinances and decrees. Therefore the legislative basis for a certain administrative activity may be very general.

This is true for almost all administrative orders with the exception of taxes (taxing power). According to the Swiss concept of democracy and of the separation of powers, taxes have to be regulated in a law which is put under the facultative or obligatory referendum of the people (Art. 164 of the Fed. Cons.). The statute must regulate who has to pay taxes, as well as the amount one has to pay. In other cases where important limits to individual freedom are imposed, the constitution also requires clear statutory provisions, allowing the administration to infringe into fundamental rights.

In some exceptional cases administrative activity is lawful even though it has no clear power. If public authorities use their police power to uphold law and order in order to prevent a clear and present danger, their activity is lawful even without a specific legislative basis. If the administration is acting within its discretionary power conveyed to it by a certain statute, this activity cannot be examined by any court as long as it observes the principle of proportionality, the activity is in the public interest and within the framework imposed upon the administration by the law.

Activities outside judicial jurisdiction are those which have only an internal impact on public authorities or civil servants and have no external effects on private citizens. Citizens who have close legal relations to the administration, for example civil servants to their government, students to the university, patients to the hospital, prisoners to the prison or children to their public school, have to observe obligations according to the aim of the administrative task to which they are related. Laws regulating those relationships convey usually far reaching discretionary power to the management, which therefore can impose duties without a clear legal basis. However persons under such regulations are not exposed at the whim of their authorities without any protection. The power of those agencies is always limited by the very statutory purpose the agency is obliged to pursue.

The principle of legality includes also the principles of constitutionality. However, for constitutional reasons the Swiss Federal Tribunal cannot review laws passed by the federal legislature (Art. 191 of the Fed. Cons). Still the constitutional rights must be observed when the law has to be interpreted, which means that laws have to be interpreted according to the Constitution. The Constitution also has to be observed within the discretionary power of the administration, and of course the Federal Constitution is binding on the cantonal administration and the cantonal laws, because those laws are subject to constitutional review.

The principle of legality differs to a certain extent from the *ultra vires* concept of the common law tradition:

1. An administrative order is considered to be illegal not only if it violates a statute but also if it has no legal basis. There is no concept of administrative prerogative power.
2. The unlawfulness of an administrative order is healed if it is not contested within a certain delay – it becomes lawful and cannot be collaterally reviewed.

C. The Principle of Due Process (Rechtliches Gehör/Droit d'être entendu)

The principle of due process has been developed by the Federal Tribunal under Article 4 of the old Constitution, providing for every citizen equal rights. Equal rights are protected when citizens' rights can only be limited with a legal basis, when administrative orders imposing rights and obligations on the individual are prepared in a due process issued in due form and subject to appeal to higher authorities. Today access to justice and due process of law are guaranteed by the Articles 29, 29a and 30 of the new Federal Constitution, not to forget the important guarantees of Articles 6 and 13 of the European Human Rights Convention.

Based on these constitutional principles the Federal Tribunal did impose on cantonal administrations some minimal obligations concerning the due process and natural justice for issuing and reviewing administrative orders. Most importantly, the cantons are obliged to inform the individual during the entire procedure establishing the facts for the preparation of an administrative order in case this order is limiting his or her rights or imposing new obligations on him or her. Parties concerned by the order must be given the chance to argue the case before the administrative authority, to propose new evidence and to be informed of arguments, fact-findings and evidence given to the authority by third parties or by civil servants. In other words, the individual subject to an administrative order has the 'right to be heard' by the administration (which does not include the formal right to get an oral hearing).

Since the Federal Tribunal stated its views concerning individuals' rights to be heard in administrative procedure, some cantons introduced legislative acts regulating all the different administrative procedures. The Federal Administrative Procedure Act defines the notion of the administrative order, regulates the competence and the duties of the authorities for the relevant fact-finding and to issue such orders, stipulates who may be parties in administrative procedure, states the rights and duties of the parties during the administrative procedure, and contains prescriptions concerning the due form in which administrative orders have to be issued and the means available for the administration to enforce administrative orders if the duties are not observed by the persons concerned.

This principle does not only regulate the procedure elaborating the administrative order; it also introduces the right of appeal against administrative orders to be quashed or newly enacted by higher administrative or judicial authorities in case of unlawfulness. The right to appeal and the procedure before such higher authorities as well as their competence to review the order or to issue new orders is regulated in the statute concerning the organization of the Federal Tribunal

(*Organisationsgesetz/loi fédérale d'organisation judiciaire*). Usually the individual can appeal against an administrative order to an administrative authority. However, only in the last instance may such an individual appeal to the administrative court or the executive. Some cantons have introduced judicial review of decisions of the executive. On the federal level and in most cantons administrative orders can only be reviewed by the administrative court, if they have been issued or reviewed by an authority lower than the executive level. Therefore some administrative orders can only be reviewed by the Federal Tribunal, and some only by the government. If the administrative order deals mainly with political questions, as for instance, the protection of the interests of Swiss citizens abroad, it is only subject to governmental review; however, when the administration has to deal mainly with legal questions in issuing the administrative order, the appeal goes to court.

The most important and most difficult question to decide is, who has a 'case' or who has legal standing. Unlike the American System of 'case and controversy', the right to appeal or the 'standing' (*Beschwerdebefugnis/qualité pour recourir*) to appeal as it is called in Switzerland does not belong only to the individual who has been directly affected by an unlawful order. The question of whether an order is unlawful will in any case only be decided with the judgment of the higher authority. The question of whether an individual has a 'case' does not depend on whether he or she has suffered a violation of their rights, but on the question of whether he or she has a personal interest which deserves a special protection, entitling him or her to ask for judicial review. It is obvious that such a vague determination of an individual's right to file a suit is subject to a number of court decisions, which are usually very difficult to interpret.

The courts have even held that an individual has the right to appeal against a permit issued to his or her neighbor allowing him to build a house on adjacent real estate. Anyone who lives within three miles of a projected atomic plant may appeal against the administrative permission; competitors can appeal against permissions given to their competitors to import products subject to import regulations or against the owner of a pharmacy who has received permission to operate on the public ground of a railway station.

The question of the right to appeal is even more important if one considers that, unlike American courts, the Swiss Federal Tribunal has no certiorari power. If the individual can appeal, and if according to the law the court must review such cases, the Federal Tribunal has to decide on the merits of the case.

The system of the *amicus curiae* known in the United States is excluded in Swiss court procedures. The individual appealing a case of important public interest, such as environmental interests, cannot ask for an *amicus curiae*. He or she must defend him/herself on the basis of his or her own interests. Therefore a considerable number of organizations defending different public interests, such as environmental organizations or groups protecting nature, ask for express statutory rights to appeal against administrative orders hazardous to clean air, protection of nature, forests, ecological systems, and so on. Until now the Bill for the Protection of Nature, the environment protection statute as the statute regulating equal rights of women did provide such a right for organizations founded to seek better protection of nature and historical monuments in the interests of the country. The very reason for the standing of such organization is to be found in the fact, that due process and access to justice in Switzerland are not only considered to protect individual rights but also to guarantee better implementation of public interests.

The fundamental guidelines for the idea of due process in Switzerland are

1. Guaranteed fair and equal treatment of the individual by the administration.
2. Credibility of administrative procedures.
3. Optimizing fact-finding of the administration.
4. Guaranteed objective application of the law and the public interest by the administration.

D. *The Principle of Proportionality* (Verhältnismässigkeitsprinzip/ Principe de proportionalité) – *Appropriateness*

The principle of proportionality is certainly one of the main guidelines of Swiss administrative law. It may be compared to the very principle of reasonableness of the Courts of the UK. The principle of proportionality is according to the Swiss tradition considered to be part of the very basics of the Rule of Law and now explicitly guaranteed by Articles 5 and 36 of the new Federal Constitution. Proportionality has to be observed in using the discretionary power delegated by the statutes to the administration, in expropriation cases, and when fees for public activities are charged, as in cases of university lectures, transportation of letters by the post, fees which have to be paid for an official permission, such as 'construction permission', 'driver's license' etc. Proportionality has to be observed in using disciplinary and penal power, when administrative orders have to be enforced by public officials. Proportionality also guides the police power as well as the procedure preparing administrative orders and preventive measures necessary to protect important public or even private interests.

In some cases administrative orders can be reviewed by the administration itself without being requested by the individual. If a school issues a diploma to the wrong student in error, it may abolish this decision if the student wrote a very bad examination paper and if it would endanger public interest in the exercise of his profession, for instance as a medical doctor. If he or she failed the examination by only one or two points and if it was the last chance for him or her to pass this examination, the abolition of the exam may be considered non-proportional, particularly if the student has already taken up his or her profession, unless he or she had been aware of the administration's error.

The principle of proportionality is very important because administrative laws in Switzerland usually contain large and vague provisions giving the administration a great discretionary power. This power should therefore be exercised and used with restraint. It is considered to be the main protection to avoid that any person is at the whim of public power.

An administrative order may be non-proportional when the interest to be promoted is of much less importance than the public or private interest violated by such administrative order. If the administration plans for the construction of an important road and if this road would alter the natural environment, then both public interests (goods traffic and protection of nature) have to be weighed against one another.

According to the principle of proportionality, the interest for the construction of a new road must be outweighing in order to justify the violation of the protected environment.

Interests also have to be balanced if the public interest is contrary to private interests and especially in cases where private interests are protected by constitutional rights. When it is within a reasonable public interest, an expropriation of private property for public use clearly outweighs private interests. Public interest does not outweigh private interest if a local community expropriates private land only for financial aims, for instance, to sell the land later at a higher price. However, public interest is accepted if a local municipality needs a private land to be able to achieve its project to build a public swimming pool.

Proportionality is not only a question of balancing different interests, it must also be guaranteed when means and aims have to be compared with each other. Means have to be proportional to the administrative aims. They must be necessary to achieve the goals provided by the statute. If the same goals could be achieved by less burdensome means, the administration has to decide on the least burdensome mean. When the administration must get private land in order to construct a road, it can only expropriate the part of the land that is absolutely necessary. If this means that the private owner must only give a small part of his land, the administration cannot, according to the principle of proportionality, expropriate the whole land. The principle of proportionality obliges the administration to use only those means that are absolutely necessary to accomplish the aim.

E. The 'Estoppel' Principle: The Obligation of the Administration to Act in Good Faith (Prinzip von Treu and Glauben/Principe de la bonne foi)

The principle that nobody has a right to *venire contra factum proprium* also binds the public administration. All public authorities have to act in good faith (Arts. 5 and 9 of the Federal Cons.). When administrative agencies give some information to private individuals, private persons must be able to rely on this information. According to case law, individuals can rely on administrative information when the information has been given by the authority in charge of the specific subject, when the authority has given written information, when the information does not contain any reservation and when the individual relying on the information had already taken some dispositions.

Persons can rely on information or administrative orders if they have been issued by the competent administrative authorities even when this information or the administrative order requires decisions not provided by a specific statute. However this is only the case when the individual did not have any doubts as to the competence of the administration and if it already took specific measures relying on the decision of the administration.

This principle of good faith and reliability on administrative activities provides for citizens a certain security with regard to the administration. It can estop administrative decisions violating prior assurances. This legal security is very important for an administration which acts within a democratic environment and which has to respect the dignity and freedom of the people. This guarantees that administrative activities are foreseeable. Individuals can calculate and foresee in which case and with what means and for what aims administration will become active.

According to court decisions, the administration is obliged to give a grant, if this grant has been assured; if the mayor of a town assured the permission to build a house, the town may be bound by this assurance, as long as the mayor was competent to give such assurances and the individual did already take dispositions according to this assurance. However if this would overwhelmingly harm public interest, the administration may have 'continuing jurisdiction' over the case, and have the right to revoke or adopt an administrative order.

There is one important exception to the reliance of individuals on administrative decisions or assurances; that is the social welfare insurance. If an individual receives a social welfare payment which is above the amount he or she is entitled to, then he or she must pay back the difference, even if he or her had already spent it. However, if this measure would cause serious hardship to the individual, then the administration has no right to demand for that money to be returned. The reason for this jurisprudence is to be found in the very fact, that social security is based on solidarity among the entire population. It would violate the solidarity principle if one individual would be privileged because of some false decisions of the administration.

The good faith principle also respected within the administrative law in Germany, but not in France and is not followed by the administrative law of the European Union. Thus, Switzerland once entering the European Union may have to review this principle considered by the Swiss legal tradition as being part of our natural justice.

IV. NEW PUBLIC MANAGEMENT

Administration has long been considered as the legally controlled body to implement the will of the legislature within the framework of the specific legal system. Administration was organized through a hierarchical structure controlled by the executive accountable by checks and balances to parliament. Administration had no power to decide how to achieve major legislative goals. The goals as well as the legal, personal and financial means to pursue certain policies were imposed on the administration. The enormous tasks of administrative agencies however, did so much increase administrative power, that the executive is no longer able to control all important powers of the administration. With the principle of new management this concept has changed radically. According to the principles of new public management the legislature and the executive should no longer prescribe all inputs on administrative activities. Administration should be directed by output goals defined by the legislature or by the executive. Legislature and executive should decide on the 'What' and not anymore on the 'How'.

In order to achieve the goals defined by the legislature the administration should have at its disposal the financial means provided in a global budget leaving specific financial decisions with regard to means to be necessary to achieve these goals up to the administration. The administration should have more discretionary power with regard to the employees in order to motivate civil servants to serve the goals of the administration and to be available to their clients who should neither be considered as subjects nor as citizens. This objective has been implemented in Switzerland by new legislation at cantonal and federal level with regard to the employment of persons to fulfill public services. In fact, the old statute for civil servants which has engaged employees as civil servants by a unilateral administrative order to be renewed every four years has been replaced by a new bill regulating the public contract of employment between administrative agencies and employees. Several public services have been given far reaching budgetary autonomy, and some services have been partially privatized through special statutes based on an almost totally private trusteeship.

V. THE PROTECTION OF PROPERTY (*EIGENTUMSGARANTIE/ PROTECTION DE LA PROPRIÉTÉ*)

I shall now explain how personal property is protected by the Constitution and the statutes, and then I will show on which basis the administration can levy taxes.

A. *The Protection of Real Property and of Vested Rights* (Wohlerworbene Rechte/Droits acquis)

Immovable property is better protected than financial rights, such as the income of the fortune not invested in real estate. A similar protection is given to rights with financial consequences historically vested in individuals, such as the centuries old right to have a 'pub' in a house, or to use the water of the river. Vested rights can be given now with a special license (concession). With a concession, the State delivers a right owned by the State to be utilized economically, such as the right to install and use a waterpower plant in order to transform water into electricity. The financial interest of such a vested right must be compensated, if the right is taken away from the individual. Therefore, vested rights can only be limited if the financial value of the acquired right (*wohlerworbenes Recht/droit acquis*) is fully compensated.

The property of the State and of individuals is regulated by private law. According to the French public law system state property is only controlled by public law. Therefore one can only acquire property by buying it from a third person; this is also true for the State. However, in some cases the public needs property in order to execute a task which is in the public interest, for instance if it has to construct new school buildings, hospitals or roads. In such cases it can acquire property that is not sold on a private law basis by the means of expropriation based on a special expropriation procedure provided in federal or cantonal expropriation bills as in real estate (*Enteignung/expropriation*).

Any expropriation by public administration is only possible if it is provided for a public purpose defined in a special statute. It must be in the public interest and the owner has to get full financial compensation. The principle is that the expropriated should be in the same economical condition as that before and after the expropriation. The administration wishing to expropriate privately owned land has according to the statute regulating the procedure of expropriation to seek the legal basis, justify the action in the public interest and then compensate the individual.

The procedure of expropriation is regulated by federal statutes for federal constructions and in cantonal statutes for the execution of cantonal tasks in the federal or cantonal public interest. The procedure gives the private owner the opportunity to appeal against the expropriation, on the grounds that the expropriation is not in the public interest or that there is no legal basis justifying such an expropriation. This appeal may be finally decided by an independent agency, normally by the court. If the expropriation is justified, the individual can appeal against the decision if he or she is fully compensated for the expropriation. The compensation is usually measured by an independent committee. This committee has to assure a full economic compensation, that is, the individual is entitled to the monetary value of the property after the expropriation. If this is not the case, he has a right of appeal to a court.

Compensation must also be paid for a partial expropriation or for the expropriation of neighbor rights such as· the right not to be injured by neighbors through noise or other emissions being caused on the neighboring real estate.

The State does not always need the ownership of the property in order to execute its task. For instance, zoning laws can distribute the use of the land without State ownership. Land may stay privately owned, but the public authority can decide that some land can only be used for agricultural use or that some real estate has to be used for housing and that other land will be used for industrial plants. With such regulations the use of privately owned land may be limited to the extent that it is almost a full expropriation. Prices for real estate may fall heavily. If the zoning law has reduced the use of the private property in a way coming close to an expropriation the State must give compensation. According to court decisions, this is the case when, for instance, land which is fit to be used for housing can only be used for agricultural purposes due to a zoning regulation.

The question of whether land can be used for housing does not only depend on the will of the private owner: the land must be close enough to a village; it must be on a road; it must have water and energy supplies; and drainage must be assured. As long as the real estate is not integrated into the urban planning, the private owner has no right to be linked with new roads, water or energy supplies. He may not even build the necessary installations at his own cost. He or she has, therefore, no right to construct any buildings and to get compensation if the zoning law forbids him or her to use his or her land for construction.

The old history of the small Swiss communities which were based on corporative ideas still influences today's use of land property. If someone owns a private forest for instance, he or she must take care of the wood and has no right to cut the trees without permission. According to the Swiss Forest Law, the amount of wood existing in Switzerland must remain; if permission is given to cut some trees, new trees must be planted elsewhere. Also the Swiss Agricultural Law provides for ways in which land is supposed to be utilized for agricultural aims. Private owners are obliged to cultivate their land. Private law tries to prevent the distribution of the agricultural land in small pieces upon the death of the owner with different measures.

In the mountain areas trespass on all the land is allowed during a few months of the year in order to feed the cattle. If a farmer would like to build a hedge around his property he must get permission and pay a certain amount of money for compensation to his village.

In several cantons there still exist old corporations of citizens who own a lot of the land and of the forest of the village. They regulate the common use and common cultivation of this land through their corporation.

B. *State Responsibility* (Staatshaftung/Responsabilité de l'etat)

Property rights can be violated not only by unlawful expropriation but also by the civil servant's negligence. Wrong information given by the administration can cause considerable damage if the individual took dispositions according to this information.

Has the administration a duty to repair these torts? Article 61 of the Swiss Code of Obligations provides, that for non-commercial activities the civil servants are personally accountable for such damages unless the cantonal legislation provides direct compensation by the state. Today all cantons have introduced special bills providing cantonal compensation for damages caused unlawfully by their civil servants. If the damage is caused by a civil servant of a federal authority the federal law on state compensation has to be applied.

According to the court decisions, the State is only responsible for the damage caused by its civil servants if this State responsibility is regulated by a special statute. If there is no statute or if the responsibility is excluded, the State does not have to repair the damage caused by its civil servants.

However, according to the private law, cantons are responsible for damages caused by their activities that have economic and no administrative aims. In cases of cantonal commercial activities, such as energy supply, which is regulated by private law, the owner of the industry is responsible for damage caused by its employees. State responsibility also takes place according to Article 58 of the Swiss Code of Obligations. If a defective construction causes damage, then the owner of the construction has to compensate the damage. If the owner of a construction such as a road is a State, then it is responsible for damage caused by its defects.

In most cantons, and in the Confederation, not only the codes of private law but also special statutes regulate State responsibility. These special bills have been introduced in the last 40 years. Although these bills provide different solutions with regard to State responsibility, they all improve the situation of the individual who has been damaged by State activity. According to several statutes an individual has to prove that the damage was caused by persons empowered to execute a State activity and that such action was unlawful and was done negligently. In some cases the individual need not even have to prove that the State authority or the employee has acted negligently; he or she must only prove that the action was unlawful. The most important consequence of these statutes is the fact that in every case the State is responsible for the activity of its employees, and must repair their damage. The injured person can directly sue the State. Damage that must be compensated can be caused by wrong information given on behalf of the State, by an arbitrary decision or in performing a task (e.g. an operation on a patient in a public hospital) or by negligently non-intervening, where a state activity is legally mandatory.

In some cases the State may have an obligation to repair damages resulting from its action, even though this action was legal. If a village in the mountains is in danger because of possible avalanches, specialists must try to loosen small avalanches.

Such activity is certainly legal. However it may cause some damage. For such types of legal action however, some cantonal laws provide the citizen an opportunity to be compensated.

C. Taxes

According to a decision of the Federal Tribunal, property must be protected from unreasonable tax laws. The State has no right to levy such high taxes as to diminish the substance of fortune, and tax systems have to respect property as an institution.

However, the best guarantees against high taxes are not the property rights, but the right of every citizen to participate in tax decisions. According to the Swiss court decisions, taxes must be determined in the law accepted by the people themselves (no taxes without consent by the voters). The legislature must decide who has to pay taxes as well as the amount to be paid. The legislature in each canton is enacted either by the parliament and the people, or by the parliament alone notwithstanding the right of the people to ask for a referendum. Therefore, the Anglo-Saxon principle 'no taxation without representation' has been changed in Switzerland into the system 'no taxation without the people'.

SELECTED BIBLIOGRAPHY

Note: For this edition we decided not to include court decisions and specific literature with footnotes. Readers can consult all federal or cantonal websites in order to find the relevant legislation or the relevant court decision. With regard to literature, including articles in periodicals, the reader can use the library of the Institute of Federalism, including its database on legislation. The library, the database on legislation as well as all links to cantonal or federal information (German, French, Italian and some in Romansh) can be found on the website of the Institute of Federalism including its search engine and links: <www.federalism.ch>.

Biaggini, G., *Theorie und Praxis des Verwaltungsrechts im Bundesstaat*, Basel/Frankfurt a.M. 1996.

Fleiner–Gerster, T., *Grundzüge des allgemeinen und schweizerischen Verwaltungsrechts*, 2nd edn., Zurich 1980.

Grisel, A., *Traité de droit administratif*, 2 vols., Neuchâtel 1984.

Häfelin, U. and G. Müller, *Allgemeines Verwaltungsrecht*, 4th fully revised edn., Zurich 2002.

Imboden, M. and R. Rhinow, *Schweizerische Verwaltungsrechtssprechung*, 2 vols., 6th edn., Basel/Frankfurt a.M. 1988.

Knapp, B., *Précis de droit adminstratif*, 4th edn., Basel/Frankfurt a.M. 1991.

Koller, H., G. Müller, R. Rhinow and U. Zimmerli (eds.), *Schweizerisches Bundesverwaltungsrecht*, Basel/Frankfurt a.M. 1996.

Moor, P., *Droit administratif*, Volume I: *Les fondements généraux*, 2nd edn., Bern 1994; Volume II: *Les actes administratifs et leur contrôle*, Bern 1991; Volume III: *L'organisation des activités administratives/Les biens de l'Etat*, Bern 1992.

Rhinow, R. and B. Krähenmann, *Schweizerische Verwaltungsrechtssprechung*, Ergänzungsband, Basel/Frankfurt a.M. 1990.

Schürmann, L., *Wirtschaftsverwaltungsrecht*, Bern 1994.

Schwarzenbach–Hanhart, H. R., *Grundriss des Allgemeinen Verwaltungsrechts*, 11th edn., Bern 1997.

Tschannen, P., U. Zimmerli and R. Kiener, *Allgemeines Verwaltungsrecht*, Bern 2000.

Zimmerli, U., W. Kälin and R. Kiener, *Grundlagen des öffentlichen Verfahrensrechts*, Bern 1997.

Chapter 4
Law of Persons

*François Knoepfler**

I. GENERAL

In Swiss law, the word '*person*' is synonymous with being a holder of rights. 'Legal personality' means all the attributes of a person that are protected by law. It includes the ability to enjoy rights and the capacity to exercise rights and assume obligations. According to Swiss law, all individual human beings (physical or natural persons) and to a certain extent corporate bodies – private as well as public – such as corporations and associations (legal persons) possess a legal personality. The law of persons is codified in the first Book of the Civil Code. It includes an introduction and two chapters. The first chapter covers natural persons (Arts. 11–51 CC), while the second one deals with legal persons (Arts. 52–89 CC).

II. NATURAL PERSONS (*Personnes physiques/ Natürliche Personen*)

A. Beginning and End of Personality

1. General

Personality begins at birth, provided the child is born alive (i.e. breathing and with the heart beating). Swiss law does not require proof of likelihood of living (viability) (Art. 31 CC).

2. *Nasciturus*

For the lawyer, even an unborn child may have a certain degree of legal personality, provided it is subsequently born alive (Art. 31 II CC). It would, however, be more correct to state that under certain circumstances the unborn child possesses a legal personality.

    Legally, the moment of conception is not decisive. Among the different possibilities, the most favorable one can be chosen since the law gives an advantage to the

*Professor Dr., University of Neuchâtel. The author expresses his gratitude to Mr. Davide Gozzer, assistant at the university, for verifying the notes.

F. Dessemontet and T. Ansay (eds), Introduction to Swiss Law, 47–58.

nasciturus. The child may choose the date eneabling him or her to benefit from the rights of the nasciturus. Proof to the contrary is possible.

The Civil Code does not guarantee a right to life that is provided for in the Penal Code (for example, abortion, Articles 118–121, but in the process of being changed). In the case of inheritance the nasciturus becomes important (Art. 544 CC).

3. Death

The legal personality of a human being ends only at death (Art. 311 CC). The Code does not define death. Traditionally, death occurred when the heart stopped and breathing ceased. Taking into account contemporary possibilities of maintaining life, death is now defined as the point when brain functions definitively and completely cease.[1]

When a person has disappeared under such circumstances that his or her death seems certain,[2] his or her death is taken as established, even though his or her corpse has not been found (for example when someone is buried by an avalanche in the presence of eye-witnesses and the body cannot be found) (Arts. 34 and 49 CC).

When two persons die in the same accident or under different circumstances, the time of each death may be important, especially regarding the consequences as to inheritance law. The burden of proof of birth or death lies with the claimant (Art. 32 I CC). If the moment of death of several persons cannot be established, the law presumes that all died at the same moment (Art. 32 II CC). This presumption can be disproved by evidence to the contrary.[3]

4. Consequences of death (*Effets de la mort/Wirkung des Todes*)

The legal personality of a human being ends at the moment of death, but all legal acts carried out by the person before his death remain valid (last will and testament) (Art. 31 I CC). Though it may appear that certain elements of legal personality continue after death, these are in fact either survivors' rights[4] (wills, recognition of a child) or rights relative to the deceased himself or herself (protection of the corpse).

In Swiss law posthumous marriage does not exist. Death terminates the marriage, whereas a declaration of absence only gives the right to sue for dissolution of the marriage.

B. *Civil Capacity* (Capacité civile/Handlungsfähigkeit)

Civil capacity is composed of two aspects: legal capacity (enjoyment of rights) and capacity to act (exercise of rights). Every person enjoys rights, but not every person can exercise a right. A child, for instance, can own a house, but cannot sell the house.

1. ATF 98 Ia 508; ATF 123 I 112.
2. ATF 56 I 550; ATF 75 I 328.
3. ATF 104 II 202.
4. ATF 74 II 225.

1. Legal Capacity (*Jouissance des droits civils/Rechtsfähigkeit*)

The law defines legal personality as the capacity to have rights and duties (Art. 11 II CC).

Certain inequalities are due to sex, such as the rule prescribing a delay for divorced people who wish to remarry (Art. 103 CC).

Impaired mental health can justify inequality of treatment. Restrictions are therefore made in the interest of third parties as well as of the mentally ill person (Art. 97 CC, marriage; Art. 467 CC, will).

In 1976 the law abolished differences between children born out of wedlock and those born within marriage. The term *'illegitimate child'* has been deleted. Differences, however, remain in cases concerning the establishment of paternity (Art. 260 *et seq.* CC), name (Art. 270 CC), and parental authority (Art. 296 CC).

Except in matters of private international law, civil law, in contrast to public law, does not take nationality into account. However, there are some exceptions like the legislation which restricts the rights of foreigners to acquire real estate in Switzerland (Lex Friedrich).

2. Capacity to Act (*Exercise des droits civils/Handlungsfähigkeit*)

The second aspect of civil capacity is the capacity to exercise rights. A certain age is required to enjoy the right to marry (Art. 96 CC), the right to adopt (Art. 264a CC), the right to make a will (Art. 467 CC), and the right to dispose of property by way of a testamentary disposition (Art. 468 CC).

The law makes this capacity to acquire rights and to assume obligations subject to some conditions.

a. Majority

Majority is attained at eighteen years of age (Art. 14 CC).

b. Discernment

The ability to make reasonable judgments (discernment) comprises an element of intellectual capacity and an element of will (willingness).[5] It is a relative concept appreciated in concrete cases. Its existence is presumed.[6] Positively, discernment is defined as the ability to act reasonably (Art. 16 CC). Absence of discernment arises from the youthful age of the person,[7] mental illness, alcoholism, feeble-mindedness or other similar reasons. Lack of discernment may therefore be temporary or permanent.[8]

---

5. ATF 77 II 97.
6. ATF 43 II 739; ATF 117 II 231; ATF 124 III 5.
7. ATF 102 II 363; ATF 104 II 184; ATF 106 V 22
8. ATF 74 II 202.

c. On Suspension of Rights

A person can be placed under guardianship in case of insanity, prodigality, alcoholism or imprisonment, as well as at his own request (Art. 369 *et seq.* CC). Such a person has his rights suspended. If any of the above conditions are present, capacity to act can be restricted or cease to exist altogether.

3. Extent of Capacity to Act (*Étendue de la capacité civile/Umfang der Handlungsfähigkeit*)

a. Restricted Civil Capacity (Capacité resteinte/Beschränkte Handlungsfähigkeit)

This concerns persons who actually have full capacity but are subject to certain restrictions. Their capacity constitutes the rule, and incapacity, limited to specific transactions, is the exception. For instance, during marriage, both the husband and the wife have their civil capacity restricted for certain acts for which the consent of the other spouse is necessary, e.g. contract of guarantee (Art. 494 CO), hire-purchase (Art. 226b CO), adoption by a married person (Art. 264a CC), lease (Art. 226m CO).

Where there is not sufficient ground for placing a person under guardianship and yet his or her own interests demand that his legal capacity be restricted, a quasi-guardianship can be appointed. This person will then have restricted civil capacity (Art. 395 CC).

b. Restricted Incapacity (Incapacité restreinte/Beschränkte Handlungsunfähigkeit)

Persons who have the ability to make reasonable judgments but who are not of age or who suffer another cause of restriction have restricted incapacity. Their incapacity is the rule; capacity is the exception (Art. 19 CC). Persons with restricted incapacity can only enter into valid transactions with the consent of their statutory guardian. The consent may be prior to the act, coincide with it, or be subsequent to it. It may be express, or tacit. A minor may himself or herself ratify the act as soon as he becomes of age.[9]

Persons with restricted incapacity may enter into transactions by which they merely benefit without incurring obligations or liabilities. They may, for example, accept gifts. They may exercise strictly personal rights (Arts. 19 II, 123 to 126 CC). They also have full liability in tort (Arts. 19 III, 411 II CC).[10]

c. Total Incapacity (Incapacité totale/Totale Handlungsunfähigkeit)

Those persons who are deprived of making a reasonable judgment (discernment) are totally incapable of exercising rights. Their acts are void and have no legal effect (Art. 18 CC, with some exceptions: Arts. 120 no. 2, 123, 519 *et seq.* CC).

---

9. ATF 75 II 337.
10. ATF 90 II 9; ATF 99 III 4; ATF 102 II 363; ATF 112 V 97.

C. *Name* (Nom/Name)

Every person must have a first name and a family name. The family name is an important part of the legal personality. A title of nobility is not a part of the name except nobiliary particles such as '*de*' or '*von*' before the name.

The family name can be acquired either by origin or be derived.

A name obtained by origin is acquired by filiation. The child of married parents bears the name of the father (Art. 160 I CC). The child of an unmarried woman bears the name of the mother (Arts. 259, 270 II CC).

A name acquired by marriage is derived (Art. 160 CC). The wife can either take the name of her husband or keep her name followed by her husband's name. After a divorce, the wife keeps the name she had during the marriage (Art. 149 I CC). She can however declare within six months that she wants to bear the name she had before the marriage. In some cases the spouses may bear the wife's name as family name (Art. 30 II CC). An adopted person takes the family name of the adopting family (Art. 267).[11]

A person may request a change of name on material grounds (Art. 30 CC), such as a child living with unmarried parents who wants to take his or her father's name[12] or a person bearing a name that lays him open to ridicule.[13]

The first name is chosen by the parents. The choice is not completely free (Art. 301 IV CC).[14]

Each natural as well as legal[15] person has a right to the protection of his or her name.

This right is an integral part of the legal personality (see E below). This protection has two aspects:

- to guarantee that each individual can bear his own name (Art. 29 I CC);
- to ensure that the name of a person is not borne by another person (Art. 29 II CC).[16] In the commercial field, breach of the right to a name can additionally be protected by the laws on unfair competition and trademark. In the field of the arts, protection covers the pseudonym.[17]

D. *Domicile* (Domicile/Wohnsitz)

The civil domicile may be different from fiscal or administrative domiciles (Arts. 23 to 26 CC). Civil domicile has many applications in Swiss law. For example a person is generally sued before the court of his domicile (Art. 30 II Fed. Cons. and Art. 3 Federal Law on the Civil Courts).

11. ATF 105 II 65; ATF 108 II 1.
12. ATF 105 II 241; ATF 117 II 6.
13. ATF 98 Ia 455; ATF 108 II 247; ATF 120 II 276.
14. ATF 116 II 504; ATF 118 II 243; ATF 119 II 401.
15. ATF 117 II 513.
16. ATF 102 II 305; ATF 108 II 241; ATF 112 II 369; ATF 116 II 463.
17. ATF 92 II 305.

Civil domicile is determined by residence in one place with the intention of settling there. The Federal Tribunal stated that the domicile is the place where a person has the center of his or her life and his personal interests. Intention is confirmed by the facts.[18] Places of school attendance or hospital stay do not constitute domicile, regardless the length of the stay (Art. 26 CC).[19]

Every person must have a domicile and one only. When a person changes his residence, he or she theoretically keeps his or her old domicile until he acquires another one (Art. 24 CO).[20] When a person leaves his or her domicile abroad without creating a new one in Switzerland, his or her place of residence in this country is presumed to be his or her domicile (Art. 24 II CC).[21]

The law distinguishes between the independent domicile – domicile of choice – and the dependent domicile. Normally a person may choose and change his or her domicile freely. In some cases the law determines where the domicile of a person should be. Children and persons under guardianship have dependent domiciles. The spouses can have different domiciles.

E. Protection of Legal Personality (Protection de la personnalité/Schutz der Persönlichkeit)

The law protects legal personality, including those rights of life, limb, body, health, reputation, and the right to personal freedom. The provisions of the Civil Code on the protection of legal personality (Arts. 27 to 29 CC) are complemented by the Penal Code and the individual liberties mentioned in the Federal Constitution.

There are legal safeguards to protect (the legal) personality against oneself and others.

1. Protection against Oneself

Personal freedom is a fundamental right but not an unlimited one. Life in society justifies restrictions as long as the basic rights of the person are not infringed upon. Persons may limit their freedom if this limitation neither violates the law nor offends public policy. Experience has shown that under outside pressure persons themselves sometimes agree to restrictions on their own legal personality. In order to protect the weak from their own actions, Article 27 CC states: 'No one may renounce his freedom or restrict himself in its use to a degree that violates the law or offends public policy'. A commitment for life or an agreement to comply without restriction with another person is illegal.[22] A person cannot promise never to marry nor to change his/her political ideas or his/her religion. The questions in the field of contracts (employment, leases and so on).[23] There are some examples of permissible

---

18. ATF 92 I 218; ATF 97 II 1; ATF 106 Ib 353; ATF 119 III 51; ATF 120 III 7; ATF 125 V 76; ATF 125 III 100.
19. ATF 82 III 12; ATF 106 Ib 193.
20. ATF 94 I 318; ATF 108 Ia 252.
21. ATF 80 II 107; ATF 93 II 7; ATF 113 II 5.
22. ATF 93 II 290; ATF 112 II 434; ATF 114 II 162; ATF 120 II 35.
23. ATF 114 II 162; ATF 120 V 299.

limitations in law such as contracts in restraint of trade (Art. 340 CO) or contracts of sale on credit (Art. 226a *et seq.* CO). A court may cancel a contract that has deeply damaged a person who was inexperienced or in severe financial difficulties at the time the contract was signed (overreaching; lésion/Übervorteilung) (Art. 21 CO).[24]

2. Protection against Others

According to Article 28 CC, '*where anyone is being injured in his or her person or reputation by another's unlawful act, he or she can apply to the judge for his or her protection from any person who takes an active part in effecting the injury.*' Through these words the law protects a large variety of rights.

a. *Life, Body and Mind*

This important right relates to protection of physical and psychological well being. Different injuries are allowed, but only in a few cases:

- consent of the person, if the consent is not void according to Article 17 CC,[25]
- existence of an overriding private or public interest, as long as it has a statutory basis; for example, blood tests or compulsory vaccination.[26]

Furthermore every person has the right to decide what shall happen to his body after death.

b. *Honour and Dignity*

The law widely protects a person's honour, including social respect and reputation. Honour may be damaged by accusations, libel, slander and wrong information. The injury is not illegal provided that it is the only way of satisfying a justifiable interest.[27]

c. *Privacy*

The law distinguishes between public, private and intimate life. Protection of privacy applies to all situations, but the limits of protection are not the same for a well-known person and less known people.[28] The former is expected to receive less protection than the latter. Protection includes all ways of discovering private information (opening letters, listening in on telephone calls and so on). Protection has had to be increased because of technical developments such as data banks, internet,

24. ATF 86 II 365.
25. ATF 114 Ia 350; ATF 117 Ia 197.
26. ATF 112 Ia 248; ATF 114 Ia 350; ATF 120 II 225;ATF 127 III 481.
27. ATF 111 II 209.
28. ATF 97 II 97.

sound-recordings and long distance photography. An event which was public when it happened can belong to intimate or private life after a few years. It will then become an injury to reveal it.[29]

d. Visual Image and Voice

The right of a person to his or her own visual image is recognized independently from that of honor and privacy. In cases of public interest, the picture of a person may be freely published (for example, pictures of politicians in Parliament). For protection the following steps may be requested:

- an injunction in case of an imminent injury,
- the removal of an existing injury,
- a statement declaring the illegality of an attack when the damage caused is on-going. Furthermore the injured person may ask for damages and moral compensation (Art. 49 CO).

When anyone is directly injured in his person by the presentation of facts in period-ically appearing media, in particular the press, radio or television, he is entitled to make a counterstatement (Arts. 28g to 28i CC).[30]

III. Legal Persons (*Personnes morales/Juristische Personen*)

A. *Associations* (Associations/Vereine)

An association is a group of natural or legal persons constituted and organized on the basis of a written agreement to reach a non-economic purpose.

1. Constitution

The Civil Code is extremely liberal on the formation of associations. Associations formed for political, religious, scientific, artistic or other non-economic purposes acquire legal personality as soon as they express in their articles of association such an intention (Art. 60 I CC).[31] The articles of association must be drawn up in writing and state the aim, resources, and organization of the association (Art. 60 II CC).

Associations operating a commercial enterprise to reach a non-economic aim are required to register in the trade register (Art. 61 II CC). For other associations, registration in the trade register is optional.

---

29. ATF 109 II 353.
30. ATF 113 II 369; ATF 114 II 388; ATF 115 II 4; ATF 115 II 113; ATF 118 IV 41; ATF 119 III 104; ATF 120 II 273; ATF 123 III 145.
31. ATF 88 II 209.

2. Organs

The law requires two organs: the general assembly and the board of directors. The general assembly, which includes all members, is the supreme authority of the association (Art. 64 I CC). It is convened upon the invitation of the directors in cases prescribed by the articles (by-laws), as well as on request of one-fifth of the members (Art. 64, II, III CC).[32] The general assembly gives directions as to the operation of the association, elects the directors, supervises the activities of the organs and decides on the admission and the exclusion of members. The general assembly also settles business for which other organs are not competent (Art. 65 I CC).

The board of directors is elected by the general assembly and can comprise one or several persons.[33] The board of directors assumes the responsibilities for the directives and carries out the decisions of the general assembly (Art. 69 CC).

3. Membership (*Sociétaires/Mitgliedschaft*)

Membership may be acquired either by participation in the constitution of the association or subsequently. No one can be forced to join an association, and the association is free to refuse a candidate, even if the latter fulfils the conditions required for admission. Nevertheless, admission and exclusion shall not lead to an excessive limitation of competition. The articles or the by-laws determine the procedure of admission, which is generally within the competence of the general assembly.

Members of an association have various rights, such as the right to vote, the right to ask that the general assembly be convened, to be informed about the activities of the association, to demand the annulment of the assembly's resolutions which are contrary to the law or to the articles of association or by-laws, as well as the right to maintain the stated non-economic aim.[34]

As far as duties are concerned, the members have an obligation of loyalty towards the association, whose interests they must not prejudice. They must also pay the annual dues set out in the articles of associations or made necessary by the financial situation of the association (Art. 71 CC). The articles of association can prescribe other obligations for the members.

Membership is lost by resignation or by exclusion. Each member may leave the association by giving six months' notice (Art. 70 II CC). The articles of association may shorten this period, but not extend it. In certain cases, the courts may admit a resignation takes effect immediately.[35]

If the articles of association do not provide for the contrary, a member can only be excluded on material grounds, for example, for non-payment of membership dues. The articles of association can, however, state grounds of exclusion or even permit exclusion without indicating any grounds (Art. 72 CC). The exclusion must in any case comply with the requirements of form and must not be arbitrary.[36]

---

32. ATF 71 I 384.
33. ATF 73 II 1.
34. ATF 86 II 389; ATF 108 II 15.
35. ATF 71 II 194.
36. ATF 90 II 194.

Exclusion of members comes within the competence of the general assembly. If, according to the articles of association, exclusion falls within the competence of another body, then appeal against the exclusion may be addressed to the general assembly (Art. 72 CC).

4. Termination (*Dissolution/Auflösung*)

The general assembly may decide to dissolve an association at any time (Art. 76 CC). The association will be dissolved *de jure* in the event of insolvency or if the aim can no longer be attained (Art. 77 CC). Finally, if the aim of the association becomes illegal or immoral, dissolution may be pronounced by a judge at the request of the competent authority or any interested party.

B. *Foundations* (Fondations/Stiftungen)

Foundations are constituted by setting apart an endowment for a special stated purpose (Art. 80 CC). Whereas associations are composed of members, foundations consist exclusively of juridically independent assets, provided with its own organs and subject to the supervision of a public authority. Once established, the endowment cannot be diverted from the purpose chosen by the founder.

The foundation is constituted by a declaration or by a last will and has to register in the trade register (Art. 81 II CC). Upon registration it acquires legal personality.

Any natural or legal person may set up a foundation. Creditors, as well as disinherited heirs, can oppose the foundation in order to protect their rights (Art. 82 CC).[37]

The fund allocated to a foundation most frequently consists of property rights, but it may also include credits, even credits against the founder.[38] The amount of the fund has to be large enough to reach the aim pursued by the founder. If the fund is insufficient, it will be transferred to an already existing foundation pursuing an identical or similar aim (Art. 83 III CC).

The aim of the foundation is an essential element. It must be possible, legal, ethical and in conformity with public policy.[39] It has to be stated in a precise manner in the charter of the foundation.

All foundations must have at least one administrative organ. Its constitution, as well as the way of administration, must be specified in the charter of the foundation (Art. 83 I CC).

The beneficiaries of the foundation may lodge a complaint with the supervisory authority if the organs of the foundation do not respect the charter. They even have the right, if the charter so prescribes in a precise and objective manner, to claim the benefits accruing to them.

Foundations are placed under the supervision of a public body (Confederation, canton, commune) to which their aim corresponds (Art. 84 I CC). The prime function

37. ATF 90 II 365; ATF 96 II 273; ATF 99 III 41.
38. ATF 75 I 269.
39. ATF 76 I 39.

of this supervision is to ensure that the assets of the foundation are used for the purposes for which they are destined (Art. 84 II CC). The authority intervenes upon receiving a complaint or *ex officio*. It also has the responsibility of supervising the management of the foundation, of pronouncing of decisions following complaints and of suspending or dismissing the administrative organs.[40]

The same authority also intervenes in case of a failing in the organizational structure of the foundation. Thus, if the charter of the foundation becomes insufficient for the proper functioning of the foundation, the competent public authority takes the necessary steps, which may go as far as preparing a new charter (Art. 83 II CC).

In principle, the organization and the aim of the foundation are unalterable. However, when a modification of the organizational structure is absolutely necessary to preserve the endowment or conserve the aim of the founder, the competent authority will take action after consultation with the highest organ of the foundation (Art. 85 CC). The foundation's aim may also be modified according to the same procedure when the character or the scope of the original aim has varied to the point where the foundation has evidently ceased to meet the original intentions of the founder (Art. 86 I CC).

The foundation will be dissolved when its aim can not longer be fulfilled. If the aim has become illegal or contrary to public policy, the dissolution will be pronounced by the court[41] at the request of the supervisory authority or of any interested party (Arts. 88 and 89 I CC). Absent any provision to the contrary in the charter of the foundation, the assets of the dissolved foundation will go to the public institution to which its aim corresponds (Art. 57 I CC). However, the original destination of the assets must be maintained as far as possible (Art. 57 II CC).

Apart from the foundations described above, there exist special foundations, such as public law, ecclesiastical, or family foundations. These may be subject to special rules.

---

40. ATF 99 Ib 255; ATF 120 II 374.
41. ATF 76 I 39.

SELECTED BIBLIOGRAPHY

Bucher, A., *Personnes physiques et protection de la personnalité*, 4th edn., Basel 1999.

Bucher, E., *Kommentar zum schweizerischen Privatrecht* (Berner Kommentar), *Das Personenrecht, Die natürlichen Personen*, Bern 1993.

Bucher, E., *Kommentar zum schweizerischen Privatrecht (Berner Kommentar), Einleitung und Personenrecht, Kommentar zu Art. 27 ZGB*, Bern 1993.

Deschenaux, H. and P.-H. Steinauer, *Personnes physiques et tutelle*, 4th edn., Bern 2001.

Gauch, P. and J. Schmid, *Kommentar zum schweizerischen Zivilgesetzbuch (Zürcher Kommentar), Einleitung, Personenrecht*, Zurich 1998.

Grossen, J.-M., *Traité de droit civil suisse*, Vol. II, 2: *Les personnes physiques*, Fribourg 1974.

Gutzwiller, M., *Schweizerisches Privatrecht*, Basel 1988.

Heini, A., *Das schweizerische Privatrecht*, Vol. II: *Die Stiftungen*, Basel 1967, p. 571 *et seq.*

Heini, A., *Das schweizerische Vereinsrecht*, Basel 1988.

Honsell, H., *Kommentar zum schweizerischen Privatrecht (Basler Kommentar), Schweizerisches Zivilgesetzbuch, Art. 1–359 ZGB*, Basel 1996.

Pedrazzini, M. and N. Oberholzer, *Grundriss des Personenrechts*, Bern 1993.

Perrin, J.-F., *Droit de l'association*, Fribourg 1992.

Riemer, H.M., *Kommentar zum schweizerischen Privatrecht (Berner Kommentar), Allgemeine Bestimmungen: systematischer Teil und Kommentar zu Art. 52–59 ZGB*, Bern 1993.

Riemer, H.M., *Kommentar zum schweizerischen Privatrecht (Berner Kommentar), Die Stiftungen: systematischer Teil und Kommentar zu Art. 80–89bis ZGB*, Bern 1975.

Riemer, H.M., *Kommentar zum schweizerischen Privatrecht (Berner Kommentar), Die Vereine: systematischer Teil und Kommentar zu Art. 60–79 ZGB*, Bern 1990.

Tercier, P., *Le nouveau droit de la personnalité*, Zurich 1984.

Tercier, P., *Le droit de la personnalité: chronique de jurisprudence*, Bern 1997.

Tercier, P., *Schweizerisches Privatrecht*, Vol. 2: *Einleitung und Personenrecht*, Basel 1996.

Chapter 5
Family Law

Jacques-Michel Grossen*
Olivier Guillod**

1. INTRODUCTION

In Switzerland as in most other countries of the world family law finds itself, literally, between tradition and change.

A new Federal Constitution (Cons.)[1] took effect on 1 January 2000. It provides a complete list of individual rights and freedoms, among them the right of children and youngsters to have their integrity specially protected (Art. 11 Cons.), the right to private and family life (Art. 13 Cons.) and the freedom to marry and have a family (Art. 14 Cons.). In addition, Article 41 of the Constitution provides that the State shall ensure the protection and promotion of the family (which is simply defined as '*a community of adult people and children*') and Article 116 directs the State to duly take into account family needs in all its policies.

The original provisions of the Second Book of the Swiss Civil Code from 1907, which regulate family law, are in the process of being completely revised. The whole child law has undergone considerable changes, brought about by Federal Laws of 30 June 1972 (adoption, Arts. 264–269e CC) and 25 June 1976 (other aspects of child law, Arts. 252–263 and 270–327 CC). The law relating to the incidents of marriage, including matrimonial property was revised by a Federal Law of 5 October 1984 (Arts. 159–251 CC). The provisions on the requirements for contracting a marriage, on void marriages and on divorce (Arts. 90–158 CC), were totally amended by a Federal Law of 26 June 1998, that went into force on 1 January 2000. The last stage of the whole family law reform which deals with guardianship (Arts. 360–456 CC) is now under way.[2]

But this is of course only one aspect of the matter, albeit an important one. Whatever changes the legislature may choose to make or to oppose, there remains the fact that the societal background of family law is very different from what it was

---

* Professor, University of Neuchâtel.
** Professor, University of Neuchâtel.
1. Recueil systématique, (RS) 101. The Constitution, like all Swiss laws, can be accessed in full text through the internet: <www.admin.ch/ch/f/rs/rs.html> (French version).
2. Office fédéral de la justice, *Révision du droit de la tutelle. Rapport explicatif avec avant-projet relatif à une révision du code civil (protection des adultes)*, Berne 1998. Provisions on civil commitment were added by a Federal Law of 6 October 1978.

F. Dessemontet and T. Ansay (eds), Introduction to Swiss Law, 59–76.
© 2004 Kluwer Law International. Printed in The Netherlands.

until recently. The number of marriages has decreased while the number of divorces has soared. Cohabitation has become a common and widely accepted form of family life. Single-parent households are numerous. The fertility rate is low (1.48 child per woman in 1999), especially among Swiss women, and the proportion of elderly people among the whole population has consistently increased (nearly 16 per cent of the population was over 65 in 1999).

In 1998, there was in Switzerland 17,868 divorces, a figure that has been consistently increasing since the eighties (for instance +40 per cent from 1990 to 1998).[3] The rate of divorce (i.e. the proportion of marriages contracted in 1998 that would end up in a divorce if the number of divorces remained stable in the future) amounted therefore to 42 per cent, one of the highest figures in Europe. Marriage, on the contrary, seems less attractive: the numbers have been declining over the last ten years, from a peak of 47,567 in 1991 to 39,758 in 2000. It nevertheless remains by far the favorite option of couples who want to have children: only 10 per cent of children were born out of wedlock in 1999, a rate that has been slowly increasing for the last ten years but remains one of the lowest in Europe.[4]

Whether the transformation has been for the better or for worse is of course a matter of controversy. But nobody would dispute that the transformation has taken place. Nor would anybody fail to admit that the prevailing views of our time are hard to reconcile with the traditional family law pattern. Present discussions relate to cohabitation and same-sex partnership, new reproductive technologies and strains on social security benefits.

This – for the theme cannot be pursued for itself – is mentioned only by way of introduction, as a *caveat* and as an excuse. If it ever was, it is no longer safe to rely on a mere reading of the Civil Code to get an idea of Swiss family law.

II. HUSBAND AND WIFE

A. *Marriage and Cohabitation*

Marriage was traditionally regarded as the only possible foundation of a legally recognized family. Today a majority of Swiss people would probably maintain that it still is the normal basis of a family and the Code, as it reads, would be on their side.

But cohabitation without marriage has become a more frequent and, socially, a more acceptable way of life. The courts have taken into account this moral and social evolution and have adopted a new, more positive, approach of cohabitation in a number of recent decisions.[5] Even though these judicial developments do not

---

3. In 1999, there were 20,809 divorces. That big increase was due to the courts completing many divorce proceedings before the new divorce law took effect on 1 January 2000. For the same reason, the number of divorces in 2000 was exceptionally low: 10,511. The 1998 data are, therefore, closer to the real rate of divorce presently in Switzerland.
4. All these figures are taken from the *Annuaire statistique de la Suisse 2001*, Zurich 2001. Many of them can be found on the internet: <www.statistik.admin.ch>.
5. See especially B. Pulver, *L'union libre, Droit actuel et réformes nécessaires*, Lausanne 1999, and the German translation and update: B. Pulver, *Unverheiratete Paare. Aktuelle Rechtslage und Reformvorschläge*, Basel 2000.

amount to a legal recognition of cohabitation, they allow finding pragmatic and fair solutions to a wide range of problems.

In the spring of 1999, the Swiss Government released a report on the opportunity to legislate on same-sex partnership.[6] It highlighted four options: opening marriage to same-sex couples; making specific adjustments in the legislation to suppress the most blatant discriminations; creating a registered partnership with effects similar to those of marriage either for all cohabiting couples or only for same-sex couples). The last of those four options was finally retained as a basis for the first draft of a Federal Law on the registered partnership of same-sex people (*partenariat enregistré entre personnes du même sexe/registrierte Partnerschaft gleichgeschlechtlicher Paare*) that was circulated in November 2001[7] in order to gather the reactions of all interested parties throughout the country. A formal Bill should be introduced in Parliament in 2002 or 2003.

If marriage remains central to the idea of the family, it does not mean that the very concept of marriage has been left unchanged through the ages. Marriage is not an abstract, self-defining notion. Each society creates its own marriage concept or adds its own touch to the understanding it has inherited from the past.

B. Engagement to Marry

Four articles of the Civil Code (Arts. 90–93) relate to the engagement to marry (*fiançailles/Verlöbnis*). The agreement to marry does not give rise to an action for specific performance of the agreement. In case of breach of the engagement to marry, each party can claim the return of the presents it gave to the other; upon request, the court may also grant fair compensation to the party who made *bona fide* expenses in view of the marriage. Both claims must be filed within one year from the date of the breach. They have become an extremely rare occurrence and in fact add very little to the general provisions on torts, restitution or the protection of the person.

C. Making a Marriage

1. Conditions

A valid marriage requires that the parties have legal capacity to marry and that there is no impediment to their proposed marriage.

Capacity to marry belongs only to those persons who have discretion (*discernement/ Urteilsfähigkeit*), i.e. the capacity to act rationally (Art. 16 CC), and who are at least 18 years old (Art. 94 I CC). A person under guardianship must seek the consent of her guardian but she may appeal against the guardian's refusal (Art. 94 II CC).

---

6. Office fédéral de la justice, *La situation juridique des couples homosexuels en droit suisse. Problèmes et propositions de solutions*, Berne 1999.
7. *Avant-projet de loi fédérale sur le partenariat enregistré ente personnes du même sexe et rapport explicatif*, Berne 2001.

According to Article 95 CC, impediments may derive from consanguinity (relatives in the direct ascending or descending line, sisters and brothers) and affinity (among one person and the child of her spouse). The subsistence of a previous marriage is, of course, another impediment (Art. 96 CC).

2. Celebration

The 1998 revision has not kept the traditional requirement of banns, i.e. publications which should – at least in theory – afford an opportunity for discovering the impediments that might exist. The engaged couple simply asks the registrar of civil status for an authorization to solemnize the marriage (Arts. 98–99 CC). Once in possession of that document, the couple may ask any Swiss registrar (*officier de l'état civil/Zivilstandsbeamte*) to proceed (Arts. 100–102 CC). The solemnization of marriage takes the form of a compulsory civil marriage. A religious ceremony, if wanted, may take place only after the parties have gone through the lay form of solemnization (Art. 97 III CC).

3. Voidable Marriages (*Annulation du mariage/Ungültigkeit der Ehe*)

It is commonly accepted that the consequence of some defects is that no marriage will be deemed to exist. For instance, where there has been no solemnization before a registrar, or where one of the 'spouses' did not attend the ceremony, no marriage has taken place and, if need be, it will be open to anyone having an interest in the issue to ask, at any time, for a judicial declaration that the two persons concerned have never been joined in matrimony.

Under the title 'voidable marriages', however, the Civil Code (Arts. 104–110) deals primarily with defects (subsistence of a previous marriage, lack of the capacity to marry, consanguinity, affinity, fraud and coercion) which will only result in the marriage being invalid if a court so decides. According to Article 109 CC a marriage does not become invalid unless and until it is so declared by the court. The law makes a distinction between 'absolute' (Arts. 105–106 CC) and 'relative' (Arts. 107–108 CC) grounds for annulment that merely serves two purposes. It helps determining who has *locus standi* and whether limitation periods apply. Suits for voiding a marriage have become a rare occurrence (11 cases in 1998, 14 in 1999).

As a matter of principle, jurisdiction, procedure and the effects of the judgment are governed by the same rules as in the case of divorce (Arts. 109–110 CC).

D. *Effects of Marriage as between the Spouses*

In the Common Law countries the duties which marriage may entail as between the spouses are not regarded as a suitable subject for legislation. Even the courts are not prone to interfere with what they consider as a matter of morals, a matter at least which they think is preferably left to the day-to-day or more permanent arrangements of the spouses. Not so in the Civil Law countries, where there is an old habit of prescribing legal rules of good matrimonial behaviour. There can be no doubt those Articles 159–180 of the Swiss Civil Code belong to the latter tradition.

Contrary to the older set of rules which clearly expressed the traditional differentiation of sex roles, the provisions that went into force in 1988 do not impose any task allocation system. Starting from the proposition that marriage should be conceived of as a partnership between equals, they ensure the spouses' freedom to organize their married life (including the allocation of roles) as they wish.[8]

To take but a few examples, the spouses choose together the matrimonial home (Art. 162 CC), they must care jointly for the proper maintenance of the family after agreeing on how each of them will contribute to it (Art. 163 CC) and they are free to enter any legal transaction with each other or with a third party (Art. 168 CC).

Whenever a spouse acts for the current requirements of the family (for instance buying food, clothes or domestic appliances), both spouses are jointly and severally liable to the third party *(représentation de l'union conjugale/Vertretung der ehelichen Gemeinschaft)*. Beyond current requirements of the family, a spouse represents the conjugal union only if she is authorized by the other spouse or by the judge (Art. 166 CC).

Since much depends on the free decisions and agreements of the spouses, the legal provisions make sure that one spouse is not left without any legal remedy, or with the sole possibility of petitioning for divorce, if and when the other spouse ignores, deliberately or not, the implications of the partnership.

Accordingly, the spouse who manages the household and looks after the children is entitled to a fair and periodical amount for his free disposal (Art. 164 CC) whereas the spouse who has contributed to the maintenance of the family considerably more than was required of her is entitled to receive fair compensation (Art. 165 CC). Article 169 CC provides that any legal transaction seriously restricting the family's right of use of the abode may only be made by the spouses jointly.

The 1988 reform left almost intact the chapter (Arts. 171–180 CC) on the measures for the protection of the marriage *(mesures de protection de l'union conjugale/Eheschutz-massnahmen)* which is a peculiarity of Swiss law. There are diverging views on whether these measures really achieve their purpose, or whether the intervention of a judge in the life of a married couple can be justified. In spite of their name, the judicial measures serve not only to protect the marriage as such but also, and perhaps much more, to protect the individual (personal and financial) interests of either spouse and of their offspring, when those interests are injured or imperilled by the other spouse.

E. *Matrimonial Property (*Régime matrimonial/Ehegüterrecht*)*

1. Ordinary, Extraordinary or Contractual Regime

A matrimonial regime can result from a contract, i.e. a marriage settlement *(contrat de mariage/Ehevertrag)*, a judgment or from the operation of law (Art. 181 CC).

---

8. See A. Leuba, *La répartition traditionelle des tâches ente les conjoints, au regard du principe de l'égalité entre homme et femme*, Berne 1997.

The last is by far the most frequent: according to various estimates, more than 95 per cent of married couples have their property relationships governed by the so-called 'ordinary system' of participation in acquisitions (*participation aux acquêts/ Errungenschaftsbeteiligung*; Arts. 196–220 CC).

The so-called 'extraordinary system' of separation of estates (*séparation de biens/ Gütertrennung*; Arts. 247–251 CC) is the regime of a few thousand couples either by operation of law (for instance because one of the spouses went bankrupt, Art. 188 CC, or in the case of separation, Art. 118 I CC) or by the decision of a court, at instance of a spouse (Art. 185 CC) or of the supervising authority for the enforcement of payments (Art. 189 CC).

Marriage settlements, either ante-nuptial or post-nuptial (Art. 182 I CC), are made by far less than 5 per cent of couples. The couple's freedom of choice is not as extensive as in some other Civil Law jurisdictions. It is confined to statutory models (Art. 182 II CC), either separation of estates (Art. 247 *et seq.* CC) or one of the several types of community of property (*communauté de biens/Gütergemeinschaf*; Arts. 221–246 CC). A marriage covenant can also serve the purpose of modifying some features of the system of participation in acquisitions or community of property, for instance the statutory division (50 per cent–50 per cent) of profits and losses (Arts. 216–217 CC; Arts. 241–242 CC) and the statutory definition of a spouse's own property (Art. 199 CC; Art. 225 CC). Sometimes, it is combined with an agreement on inheritance (*pacte successoral/Erbvertrag*; Art. 512 CC), or made at the same time as such an agreement.

2. The Ordinary Legal Regime

Since 1988, spouses are placed under the system of participation in acquisitions, unless they have provided otherwise by a marriage covenant. That system is supposed to meet both the demand for sharing and the demand for equality. Its main characteristics are:

1) The system encompasses two kinds of property: each spouse's acquisitions (*acquêts/Errungenschaft*), i.e. property which the spouse acquires as income during the matrimonial property system (Art. 197 CC) and each spouse's own property (*biens propres/ Eigengut*) especially property which belonged to the spouse before marriage and property which comes to the spouse during marriage by succession or other gratuitous title (Art. 198 CC).
2) Each spouse keeps the ownership, administration, use and disposal of all her belongings (acquisitions and own property) during marriage (Art. 201 CC), like in the system of separation of estates.
3) Each spouse is liable for his or her debts with his or her whole property (Art. 202 CC).
4) At the end of the regime, each spouse (or his/her heirs) keeps his own property and is entitled to one half of the other spouse's acquisitions (Art. 215 CC) unless a marriage covenant provides for a different division.

F. *Divorce* (Divorce/Ehescheidung) *and Judicial Separation* (Séparation de corps/Trennung)

1. Grounds for Divorce

The 2000 reform has adopted the 'no-fault divorce' concept. The basic ground for divorce is indeed the mutual agreement of both spouses (*divorce sur requête commune/Scheidung auf gemeinsames Begehren*; Arts. 111–112 CC). A divorce asked by both spouses is granted quickly: spouses who have signed a written agreement dealing with all subsidiary effects of the divorce submit their agreement to the judge at a single hearing. After two months, they must simply confirm their decision in writing and the judge will grant them a divorce.

Divorce may also be asked by a single spouse (*divorce sur demande unilatérale/Scheidung auf Klage eines Ehegatten*) in two cases: when the spouses have led a separate life for more than four years (Art. 114 CC; there is no hardship clause) and when serious grounds not attributable to the plaintiff make the continuation of life in common intolerable (Art. 115 CC). It should be stressed that the ground on which the divorce decree is based as well as the conduct of each spouse bear no influence on the subsidiary effects of divorce, especially on its financial consequences.

2. Personal Consequences of Divorce

When marrying, a woman normally takes the name of her husband ('family name') but she may keep her former name and place it in front of the family name. For grounds worthy of consideration, the engaged couple may request that the bride's name be the name of the family (Arts. 30 and 160 CC). Upon divorce, the spouse who acquired a new name by marriage retains it, unless she asks within one year from the divorce to the registrar of civil status to regain the name she bore before getting married (Art. 119 CC).

A divorced person loses the statutory right of inheritance towards her ex-spouse and cannot claim any benefits from testamentary dispositions made before the suit for divorce was brought (Art. 120 II CC).

3. Financial Consequences of Divorce

The financial consequences of divorce will have to be decided by the divorce court (and as a rule the decision must be made at the same time as the divorce itself). They may also, and indeed frequently are, dealt with in an agreement made by the parties or their counsel and submitted to the court for confirmation (Art. 140 CC).

Article 121 CC gives power to the court to issue rules for the future use of the family home, based on the situation of the family, especially the children. The court is not bound by contractual or property rights on the abode. The judge may for instance transfer the lease from the husband to the wife who gets sole parental power over the minor children and lives with them. In such a case, the husband would

nevertheless be severally and jointly liable for paying the rent for a maximum period
of two years. For similar grounds, the court could also grant use of the home owned
for instance by the wife to the husband caring for minor children, by way of a right
to residence fairly limited in time (presumably at the latest until the youngest child
living with his father reaches 18).

Old-age entitlements accumulated in a pension fund by the working spouse during the marriage (through fixed premiums deducted monthly from her wages) shall
be divided in half upon divorce (*partage des prestations de sortie/Teilung der
Austrittsleistungen*; Art. 122 CC). The other spouse will not get money in cash but
the amount shall be put in a pension fund that will pay him retirement benefits in the
future. The purpose of the rule is to secure a better position towards social security
for the financially weaker spouse (usually the wife still today)[9] who did not earn a
living during the marriage but who looked after the children and kept the household.
Such a compulsory pension sharing will not take place in only two situations: when
the home-keeping spouse renounced it during the divorce proceedings (provided her
or his maintenance during old age is secured in another way) and where the division
would prove grossly unfair (Art. 123 CC). When the working spouse is already
retired, the division of future entitlements becomes impossible and that spouse must
then pay a fair contribution in cash to the other (Art. 124 CC).

Financial contributions (*entretien après le divorce/nachehelicher Unterhalt*) from
one ex-spouse to the other do not depend any more on fault but are based on need.
As long as a divorcing spouse is unable to maintain himself properly after divorce,
he will be entitled to a fair contribution from the other spouse (Art. 125 CC). The
amount and duration of the contribution will be agreed upon by the divorcing
spouses (under the supervision of the judge who must ratify their written agreement)
or decided by the court after adequate consideration of all relevant circumstances
(the duration of the marriage, the way each spouse contributed to the maintenance of
the family, the standard of living enjoyed, the age, health, earnings, education and
professional activity of each spouse, etc.).

In the normal case monthly instalments (Art. 126 I CC), adjusted yearly for inflation
(Art. 128 CC) will be decreed, but a cash settlement is also possible (Art. 126 II CC).
In order to secure payment, the court may give an injunction to the debtor's
employer to pay each month part of the wages directly to her employee's ex-spouse
or decide other security (Art. 132 CC). Public services in each canton will continue
to provide assistance in getting the alimony paid and to give advance payments
(Art. 131 CC).

If the party entitled to the annuity later remarries, she forfeits her right to it, unless
the spouses decided in the divorce agreement that the annuity would be paid for a
longer period (Art. 130 CC). Unless the spouses agreed otherwise (Art. 127 CC), the
contribution for maintenance may be diminished, suppressed or suspended if
the personal circumstances of one of the parties change deeply, for instance where

9. Statistics indicate that 62% of women and 90% of men aged between 20 and 49 are professionally active. Among women, only 53% had a full-time job against 85% of men.
Statistically, being a mother reduced the professional activity but being a father made no
difference: see Office fédéral de la statistique, *L'enquête suisse sur la famille 1994/95*,
Berne 1998, p. 145 *et seq.*

the party entitled to it cohabits with a stable partner (Art. 129 I CC). Within five years from the date of the divorce, a contribution could be awarded or increased by the court if it had not been possible at the time of the divorce to grant a contribution large enough to cover one spouse's basic needs and if the financial situation of the other has notably improved since the divorce (Art. 129 CC).

4. Consequences of Divorce for Children

Until 1999, the judge had to choose between the mother and the father regarding parental authority over the children after divorce. The result was that parental authority was conferred upon the mother in about 90 per cent of the cases. The 2000 reform introduced the possibility for the court to grant shared parental power (*autorité parentale conjointe/gemeinsame elterliche Sorge*) to the divorcing spouses (Art. 133 CC). However, joint parental power is not the rule but may be decided by the court only when three conditions are met: both spouses request it; they have agreed in writing on all aspects of the future care of their children, including maintenance; and joint parental power appears to be in the best interest of the children. In that matter, any order made by the divorce court may be modified later, as soon as important circumstances change (Art. 134 CC).

The parent who has neither parental authority nor custody is usually granted access, and he must contribute to the expenses of bringing up and educating the child. In ordering access and maintenance the divorce court must apply the provisions of child law (Art. 133 I CC).

Children (provided their age and understanding allow it) must be heard on all matters that directly concern them, either by the judge or by an appropriate third party designed by the court (Art. 144 CC). That right already derived from Article 12 of the UN Convention on Children's Rights, which is deemed self-executing by the Swiss Federal court.[10] Where serious grounds make it desirable (for instance when the parents disagree on who should keep parental power after divorce) or when the child asks for it, the court shall appoint a curator (*curateur/Beistand*) with the task of speaking for the child (Art. 146 CC). The curator will be entitled to take part to the procedure for all matters concerning the child and will have standing to appeal (Art. 147 CC).

5. Judicial Separation

Due to the religious diversity of the Swiss population, judicial separation has been kept as an alternative to divorce (Arts. 117–118 CC). The grounds for separation are rigorously the same as the grounds for divorce. A judicial separation has no bearing on the right of each spouse to file for divorce.

Whatever the advantage or inconvenience of having judicial separation as an alternative to divorce, decrees of the first sort are no longer frequent. In 1998 the courts made 603 decrees of judicial separation but 17,868 divorce decrees.

---

10. ATF 124 III 90, available on the internet: <www.bger.ch>.

III. PARENT AND CHILD

A. Fundamental Principles of Child Law

The reform of child law in the 1970s aimed at abolishing illegitimacy, conferring equal rights on father and mother, and establishing the welfare of the child as the dominant principle in the whole field. As to adoption, the main objective was the complete assimilation of the adopted child to a natural child (through the so-called system of full adoption; *adoption plénaire/Volladoption*). More recent reforms have implemented the right of the child to be heard in all matters of direct concern to him, in accordance with Article 12 of the UN Convention on Children's Rights of 20 November 1989 which came into force on 26 March 1997 for Switzerland.

B. Establishment of Parentage

1. Maternal Filiation

A child's maternal descent is established by the fact of birth (Art. 252 I CC). It can also result from an adoption decree (Art. 252 III CC).

Surrogate motherhood, embryo and egg donation are prohibited by Article 4 of the Federal Act on Medically Assisted Procreation (AMAP).[11]

2. Paternal Filiation

In the situation which is by far the more frequent, namely, where the mother is married, there is a legal presumption (*présomption de paternité/Vaterschaftsvermutung*) that her husband is the father of any child born during the marriage or within 300 day of the husband's death (Art. 255 I CC). The presumption of the husband's paternity is refutable, but the corresponding action may be brought only within a definite period of time (Art. 256c CC), by a strictly limited group of persons (Arts. 256 and 258 CC), on legally specified grounds (Arts. 256a and 256b CC).

Paternity may also be legally ascertained through a formal acknowledgement by the father (*reconnaissance/Anerkennung*; Art. 260 CC). However, any interested party (Art. 260a CC, with the exception provided for in Art. 259 II CC) may bring an action to oppose the acknowledgement, within time limits and on legally specified grounds (Arts. 260b and 260c CC). Paternity may further be established by a judgment following paternity proceedings (*action en paternité/Vaterschaftsklage*; Arts. 261–263 CC), or by an adoption decree (Art. 267 CC).

In vitro fertilization or insemination with the sperm of a donor is restricted to married couples (Art. 3 AMAP). Paternity of the husband who consented to the medical procedure cannot in such a case be disavowed. No paternity suit may be brought against the sperm donor (Art. 23 AMAP) but at 18, the child has the right to know his identity (Arts. 119 Cons. and 27 AMAP).

11. From 18 December 1998, in force since 1 January 2001.

3. Scientific Evidence of Paternity

Over the years courts have come to accept a number of scientific methods of proving (or disproving) paternity: blood tests, serostatistical investigation, anthropological evidence, methods founded on the duration of pregnancy, DNA fingerprinting, etc. Today, only DNA fingerprinting is used because it gives the most reliable results.

Article 254 II CC provides that parties or third parties have a duty to cooperate with the scientific investigations which are necessary to the ascertainment of a paternity relationship, provided only that they can be submitted to such investigations without risk to their own health.

C. Effects of Parentage

1. Child's Name

The child of a married couple bears the surname which is common to both parents. Where the mother is not married to the father, as a rule the child bears the mother's surname (Art. 270 CC). Where there are material grounds for a change (cohabitation of the mother and father is not *per se* such a ground),[12] the child may however be authorized to change his name (Art. 30 I CC). If parental authority is conferred on the father, the child will normally be allowed to take the father's surname (Art. 271 II CC). The general aim of the law is to ensure that the child will have the name which it is in his best interest to bear, or at any rate, which will cause the least embarrassment to him.

2. Access (*Relations personnelles/Persönlicher Verkehr*)

Access is the reciprocal right of a minor child and of a father or mother who has neither parental authority nor custody of the child to have adequate personal contact (Art. 273 CC). Under exceptional circumstances, and provided the best interest of the child so requires, a right of access may be granted to another person, for instance a grandparent, or a former foster-parent (Art. 274a CC).

Even when it is claimed by a father or mother, the right of access is not unconditional. The law (Art. 274 CC) mentions a few situations where it would have to be denied from the start or suspended. One of them arises when a parent who has not shown any interest for his child for years suddenly feels that he should have access. Another is where the well-being of the child is endangered by the personal contact. In a more general way any serious ground may lead to a refusal or a suppression of access.

3. Maintenance (*Obligation d'entretien/Unterhaltspflicht*)

The importance of the problem and the extent of the litigation which surrounds it are reflected in the number of provisions to be found in the (otherwise rather laconic)

12. ATF 121 III 145; ATF 124 III 401.

Swiss Civil Code. Nineteen articles, numbered 276 to 294, deal with the duty to maintain the child.

Among the many questions which are touched upon, reference should be made to the duty to maintain the child after he or she has attained the age of majority (Art. 277 CC), maintenance pending suit (Arts. 281–284 CC), possibility to increase or reduce maintenance where the circumstances of the parties have undergone material changes (Art. 286 II CC), maintenance agreements (Art. 287 CC), lump sum agreements (Art. 288 CC), and enforcement measures (Arts. 290–292 CC). Encouraged by Article 293 CC, a number of cantons have established a duty of the State or municipality to make advance payments. All cantons are under an obligation to see to it that the procedure applying to maintenance is simple and speedy (Art. 280 CC).

*D. Parental Authority (*Autorité parentale/Elterliche Gewalt*)*

1. Subjects

Parental authority is the responsibility of the father and mother to give proper care and education to their minor (i.e. less than 18 years old according to Art. 14 CC) children as well as to make the necessary decisions for them (Arts. 296 and 301 I CC).

During marriage parental authority is exercised jointly by the father and mother (Art. 297 I CC).

Where the mother is not married to the father, parental authority belongs, by operation of law, to the mother (Art. 298 I CC). However, mother and father can ask the guardianship board to grant them joint parental authority on the same conditions as divorcing parents (Art. 298a CC). In case the unmarried mother is herself a minor, or she has been deprived of her parental rights, the guardianship board has to decide whether the welfare of the child requires that a guardian be appointed or whether it would be better to confer parental authority on the father (Art. 298 II CC).

Parental authority cannot, of course, have quite the same meaning in the case of a small child and in that of a 'young person'. Without really organizing a distinctive legal status for adolescents, the law stresses that a child must be left the measure of freedom corresponding to his stage of maturity (Art. 301 II CC).

2. Contents

The characterization of parental authority has long divided the legal writers. Is it a right, or a bundle of rights, or a set of rights and duties, or a social function? The qualification must depend, to a certain extent, on the perspective: *vis-à-vis* the children the duties are more obvious than the rights.

Generally it is the duty of the parents to provide the child with the setting, the examples and the means which will permit him to develop his personality, to become gradually independent and to play a role consonant with his aims and talents (Arts. 301–302 CC). Inasmuch as rights exist (right to custody, right to educate) they are really subordinate to the purposes of parental authority ('duty impregnated rights', to use the expression coined by a learned author). Parental authority also entails the statutory right to represent the child in transactions with third parties, always bearing the welfare of the child in mind (Art. 304 CC).

Parental authority ends with the child's eighteenth birthday, save for the right to determine the religious education which ceases when the child has completed his sixteenth year (Art. 303 CC).

3. Child's Property

While it has maintained the principle that the child's property is administered by the parents having parental authority (Art. 318 CC), the 1976 reform of child law has abolished the time-honoured usufructuary rights of the parents over such property. Parents may, however, use the income produced by the child's property – as far as fair and equitable – to cover the expense of maintaining and educating the child and of providing him with professional training (Art. 319 CC).

The child is free to dispose of his wages, though he is expected to contribute to the cost of his maintenance if he lives with his parents (Art. 323 CC).

4. Protective Measures (*Mesures de protection de l'enfant/ Kindesschutzmassnahmen*)

If and when the person or the property of a child is in danger, protective measures of various kinds must be taken by the guardianship board (Arts. 307–316 and 324–325 CC). Parents may in particular be deprived of their parental authority (Arts. 311–312 CC), of the custody of the child (Art. 310 CC), or of their right to administer the child's property (Art. 325 CC).

State intervention must, however, be kept within the limits of what is necessary and, before going to the extreme of the gravest measures, the proper authorities must consider whether more lenient action (for instance instructions on specific matters, with or without supervision; Arts. 307 and 324 CC) would not be sufficient.

It is important to note that protective measures do not necessarily imply a blame on the parents. They may have to be taken regardless of whether or not the parents are at fault.

E. Adoption (Adoption/Adoption)

1. Conditions

The welfare of the child is the first and paramount consideration whenever an adoption order is applied for. While no authority can be expected to foresee the future, a careful examination of all the circumstances is required, leading to a reasonable belief that the adoption concerned will serve the best interest of the child (Art. 264 CC).

A child may be adopted only if he has been in the care and control of his prospective adoptive parents for at least one year (Art. 264 CC, as amended by the Federal Law of 22 June 2001, about the Hague Convention on foreign adoption).[13] The main

---

13. *Feuille Fédérale 2001*, p. 2770, available on the internet: <www.admin.ch/ch/f/ff/index. html>.

purpose of this waiting period is to make sure that the decision rests on a firm basis of information and experience.

If the prospective adoptive parents already have children, the competent authority must further consider whether the proposed adoption might cause undue prejudice to the interests of those children (Art. 264 CC). A mere reduction in the rights of inheritance is not regarded as undue prejudice.

The adoption of an adult person is not excluded but the law makes it dependent on stricter conditions: An adult may only be adopted under special circumstances, and only by persons who have no issue (Art. 266 CC).

Joint adoption is open only to a married couple but an unmarried person can adopt singly. In the former case the spouses must have been married for five years or both have reached the age of 35 (Art. 264a II CC). In the latter case the single person must be at least 35 (Art. 264b CC). It is also possible for a married person to adopt the child of his or her spouse (Art. 264a III CC). In any case, the child must be at least 16 years younger than either of his adopting parents (Art. 265 I CC).

2. Consent

Where the child has discretion, which has repeatedly been accepted by courts from 14 years on,[14] his consent is required (Art. 265 II CC). The consent of the child's natural parents is normally required as well (Art. 265a CC). It can be dispensed with on the part of a parent who is unknown, unreachable or incapacitated or has – with or without fault – shown no concern for the child (Art. 265c CC).[15]

3. Procedure

Adoption is no longer made by contract. It takes the form of a decree of the competent authority of the canton concerned (Arts. 265d and 268 CC). This must be preceded by an examination of all the circumstances of the prospective adoption (Art. 268a CC). The Federal Law of 22 June 2001, about the Hague Convention on foreign adoption, provides for a special procedure with added safeguards for the child in case of foreign adoption.

4. Effect

The adopted child is in the legal position of a natural child of his adoptive parents (Art. 267 I CC). His former kinship relationships are abolished, except where the adoptive parent is a stepfather or stepmother (Art. 267 II CC). Since a 1992 constitutional amendment (Art. 119 Cons.), the child is entitled to know his origins, i.e. the identity of his natural parents (Art. 268c CC as amended by the Federal Law of 22 June 2001, about the Hague Convention on foreign adoption).

---

14. See e.g. ATF 119 II 7.
15. It is one of the most controversial issues in adoption: see e.g. ATF 113 II 381; ATF 111 II 322; ATF 107 II 22.

As an exception to the general rule, the adoption of an adult does not affect his nationality (Art. 267a CC).

IV. GUARDIANSHIP AND OTHER PROTECTIVE MEASURES

A. *General Principles*

Under the general heading 'guardianship' (*tutelle/Vormundschaft*), Articles 360–456 of the Swiss Civil Code provide for a variety of protective measures, not only as to guardianship in the strict sense (*interdiction/Entmündigung*, Arts. 369 *et seq.* CC) but also less incisive forms of protection, such as curatorship (*curatelle/ Beistandschaft*, Arts. 392 *et seq.* CC)) or the appointment of a legal adviser (*conseil légal/Beiratschaft*, Art. 395 CC). The common denominator is that all these measures are intended to help people incapable of properly handling their own affairs. In accordance with the principle of proportionality, the competent authority must choose in each case the most lenient measure compatible with the purpose of aiding the person involved.

Most of the provisions concerned have remained unchanged since they were adopted in 1907, but a statute of 6 October 1978, in force since 1 January 1981, has modified and supplemented the conditions on which a person may be deprived of his freedom for his own protection (Arts. 397a–397f CC). As stated in the introduction of this chapter, a global reform of the law on guardianship is under way, as the last stage of the current updating of the whole family law.

B. *Guardianship*

1. Cases of Guardianship

Every minor not under parental authority has to be provided with a guardian (*tuteur/Vormund*, Art. 368 CC), as must every person who is interdicted. The causes of interdiction are lunacy, mental deficiency, prodigality, drunkenness, immorality, mismanagement, and a one-year or longer prison sentence (Arts. 369–371 CC). In addition, the person must be incapable of managing his own affairs, risk falling below the poverty line, need permanent care and supervision or be a danger to the community.

A person may be interdicted at his own request in case he is prevented from managing his affairs properly because of old age, physical infirmity or inexperience (Art. 372 CC).

2. Appointment of Guardian

The guardianship board must appoint as guardian a person of full age with the necessary abilities (Art. 379 CC). In the absence of material grounds to the contrary, the board is directed to give preference to the nearest relatives or to the spouse of the ward (Art. 380 CC). Under the same condition, the board will appoint the person preferred by the ward or his parents (Art. 381 CC).

In theory at least, some people are under an obligation to accept the office of guardian (Arts. 382–383 CC). In fact, boards choose with increasing frequency to appoint professionals, for instance, social workers active in a children's department or in a special guardianship office.

3. Role of Guardian

The guardian's tasks may be divided into three broad categories: care of the ward's person, administration of his property, and legal representation (Arts. 398–416 CC). The ward having discretion remains entitled to exercise alone strictly personal rights (Art. 19 II CC), like consenting to medical treatment.

While the guardian may often act on his own initiative and take the course of action which he thinks proper, there are cases where he must seek the consent of the guardianship board (Art. 421 CC), or even a confirmation of that consent by the supervisory authority (Art. 422 CC). A few acts are even prohibited (contract of guarantee, donation, and creation of a foundation: Art. 408 CC).

C. Curatorship

As distinct from a guardian, a curator (*curateur/Beistand*) is appointed to deal with a specific matter or to take care of property (Arts. 392–393 CC).

In spite of its being placed in the Second Book of the Swiss Civil Code the subject has only a tenuous connection with family law. One case in point would be where there is a conflict between the interests of a minor and those of his legal representative (Art. 392 CC).

D. Legal Adviser

The legal adviser (*conseil légal/Beirat*) of Article 395 CC was inspired to the Swiss legislature by the (now abolished) French institution of the '*conseil judiciaire*'. The underlying idea is that some people may need a form of permanent help which does not entail as wide a restriction on their capacity as that following the appointment of a guardian.

The legal adviser may have the task of giving his advice and consent to contracts of a particular importance and/or of managing property. He is not normally supposed to take care of the person he is expected to assist.

E. Civil Commitment (Privation de liberté à des fins d'assistance/ Fürsorgerische Freiheitsentziehung)

A person who is insane, feebleminded, alcoholic, addicted to drugs or in a serious state of neglect may be committed to a mental or other health-care facility against her will if the necessary care cannot be provided otherwise (Art. 397a CC). The decision is made by the guardianship board save in cases of emergency and mental illness where other qualified authorities designed by each canton are competent (Art. 397b CC).

A number of procedural safeguards (right to be heard, right to judicial assistance, right to appeal to a judge at any time, etc.), as required by Article 5 of the European Convention on Human Rights, are provided for in Articles 397c–397f CC. The State is liable on a no-fault basis in case of illegal commitment (Art. 429a CC).

The decision to commit somebody to a mental institution does not allow the latter to treat the patient against his or her will.[16]

---

16. ATF 125 III 169; ATF 126 I 112; ATF 127 I 6.

SELECTED BIBLIOGRAPHY

Honsell, H., N. Vogt and Th. Geiser (eds.), *Kommentar zum Schweizerischen Privatrecht. Schweizerisches Zivilgesetzbuch I (Art. 1–359)*, Basel/Frankfurt 1996.

Tuor, P., B. Schnyder and J. Schmid, *Das Schweizerische Zivilgesetzbuch*, 11th edn., Zurich 1995 and 1999 Supplement.

For regular updates on Swiss family law, see the Swiss contributions to the yearly *International Survey of Family Law* published on behalf of the International Society of Family Law.

Chapter 6
Law of Inheritance*

*Audrey Leuba**

I. INTRODUCTION

The law of inheritance is regulated in the third Book of the Swiss Civil Code. Except for a few minor changes, this part of the Swiss Civil Code has undergone only one important modification since 1907: the partial revision of 1984, in force since 1988. This revision has considerably increased the rights of the surviving spouse (among others, increase of the intestate share and of the compulsory portion,[1] right to the ownership of the house or apartment where the spouses lived at the time of death).

II. PRINCIPLES GOVERNING THE LAW OF INHERITANCE

A. The Immediate Transfer of the Estate as a Whole

Swiss law is dominated by the principle of the transfer of the estate as a whole (Art. 560 CC). Subject to certain statutory exceptions, all rights that belonged to the deceased and all debts due to him pass as a whole to the heirs, even if they did not have knowledge of the estate. The estate vests immediately in the heir or heirs, without any time interval.

B. The 'Saisine'

When the succession opens, i.e. at the death of the deceased, the inheritance vests in the heir or heirs by operation of law. The heirs are 'seized' (*saisi*) of the ownership of the estate. The 'saisine' takes effect irrespective of the heirs' intention with respect to the inheritance and the heirs' acceptance to this is not required.

---

* The text has been adapted from a previous version written by M. Jean Guinand, formerly professor, University of Neuchatel. The author thanks Ms. Martine Rehm–Fuchs for the help.
** LL.M. (Harvard), Dr. iur. Associate Professor, University of Neuchatel.
1. Swiss Law limits the testator's freedom to dispose of his estate by giving to certain heirs a fixed portion of the estate (the compulsory portion). See below IV C.

F. Dessemontet and T. Ansay (eds), Introduction to Swiss Law, 77–92.

The consequences of the principle of 'saisine' are softened by the right given to the heirs to disclaim the inheritance (Art. 566 CC). A disclaimer can be made by a written or oral declaration to the competent probate authority (Art. 570 CC). The disclaimer must take place within a period of three months. For statutory heirs, the period runs from the day when they acquire knowledge of the death of the deceased, unless they can prove that they did not have knowledge of their rights of inheritance until later; for appointed heirs,[2] it runs from the day when they were officially notified of the dispositions in their favor (Art. 567 CC). The competent probate authority can on material grounds grant an extension or a renewal of the time allowed for a disclaimer (Art. 576 CC). A disclaimer is automatically presumed by law, if the deceased was insolvent at the opening of the succession and his insolvency was common knowledge or officially declared (Art. 566 II CC). A heir loses the right to disclaim where he or she has within the time limit interfered with the inheritance or done acts which were not required for the mere management of the estate and the carrying on of the affairs of the deceased, or where he or she has appropriated or concealed anything forming part of the estate (Art. 571 II CC).

The principle of 'saisine' is also affected by the right given to the heirs to limit their responsibility for the debts of the estate.[3]

C. *The Joint Ownership of the Estate* (Gesamteigentum/Propriété commune)

Where there are several heirs, all the rights and obligations comprised in the inheritance are undivided among the heirs until partition (Art. 602 I CC). They are joint owners of the property forming part of the estate. They are liable jointly and severally for the debts of the deceased (Art. 603 I CC).

Except in an emergency situation, the heirs deal jointly with the inheritance and in conformity with the unanimous decision of all the heirs.[4] They can appoint or ask the Probate authority to appoint an agent to represent the heirs until partition (Art. 602 III CC).

D. *The Necessity of an Heir*

The inheritance must always vest in an heir. Swiss law requires that there must be an heir. In the absence of a will of the deceased, the law designates the person who will receive the inheritance (intestate succession).

III. INTESTATE SUCCESSION

The heirs designated by law are, in principle, those related to the deceased. The relationships may be based on marital or parental ties. In the absence of a person with a

2. By will or testamentary agreement, a testator may appoint one or several persons to receive the entire estate or a part of it. See below IV B1.
3. See the official inventory and the official liquidation under VI B1 below.
4. ATF 121 III 118; 93 II 11.

marital or a sufficient parental tie with the deceased, the inheritance devolves to the Canton of the deceased's last domicile or to the Commune entitled under the law of that Canton (Art. 466 CC).

A. Parental Ties

The law splits the relatives into groups which are called 'parentels' (*verwandte/ parents*). A parentel includes all persons having a bond of affiliation to a common ancestor. With the mother, affiliation arises from the birth. With the father, paternity results from his marital link to the mother at the time of the child's birth. It may also be established by an acknowledgement of the child, a judgment following a paternity proceedings or an adoption decree.

The Civil Code recognizes three parentels. In the absence of a surviving spouse and of an heir among the first three parentels, the inheritance devolves to the State (Art. 466 CC). The parentels are:

    a. the first parentel (Art 457 CC): which includes the deceased's descendants,
    b. the second parentel (Art. 458 CC): which groups the deceased's parents and their descendants (brothers, sisters, nephews and nieces of the deceased),
    c. the third parentel (Art. 459 CC): which includes the grandparents and their descendants (uncles, aunts, cousins of the deceased).

Several principles determine the order in which the members of the parentels inherit and the part devoted to each of them:

    a. members of the parentel nearest to the deceased rule out members of more removed parentels. So for example, the deceased's grandchild (first parentel) rules out his father (second parentel), the deceased's brother (second parentel) rules out his grandfather (third parentel);
    b. among the members of a parentel, those nearer in degree take priority over the others. So the deceased's son rules out the grandson, the deceased's father rules out his brother;
    c. among a parentel, the heir who does not inherit (due to prior death, disinheritance, unworthiness, or disclaimer) will be represented by his descendants. So the portion that should be devolved to the deceased's son passes to the son's only daughter when he is predeceased;
    d. among a parentel, the inheritance is divided in stirpes. A stirpe includes a descendant and his descendants. The inheritance is divided equally among the stirpes. In the absence of a heir in one stirpe, the entire estate passes to the other stirpe;
    e. in the second parentel and, in the absence of a heir in the second parentel, in the third parentel, the inheritance is equally divided between the maternal line and the paternal line, irrespective of the fact that one line may not count the same number of heirs as the other line. In the absence of an heir in one line, the entire estate passes to the other line.

B. *Marital Ties*

In order to inherit, the spouse must still be married to the deceased at the time of the death. An ex-husband and an ex-wife may not inherit from each other after divorce. At divorce, they lose their statutory rights of inheritance towards each other and all benefits under a will adopted before the introduction of the divorce (Art. 120 II CC).

The portion devolved by law to the surviving spouse varies according to the parentel to which the other heirs belong (Art. 462 CC). If a deceased leaves descendants, the surviving spouse receives one-half of the estate. Where the surviving spouse competes with the heirs of the second parentel, she or he receives three-quarters of the estate. If there is no heir in the second parentel, the surviving spouse takes the whole of the estate.

The death dissolves the matrimonial 'régime' of the spouses, except the 'regime' of separate property. Under the ordinary legal 'régime',[5] each spouse is entitled to one half of the other spouse's acquisitions made during the 'régime', unless a marriage covenant provides for a different division. So when the succession opens, the surviving spouse is entitled to one half of the acquisitions, the other half passing to the estate.

At the time being, same sex partners are not considered statutory heirs since they have no marital ties. This position might change. A first draft of a federal law on the registrered partnership of same sex people was circulated in November 2001 among the interested groups throughout the country. It proposes to give same sex partners the opportunity to enter a registered partnership which would, among other advantages, give the surviving partner the same inheritance rights as a surviving spouse.[6]

C. *The State*

In the absence of a surviving spouse and in the absence of an heir among the fist three parentels, the estate passes to the Canton of the deceased's last domicile or to the Commune entitled by the law of that canton (Art. 466 CC).

IV. TESTATE SUCCESSION

A. *Principles of Testamentary Dispositions*

1. Testamentary Capacity (Arts. 467–468 CC)

A person must be able to make reasonable judgments at the very moment she makes her will[7] and be at least eighteen years old (which is the normal minimum age at

---

5. For more details, see Ch. 5 on Family Law.
6. The project can be reached via the website of the Swiss Federal Office of Justice: <www.ofj.admin.ch/themen/glgpaare/veber-com-f.htm>.
7. Ability to make reasonable judgments is presumed under normal circumstances. Inability is however presumed where the health of the person at the time the will was made allows to consider that he or she was usually in a state of inability to make reasonable judgments (ATF 124 III 5, 7–8).

which one has capacity to enter into transactions). To enter a testamentary agreement (bilateral), a testator must in addition not be under guardianship.

2. Interpretation of Testamentary Dispositions

The interpretation aims at the restoration of the deceased's real intent expressed in the testamentary act.[8] The Supreme Court considers that an unequivocal text shall not be subject to interpretation with elements that do not figure in the act itself.[9] This point of view has been criticized by several legal scholars.[10]

3. Invalidation of Testamentary Dispositions

A testamentary disposition may be flawed by the testator's lack of capacity, by the fact that the will was made under undue influence or error,[11] by the illegal or immoral character of the disposition or by the non-respect of the formalities imposed by law.[12] Heirs and legatees may bring action to invalidate the disposition. If the claim is well-founded, the disposition is invalidated with an *ex tunc* effect.

The action must be brought only within the period set by Article 521 CC, i.e. one year from the date on which the heirs acquired knowledge of the testamentary disposition and the grounds for invalidation, in any case no later than ten years from the date of the opening of the will. It can be brought within thirty years against a beneficiary who has acted fraudulently, where the will or agreement is voidable by reason of illegality or immorality or due to the testamentary incapacity of the testator. There is no statute of limitation to plead the invalidity as a defence to an action to enforce the testamentary disposition.

B. Formalities Required for Testamentary Dispositions

To make a will or enter a testamentary agreement, some formalities imposed by law should be respected.[13] One distinguishes the formalities for a unilateral act (will) and those for a bilateral one (testamentary agreement).

8. The interpretation of a testamentary agreement should take into consideration that it is a bilateral act. For details, see among others P. Weimar, *Das Erbrecht, Berner Kommentar, Die Verfügungen von Todeswegen – Einleitung*, Berne 2000, pp. 106–107.
9. For example ATF 120 II 182, 184.
10. For details, see among others P. Breitschmid, *Kommentar zum schweizerischen Privatrecht, Schweizerisches Zivilgesetzbuch II, ad art. 469 ZGB*, n. 22–30; also P. Weimar, *op.cit.*, pp. 104–124.
11. Every kind of error, including an error on the motives of the act, is relevant as long as the error has decisively prompted the testator to adopt the will. It must be proved that had he known the error, he would have revoked the disposition: ATF 119 II 208.
12. With regard to the formalities imposed by law for testamentary dispositions, see IV C.
13. ATF 117 II 239, 245–246; where the formalities have been omitted, interested heirs and legatees can bring an action to invalidate the testamentary disposition. The invalidation can be claimed within one year from the date when the plaintiff had knowledge of the testamentary disposition and of the ground for invalidation, and in any case no later than ten years from the date of the opening of the will (Art. 521 CC). There is no statute of limitation to plead the invalidation as a defence.

1. Wills (*Letzwillige Verfügung/Testament*)

A will is a unilateral legal act. It expresses a person's intention regarding his property which takes effect at his death. Swiss law recognizes three kinds of wills: namely holographic, public and oral wills.

A holographic will is completely hand written by the testator himself, and signed by him at the end of the document (Art. 505 CC). The testator must mention the year, month and day it was made.[14] Where the testator omitted the date or indicated an inexact date, the will may be invalidated if the date is relevant to the validity of the will and the exact date cannot be established by any other means. The date is relevant to know if the testator had reasonable judgment at the time the will was adopted or, where the testator has adopted several acts, to decide which one is the latest (Art. 520a CC). A holographic will may be deposited at the office designed for this purpose, but it is not a condition of validity.

A public will is one made in the presence of two witnesses[15] before a notary or another official authorized for this purpose under cantonal law (Arts. 499–504 CC). The will must necessarily be deposited for safe custody at an office designated for this purpose or at the notary or official's office.

An oral will is a susbsidiary form. It can only be made where the testator is unable to make a public or a holographic will due to exceptional circumstances such as imminent danger of death, absence of means of communication, epidemic or war (Art. 506 CC). The testator must declare his last wishes in the presence of two witnesses and charge them to write down and to inform the probate authority of his last wishes.

A will may be revoked at any time. A revokation has to respect one of the forms prescribed by law for the making of the will (Art. 509 CC). Where a testator makes a will without expressly revoking an earlier one, it is deemed to supersede the earlier one in its entirety, unless it purports clearly to be only a complementary disposition (Art. 511 I CC). A testator may revoke, wholly or in part, his will by destroying the document with *animus revocandi*. The crossing of some words is considered by the Supreme Court as a partial destruction, the mention of the day the crossing occured being then not a condition of validity.[16] Where the testator alienates *inter vivos* the object of the legacy stated in his will, a revocation is presumed (Art. 511 II CC).

2. Testamentary Agreement (*Erbvertrag/Pacte sucessoral*)

A testamentary agreement is a bilateral act between the testator and another person, with several or all clauses expressing the intention of the testator regarding the devolution of his estate at his death. It must respect the formalities required for a public will (Art. 512 CC). Except for a few exceptions, it cannot be revoked unilaterally.

---

14. Since 1996, the mention of the place where the will was made is no longer required. The law has been amended subsequently by the parlementary initiative of the national councellor Jean Guinand (Lex Guinand), FF 1994 III p. 519.
15. Where the testator does not read the document by himself, the official must read it out to him in the presence of two witnesses: ATF 118 II 273.
16. ATF 116 II 411; about the ambiguous distinction made between the revocation of a will by written words and the revocation by signs, see M. Stettler, 'La révocation et la suppression du testament', in *Mélanges Schüpbach*, Neuchâtel 2000, p. 155.

There are two kinds of testamentary agreements:

a. the agreement of attribution: the testator binds himself to leave his estate or a specific good to the other contracting party or to a third person (Art. 494 CC);
b. the agreement of renunciation: the testator can enter an agreement with one of his heirs whereby the latter voluntarily renounces to his rights of inheritance, with or without a monetary compensation (Art. 495 CC).

C. Kinds of Disposition

The law lists several kinds of dispositions that can be made by will or by testamentary agreement. A disposition made with a kind not provided for in the Civil Code is void *ab initio*. So, for example the constitution of a trust by testamentary disposition is not possible under Swiss Law and would be void.[17]

The most important kinds of dispositions are:

1. Appointment of Heirs (Art. 483 CC) (*Erbeinsetzung/Institution d'héritier*)

A testator can appoint one or several persons to receive the entire estate or a part of it. The heir nominated can be a natural or legal person. A statutory heir may also be appointed. Unless otherwise provided by the testator, the parts devolved are presumed to be equal.

2. Legacies (Art. 484 CC) (*Vermächtnis/Legs*)

A testator can leave by will or by an agreement of inheritance a legacy to one or to several beneficiaries. As a legacy the testator can leave a specific object, a fixed amount of money or the usufruct either in the whole or in part of the estate. He may charge his heirs or other beneficiaries to give a beneficiary some benefit out of the estate or release him from some liability. Unlike the appointed heir, the legatee is not liable for the deceased's debts or for the debts incurred through the liquidation of the inheritance.

It can be difficult to distinguish appointment of heir from legacy. As a remedy, the law holds the attribution of the whole or a share of the inheritance to a beneficiary to be an institution of an heir (Art. 483 II CC). *A contrario*, the attribution of a determined value or a specific object is deemed to be a legacy.[18]

Where a testator leaves a specific object to legatee, the heir in charged with handing it over is not bound to do so if the thing beaqueathed does no longer exist as a part of the estate. A contrary intention of the testator may be proved (Art. 484 III CC).[19]

---

17. See Ch. 7, VI on Property.
18. ATF 50 II 332, 334.
19. ATF 101 II 25; 91 II 94.

3. Burdens and Conditions (Art. 482 CC) (*Auflagen und Bedingungen/Charges et conditions*)

A testator can attach conditions in his will or in the testament agreement. He or she can charge the heirs or other beneficiaries with the execution of some specific action or ask them to refrain from doing it.[20] The Supreme Court has considered that the testator may bind the heirs' inheritance right or part of it to the condition that the will not be contested,[21] as long as their compulsory portion is not touched.[22]

Burdens and conditions are voidable if they are immoral or illegal (Art. 482 II CC), the action may be brought by any heir or beneficiary who is an interested party. Meaningless, frivolous or merely vexatious burdens and conditions are deemed to be non-existent (Art. 482 III CC).

4. Substitutions

A testator can in his will or by testamentary agreement appoint one or several persons to take the inheritance in the event of one or more heirs predeceasing him or disclaiming the inheritance (Art. 487 CC). A substitution can also be made with regard to a legacy.

A testator can also charge a 'limited heir' (*grevé*) to pass the inheritance to a 'remainder heir' (*appelé*) (Arts. 488–492 CC). The remainder heir succeeds to the testator, albeit the fact that he takes the inheritance from the limited heir. The transfer of the inheritance to the remainder heir happens, in the absence of a testator's contrary intention, at the death of the 'limited heir' (Art 489 CC). The limited heir becomes owner of the estate and has all rights and duties attached to it (Art. 491 CC). He is however charged with the obligation to transfer the inheritance to the remainder heir at some point. As owner, the limited heir can alienate the inheritance to a third party without the consent of the remainder heir. At the commencement of the subsitution, the remainder heir can however claim the recovery of the inheritance against the third party, except for the the latter's *bona fide*.

To protect the remainder heir's rights, the law requires the limited heir to give a guarantee, before he or she may receive the inheritance (Art. 490 II CC). By testamentary disposition, the testator can free the limited heir from this obligation.

This kind of substitution is limited in its scope: the testator cannot impose a similar obligation on the remainder heir (Art. 488 II CC). A similar substitution cannot charge the compulsory portion due to some heirs.

Substitution can be made with regard to a legacy as well.

5. Appointment of an Executor

A testator can appoint one or serveral persons to execute his last wishes. He will do so for example where the liquidation of the inheritance is difficult or where there is

---

20. There is no presumption in favor of a charge or in favor of a condition. Where there is a doubt, the provision must be interpreted: ATF 120 II 182.
21. ATF 117 II 239, 246: the clause does not apply when the claim is brought because of a problem of form of the testamentary act.
22. For details on the compulsory portion, see under IV D.

a discord among heirs. The executor can be a natural or corporate person. He or she can be an heir. The person appointed must declare within fourteen days from the notice of the appointment whether he or she is willing to accept the appointment. Silence is taken to mean consent.

In the absence of any other provision by the testator, the executor has to manage the estate, pay the debts of the testator, give effect to the legacies and carry out the division of the inheritance according to the directions given by the testator or the provisions of law (Art. 518 CC).

D. The Limitations Imposed by the Compulsory Portion (Pflichtteil/ Réserve)

Swiss Law reserves a compulsory portion of the estate to certain heirs. As a result, the testator's freedom to dispose of his estate is reduced to the part not covered by the compulsory portions (Art. 470 CC).

1. Beneficiaries and Extent of the Compulsory Portion

There are three categories of beneficiaries: the descendants, parents and surviving spouse of the deceased (Art. 471 CC). Since 1988, brothers and sisters do not have a compulsory portion any more.

A compulsory portion is a fraction of the intestate share of the heir. This fraction is fixed by law for each beneficiary. The fraction is 3/4 of the intestate share for the descendants and 1/2 for the surviving spouse and the parents. So where both surviving spouse and descendants are heirs, the compulsory portion is 1/4 of the estate for the spouse and 3/8 for the children. Or where surviving spouse and the deceased's parents are heirs, the compulsory portion is 3/8 of the estate for the spouse and 1/8 for the parents.

The compulsory portion of descendants who are common to the deceased and the surviving spouse is not protected in two situations: first, where the testator leaves to the surviving spouse *mortis causa* the usufruct in the whole of the share devolved to the common decendants (Art. 473 CC), second, where the testator leaves to the surviving spouse a larger part of the benefits accrued during the marriage than what is due by law (Art. 216 CC).

2. Protection Given to the Compulsory Portion

Gifts or other kinds of gifts,[23] *inter vivos* or *mortis causa* are subject to a reduction where they encroach upon the heirs' compulsory rights.[24] All types of gifts *mortis causa* but only certain gifts *inter vivos* may be subject to a claim for reduction.

---

23. In case of an agreement with obvious and intended disproportion between the parties' reciprocal obligations (*donation mixte*), the gratuitous part might be reduced to the part corresponding to the testator's liberty of disposition: ATF 120 II 417, 420–422; 116 II 667.
24. For details about form and extent of the abatment, see S. Spahr, *Valeur et valorisme en matière de liquidations successorales*, Fribourg 1994.

The latter gifts are among others[25]: a) gifts made five years before the deceased's death, b) gifts made by the deceased with the obvious intention of evading the rules restricting his freedom of disposition c) gifts made by the deceased as a satisfaction of the donee's right of inheritance, but not brought into the hotchpot at the opening of the succession (Art. 527 CC).[26]

A claim for 'reduction' may be brought within one year from the date on which the heirs first learned of the infringement of their rights, in any case no later than ten years from the opening of the will (for testamentary dispositions) or from the death of the donor (for gifts *inter vivos*) (Art. 533 CC).[27] To calculate the compulsory portion, gifts are taken at their value at the death of the donor (Arts. 474 I and 537 II CC).

3. Disinheritance[28] (*Enterbung/Exheredation*)

The testator can by will deprive a heir of all or a part of his compulsory portion, but only where the heir has committed a serious offense against the deceased or one of his next-of-kin or where he has seriously failed in the duties imposed upon him by law towards the deceased or his family (Art. 477 CC). Such disinheritance is valid only when the testator has stated the reason in his will (Art. 479 CC). The disinheritated can request a reassesment from the judge. If the claim is well-founded, he gets his compulsory portion.

The testator can dispose freely from the portion of the disinherited person. The compulsory portion of the disinherited heir's descendants is however protected (Art. 478 III CC). In the absence of any contrary disposition by the testator, the portion of the disinherited heir passes to the intestate heirs as if he had not survived the deceased (Art. 478 II CC).

Swiss law knows another cause allowing the testator to deprive an heir of his compulsory portion. Where the testator's descendant is insolvent, that is when the creditors hold certificates of unsatisfied claims against him, the testator can deprive the heir of half of his compulsory portion, provided the portion is given to the descendant's children whether born or not at the time of the testator's death (Art. 480 CC).[29]

---

25. For details, see among others P. Eitel, *Die Berücksichtigung lebzeitiger Zuwendungen im Erbrecht*, Berne 1998; L. Vollery, *Les relations entre rapports et réunions en droit successoral, L'article 527 chiffre 1 du Code civil et le principe de la comptabilisation des rapports dans la masse de calcul des réserves*, Fribourg 1994.
26. It includes gifts which should have been brought into hotchpot, had the testator not expressly stated the contrary: ATF 116 II 667; see also ATF 126 III 171.
27. The statute of limitation starts to run at the time when the heir has a sufficient knowledge of the facts which allow him to claim for 'reduction'. An approximate knowledge of the amount of the estate is sufficient: ATF 121 III 249, 250–252.
28. For more details see among others P. Weimar, *Das Erbrecht, Berner Kommentar, ad art. 477–480 ZGB*, Berne 2000; see also F. Bellwald, *Die Enterbung im schweizerischen Recht*, Bâle 1980.
29. ATF 111 II 130.

V. TRANSFER, CONSERVATION AND RESTORATION OF THE ESTATE

A. *Intervention of the Probate Authority*

The competent probate authority is required to take all necessary measures to secure the distribution of the inheritance (Art. 551 *et seq.* CC). In accordance with law, the probate authority may be required to affix a seal (Art. 552 CC), make an inventory (Art. 553 CC) or administer the estate officially (Arts. 554–555 CC).

When a will is found at the death of the deceased, it must be handed without delay to this authority, even if it appears to be invalid. The official who has drawn up the will or in whose care it was deposited, as well as any person who has taken charge of it or found it among the testator's effects is personnally responsible for it (Art. 556 CC). Non compliance may lead to civil and criminal liability and an heir so liable can be held unworthy to take a portion of the inheritance or benefit under a testamentary disposition (Art. 540 no. 4 CC).

The probate authority must open the will within a month of its delivery. It must deliver a copy of the will to all parties involved. After one month, those nominated heirs whose claims have not been openly contested by the statutory heirs or by beneficiaries under an earlier will can obtain a certificate of inheritance from the probate authority (Art. 559 CC).

B. *Claim to Recover Inheritance*

Where part of the deceased's estate is in the possession of a third party, the heirs who consider that they have as statutory or instituted heir a better right to it than the third party can claim the recovery of the inheritance.[30] The heirs must claim jointly. The claim can indicate in general terms what is subject to the recovery, due to the fact that it can be difficult to know exactly in advance what belongs to the inheritance.

The claim must be brought within one year from the date on which the plaintiff first learned of the defendant's possession and of his own better title on the estate, in any case no longer than ten years from the date of death of the deceased or the opening of the will (Art. 600 I CC). In case of a *mala fide* defendant, the statute of limitation is thirty years (Art. 600 II CC).

VI. LIMITATION OF LIABILITY FOR DEBTS AND PROTECTION OF THE CREDITORS

A. *Limitation for the Debts*

At the commencement of the succession, the heirs become personnaly liable for the decedent's debts. Should they wish to avoid this consequence the heirs are entitled

---

30. ATF 119 II 114.

under the law to disclaim their inheritance or to limit their liability. The heirs have two options to limit their liability: the official inventory and the official liquidation.

Each heir can demand an 'official inventory' as long as he is entitled to disclaim inheritance (Art. 580 I CC). The demand must be made to the competent probate authority within a month of the commencement of the succession and for the instituted heirs from the communication of the will. The inventory is made according to the rules laid down by cantonal law and consists in a statement of the assets and debts of the estate, with a valuation of every asset. After the closing of the inventory, each heir is called upon to declare within one month what his intention is (Art. 587 CC). He has the right to disclaim the inheritance, demand its official liquidation or accept, either unconditional or subject to the official inventory (Art. 588 CC). In the latter case, his liability is limited to the debts stated in the inventory. He is liable then not only to the extent of the assets but also to the extent of his own private property (Art. 589 CC).

Within the statute of limitation provided for a disclaimer, each heir can make a demand to the probate authority for the 'official liquidation' (*amtliche Liquidation/liquidation officielle*) of the estate, but only as long as one of his co-heirs has not accepted the inheritance unconditionnally (Art. 593 CC). The heirs are then not liable for the debts of the estate. They will get only what remains of the estate after liquidation. The operations of liquidation will be performed by the competent probate authority or at its request by one or more administrators.

B. Protection of the Creditors

The commencement of the succession may endanger the situation of the creditors deceased or the heirs. The law takes it into account.

1. Protection of the Deceased's Creditors

Two situations should be mentioned:

1. Where the deceased's creditors have reasonable grounds to think they might not be paid, they can request the official liquidation of the inheritance, which will ensure them that the testator's debts will be paid before any distribution of the assets (Art. 594 I CC). Heirs' insolvency or foreseeable difficulties with the recovery of the debt outside Switzerland might be considered to be such reasonable grounds. With the official liquidation, creditors are ensured that the deceased's debts will be paid before any distribution of the estate.

   Creditors shall first demand all heirs known to them to pay their debts or to furnish a guarantee. Creditors shall give a reasonable time to perform to the heirs and indicate that an official liquidation will be instituted in case of a failure do pay within the given time.[31]

---

31. M. Karrer, *Kommentar zum schweizerischen Privatrecht, schweizerisches Zivilgesetzbuch II*, Art. 594 ZGB, n. 6; P. Piotet, *Traité de droit privé suisse IV, Droit successoral*, p. 741.

The demand shall be adressed to the competent probate authority within three months from the death or the will's opening. Creditors must give reasonable evidence that there is a risk of default in payment.

2. Where heirs disclaim an insolvent inheritance, they are nevertheless held liable to the creditors of the estate to the extent of the property which they have received from the deceased within the five years preceding his death and which they would have had to bring into hotchpot if they had claimed in the partition of the inheritance (Art. 579 CC). Heirs who have acted *bona fide* are liable only to the extent by which they are enriched at the time.

2. Protection of the Heirs' Creditors

Two situations should be mentioned:

1. Where an insolvent heir has disclaimed for the purpose of depriving his creditors of the estate, the creditors themselves or the official in bankruptcy can within six months oppose the disclaimer, unless their claims are duly secured (Art. 578 I CC). The estate is then submitted to official liquidation (Art. 578 II). Surplus assets are first assigned to satisfy the creditors who have opposed the disclaimer and secondly for the payment of the other creditors. The rest, if any, falls to the heirs in whose favor the disclaimer was made (Art. 578 III CC).
2. Where a testator has exceeded his right of disposition to the prejudice of an heir who is insolvent, the administrator in the bankruptcy of the insolvent heir or his creditors who at the date of the commencement of the succession hold certificates of unsatisfied claims against his estate can bring the action in reduction (Art. 524 CC). The administrator or the creditors must first request the heir to claim for reduction.

VII. PARTITION OF THE ESTATE

A. *General Principles*

1. The time of partition is not imposed by law. The heirs can agree to keep the assets of the estate and the liabilities among them for a given time. Each heir can in principle demand the partition of the estate at any time (Art. 604 CC).
2. The mode of partition is settled by agreement amongst the heirs. The legal rules apply only where there is no agreement. The deceased's instructions as to the mode of partition are binding on the heirs, unless all heirs agree not to respect them (Art. 608 II CC).

    In the absence of a contrary intention of the deceased, the attribution of a specific asset to a heir is not held to be intended as a legacy additional to his hereditary portion but as an instruction for the partition of the estate (Art. 608 III CC).[32]

---

32. ATF 115 II 323, 326–327; 103 II 88, 92–93.

3. In general, partition has to be made in kind. Sale of elements of the estate must be the *ultima ratio*.

Where the house or the apartment, in which the spouses lived, or the household effects are part of the inheritance, the surviving spouse can demand that they become his or her property in return for appropriate compensation (Art. 612a CC).[33]
4. A specific law deals with the partition of farming estate.[34]

B. *Hotchpot* (Ausgleichung/Rapport successoral)

In order to implement an equality of treatment among statutory heirs, Swiss law imposes that gifts made by the deceased to his descendants by way of advance on their share in the inheritance shall be brought into hotchpot, if no contrary intention expressly stated by the deceased (626 II CC). Gifts made to the descendants to establish, consolidate or develop their situation in life are held to be made in advance on their share.[35] Gifts made to heirs other than the descendants, or gifts to the descendants not made in advance on their share, shall not be brought into hotchpot, except for a contrary intention of the deceased (Art. 626 I CC).

The Federal Tribunal considers that a descendant given a share different from his statutory share shall not be compelled to bring into the hotchpot the gifts made to him by the deceased, except for a contrary intention expressed by the deceased.[36] This point of view has been criticized by several legal scholars.[37]

Gifts are brought into hotchpot at the value at the date of the opening of the estate or, where the donnee has already sold what he received before that date, at the price at which the items were sold (Art. 630 I CC).[38] The heir can chose whether he will bring the item he has received into hotchpot in kind or keep it and forfeit his share or part of it according to the value of the item received (Art. 628 CC).

C. *Procedure of Partition*

The Swiss Civil Code sets out three forms of partition procedure:

1. The heirs can make a partition agreement in which they agree to the mode of partition and to the arrangement and distribution of the 'batches' (lots). A partition agreement is valid only if made in writing (Art. 634 II CC). It can be invalidated under the same conditions as any other contract (Art. 638 CC).

33. See among others C. Wildisen, *Das Erbrecht des überlebenden Ehegatten*, Fribourg 1997.
34. RS 211.412.11 which may be reached via the website of the Swiss federal administration: <www.admin.ch>.
35. ATF 116 II 667.
36. ATF 124 III 102.
37. Among others, J. Guinand and M. Stettler, *Droit civil II, Successions*, 4th edn., Fribourg 1999, n. 399
38. For more details, see among others S. Spahr, *Valeur et valorisme en matière de liquidations successorales*, Fribourg 1994.

2. Where the heirs cannot agree, any one of them can require the competent probate authority to dispose of the batches. This will be carried out by taking into account local customs, the circumstances of the heirs and the wishes of the majority of them (Art. 611 II CC).
3. The heirs can call the court to order partition (Art. 604 CC).

   Even after partition the heirs remain jointly and severally liable for the debts of the estate. Their joint liability ceases, however, at the expiration of five years from the date of partition (Art. 639 II CC).

VIII. COMPETENT JURISDICTION

Claims based on rights of inheritance are introduced at the last domicile of the deceased or, for the devolution of a farm or a farming land, at the place where it is located.

The probate authority of the last domicile of the deceased is competent to take all necessary measures to secure the distribution of the inheritance; if the deceased did not die at his domicile, the probate authority of the place of his death must take all necessary measures to preserve the property left there by the deceased.

IX. TAXATION OF THE ESTATE

There is no federal law on inheritance taxation in Switzerland. Cantons are competent to tax the transfer of the estate to the heirs where the deceased had his last domicile in the canton or where the deceased's real property is located in the canton. The amount of the taxes can vary widely from one canton to another. It is almost always proportional to the degree of kinship between the deceased and the heirs.

The taxation is calculated on the share or on the legacy received. In a few cantons, there is an additional taxation on the whole estate before distribution. A large majority of cantons exempt the descendants and the surviving spouse from taxation. A few others have pending legislative propositions to exempt them. The canton of Schwitz does not have any inheritance tax.

SELECTED BIBLIOGRAPHY

Druey, J. N., *Grundriss des Erbrechts*, 5th edn., Berne 2002.

Guinand, J. and M. Stettler, *Droit civil II*, 4th edn., Fribourg 1999.

Honsell, H., P. N. Vogt and T. Geiser (eds), *Schweizerisches Zivilgesetzbuch II*, Basel/Frankfurt am Main 1998.

Piotet, P., *Droit successoral, Traité de droit privé suisse IV*, 2nd edn., Fribourg 1988.

Piotet, P., *Précis de droit successoral*, 2nd edn., Berne 1988.

Tuor, P., B. Schnyder and J. Schmid, *Das schweizerische Zivilgesetzbuch*, 11th edn., Zurich 1995.

Weimar, P., *Das Erbrecht, Berner Kommentar, Die Verfügungen von Todeswegen – Einleitung*, Berne 2000.

Chapter 7
Law of Property

*J.N. Druey**

I. IN GENERAL

A. Subject

When writing on the fourth part of the Swiss Civil Code, the term property will be a *pars pro toto* heading. The subject of this part is – following Gaius' doctrine and the traditional codification principles – *jus in rem (dingliches Recht/droit réel)*. The German terminology reflects the difference between 'right' and 'law', when the *jus in rem* in the sense of a subjective title is called 'dingliches Recht', whereas the body of law covering it is the 'Sachenrecht'.

Therefore, in addition to property in the strict sense (*Eigentum/propriété*) this part of the Code deals with servitudes (*Dienstbarkeiten/servitudes*) and mortgages (including other liens; *Pfand/gage*). Furthermore, it contains chapters on each of the two concepts aimed at securing publicity to the *jus in rem* according to the system, i.e. possession (essentially meaning actual control of the object) and the land register (fulfilling this function for real property, i.e. immovables).

Besides, it has to be mentioned that for agriculturally used land a special Act is applicable (Federal Act on Agricultural Land, dated 4 October 1991). This Act contains rules on the acquisition of agriculturally used land and regulations in the field of inheritance law.

B. Background

The Swiss system of property law illustrates more clearly than any other national system the clash between the Roman and the Germanic tradition which marked legal development in many European countries. Geographically, it appears to be a paradox that the influence of the Roman system was stronger on the neighbor in the north, i.e. the German Code, and that the Germanic roots remained better conserved in Switzerland. However, its explanation is found in the long-lasting tradition of free land ownership by the farmers, which characterizes the history of important parts of

* Professor, University of Economic, Legal and Social Sciences, Saint-Gall University.

F. Dessemontet and T. Ansay (eds), Introduction to Swiss Law, 93–106.
© 2004 Kluwer Law International. Printed in The Netherlands.

Switzerland, particularly in the mountainous regions. This brought about a conservative attitude towards the institutions of property.

This same attitude expressed itself also in an accentuated local specificity of each region sticking strongly to its accustomed rules and procedures. This made the task of unification which Eugen Huber undertook at the end of the last century, an especially cumbersome one in the field of property. But it was also of a particular importance. Traditional concepts had suffered from the rationalization wave which flooded the country after the French revolution and made traditional property law in the cantons highly insecure. Certainty and precise rules were crucial, given particularly the land mortgage practices which became a central feature of the economic life of the country.

Unification in the Code, for this reason, fell somewhat short of regulating all aspects, leaving certain gaps for individual legislation of the cantons, such as relations among neighbors, identity of objects composed of several elements (cf. below IV), interest limits on mortgage-secured loans, and pre-emption rights to agricultural land.

II. Land and Chattels

As under other systems, land and chattels in Switzerland considerably differ as to their legal treatment. Conforming to the roots of this field of law, real estate had to draw to itself much of the legislators' attention. Thus the limits of the socially tolerated use of objects are much more intensively spelled out with respect to land, and the possibilities of establishing servitudes or mortgages are offered by real property law in a way that is clearly more generous.

This has much to do with the institution of the land register which permits to create differentiated legal situations for the objects without running into problems with the principle of publicity governing Swiss property law (claiming that an object's 'real' status be expressed in facts discernible by outsiders; cf. below V), since all those different claims to one piece of land are reflected in the register which is accessible to the persons interested.

No register exists for chattels and therefore the publicity function is attached to physical control (possession) of the object. Hence possession is deemed to express, in the case of chattels, the existence of a *jus in rem*. This, however, being a uniform concept (you either have control or you do not), possession is not able to express a variety of different legal titles to the same object.

One should nevertheless realize that the basic ideas of property with respect to land or chattels are identical. It confers the same sorts of rights as to both, and, as to creditor's rights, therefore, it means the same to mortgage a piece of land or to pledge a piano or a gold watch (Swiss law uses the same term, *gage* in French and *Pfand* in German, for both). The Swiss Code, less inclined as it is to abstractions when compared to the German Code, contains numerous rules promulgated only for land, but which are actually of a general character and are applied to chattels as well.

III. *Jus in Rem* and Personal Right

The law observes the fundamental division between *jus in rem* and *jus in personam* (i.e. former being a right opposable and to be respected by everybody, while the latter refers to the right resulting from a relationship to particular persons and being limited in its impact to persons having such privacy. Although this distinction not seldom is a windfall matter, it has the serious consequence in cases of bankruptcy that the right is opposable to third party creditors and the holder's title can withstand another person's bankruptcy.

In order to smooth this distinction out, the law provides a sort of shelter against third party rights for quite a few additional positions which from their nature are not a *jus in rem*. A right of pre-emption, for instance, would mean that the holder has no title against a buyer of the house, since the pre-emption right by its nature is a mere personal claim against the grantor (usually the previous owner), and not extended to his successor. But the Code, in order to protect the holder, grants him a right to have the pre-emption right inserted in the Land Register. Thereby, his right becomes opposable to a third party, essentially similar to the *jus in rem* (Art. 959 CC).

The tendency to stretch the *jus in rem* concept also appears in cases of the bankruptcy of a bank. The securities administered by the bank for its clients remain the clients' property and may be sorted out when it comes to the worst for the bank. This is true despite the fact that the relationship of the clients to those values is only indirect and the element of control, which constitutes the right *in rem*, is hardly granted, all the more so when the securities are not even deposited with the client's bank, but concentrated in a third place.

IV. The Identity of Objects

For good reason the Code and legal reasoning in Switzerland pay much attention to the question of what is to be considered as one single object. This problem arises when a thing is composed of a plurality of elements. The Code distinguishes two categories depending on whether the link between such elements is of a stringent nature and therefore may not be dissolved by (normative) disposition of a private person or whether it is a mere legal assumption leaving it open to the owner legally to separate the elements.

In this matter the law primarily follows an economic approach. The criterion which decides whether we are confronted with one single entity in the sense of property law or rather with a majority of objects turns on the presumptive function which can be attributed to the object(s) from their nature. Conforming with the concept, an approach from the outside is applicable: we must see how it looks for a third party without reference to the holder.

Such function may be derived from the circumstance that separation of elements could create extra cost or could be detrimental to the value of the elements (according to one theory it must be a prejudice to the main element). This shows that the elements are thought by the owner to stay together. Thus, a tube in a wall or the stone in a ring will usually have to be considered as necessarily linked with the house or the ring, respectively; from the legal standpoint, they cannot have a 'real' status of their own (as long as they are not in fact separated) (Art. 642 CC). Occasionally, however there will be no functional symbiosis despite the physical tie, and then we legally have no entity; this is true, for example, of electrical installations fixed on a house wall but not serving the house itself.

This necessary identity of an object also exists in Swiss law where its appearance does not allow one to discern a difference in the legal situation of its elements that is where it forms a homogeneous totality. Thus the parts of a pile of wood or a set of balls cannot belong to different persons, and this is all the more the case for the content of a gasoline tank or a wine-cask. But what about a library, the books differing among each other and the elements therefore being identifiable? Since an economic standard is applicable, we should also treat it as one entity in all cases where the whole is clearly worth more than the sum of its parts.

The consequence of such uniform legal treatment is for instance felt when pieces of machinery and the like are delivered with the passing of title reserved until full payment of the price: as soon as those devices are built into another entity of more importance in itself (the engine into the car) the title reservation will lose all its effect. Only if the element built is to be considered as the main part will its owner become the owner of the whole unit (Art. 727 II CC). If the parts after their unification are more or less equivalent in functional importance, they become the co-property of their prior owners according to the value share of the parts (Art. 727 I CC). The same applies in the case of mixing various materials into a homogeneous bulk (same provision).

A special rule governs such combination cases when land is involved. Following the Roman accession doctrine, the land itself is always considered as the main part in the above-mentioned sense. The owner of the land therefore automatically becomes the owner of the buildings and plants as well as of the sources located on it (Art. 667 CC). One of the exceptions to this rule will have to be discussed below, which is the case of the building right (see below XII).

If the tie between elements is looser, this is reflected by an accordingly looser link in law. It is the case of the so-called accessories (*Zugehör/accessoires*), which will only follow the main part in any transaction (a sale, a mortgage) unless the contrary is stipulated. The legislators took great pains in circumscribing the criteria for this quality of being an accessory in a very differentiated manner (Art. 664 *et seq.* CC), but it will hardly be less precise to simply state that it is a gradual problem of the intensity of the tie. In this sense legal opinion will consider as an accessory the additional lenses to a camera, the replacement wheel of a car, or the box specifically destined (even if not specifically formed) for a pair of glasses.

The concept of accessory indicates in itself that the object is in a service relationship to the main object. This is why this quality is denied, e.g. for the cattle on a farm; borderline cases will be the loudspeaker-boxes of a stereo set, probably depending on the respective values, or the shades in an apartment (as they are customarily bought by each inhabitant party itself, they may not have sufficient tie with the building, not more than other personal furniture which clearly is not an accessory to the building).

V. THE TRANSFER OF PROPERTY

Property, like the other rights dealt with in this chapter (see I, above), is transferred from one person to another by transfer of physical control over the object on the basis of a valid contract. When land is the object, transfer of control is replaced by an inscription in the land register. Contrary to French law, for example, a sales contract itself is not able to cause the passing of title, but a strict separation is made between the 'personal' and the 'real' aspect of the transaction. The 'real' transfer has to comply with the externalization principle (publicity test) governing property law in Switzerland as in Germany and elsewhere. This means that every sale or donation will confer ownership only when the object itself is transmitted. But it does not mean, of course, that every transfer of the object is the passing of title. If passing is not intended, it will not take place; if, for example, a carpet is delivered for a few days' examination at home, ownership remains with the furnisher (without having to fulfill the requirements of title reservation; cf. below XI).

The rules providing for a transfer of title therefore can only establish the personal obligation to perform the real transfer. These rules will usually emanate from a contract, but there can also be another private disposition such as a will or exercising of an option right. Furthermore it can be a right granted by the law itself, particularly in cases of servitudes and mortgages. If a contract on such a matter concerns land, it is subject to strict form requirements; as a general rule, it has to be established by a notary deed.

A particularity of Swiss law, which otherwise in this field is strongly influenced by German law, appears in the situation where the underlying contract is invalid. Then, according to Swiss case law, the transaction is also invalidated on the 'real' level. Thus the distinction between the two aspects is not followed in Swiss law up to its last consequence, which would be that a deficiency on the level of the contract, constituting the personal right to have the property transferred, should not 'contaminate' the *jus in rem* after the transfer was operated.

Great practical importance has been attached in Switzerland to pre-emption and option contracts concerning land. Pre-emption rights (*Vorkaufsrecht/droit de préemption*) often are stipulated among neighbors to control third party acquisitions of the land. The person entitled usually has the right to buy at the price and conditions offered by a third party, if the owner is prepared to sell. In some circumstances, pre-emption rights are granted by the law itself, such as for a co-owner in case one of the other owners wants to sell his share, or for either the owner of real estate which is encumbered with another's right to construct a building thereon or the holder of this right in case one of them wants to sell the land or the right. Option rights (*Kaufsrecht/droits d'emption*) have received a somewhat bad reputation, since they are often used to get land dealers in a 'put–call' situation by which they will profit from a rising of value since the price is fixed in the option contract, but no risk will be incurred if prices fall, because no important option fee is provided. Inexperienced sellers, not seldom, are abused by this sort of bargain. At the same time, they serve to avoid transfer taxes.

The taxation of a transfer only takes place in the cases where land is involved.

The rate is in the range of 2 per cent of the value and is usually shared equally by the parties to a sale contract. Further, there is a tax on the seller's profit that results from the sale of land. Its rate depends on the amount of the profit (progressively) and the duration of ownership (digressively). In addition, taxation exists in some cases of transactions of securities and of other goods (essentially if performed between professionals).

VI. FIDUCIARY RIGHTS ('TRUSTS')

The trust is not known as an institution by Swiss law. However, the practice of banks and others is very familiar with the so-called fiduciary (*Treuhand*) legal position. The position of the fiduciary holder (which has some analogy to that of a trustee) comprises full rights against third parties, but he is bound to follow the instructions of another person and may in turn devolve the risks on him. This other person has a position somewhat comparable to that of the settlor in the law of trusts, but also with that of the beneficiary. He may be called an 'owner' in an economic sense.

Thus, the phenomenon of the fiduciary turns on the very distinction between 'personal' and 'real': the fiduciary is the legal instrument to differentiate between these two levels. The internal ('personal') aspects are irrelevant for third parties; the fiduciary for them is the full holder of ('real') rights.

Such relationships call for a good deal of trust not only on the part of the economic owner in the background that the fiduciary will not misuse his powers, but also on the part of the fiduciary that the 'settlor' will reimburse him for the costs and liabilities he often incurs in the course of fulfilling such functions. Therefore, this relationship is qualified by Swiss law to be a mandate, which implies that it may be cancelled by either party at any time with immediate effect (Art. 404 CO). Regarding legal claims against third persons, the fiduciary has acquired in his own name but for the account of the 'settlor', the 'settlor' will not run a risk in the case of bankruptcy of the fiduciary if he has fulfilled all his obligations arising out of the fiduciary contract (Art. 401 II CO). The same applies to chattels (Art. 401 III CO), but according to a recent Supreme Court decision the settlor has no privilege in the fiduciary's bankruptcy for claims resulting from values transferred from the settlor to the fiduciary.

VII. LEGAL PROTECTION OF PROPERTY

Property protection is not only regulated in the Civil Code, but it is also expressly stated in the Federal Constitution (Art. 26). These two sources are in this respect more in a symbiotic than in a hierarchical relationship, since the Constitution, although formally standing on a higher level than the Code as a simple law, does not define property – this is primarily to be answered by the Civil Code.

The constitutional guarantee of property falls short of total protection. It has two wings. First is what is called an 'institutional' guarantee in the sense that the institution of private property may not as such be abolished. This would materialize even if the possibility of private ownership would be substantially hindered only in specific areas, say in a whole industrial branch. In practice, this aspect is of much lesser importance than a second one, granting a right to full remuneration where an expropriation has occurred, but where governmental dispositions caused substantial losses to the value of private property, such as in the context of urbanization plans (Art. 26 II Fed. Cons.)

On the level of civil law, the Code defines the right flowing from property as being the right to use and the right to dispose of the object. 'To dispose' contains a factual element (to change or to destroy) and a legal element (to transfer property or other rights regarding the object to other persons) (Art. 641 I CC).

The claims by which one enforces those rights are patterned on Roman models, the *actio negatoria* (injunction not to infringe on one's property use) and the *rei vindicatio* (claim against a holder without title to return an object). In addition, the owner may receive from the court a declaratory judgment, i.e. a ruling not issuing an order but simply stating what the plaintiff's rights are. Injunctive relief is also granted to a person who is not able to show a title to the object, on the sole basis of having it under actual possession (Art. 928 CC). It clearly shows two different levels: the real claim (*dingliche Klage/action pétitoire*) can only be engaged by the owner, whereas the possessory action (*Besitzklage/action possessoire*) can be engaged either by the owner or by the holder.

VIII. PROTECTION OF GOOD FAITH ACQUISITION

It is an ongoing theme of Swiss property law that good faith acquisition should be protected. This is again an outflow from the publicity principle. The appearance should, as a rule, be decisive for the legal situation. This approach, however, has not been followed to the end, but had to some limited degree been superseded by the protection of a former holder of title.

The result of the compromise is a distinction depending on the circumstances under which the former holder lost his control. Should he have abandoned it by his own decision, he has to bear the risk. For example, if he has given a painting to an exhibition or transmitted his securities to the bank for storage, he will have no right to the object against a buyer who acquired it from the exhibition or the bank or from an intermediary party in good faith (Art. 933 CC). The situation of the former holder is better if the object left the domain of his control without his consent, for example if it were stolen. Then he has a claim even against a good faith buyer for five years. But full payment of the price is due if the objects were bought in a place which was publicly and professionally offering goods of the respective sort (Art. 934 CC). And no claim exists for money and bearer shares (Art. 935 CC).

The case is simpler for land. The land register is a device operated by special officials of the State. They have a duty to examine the transactions brought to them for entry (cf. below XV). Therefore, the register is expressly endowed by the law with public trust. This means that any acquirer of a right *in rem* is protected in his confidence that the preceding entries in the register are correct (Art. 973 CC).

It should be noted in this context that Article 3 of the Civil Code states a presumption in favor of good faith. Hence bad faith has to be specifically proved by those alleging it.

IX. COMMON OWNERSHIP AND APARTMENT PROPERTY

There are two forms of property common to several persons. One is used where the group is in itself a body, such as partnership or a community of heirs (*Gesamteigentum/propriété commune*). The exercise of property rights is then a function of the respective organization.

The other form is a co-property by shares (*Miteigentum/copropriété*). This applies where no community except for ownership exists. Title of each co-owner is expressed as a fragment of the whole. Each has rights to the object so far as they are in harmony with the corresponding rights of the others. He may sell his share but he may also request that the object as a whole be either divided or sold (Art. 651 CC). Rather complicated are the rules concerning the administration of objects held in such co-property by shares.

An amendment which was attached in 1965 to the Code's rules on co-property by shares (Art. 712a *et seq.*) created quasi-ownership to specific flats of a building. When the Code was inaugurated in the beginning of the century, it was thought that ownership to parts of a building was incompatible with the mentioned (IV, 6th para.) principle of accession making each piece of land and its constructions a necessarily individual unit. Economic need for a flat ownership system has since then grown to be important. The amendment now renders it possible to buy co-property of a parcel of land in a share approximately corresponding to the value of a flat in proportion to the rest of the dwelling space. Combined with this is an exclusive using right to the specified apartment.

All parts not reserved by exclusive using rights, i.e. not belonging to the dwelling space, such as staircases, cellars, garden, and garage (if they are not themselves individually closed and reserved spaces), are the property of the co-proprietors in undivided co-ownership. These common parts are administered by an organization mandatorily prescribed by the law and consisting of the assembly of the owners as the 'legislative' body and of an administrator. Concerning repairs and maintenance of those parts the community of co-proprietors can bring action and enforce payment in its own name and an action can be brought against it or payment can be enforced.

The need for this institution of flat ownership has been confirmed by the number of houses which today are legally split in this manner.

X. THE DUTIES TO THE NEIGHBOR

The Civil Code extensively deals with neighborhood law. In addition, we find a lot of rules dealing with those problems in public law regulations mostly located on the cantonal or community level, which are laid down in construction laws, town and city planning decrees and the like.

Although the Federal Civil Code is intended to be the exclusive source in the fields of private law covered themselves, there is space and need for local law in the matters of property, because the Code's rules call for implementation (cf. in particular Arts. 641 I, 686, 695). Each canton therefore has established an introductory law to the Civil Code to set forth such implementation rules, and this mostly proves another rich source, particularly concerning neighbors' interferences.

The civil neighborhood law is dominated by a general paragraph prohibiting any excessive use of one's land to the detriment of the neighbors (Art. 684 CC). This is directed against nuisance by noise or by odour or otherwise hurting the neighbors' feelings (a slaughterhouse for example and in cases of physical interference, such as water or stones moved on the neighbor's ground). Pursuant to recent trends we should include the case of not actively causing disturbance but impairing the chances of free use of the neighboring property, such as by depriving it of sunlight or impeding access for business customers. The standard is always set by a weighing of interests on both sides. A contemporary and frequent use of this is made to prevent neighbors from installing cellular phone's antennas.

The law also insists on the opposite aspect. Several provisions state duties of tolerance for a neighbor's activities. If one's land is not adjacent to a road or water tap, he may conduct a way or a pipe over the neighbor's land, etc. Old local traditions maintain their validity in this field, like a right to use the neighbor's land for construction scaffolds or for turning the ploughshare on it, or a right to transport wood over it in wintertime.

Abuse of ownership to the detriment of a neighbor is sanctioned by the right to injunction. Furthermore, damages can be claimed (Art. 679 CC), and this right to damages is, contrary to the general rule (Art. 41 CO), independent of fault or negligence on the part of the liable person. This is why the delimitation of the area of application of this article became a subject of lively discussion. Some uncertainties left by the Code have now been cleared up. The claim may be raised not only by the proprietor himself, but also by other persons having a steady relationship with the land, such as the lessee of an apartment situated on it. A claim is also possible against those persons, if the nuisance is caused by them. Damages under this section can only be asked for if the unlawful behavior is to be qualified as a use of the land, thus as a transgression of ownership rights. This is not the case, for example, of a shot by a child standing on one's ground, if the land is not regularly used for such purposes.

XI. PROPERTY RESERVED TO THE SELLER (*Eigentumsvorbehalt/Reserve de propriété*)

The seller has an interest in keeping the goods sold as a lien for payment of the price as long as this is not fully affected. The only protection for the seller under Swiss law in this respect is to withhold delivery of those goods until payment. This stands, however, in opposition to widespread commercial practice in particular (but not only) for certain consumer goods ('buy now, pay later'). To pledge the objects sold is barred by the publicity principle, which demands physical transfer to the creditor in order to give him a title *in rem* (below, XIV). And the same is true of course for the passing or non-passing of ownership: the publicity rule not only requires that control be transmitted as a condition for transferring title, but also that the acquirer necessarily becomes the owner in order to bring the legal situation in harmony with the appearance.

But the mentioned needs of commerce (which are not so recent as today's aggressive business practices may lead us to assume) brought about an exception to this system. Reservation of title despite physical transfer is allowed. However, being an exception, the legislature has thoroughly confined this possibility (Art. 715 *et seq.* CC).

First, reservation of title is strictly limited to the case of securing the seller for the remainder of the sales price. It ends with full payment. Second, it ends when the object is built into another (above, IV). Third, it also ends (contrary to the rule in Germany) when the object (maybe without authorization) is sold. Fourth, the agreement by which a transferor reserves the property has to be concluded before the goods are transferred to the receiver. Fifth and mainly, the reservation is only valid if it has been inscribed – before adjudication in bankruptcy – into a register specially established for this purpose. Still, this inscription will not hinder the good faith acquisition of any rights *in rem* by another person, such as the lessor of business rooms (cf. Art 268a CO). Furthermore it causes the seller administrative inconvenience, since the reservation ends in case of moving of the buyer, unless the insertion is renewed in the new local register within three months.

XII. SERVITUDES (*Dienstbarkeiten/Servitudes*)

The shortness of the following remarks is in disproportion to the great importance which servitudes concerning land have in Switzerland. There is hardly a page in the land register which does not show a list of rights and charges of this sort. Servitudes are often written in favor not of a specifically named person, but of the current owner of the land (praedial servitudes, *Grunddienstbarkeiten/servitudes foncières*; Art. 730 *et seq.* CC). This applies in particular to rights and duties which are stipulated between neighbors. They have the purpose, for example, to ensure that construction on an adjacent ground will not be above a certain height or that the owner's building may come closer to the boundary than neighbors' right would permit or that the boundary area of the garden is shaped in a certain manner.

Another type of servitudes, growing in importance is granted in favor of a specific person. These rights fulfill a very different economic function. They grant a claim to exploit the land under one or another aspect, to a degree which may come close to full property rights. This is especially so for the most important of these rights which is the right to construct a building on another's land (*Baurecht/droit de superficie*; Art. 779 *et seq.* CC). Contrary to the general rule, such a right enables the entitled person to be the owner of the respective constructions. Servitudes of this kind are usually provided for a long period, limited by the Code to one hundred years (Art. 779 I CC). At their expiration the property reverts back to the owner of the land, but he has to reimburse the remaining value of the buildings (Art. 779 d CC). Due to the scope of rights granted, the construction right has to be stipulated by notary deed, whereas most of the other servitudes can be set forth in an informal document signed by the parties. The construction right is furthermore handled in the register of land like a property on its own; it can therefore be mortgaged as the land itself.

The discussion on the subject of the so-called beer servitudes has become classic in Switzerland. The Swiss breweries usually have exclusivity agreements with restaurants and pubs prohibiting them from drawing their supply of beer from any other supplier. To legally fortify those contracts the breweries used to place a servitude on the land of the restaurant, etc. stating this exclusivity. It is recognized today that this transaction cannot be the subject of a servitude, which pursuant to its concept is to rule in one way or another on the use of the property – the buying of one or the other label of beer obviously not being a 'use' in this sense.

Servitudes concerning chattels are limited to one type, which is usufruct. This institution is of great importance because the spouse is often granted a testamentary right of this sort in inheritance law (Art. 473 CC).

XIII. MORTGAGE OF LAND

Mortgages concerning land are, in Switzerland, economically speaking, of a stable nature. Interest rates are low and amortization requirements usually are mild (none is provided by the Code). It is therefore very frequent that construction loans, secured by a mortgage, are maintained for several decenniums.

The repayment claim and the mortgage right may be bonded in a security (*mortgage certificate, Schuldbrief/cédule*) or not (*Grundpfandverschreibung/hypothèque*). The bond is aimed at facilitating mortgaged credits to a maximum, giving the creditor the possibility of easily selling the claim. This claim is given an abstract character, not depending on the objections the debtor might oppose to the first creditor (Art. 855 CC). If the credit is not bonded the advantage is – apart from lesser costs and smaller risks for the debtor – that the secured credit may vary in sum. This form, the hypothèque, therefore is used for overdrafts and other fluctuating credit facilities granted by banks to their clients. The mortgaged claim, which necessarily is to be specified, is identified in this situation by a maximum sum resulting from the accumulated business between the parties and not by a particular bargain (cf. Art. 794 II CC; 'maximum mortgage' as opposed to 'capital mortgage'). An agreement to create a mortgage on land has to be stipulated by notary deed (Art. 799 II CC). Besides, there are several mortgages created by law, such as for certain cantonal taxes and for the unpaid seller of the land. The possibility for craftmen and entrepreneurs to obtain a mortgage on theirs works on a building site (Art. 839 *et seq.* CC) is well known and often used in practice.

A special form of securing by bonded mortgages is a peculiarity very popular in Swiss practice, namely, not to make the creditor himself the owner of such a bond, but to pledge it in his favor. Formally, the debtor is at the same time the owner of the bond, and the creditor has such bond in his hands as a chattel security. Many banks see advantages connected with this form.

Extended discussions took place during the preparation of the Code concerning the question of hierarchy of several mortgages on the same land. The Roman principle which was again taken up by the German Code a few years before the Swiss Code was created is the criterion of priority in time. Deviating from that, the Swiss Code chose the system of a fixed rank of the mortgage rights; therefore a lower placed mortgage right will not automatically advance into a higher rank, if a higher mortgage is cancelled. However, such a right to succeed may be provided for contractually by the parties and this has become frequent in contracts: nevertheless, these clauses for various reasons have been shown to have little practical impact. One reason is that such succeeding clauses have no effect if there is in the higher rank a bonded right, which by its very nature is usually 'immortal' (instead of cancellation it is usually sold).

XIV. PLEDGE OF CHATTELS

The pledging of chattels plays an incomparably minor role than the mortgaging of land. One of the reasons lies in the legal system. The publicity principle calls for physical transfer of pledged chattels; therefore, the debtor is deprived of the use of the property. The main applicable case is the mortgage of securities to the bank where they are deposited. Some exceptions are granted in special laws for chattels of particular importance, such as livestock, railroads, airplanes and ships. These are treated as if they were land; mortgages thus are made public in a register especially instituted for these chattels. In addition, not only chattels but also debts can be pledged (Art. 899 *et seq.* CC). The agreement to create the pledge must be in writing if the debt is not fixed in a negotiable security.

The publicity rule is an actual obstacle to economic development as evidenced by the tendencies to circumvention with which the law has to deal. This has already been mentioned in the context of reservation of ownership (above, XI).

The objects which come under the control of the creditor in fulfilling any duties can serve him as a lien for any claims arising for those activities ('right to retention', Art. 895 *et seq.* CC). Unless the parties have the status of a merchant (cf. Ch. 10 on Commercial Law) a connection between the claim and the business which brought the object to the creditor is required. This is the case, for example, when a transportation firm retains the goods transported for payment of its fee or for refund of customs duties. The nexus is not met – to take up our previous example – for a bank credit with respect to securities of the same client administered by the bank, since two different relationships are involved, one a storage and the other a credit contract. This is why the banks insist on special mortgage agreements if they want the securities as a lien.

A clause forfeiting an object to the creditor in case of non-payment of a debt is invalid. And excess value of a pledged or retained object has to be paid to the owner when realized (Art. 894 CC).

XV. THE LAND REGISTER (*Grundbuch/Registre foncier*)

The land register has the function to secure and perfect publicity concerning the rights *in rem* on pieces of land. It is administered locally and contains a folio for each parcel. Although access to the register for every interested person is expressly provided for (Art. 970 CC), practice is rather restrictive. This became a political matter when representatives of the Iranian regime were denied access to the records while investigating on the Swiss properties of the ex-Shah.

Apart from the numerous provisions of the Code on this subject (Arts. 942 to 977), there exists a special decree of the Federal Council regulating the activities of the officials of the land register (*Arrêté du Conseil Fédéral concernant le Registre foncier*, of 10 February 1910, as amended). These officials became a qualified staff, examining with growing intensity the matters brought before them. Although they are deemed only to apply a *prima facie* scrutiny, they do deny entry requests due to defaults seen in the basic document (e.g. the contract of sale) or because the entry is in their view otherwise against the law. The case can then be appealed to a governmental agency of second instance in the canton, and in the last resort, to the Federal Tribunal. The registrar's examination also extends to other points. He ensures, for example, that the holder of the pre-emption right is informed in case of a sale, and he aids in the enforcement of a Federal Law against land purchases by foreigners by notifying the proper government branch beforehand.

The land register is based on an exact survey map of the parcels. The respective geodesy, despite its start at the beginning of the century, has up to now only covered somewhat more than half of the country's cultivated land. This means that there remain substantial areas where the land register still does not exist, due to the Swiss inclination to precision. In such regions, we only find substitute and sometimes old-fashioned systems which will not be administered in the same degree of public faith as that attached to the official land register (Art. 973 CC).

Public faith, as a feature of the land register, has the effect of protecting the rights *in rem* acquired in good faith based on a land register entry. Thus, for example, the buyer who drew from the land register that his selling contract partner was the true owner is protected. *Not* protected, however, are other parties like a person's creditors who trusted a register entry wrongly showing this person as the owner of a real estate. And the good faith rule does not mean that wrong entries are fixed forever. The person interested in a correction in order to insert a right *in rem* of his own may initiate court proceedings (Art. 975 CC). This is the case of a seller when the sales contract for which a purchaser was entered is subsequently invalidated.

Thus, the land register can be considered as a tool bringing the publicity principle to its possible summit and therefore as an apotheosis of the very idea underlying Swiss property law. Paradoxically enough, this institution made an evolution which now tends to betray the idea. As an easy and reliable information instrument, the scope of its content has been broadened more and more. An increasing number of rights of a 'personal', not 'real' nature have obtained access to its columns. One may insert into the register a pre-emption right or an option, but also a lease contract and many other types of agreements concerning the whole or parts of the land, and thereby securing them a 'quasi-real' effect against third parties (Art. 959 CC). The same is true for rights in litigation (Art. 960 CC). The Federal Tribunal held that these rights are enforceable in bankruptcy: the *experimentum crucis* for the right *in rem* is thereby successfully passed.

SELECTED BIBLIOGRAPHY

Deschenaux, H., 'Das Grundbuch', in: *Schweizerisches Privatrecht*, Vol. V/3, Basel 1988/1989.

Haab, R., A. Simonius, W. Scherrer and D. Zobi, in: *Zürcher Kommentar*, Vol. IV/1: *Das Eigentum*, Zurich 1977.

Hinderling, H., 'Der Besitz', in: *Schweizerisches Privatrecht*, pp. 403–517.

Homberger, A., in: *Zürcher Kommentar*, Vol. IV/3: *Besitz und Grundbuch*, 2nd edn., Zurich 1988.

Liver, P., 'Das Eigentum', in: *Schweizerisches Privatrecht*, Vol. V/1, Basel 1977, pp. 1–401.

Liver, P., in: *Zürcher Kommentar*, Vol. IV/2a: *Die Dienstbarkeiten 641–654 ZGB, Grundlasten*, 3rd edn., Zurich 1981.

Meier–Hayoz, A., in: *Berner Kommentar*, Vol. IV/1: *Systematischer Teil* and Arts. 641–654 ZGB, 5th edn., Bern 1981.

Piotet, P., 'Dienstbarkeiten und Grundlasten', in: *Schweizerisches Privatrecht*, pp. 519–666.

Rey, H., *Grundriss des Schweizerischen Sachenrechts*, Vol. 1: *Die Grundlagen des Sachenrechts und das Eigentums*, Bern 1991.

Rey, H., *Grundriss des schweizerischen Sachenrechts*, Vol. 1: *Die Grunglagen des Sachenrechts und des Eigentums*, 2nd edn., Bern 2000.

Riemer, H.M., *Grundriss des schweizerischen Sachenrechts*, Vol. 2: *Die beschränkten dinglichen Rechte*, 2nd edn., Bern 2000.

Simonius, P. and T. Sutter, *Schweizerisches Immobiliarsachenrecht*, Vol. 1, Basel 1995; Vol. 2, Basel 1990.

Stark, E.W., in: *Berner Kommentar*, Vol. IV/3: *Der Besitz*, 2nd edn., Bern 1984.

Steinauer, P.-H., *Les droits réels*, Vol. 1, 3rd edn., 1997; Vol. 2, 2nd edn., 1994; Vol. 3, 2nd edn., 1996.

Tuor, P. and B. Schnyder, *Das schweizerische Zivilgesetzbuch*, 11th edn., Zurich 1995, pp. 549–804.

Chapter 8
Law of Contracts

Eugen Bucher

I. GENERAL REMARKS ON THE SWISS LAW OF OBLIGATIONS

A. *Historical Background and Influence Abroad*

The actual text of the Swiss Federal Code of Obligations (CO) relating to contracts and torts was adopted on 30 March 1911, then presented as a supplementary part of the Civil Code, both entered into force as per 1 January 1912. Its text is to a large extent based on its predecessor, the ancient CO as adopted in 1881 and in force since 1 January 1883 (here 'aCO'). This text is worth being mentioned not only because it is in some details preferable to the present version but because its creation preceded that of the German Civil Code (Bürgerliches Gesetzbuch, BGB) by almost two decades and necessarily influenced the latter. The characteristics of the CO recommend it as an example, representing the best of 19th century Civil Law tradition but being less complicated and more straightforward than the German code, which alone by its being focused on the artificial notion of 'Rechtsgeschäft' is not easy to be absorbed by lawyers of non-German background. Therefore the influence demonstrated by the CO is remarkable in the Spanish speaking area and in the Far East. Whilst the Japanese Codification of 1898 in most respects follows the German BGB, the influence of the Swiss CO is clearly predominant in the traditional Chinese Code (actually at least in force in Taiwan, Book II), the Code of the Republic of South Korea (Part III) and the Code of Thailand (Book II). In addition it may be mentioned that in 1926 under Kemal Atatürk Turkey adopted the Swiss Civil Code (CC) including the CO without major modifications.[1]

The contract law of the CO is, as in all areas of the continental Civil Law, based mainly on the tradition of Roman Law. The CO in particular is influenced mostly by the German 'doctrine of the Pandects' of the 19th century. Therefore the BGB is the next of kin to the Swiss CO. The Romanist basis is still of importance for the handling of the CO not only for full understanding of the intentions of the legislator

---

1. See in this context E. Bucher, 'The position of the Civil Law of Turkey in Western Civilisation,' in *Annales de la Faculté de Droit d'Istanbul*, XXXII/49 (2000), 7–23, (<www.eugenbucher.ch> no. 72).

F. Dessemontet and T. Ansay (eds), Introduction to Swiss Law, 107–143.

at the time of its creation, but also as a basis for future modernization and improvement of the CO which in some respects represents Roman Law oversimplified by the 19th century literature: A look into the texts of ancient Rome (the Corpus Iuris of Iustinian) or the Romanist texts of the years 1200 to 1800 can provide considerable inspiration for the solutions to come.

B. Evolutions to be Expected in the Future

In Germany a reform of the BGB was under discussion since 1980 and a somehow hasty and controversial reform took place with effect as per 1 January 2002. The Swiss legislator considers a reform of the law of tort (see Ch. 9) but is not inclined to touch the text of the contract-related dispositions, which are in most respects still perfectly satisfactory but nevertheless would in some aspects deserve an updating. The following aspects should be kept in mind:

- Consumers' protection is a subject as it is popular and promoted by EU-legislation, requested by the Federal Constitution (Art. 97) but neglected or systematically avoided by the legislator. First a step allowing judicial control of General Conditions (*Allgemeine Geschäftsbedingungen*) is needed. Based on the experiences made abroad the undersigned is inclined to prefer a general clause allowing judges in unacceptable cases to disregard the pre-made text of the parties' agreement to a detailed codification, the precision of which would exist more in appearance than in fact.
- In a broader context also the abolition of the rule *periculum est emptoris* (the risk passes from the seller to the buyer with the conclusion of the contract, not with the transfer of the sold object; Art. 185 I CO) may be considered as being part of consumers' protection (see below XIV B and related footnotes). Said rule exists not in its presentation but in the practical effect in the majority of the legal systems influenced by the French Civil Code ('Code Napoleon' of 1804), and the lawyers accustomed to it like the resulting legal complications. In all other systems (and in all of the German speaking areas) this rule was never adopted, and in Switzerland the view of it being outdated prevails more and more.

C. Basic Elements of Contracts

The law of contract is to a large extent the same worldwide. Certainly the rules governing contracts in the English-speaking countries differ considerably from those of the Civil Law countries. Amongst the latter, when there are divergences, they are often more in appearance or theory than in the practical effects of the solutions. The similarities between Swiss and German contract law are extensive (below II). Both German and Swiss legislation have their roots in the Roman Law tradition of the 19th century; in addition, both are influenced by the French Civil Code, the Swiss Code showing this influence more clearly.

The notion of contract in Switzerland is a broad concept embracing situations perhaps elsewhere not considered contracts. Not only is donation not a unilateral declaration of the donor but a bilateral act (contract) between the donor and the donee (Art. 239 CO); the assignment of choices in action presupposes an agreement between the assignor and the assignee (Art. 164), the transfer of movable property requires the mutual intention of the parties to transfer property (and, in addition, the physical transfer of the goods, Art. 714 CC) and the remission of a debt the consent of the debtor (Art. 115). These acts, transferring or annulling a right under the categories of Swiss (or German) law, are qualified a special kind of contract (*Verfügungsgeschäft/acte de disposition*; as far as real property is concerned: *dinglicher Vertrag/contract réel*; see also E below).

The possibility of private individuals to cause legal effects to others ('autonomy of the parties') (*Privatautonomie/autonomie privée*) is restricted to contracts in the sense of bilateral acts; unilateral acts have legal consequences only insofar as a specific legal basis to that effect exists. Examples of unilateral acts are wills ruling the succession of the testator (Art. 467 CC) or termination of a contract by giving notice (but only as far as the law or contractual provisions provide a legal basis). There is nothing like the assumption of obligations by unilateral declaration of the obligated party (though the law relating to negotiable instruments provides examples of obligations created by unilateral acts).

D. Principle of Freedom of Contract

Swiss law upholds to the maximum the principle of freedom of contract as developed in the seventeenth and eighteenth centuries. The main aspects are:

1. Freedom to conclude or not to conclude a contract and freedom of choice of the partner. There is no obligation to enter a contract unless a special legal provision prescribes the formation of a contract (as may be the case for public transportation and other public services or in the context of antitrust law).

2. Freedom to establish the content of the contractual provisions. Either party may at free discretion establish the conditions of the contract. This refers not only to the possibility of the parties determining their mutual obligations but also to the consequences of non-performance (e.g. conditions and effects of breach, etc.). Furthermore, the freedom as granted under Swiss law means that some types of contracts, perhaps excluded or restricted in other systems, are admissible even without explicit legal basis. For example:

   - the agreement terminating a previously concluded contract or altering the terms thereof (Art. 115);
   - the contract creating an obligation for one or both of the parties to conclude a contract in the future *(Vorvertrag/précontrat, promesse de contracter;* Art. 22);
   - the contract for the benefit of a third party (Art. 112);
   - the contract substituting a party to a contract by another party (below X D).

3. Freedom to depart from the types of contract as presented in the special part of the Code of Obligations (below XIV A).

E. *Contracts as Basis for Obligations: No Translative Effect*

Contracts create legal obligations and claims of the parties but do not by themselves
actuate the transfer of rights, if such a transfer is the object of the obligation (this is
true in other systems where contracts for the transfer of goods bear the fulfillment,
i.e. the transfer of property, in the act of their conclusion; see e.g. the French CC).[2]
In Switzerland (as under German law) the contract of sale does not transfer property
(as an 'agreement to sell' does not) but obliges the seller to effect this transfer at a
later stage by another act involving the same parties (which may again be qualified
as a contract; see above I C). The same is true for contracts such as one obliging the
creation of a pledge.

II. SYSTEM OF THE LEGISLATION; COMPARISON WITH FOREIGN LAW

Contract law as described here is contained in the CO,[3] Articles 1–529.[4] These
provisions are divided into two parts: General Part (Arts.1–183) and Special types of
contracts (Arts.184–551). The division into general and special contract rules
reflects the different historical background of the two sets of legal rules:

- the general rules regulating formation and termination of contract, avoidance of
  contract, sanctions in the case of non-performance and transfer of contractual
  rights (see below III–VII, X) are based on the legal theory of the seventeenth
  and eighteenth centuries and the philosophy of the Enlightenment;
- the special rules (referring to the contract of sale, donation, etc. (see XIV
  below) follow the Roman Law tradition and deal with problems specific to the
  legal relationship under particular circumstances. In addition, the dependence
  on Roman Law is shown in Restitution (Arts. 62–67), extralegal quasi-
  contractual obligations and compensation (see below VIII, IX, XI).

The historical basis of Swiss contract law is identical with that of the German Civil
Code (*Bürgerliches Gesetzbuch* of 1896–1900). The Swiss Code of Obligations
dates back to 1883; a reform of the Code at the time of the enactment of the Civil

2. The model of the French Civil Code of 1804 may be compared with the effect of a sale
   transferring title; see CC Arts. 711, 938, 1138 and 1583. The main reason for the adoption
   of this system is to provide a modern vest to the old Roman rule *periculum est emptoris*
   (the risk is with the buyer, who must pay the price even if the object of the contract
   perishes before its delivery); see E. Bucher, 'Die Eigentums-Translativwirkung von
   Schuldverträgen: Das "Woher" und "Wohin" dieses Modells des Code civil' in *Zeitschr. für
   Europ. Privatrecht (ZEuP)* 1998, 615–669 (<www.eugenbucher.ch>, no. 69). This concept
   was adopted by the majority of codifications influenced by the French CC, i.e. those of
   Romanic languages.
3. A trilingual version (English, Spanish and French) of the text of the CO was published by
   Georg Wettstein, Zürich 1928 (Art. 1–551) and 1939 (Art. 552–1182).
4. No consideration can be given to contract law as contained in special legislation (such as
   insurance contracts). For partnerships see Ch. 10, I, D.

Code in 1911 introduced changes of minor importance, many of them inspired by the German Code. According to the identity of the background of German and Swiss legislation and given the fact that the original Code of Obligations influenced the German Code and subsequently the latter the Swiss Code in its present form, contract law in Switzerland and in Germany is to a large extent congruent, if not in its presentation, at least in its practical solutions. The German Code differs from the Swiss Code of Obligations in terms of system and abstraction. For example, it begins with a General Part giving rules not referring to 'contracts in general' but to an abstract notion of legal act (*Rechtsgeschäft/acte juridique*). The Swiss approach is more practical and vivid in its presentation and certainly easier to understand for a lawyer of the English-speaking world than the text of the German Code.

The relative congruency of Swiss and German contract law means practically that a substantial part of German legal literature as well as court decisions are helpful to the understanding of Swiss law, and this to a much larger extent than in any other branch of Swiss law.

III. FORMATION OF CONTRACTS IN GENERAL

A. *Survey of the Positive Prerequisites of Validity*

The elements necessary for the formation of a contract are to a large extent identical with those familiar in the Common Law system; however, certain elements of the Common Law contracts do not exist in Switzerland (letter C).

The main requirement of valid contractual relationship is the consent of the parties, their *consensus ad idem*. The problem of formation of consensus is seen on the Continent in the same way as in the Common Law countries, under the principle of 'offer and acceptance' (below IV).

In order to distinguish from non-binding rules of conduct such as gentlemen's agreements, agreements forming a binding contract require that the parties express – even tacitly – the intention to bind themselves.

Other elements may be mentioned such as the requirement of the capacity of the persons concluding the contract (as a general rule all persons of the age of 18 years or more; Art. 14 CC) and the fact that a contract only exists as from the moment parties have not only agreed on the terms of their contract but mutually expressed the intention to enter into it and to be contractually bound.

B. *Form-requirements*

As a general rule, the formation of a contract does not presuppose formalities of any kind. With a few specific exceptions, contracts may be concluded orally or even without any verbal expression of assent, for instance, by actions implying *viz.* showing the intention to enter into a contract (Art. 1).

This is not only true on the basis of substantive law but also in procedure. Contrary to the tradition of the Statute of Frauds and to the system of the French Civil Code (see Art. 1341 *et seq.*) every contract, regardless of the amount involved, may be proved in court by all means receivable in evidence, especially by witnesses. Cantonal legislation, generally competent to regulate procedure before cantonal courts, is not allowed to require written evidence for the proof of contracts (see Art. 10 Swiss CC).

The main exceptions to this rule of absence of formal requirements are:

- an assignment requires a written document, signed by the assignor and delivered to the assignee (Art. 165 I). This refers to assignment as the act transferring the right (*Verfügungsgeschäft*; see above I E); the contract creating an obligation to assign/transfer is not subject to said form-requirements;
- the contract for the sale of land, contracts to transfer interest in land, and preliminary contracts for the sale of land require a notarial deed (Art. 216);
- an executory contract of donation (or promise of donation) requires a written contract signed by the donor (Arts. 243 I and 13);
- the contract of suretyship (guarantee) is submitted to an elaborate system of formal requirements (Arts. CO 493–494);
- If a formal requirement as established by legislation has not been realized, the contract, at the level of substantive law, is void (i.e. evidence of the oral conclusion of the contract by the party entering obligation could not validate it; see Art.11 II). However in the context of sale of land this rule in its effect is partly excluded: according to court practice a sale contract not indicating the price really paid by the purchaser and mentioning a fictitious figure instead is void, but if executed (price paid, transfer of property entered in the register) either party is 'estopped' by the rule of CC Article 2 ('misuse of a right') to claim restitution.

C. No Requirement of Consideration

The doctrine is of consideration of the Common Law countries (as well as the concept of 'cause' of French law) is not familiar to Swiss contract law. This has the following practical consequences:

- a party may informally enter a purely unilateral contractual obligation. He or she may, without consideration, validly remit debts, extend the time limit for performance or agree to any change of contractual conditions favoring the other party exclusively;
- the absence of consideration does not constitute a ground for special formal requirements corresponding to those existing for deeds;
- unilateral contractual obligations are binding even in the absence of an explicit agreement with respect to the ground of the assumption of said obligation, i.e. letting unanswered the question whether the contractual obligation (to pay) is entered into for consideration (the possibility – somewhat controversial – of an 'abstract' obligation, i.e. one not being explicitly related to the commercial basis of the transaction; someone may be obliged to a contractual payment only because he expressed the intention to enter an obligation to pay, Art. 17);
- offers to enter a contract may be binding (below IV).

On the other hand, some legal consequences which are often attached to the concept of consideration are realized with similar effect but under different presentation:

- The rule of 'privity of contract' ('consideration must move from the promisee') is unquestioned; a party foreign to a contract may not be obliged by it. As a difference, less important as to the practical outcome, but influencing the historical evolution, may be mentioned the development of the possibility of the assignment (below VIII) and third party beneficiary contracts which in Swiss law were never impeded by the 'privity argument' as in the Common Law countries;
- Legality of contract ('consideration must be legal') is an obvious requirement which is under Swiss (and German) law not understood as a positive, but as a negative condition (below D 2).

D. Negative Elements Making a Contract Void

1. Impossibility

Impossibility under Article 20 CO follows the old rule of *impossibilium nulla obligatio*, stating that a contract is void which subsequently appears to be impossible at all times to be executed and was so at the time of the conclusion of the contract.[5] A party entering into an agreement knowing that its performance will not be possible may be liable under the rule *culpa in contrahendo* (below IX D).

2. Illegality

Illegality is another ground for nullity of a contract under Article 20; the same rule applies to contracts with immoral content (against *boni mores*). Cases of application of said rules are comparatively rare (contracts for the sale of illegal drugs or of obscene publications; contracts implying an element of bribery).

In modern practice there is growing importance of contracts disapproved of by law under the aspect that the binding effect is too burdensome for one of the parties involved. Examples are excessive contractual prohibition of competition, agreements in restraint of trade[6] or the contractual exclusion to dissolve a partnership by giving notice.[7]

Traditionally in the above situations such contracts were null; more recently, however, a voidability concept, allowing the party excessively bound to seek relief by way of exception, is gaining ground. The problem is rather one of application of Article 27 of the Civil Code on the protection of the personality (Ch. 4) than of Article 20 CO.

---

5. For the consequences of subsequent impossibility, i.e. impossibility occurring after the conclusion of the contract, see below VI D.
6. In the context of a contract of employment the special provisions of Art. 340 are applicable.
7. BGE 106 II 230.

IV. FORMATION OF CONTRACT (CONSENSUS; OFFER AND ACCEPTANCE)

The constituent element of a contract is the consent of the parties to it. Their agreement may be extensive, including details of the duties of the contracting parties or consequences of hypothetical situations, or it may be limited, i.e. covering only the most basic points and leaving open all secondary questions. Validity of the contract is reached by a consensus covering a minimum only. This minimum is to be defined by the doctrine of the special types of contract (see below XIV).

Beside the rule that contracts are created by mutual assent of the parties the formula exists as a worldwide commonplace that contracts are formed by an offer and its acceptance. Although obviously correct in a restricted meaning, it becomes nonsense if read as: the coming into existence of a valid contract requires a (valid) offer and its (valid) acceptance. If the consent of the parties at a given moment is unquestioned, the validity of a contract as a consequence of the impossibility to recognize or evidence the exchange of offer and/or acceptance can never be doubted. Both with respect to the transactions of minimal importance as e.g. such concluded at newsstands and to voluminous contracts being the result of lengthy negotiations in multimillion dollar deals, the formula of formation by offer and acceptance is meaningless. Both conceptions only apply (and are indispensable) exclusively in the situation where partners enter into a contract by subsequent declarations (mostly agreements between absentees).

An offer is deemed to be a declaration of the intention to be bound under a contract with the content as specified, under condition of acceptance by the addressee. It has to include all the necessary elements of the intended contract, so that the addressee of the offer may only say 'yes' or 'agreed'.

Contrary to the Anglo-American system and in accordance with the other Civil Law countries, under Swiss law an offer, though oral, may be binding. The intention of being bound by the offer – contrary to the French tradition and others – is presumed. If the offeror does not express his intention to reserve his right to revoke the offer (Art. 7 I) it cannot be withdrawn. Nevertheless, some circumstances may show that a party does not intend to be bound. The sending out of price-lists, for example, is deemed to be not an offer but an invitation to make one (Art. 7 III).

The duration of the binding effect may be fixed by the offeror at his free discretion. If no time limit has been fixed, an offer is open for a reasonable period of time, allowing the transmission of the acceptance under normal circumstances after a short time of reflection. An offer made *viva voce* to a present partner or by phone has no binding effect if the offeror does not expressly declare his or her intention to be bound for a certain period.

The acceptance must be entirely consistent with the offer; a modification of conditions of the original offer is not an acceptance but is deemed to constitute a counter-offer.

Under certain circumstances explicit acceptance is not required; in such cases the addressee of the offer is bound to the contract (Art. 6) if he does not expressly reject the offer. This applies to contracts which are exclusively beneficial to like donations to the donee or assignments to the assignee. Existing commercial relationship between the parties may also create a presumption of acceptance therefore requiring an explicit rejection if the party receiving the offer is not prepared to accept it.

Under the provisions of Articles 8 and 9 an offer to the public in general is possible (*Preisausschreiben und Auslobung/promesse publique – Public promise/ Reward*). The obligation of the offering person is not created by an explicit acceptance of the other party but by the performance required by the promise declared to the persons possibly interested.

V. Conclusion of Contracts by Representatives

The rules governing the conclusion of a contract by other than the parties to it, but by an intermediary acting for one of them (agency, representation) follow one of two concepts, the first being predominant in non-commercial circumstances (below A, the other ruling in commerce (below B) and being valid for legal entities as corporations and for partnerships (dealt with below, Ch. 10). The two models have different sources and background: Whilst the non-commercial representation was developed by the doctrine as taught at the Universities, the other model is a creation (previous to the other) of businessmen.

A. Non-commercial Representation (Arts. 32–40 CO)

Swiss civil law fully admits the possibility of concluding contracts by an agent. Notwithstanding a Roman Law tradition reluctant to admit representation, under the influence of ideas of the Enlightenment the scholars increasingly admitted this institution, and all modern codifications accept it. A contract concluded by a person in the name of another is valid, if the latter has authorized the acting person to do so. A subsequent ratification of the conclusion of the contract equals a preliminary authorization.

In order to contrast it with the other model it must be emphasized that an only apparent and not real authorization is of no effect. The contract is not valid even if the other party had reasons to believe that the acting third person was duly authorized. In noncommercial transactions an 'agency by appearance' can only be admitted under special circumstances, i.e. if the represented person himself has created said appearance or tolerated others creating it.

In the absence of a preliminary authorization or subsequent ratification the contract is void and the person wrongly alleging to be authorized is liable in damages to the other contracting party (Art. 39). The amount of damages is generally restricted to the 'negative interest', i.e. the amount of useless costs caused by negotiating and entering the void contract, but not comprising 'positive interest', i.e. missed profits to be expected from the non existing contract. A claim in the amount of 'positive interest' may exceptionally be granted in case of fault of the non-authorized representative.

The power of representation given to the agent may be revoked at any moment, and an obligation not to retract authorization would not be valid (Art. 34). The same applies in principle in the commercial context. But third parties not duly informed of the revocation are, as long as in good faith, not concerned by the revocation.

B. Commercial Representation (OR 458–465, and Special Provisions)

The model of representation in commerce has its origin in the late middle ages in northern Italy, where the institution of *procura* was created: the *alter ego* of the principal in another town being authorized to conclude all contracts entering into the range of businesses of the principal. This historical background shows clearly the justification of the representing effect. It is not (as in the voluntaristic model, see A above) the intention of the principal to conclude a contract of a given nature, but his being prepared to be bound by the contracts of whatever content concluded by his *procurator*.

The traditional model of Procura (*fondé de procuration*/agent with power of procuration) is laid down in Articles 458–461. The range of allowed representation is defined by the legal text and is not open to modifications. All contracts within that area are valid whilst the approval by the principal of the content of the contracts as concluded is irrelevant. The only restrictions allowed are the prerequisite of the consent of one or even more other persons (i.e. their concurring signature) and a geographical limitation to local branches of the business (Art. 460).

As a general rule the Procura is established by inscription in the register of commerce. But contrary to the non-commercial rules (above lit. A) a Procura may come into existence not only without inscription in the register, but also without an explicit expression by the principal to confer such power, based on the sole fact that the principal admits the coming into existence of the appearance to authorize the person acting as an agent and to have the intention to institute him as a '*fondé de pouvoir*'.

As in the non-commercial context the power of representation given to the agent may be revoked at any moment. If the power of procuration has been entered into the register, its cancellation must equally be entered. Was no inscription performed, it nevertheless is possible to enter the cancellation of the power in order to inform all persons having knowledge of the procuration (Art. 461).

For a power of representation on a more modest level and a restriction to only limited sectors of the business the rules for 'other commercial powers' of Articles 462 and 463 apply. Entering into the commercial register of this form or representation is not foreseen.

Similar rules as established for the *procurator* apply to the power to represent a partnership (Art. 563), corporations and other legal persons (see with respect to the company limited by shares Art. 718 lit.a, for the co-operative society Art. 899, below Ch. 10).

VI. INTERPRETATION; VITIATING ELEMENTS IN THE CONSENSUS

A. Interpretation in General

The interpretation of the declaration of a party follows the 'principle of confidence' (*Vertrauensprinzip*/*principe de la confiance*), that is, the declaration is neither understood in the sense of what the declaring party may have had in mind nor in accordance with the literal meaning of the wording, but in the meaning the addressee could in good faith attribute to it. This is in some way an 'objective' approach to the problem. On the other hand, the addressee is deemed to be obliged to give all possible attention to the 'subjective element', i.e. to consider all aspects allowing the understanding of the declared intent. Under these two aspects interpretation is less strict than under the English and American tradition, i.e. focused on the 'objective' meaning of the existing texts.

B. *'Dissensus' Distinguished from 'Error'*

In case of divergence of the real intention of one party from the understanding of its declaration by the other, two situations must be distinguished. 'Dissensus' is the absence of contractual consent with the consequence that no contract at all came into existence even if the parties believed to have concluded it. Dissensus exists when two parties agree to the same term but understand it in a different way so that both interpretations are equally admissible in the particular circumstances. For example, where a Canadian and a US citizen conclude a bargain based on a dollar price there is dissensus (no contract), if in the particular situation each party is equally entitled to understand 'dollar' as his own national currency. If one understanding prevails, the contract exists but the other party may claim relief resulting from 'error' (see C below).

In case of *dissensus* the contract is non-existing, i.e. void *ab initio*.

C. *Error (Mistake; Arts. 23–27)*

'Error' *(Irrtum/erreur)* describes the situation where a party is held, based on the 'principle of confidence', to the apparent meaning of a declaration even if another meaning was intended. For instance, said Canadian, who understood the agreed price to be in Canadian dollars, is not entitled to his interpretation if under the given circumstances an objective interpretation indicates that US dollars were intended. Consequence of error is the voidability of the contract, i.e. the party succumbing to it has the possibility to bring the contract to an end by making a private declaration to that effect to the other party within one year from the date of discovery of the error (Art. 31).

In its original meaning error was restricted to the situation of the diverging intention of a party from their declaration. It had to refer to one of the three aspects mentioned in Article 24, paragraphs 1–3 (the traditional *error in negotio, error in persona* and *error in quantitate/qualitate*, which survive also in the French CC, Arts. 1109–1110 as well as in the German BGB §119). Contrary to said tradition the voidability of a contract based on error has in the Swiss Code a broader application. It introduces the principle of 'error as to the basis of the contract' *(Grundlagenirrtum/erreur sur la base nécessaire du contract)*, under which a contract is voidable if a party concluding the contract relies upon elements which later prove to be non-existent (Art. 24 no. 4). In Switzerland as elsewhere, the motives of the parties concluding a contract are generally irrelevant. But under actual

Swiss law[8] they start being relevant if the motives under consideration have such weight, that they become a precondition of the conclusion of the contract for one party: The other party, knowing that the contract would not be concluded with said precondition missing, cannot conclude the contract without the preparedness to accept the existence of said element as an implied condition of the contract. This is at least true if under general aspects the element under consideration is generally qualified as relevant and decisive, and therefore the non-acceptance of the thereto related precondition of the contract is not compatible with good faith. This concept of 'error as to the basis' actually has more importance than Article 24 nos. 1–3 setting out the traditional topics of error.[9] The 'error as to the basis' argument covers also parts of the 'frustration-cases' of the Common Law (see G below).

The party terminating a contract on the legal ground of *error* is liable for damages if their erroneous understanding was due to their own negligence in examining and understanding the given situation; the compensation has to cover the 'negative interest' (*negatives Interesse/intérêt négatif*); see VII D below), i.e. to put the other party economically in the situation they would be not having concluded the subsequently annulled contract. In exceptional cases the damages may comprise further elements ('positive interest', *lucrum cessans*; Art. 26).

D. Fraud, Duress (Arts. 28–31)

Whilst the contractual defects of *error* as explained above are the result of the given circumstances and not intentionally caused by the parties, *fraud* and *duress* are the result of machinations of one of them. *Fraud* consists in causing a mistake by intentionally misinforming the partner with respect to essential elements of the contract (Art. 28), *duress* means constraining a person to conclude a contract, be it by coercion, threats or by physical force (Arts. 29 and 30). Under such circumstances the affected party may terminate the contract by private declaration to the opposed partner. Such declaration must be given in a one year's term upon the recognition of the mistake *viz.* the termination of the coercive situation. The aggrieved party may also choose to maintain the contract by ratification, in that event still preserving claims for damages (Art. 31).

---

8. '*Grundlagenirrtum*' was introduced into the text in the reform of 1911 (Art. 24 para. 4) on the basis of doctrine and some precedents. The German BGB still does not know this type of error.
9. BGE 113 II 27 states that the precondition of *Grundlagenirrtum* is a misconception which is, known or unknown to the parties, under 'objective criteria' a precondition of the contract (with reference to BGE 109 II 324). Further examples of jurisprudence: BGE 55 II 184; 79 II 161; 97 II 45; 98 II 18/87 II 137 (sale of land for construction; construction not possible for legal or other reasons related to the land); 52 II 153/82 II 424; 114 II 131 (sale of an antique carpet not being antique, of a van Gogh painting not being painted by this artist, and of a Picasso drawing not drawn by him). Negative precedents also exist not allowing avoidance: BGE 95 II 409 (sale of land for construction with impossibility to construct; under the given circumstances the buyer was not allowed to take the possibility to construct for granted); 53 II 127; 41 II 575.

E. *Protection of Consumers*

Articles 6a and 40a to f CO, enacted in 1991 allow a consumer to terminate a contract concluded under unusual conditions such as at the consumer's home or at the occasion of an advertising ride, etc. Repudiation can be made by written declaration within a week after the conclusion of the contract.

Special legislation in favor of consumers as existing in the European Union and elsewhere does not yet exist, nor is given legislation authorizing the courts to control General Conditions introduced to mass-market contracts.

F. *Subsequent Impossibility of Performance*

In cases where performance is possible at the time of the conclusion of contract but subsequently becomes impossible without fault on either side, the obligation to perform is extinguished.[10] The performance promised in exchange does not become due or must, if executed, be restituted. If the impossibility is not due to 'circumstances for which the debtor is not responsible' (Art. 119 I), i.e. if the debtor is not in the position to prove 'that there is no fault on his part' (Art. 97 I), he is liable under the general rule of liability for non-performance.

G. *Frustration*

The concept of frustration is not known on the Continent. Arising in England in the late 19th century it seems not completely clear and coherent to Civil lawyers. 'Frustration' covers 'impossibility' of the Swiss and German tradition (see F above), but is a larger concept, comprising in addition the relief from contractual obligations under the doctrine of 'error as to the basis of the contract' (see C above). The so-called 'Coronation cases' (renting of a room with a view of the coronation procession of King Edward VII, which did not take place on the date originally scheduled) are in English doctrine generally understood to come under the frustration rule,[11] but would, under Swiss law, be qualified as problems of 'error' (though probably with a result similar to that in the English Coronation decisions).

VII. BREACH OF CONTRACT

A. *Specific Performance*

Unlike the Common Law tradition Swiss law as a general rule enables the creditor to claim specific performance of the contract. Said principle has some limited relevance in contracts for the transfer of property and contracts preventing a party from doing something (e.g. competing in a specified field). However, specific

10. Same rule in England since *Taylor v. Caldwell* (1863).
11. *Krell v. Henry*, [1903] 2 K.B.740.

performance is not available in contracts positively obliging a party to do something such as to render a service or the like.

The Roman law was intended to convert an obligation to do or to deliver something into damages when not carried out, a solution which is to some extent still preserved in the French Civil Code.[12] The Swiss Code of 1881 followed the French example, exchanging specific performance of obligations to do (or refrain from doing) something; but the Reform of 1911 abolished it and introduced, under the influence of German law (and to the regret of this writer), said possibility of specific performance. This rule is applicable even to the non-execution of pre-contracts (i.e. contracts obliging to conclude a specified contract in the future). The prevailing view accepts an action based on the pre-contract for the conclusion of the main contract. The latter is deemed to be concluded at the moment of a court decision to that effect.

B. Damages as General Remedy for Breach

The general rule is that a party to a contract not performing it correctly must pay damages compensating the failure of performance or its imperfections.

The quantum of damages equals the difference between the actual financial situation of the aggrieved party and the hypothetical situation in which he or she would have been in case of a proper performance. This so-called 'positive interest' comprises also *lucrum cessans*, that is, the profits lost as a consequence of the incorrectness of performance (see also D below). The burden of proof of the amount of the damages lies with the injured party.

The liability of the parties to a contract is in the diction of the Code a liability under the condition of fault of the party not performing correctly (Art. 97 CO). This principle is complemented and qualified by a presumption of fault: the burden of proof is on the non-performing party causing damage who may show that their non-performance, or delayed or defective performance, was caused by elements independent of their responsibility. In effect, exoneration as a consequence of evidence for absence of fault of the non-performing debtor is rare. Therefore in the outcome the liability under Swiss (and German) law is not far away from the strict liability of legal systems allowing the excuse of 'force majeure.'

C. Consequences of Delay (Arts. 102–106 CO)

'Delay' in performance is understood in a technical meaning, i.e. as default (*Verzug/demeure*), presupposing a delay either under the precise stipulation of a certain date of performance in the contract or a subsequent notice by a creditor demanding performance (Art. 102 CO).

---

12. French CC Art. 1142 CC: 'Toute obligation de faire ou de ne pas faire se résout en dommages et intérêts, en cas d'inexécution de la part du débiteur.' This rule applies as far as personal obligations are concerned but not to obligations to transfer a thing or property: property is transferred by contract of sale (see I E above), and therefore the claim of the purchaser for the delivery of the object sold is an action of the owner *in rem*.

These requirements of default are the basis of damages for delay in performance described under section B above. In addition, default has the consequence of transferring the risk to the belated party (*periculum in mora*). Once in default, he is liable for further damages even if the subsequent delay or impossibility of performance is not caused by his fault. If the default concerns a payment of money the debtor has to pay interest on arrears to the amount of 5 per cent per annum if there is not a higher interest rate stipulated in the contract. In commercial transactions bank rates may be applied if they are higher (Art. 104 CO).

The above consequences of default are independent of a fault of the non-performing party; only the consequences of damages presuppose fault. It may be noted that the contrary is true under the German Civil Code, where not only damages are the consequence of fault, but the notion of default (*Verzug*) itself depends on fault. Interest on arrears is due under Swiss law without respect to fault (BGB § 286 old and new version). The general rule of damages as exposed under section B above applies if the creditor not receiving payment in due course has suffered injury in excess of the legal or contractual rate. He may recover the amount of his loss if the debtor is not in the position to exonerate.

D. *Discharge by Breach (Arts. 107–109 CO)*

Upon the failure of a party to perform, the other party may be released from the contractual obligations and has a claim for damages. This solution, in the practical outcome, is granted by Swiss law, but it must be noted that the 'discharge by breach' does not operate automatically as it may do in the Common Law area and that full damages are not granted under all circumstances. Discharge from the contract as a consequence of non-performance is subject to the following two requirements:

The party not receiving performance in due course (1) generally has to grant a grace-period, i.e. an additional time limit for execution and (2) must upon failure of performance during the grace-period express the intention not to accept the delayed performance (renunciation, or rescission of the contract).

These two prerequisites (traditional under Swiss law since 1883, followed by the German BGB § 326 and to some extent actually adopted by the United Nations Convention on Contracts for the International Sales of Goods (1980) (CISG), see Arts. 47, 49 I b) are governed by the following rules:

(1) The additional period conceded by the creditor may be short but must be long enough that a party who has already made appropriate preparations for his performance may have an additional chance to perform. The creditor is only exempted from allowing an extension of time for execution if one of the three situations indicated by Art. 108 CO is fulfilled:[13]

    (a) the attitude of the obligor has shown that conceding an additional time is useless (e.g. the obligor has made no preparations and additional time

---

13. See also Art. 190 CO making the idea of Art. 108 CO applicable to all sales between professional dealers.

would not allow performance, or the obligor has expressed his intention not to perform, he has repudiated the contract, etc.);

(b) the performance, as a consequence of the delay, has become useless to the obligee;

(c) the contract is unambiguously stating that performance has to be effected on or before a certain time and shall subsequently be excluded.

(2) The expiration of the period of time as described under no.1, including the situation that no additional time must be conceded, does not automatically operate as a discharge of duties. Discharge depends on a renunciation by the obligee. Upon expiration of the time limit the obligee may still insist on contractual performance; if he prefers the exclusion of the belated performance he has to give notice of his decision to rescind immediately. The obligee may declare renunciation at the moment of fixing a time limit (see A) but is (contrary to the German Civil Code § 326) not obliged to do so. He may make his declaration upon expiration of the time conceded (but then must act without delay; Art 107 II CO).

Renunciation may be expressed in two ways, with different consequences as to the amount of damages. The traditional concept of the effect of renunciation is that of subsequent dissolution of the contract, i.e. rescission in the technical sense (*Rücktritt/se départir du contrat*, i.e. 'withdrawal from the contract'). This possibility (originally inspired by the *condition résolutoire* of the French CC), puts an end to the execution of the contract, both parties becoming free. The party who failed to perform must pay damages, but only on the basis of 'negative interest' (*negatives interesse/intérêt négatif*). The obligee must be put in the situation he would be in, had he never entered the contract. This quantum is generally smaller than that of 'positive interest', which is based on the aim to grant to the obligee the hypothetical benefits of correct performance of the contract. If the obligee wishes to reserve his right to 'positive interest' (including *lucrum cessans*, i.e. indemnification for lost profits, which only in exceptional cases is comprised by 'negative interest', see B above), he has to choose another way and insist on the validity of the contract while renouncing to the performance of the obligation as stipulated in the contract. Thus, the right to and the duty of contractual performance is transformed into contractual damages, replacing the original contractual duties. Both parties are held to perform the contract, but the party not having performed his or her part must pay damages in place of the performance originally due. The system of twofold possibility for renunciation of the obligee is more complicated than necessary and may be explained only by the historical evolution of legislation in the context of 'discharge by breach'. In practice, there is a clear tendency to grant full compensation (*positives Interesse*) irrespective the obligee's declarations.

A distinction must be drawn between 'main duties' and 'ancillary duties' of the party performing incorrectly. Discharge by breach as shown above operates only if a 'main duty' is not correctly performed (e.g. in the case the object sold is not delivered) but not if the performance of 'ancillary duties' fails (the object sold is not properly packed, user's instructions due under the contract are not given, etc.).

VIII. Restitution (CO Arts. 62–67)

A. General Remarks

The Swiss Code follows, as all other codifications of the continental legal tradition do, the example of Roman Law by introducing its institution of *condictio*. In its historical origin and until modern times *condictio* does not represent a clear and well defined concept, but comprises a series of types of different character, mostly covered by the general notion of obligations of quasi-contractual origin (which is shown in the French CC, Arts.1371–1381). A tendency to a more systematic approach of the phenomenon goes back to the antiquity and may be seen in the Corpus Iuris (533–535) of Justinian.

The core of *condictio* is to grant the restitution of assets which have been transferred from one person to another, because the justification of said transfer did not – contrary to the understanding of the parties at the time of the transfer – exist or disappeared after the event.

The term defining the situation in modern Codifications is 'unjustifiable enrichment' of the obligor of condiction (*ungerechtfertigte Bereicherung/enrichissement illégitime*); see the heading before CO Articles 62–67. The basis of the claim for restitution is the fact that no cause exists for the transfer of title of a thing from the obligee to the obligor or of money paid to the latter.

Three groups of cases allowing restitution may be distinguished under the aspect of the reason of the transfer of value which must be reversed:

- the reason may be an act of the obligee who transferred title or made payment erroneously assuming the existence of a good cause (restitution of a benefit granted by act of the claimant; 'Leistungskondiktion'; see B below)
- the transfer may be caused by an unjustified act of the obligor of the restitution (restitution of things acquired by unjustified acting of the obligor; 'Eingriffskondiktion', see C below);
- the transfer may be caused by chance, i.e. without interference of one of the parties ('Zufallskondiktion', see D below)

B. Restitution of a Benefit Granted by the Party Claiming Restitution

This type of restitution is by far the most common and important of all. It comprises the *condictio indebiti* of the Roman Law,[14] which became under some authors of the enlightenment and especially in the French Civil Code (as well as in the innumerable codifications following it) the restitution pure and simple, in general (the concept of *répétition de l'indu*, see CC Arts. 1376–1381) and which may explain the core of the situation justifying the claim for restitution. The party granting a payment of money or transfer of title of an object does so under the belief that he has an obligation to do so (because he is under a contractual duty, he has a duty as the heir

---

14. See Digests 12, 6 and Codex 4,5, both *de condictione indebiti*.

of a deceased person etc.) while, as he learns only later, this duty does not exist, may the contract be void or avoided *ex post,* the performance previously granted by another person, the deceased not having been obliged etc. In case of a contract being void or becoming subsequently avoided both partners to it may be at the same time entitled to restitution of what they granted under the non-existing contract.

The condition of the existence of a claim of restitution is not only the absence of a legal duty to the granting of the object to restitute, but equally the error of the claiming party at the time of the performance as to the legal duty to grant said performance, the burden of proof for both elements (absence of a duty and the erroneous belief in the existence of it) is with the person claiming restitution.

The concept of *condictio indebiti* or *répétition de l'indu* can be generalized in the sense that the error of the party giving performance does create a claim for restitution. The error must relate to the reason for giving the performance, i.e. to an element being the precondition of granting the transfer of value, but it must not necessarily refer to the existence of a legal duty to provide performance. Certainly, the error may refer to a legal aspect. The debtor of a claim assigned by the creditor to a third person paying erroneously to the original obligee and thus must not pay a second time to the latter has a claim for restitution against the payee to whom he was not a debtor. But the misconception may refer to the erroneous assumption to receive any value in exchange. Even the assumption of the coming into existence of a marriage could justify the claim for restitution of a gift if the marriage does not happen.[15]

The transfer of value (payment of money to a bank-account etc.) with the intention to grant a benefit to a third person does exclude the claim for restitution even if a valid contract of donation between the person transferring and the person receiving the value did not come into existence.[16]

The requirement to provide evidence of an error at the time of the performance is vital under general aspects of law: without it every person receiving a payment or receiving a thing would incur the risk of a claim for restitution, could she or he not be in the position to provide evidence for the existence of a thereto related duty of the other party.

C. Restitution of Unjustly Appropriated Value

In this context are considered cases of appropriation of value caused without legal justification. For example, if a person has sold foreign property in good faith, he is

---

15. BGE 82 II 433.
16. The Federal Tribunal in a series of decisions misinterpreted the legal situation in the context of donations: BGE 105 (1979) II 105; 69 (1943) II 309; 52 (1926) II 369 take the position, that the nullity of a donation for formal reasons is a ground for a claim of restitution not withstanding the fact that in said cases the intention of the donor to grant a benefit was in no way doubtful: the absence of a formally valid contract of donation does in no way constitute an error requested for claim for restitution; the absence of the preconditions of restitution constitute good title to keep what was received even without valid donation. See also E. Bucher, in: *ZSR* 1983 II, 330, 332.

not liable in tort but has to restitute the proceeds under the rules of *condictio*. The same may apply in case of infringement of foreign patent rights etc.

D. *Restitution of Value Transferred by Chance*

The transfer asking for restitution may be the consequence of acts of third parties or happen by chance: cash is erroneously mixed with the money of another person and becomes by that his or her property. Value is appropriated by insane persons not liable in tort, or cattle is grazing on foreign pasture.

IX. EXTRA-CONTRACTUAL AND QUASI-CONTRACTUAL OBLIGATIONS

A. *General Remarks*

The (prevalent German) Romanist doctrine of the 19th century had its merits, but transmitted the legal tradition in many respects in an oversimplified presentation. The codifications of the continental legal tradition qualify the obligations according to their sources. Following the concepts of the 19th century the position of the Codes is the dualism of obligations resulting either from a contract or from a tort. The CO (in this respect identical with the German BGB) adopts the distinction of *contractus* and *delicta* (Arts. 1–40; Arts. 41–61 CO), adding only *restitution* as a further possible cause (Arts. 62–67 CO) and, by doing so, excluding all further types of obligations.

The more complex way of looking at the possible grounds of obligations of the jurists from the antique Rome up to those of the 18th century who knew intermediate figures (*obligations quasi ex contractu* and *quasi ex delicto* or also such as *obligations ex variarum causarum figuris*) were regrettably not considered by the codifications.[17] In the intention to overcome the oversimplified system of the codes the doctrine, followed by court-practice, developed other types of obligation-creating situations, so in Switzerland and to some extent in Germany, Austria and other countries. As these concepts have under practical aspects considerable impact and deserve to be outlined in their basic elements:

- *faktische Vertragsverhältnisse* (obligations resulting from acts of the obligor; see B below),
- *Vertrauenshaftung* (*responsabilité fondée sur la confiance*; obligation from inspired confidence; see C below),
- *culpa in contrahendo* (in short *c.i.c.*; fault in concluding a contract; see D below).

17. Nevertheless we mention that two institutions of modern codifications (restitution, CO Arts. 62–67, above VIII; and *negotiorum gestio*, CO Arts. 419–424, below XII) follow the Roman Law tradition in which they were qualified as *obligationes quasi ex contractu* (obligations resulting from quasi-contractual relations).

Each of the three concepts covers a group of cases which cannot remain without adequate remedies. The group of *obligations quasi ex contractu* or *ex variarum causarum figures*, well established in the texts of the Corpus Iuris as well as by the literature up to the 19th century covered these cases which actual doctrine tries to re-invent and to handle under new headings.[18]

Said labels are of recent invention, but the principles represented by them have been realized in court practice long before. That does not make the theories under consideration superfluous. They are helpful as means of communication, i.e. to recall them to the legal community, to create a focus of closer consideration in doctrine and to establish a generalized view of the existing law.[19] Switzerland in comparison with other countries is ahead in recognizing the said concepts. Change and progress is easier to achieve in small areas.[20]

B. Obligations Resulting from Facts of the Debtor

As has been shown, the concept is very old. The actually used label 'faktische Vertragsverhältnisse' was created by G. Haupt in 1941.[21]

An illustrative case mentioned in literature goes back to the year 1930. A private pilot is landing (without any prior contact) on an airfield and refuses to pay the usual fee. The airman must pay notwithstanding that no prior contract was concluded nor could the landing be qualified as *delictum* (tort). In this context were mostly considered cases of taking profit of a generally offered facility (public transportation, the procurement of water, electricity, gas etc.), but the principle may possibly apply to important issues of commerce.[22]

The concept was always controversial and is actually out of fashion in Germany, but nevertheless applies without referring to the term.[23] Eventually it is not possible to renounce to said rule without instituting an area of lawlessness. The rule applies only in cases where a party takes profit of goods which are offered under contract,

---

18. In this context is fundamental C.A. Cannata, 'Das faktische vertragsverhältnis oder die ewige Wiederkunft des Gleichen', in: *Studia et Documenta Historiae et Iuris, Rom Pontificia Universitas Lateranensis*, LIII – 1987, 297 *et seq*. See also E. Bucher, 'Rechtsüberlieferung und heutiges Recht', in *ZEuP* 2000, 394–543, at 465 (<www.eugenbucher.ch>, no. 75).

19. One should bear in mind the key distinction between the legal rule as applied in practice and the recourse to the related technical short term thereto (*faktische Vertragsverhältnisse, Vertrauenshaftung*, c.i.c.). In Switzerland the application of the three formulas was subsequent to the application of the legal rule labeled by them.

20. In Germany only the use of the formula *culpa in contrahendo* is well established and broadly used, whilst all three principles are used in practice, often without reference to generalizing principles, but many of them allocated to c.i.c. notwithstanding they fit better in one of the two others: actually reluctance to explicitly accept the formula '*faktische Vertragsverhältnisse*' prevails. Cases best considered as '*Vertrauenshaftung*' are preferably qualified under the heading of '*culpa in contrahendo*'.

21. G. Haupt, *Ueber faktische Vertragsverhältnisse*, Leipzig 1991 (or *Festschrift für Siber*, Vol. 2, Leipzig 1943). Bucher, *ZEuP* 1996, 715–722 (<www.eugenbucher.ch>, no. 65).

22. See Bucher in *ZEuP* (fn. 18 above).

23. See P. Lambrecht, *Die Lehre vom faktischen Vertragsverhältnis*, Tübingen 1994.

and it cannot remain without sanctions the appropriation of a benefit for which correct people grant the contractual counter value.

In Switzerland an early case of 1937 (BGE 63 II 369) applied the rule (without referring to the then still unknown term of *faktische Vertragsverhältnisse*) by obliging an overstaying tenant to pay the contractual rent even the contract is terminated. In another case, BGE 110 (1984) II 249, the purchaser of a car annulling the contract on grounds of absence of formal requirements had to pay a quasi-contractual compensation for the period he used the car. This *landmark case* is generally followed and of considerable practical importance in the context of purchase by installments or hire-purchase-contracts (often somehow misleadingly called '*Leasing-Verträge*') which might be found void or voidable if they are not in conformity with the form-requirements of CO Articles 226a–228.

C. Obligations Resulting from Acts of the Debtor: Vertrauenshaftung; Responsabilité fondée sur la confiance[24] (Obligations Based on Trust)

The term 'Vertrauenshaftung' received general attention in 1971 as a consequence of the publication of Canaris. However, it still misses general acceptance in Germany today. It was the 1st *Zivilabteilung* of the Swiss Federal Court which in the so called 'Swissair-Case' (BGE 120 [1994] III p. 331) had to deal with a classical example for the application of the principle of 'Vertrauenshaftung': The then national airline of Switzerland had allowed or at least tolerated that a depending company establishing luxury tourist-sites used logos of Swissair and made reference to the reputation of this firm as a means of promotion. In its subsequent insolvency Swissair was held liable to the investing shareholders, because under the given circumstances the latter were allowed to believe that the mother-company would grant save investment policy as well as the solvency of the daughter-company.

Since 1994 the 1st *Zivilkammer* had the opportunity in a series of cases to refer to the *Vertrauenshaftung*. In BGE 121 (1995) III p. 350 they granted damages for useless expenditures to a sportsman, the defendant being a sports club competent to select the athletes representing Switzerland in an international competition which had promised to delegate him but failed to do so. Similar considerations where applied in a case of banking law (responsibility of the bank in the context of mistakes in the transfer of money; BGE 121 [1995] p. 310). In other cases the principle under consideration may provide arguments for adequate limitation of responsibility. With reference to the liability of a member of a law firm (constituted as a '*partnership firm*', *Kollektivgesellschaft*, under CO Arts. 552–593) it was held that a lawyer, although as a general rule engaging the liability of all member of the firm by his professional activity shall not do so in cases where his incorrect declarations were, to the knowledge of the client, purely personal and had no relation to the firm and his partners (BGE 124 [1998] III p. 364. See also BGE 124 III p. 297 following the same approach). The importance of this newly discovered principle is clearly demonstrated by the multiplicity of comparable cases in a short period of time.

---

24. Bucher in *recht* 2001, 65–81 (<www.eugenbucher.ch>, no. 76).

The range of possible application of 'Vertrauenshaftung' is considerable. It covers e.g. the case of misleading testimonial for employees. In BGE 101 (1975) p. 69 *et seq.* an employer was held liable for part of the damages caused to the new employer, because he had delivered to a bookkeeper dismissed for fraud an excellent testimonial attesting trustworthiness (the legal basis was in the then viewed *tort liability* which in fact is hardly compatible with the traditional understanding of that cause of obligations under CO Art. 41 *et seq.*). Even more important is the rule to handle *letters of intent, memoranda of understanding, gentlemen's agreements* as well as declarations providing more or less explicit guaranty of an enterprise for another legal entity (often called 'Patronatserklärungen' etc.). These cases have in common that they are neither considered in legislation nor even accessible to general rules. The content and the consequences are purely depending on the intention of the parties to these agreements *viz.* the understanding in good faith of the addressee of unilateral declarations. Essential is the interpretation of the relevant texts and the given circumstances which must be examined under the aspect of the created appearances and the therefrom resulting justified expectations.

A series of claims by the courts granted either on tort liability or on the c.i.c.-argument are more correctly qualified as resulting from the trust created by the obligor. BGE 101 II 69 held liable a patron for losses incurred by a subsequent employer who relied on the certificate issued by the former attesting perfect trustworthiness, notwithstanding that the person was dismissed on the grounds of embezzlement. The same view of creation of confidence may be applied in dealing with *letters of intent* or *memoranda of understanding* (likewise 'Patronatserklärungen' etc.) which play a considerable role in modern business.

D. Obligations Resulting from 'Culpa in Contrahendo'[25]

1. Origin and Explicit Legal Provisions

The concept of *culpa in contrahendo* (hereinafter 'c.i.c.') was created by *Rudolf* v. *Jehring*.[26] This expression suggests that a party is liable to contractual negotiations if by his *culpa* (fault, wrong) no valid contract comes into existence. The main example is voidable contract for mistake. The erring party should, in case of negligence, grant compensation to the other party for his losses resulting from the reliance on a valid contract. The concept was not new[27] but found much attention, arising controversies but finding finally widespread acceptance in Germany as in other countries even outside the German speaking area. The Swiss Code of Obligations of 1881/83 was the first codification realizing some of Jhering's concepts and including them in the actual Code:

- Article 26 CO establishes the liability of the party avoiding a contract for his mistake resulting from negligence;

---

25. Bucher, CO § 17
26. Jhering, 'C.i.c. oder Schadenersatz bei nichtigen oder nicht zur Perfection gelangten Verträgen', in *Jhering's Jahrbuch* 4 (1861), pp. 1–112.
27. Pothier in his Traité des obligations (1761–67) No. 19 refers to the problem; the *Allgemeine Preussische Landrecht* (1794) I 5 §§ 284 establishes such rules.

- Article 31 III CO establishes liability of the party having reached the contract by fraud or duress (be the contract avoided of ratified);
- Article 39 CO creates the liability of a representative concluding a contract without authority, and Article 36 II the liability of a partner revoking a given authority without taking back the proxy subsequently misused.[28]

In these cases the lawyer will refer to the legal provisions and not to the formula of c.i.c. which caused the coming into existence of the former.

The Swiss code fails to order the liability of the party concluding a contract knowing the impossibility of performance, in which case reference to the c.i.c.-principle is still indicated (both the German BGB § 307 and the Italian CC art. 1338 provide an explicit rule).[29]

2. Extended Application

The c.i.c.-concept had an impact on subsequent legislation but did not show its main importance in the field of the examples promoted by Jhering, but served as a nucleus for further development of the doctrine which did not hesitate to attach new (and justified) ideas to the term of c.i.c. German courts were first reluctant, but eventually adopted the theory in 1911 in the subsequently most influential 'Linoleumteppich-Decision'.[30] It is obvious, that even this leading case departs from the original idea: The damage was not caused to the prospective buyer by a defective contract but only at the occasion of negotiations in view of a possible conclusion of a contract.

A series of Swiss court decisions (e.g. BGE 90 II 453, BGE 92 II 334 E.4 and BGE 105 II 77) grant compensation for the fact that contracts were concluded with certain content and not with another, a result hardly compatible with the c.i.c.-concept. On the other hand, well established and justified is the rule, that negotiating contracts without intention to conclude such contract may cause a liability for losses (useless travel costs, missed other opportunities to contract) of the partner to the negotiations (e.g. BGE 77 II 137; 80 II 375). Equally, preliminary agreements to conclude a contract with form-requirements (i.e. the sale of immovables, requiring a notarial instrument; Art. 216; below XIV B 1) may cause, if not executed, a liability (e.g. BGE 39 II 227; 41 II 101 E.2; 49 II 67 E.4; 51 II 54 *et seq.*). The aforementioned decisions are partly not based on the c.i.c. argument but on tort (Art. 41 *et seq.* CO).

---

28. To illustrate the influence of the ideas of Jhering may be mentioned in addition the German BGB, § 122 (equivalent to CO Art. 26) and § 179 (corresponding to CO Art. 31 III but adding a claim for performance).
29. The Italian CC, Art. 1338 establishes the interesting rule inspired by c.i.c. (but not mentioned by Jhering), that a party to a contract is liable for damages if he fails to inform his partner of the contract being not being valid for grounds unknown to the latter.
30. *Entscheidungen des Reichsgerichts in Zivilsachen RGZ* 38 p. 239 *et seq.* A client interested to buy linoleum in a shop was injured by a roll of such carpets falling by negligence of an employee. The shop owner was held liable for damages.

X. ASSIGNMENT AND OTHER TRANSFERS

A. Preliminary Remarks

As a general rule the effects of a contract under Swiss law are less strictly limited to its parties than in Anglo-American law. Third party beneficiary contracts and assignment of contractual rights are allowed almost without restrictions, and contractual rights and obligations are more widely transferred to the heirs of the deceased contracting party. This difference may be explained by different historical evolution. The Common Law system is determined by the idea of contract as a legal relationship binding on the parties only. Contrary to this approach, continental legal thinking has, for centuries, in some way been dominated by the concept of the rights or claims of the persons involved (*subjektives Recht/droit subjectif*). This concept does not oppose to solutions involving a transfer of a legal position to another person or to make a third party the beneficiary of a contract. The clear distinction between benefits conferred by contract upon a third party and liabilities imposed by it upon third parties (excluded under all systems) allows without restriction the admission of the former.

B. Assignment of Choses in Action *(Arts. 164–175)* (Abtretung von Forderungen/Cession des creances)

1. Object of Assignment

Claims of whatever nature and origin may be transferred to a third party by assignment. In case of assignment of contractual rights, not the position as a party to the contract is transferred, but only the specific claim emerging from it. The seller may transfer by assignment his claim for the price to his banker, but he cannot transfer to him the position as seller and party to the contract. The buyer, though obliged to pay the banker, has rights from the sale (warranty, etc.) against the seller exclusively.

Legal provisions excluding assignment of specific claims exist but are not numerous (Arts. 529 I, 325 II, 306 II, 292, 262/3 CO, etc.). Furthermore the assignment of future claims of salary is not possible (Art. 325 II CO, in force since 1 July 1991). However, the transfer of contractual rights by assignment may be excluded by a clause in the contract with the debtor excluding assignment (Art. 164 I CO). The effect of such a clause is not a duty of the obligee not to assign but the incapacity to do so. An assignment would be ineffective even with respect to *bona fide* assignees.

2. Contract to Assign and Assignment

The stipulation of an obligation to assign a chose in action and the assessment of the conditions of assignment, such as a consideration possibly provided by the assignee, may be effected by a normal (i.e. informal) contract (Art. 165 II). The assignment itself, i.e. the act actually transferring the claim from the assignor to the assignee, requires a document in writing, which represents a contractual consensus of the parties (assignor and assignee) but must only be signed by the assignor (Art. 165 I).

3. The Position of the Debtor

In the transaction transferring the claim against him the debtor (*debitor cessus*) does in no way participate. His consent to the transfer is not required. Neither is there a validity requirement to inform the debtor of the assignment. This solution is opposed to that of the Common Law tradition and of the French Civil Code (Art. 1690).

A fundamental task of the law governing assignment is to protect the position of the debtor. *First*, the debtor must be protected against the risk of being obliged to perform twice because the first performance was not made to the real creditor. Therefore, the debtor not being informed of the assignment may now as before make payment with liberating effect to 'his' creditor (i.e. the assignor), notwithstanding the effects of the assignment *inter partes*. In fact, assignments not disclosed to the debtor are common and they prevail in assignments securing bank-credits: The pre-rogative rights of the assignee/banker to the claim assigned to him are independent from notification of the assignment to the *debitor cessus*.

If the debtor has been informed of the assignment by the assignor or the assignee, it prevents him from paying the assignor ('his' creditor). If he should do so he would incur the risk of being obliged to make a second payment to the 'real' creditor, i.e. the assignee (CO Art. 167). Besides this effect, the notice (given by the assignor or the assignee) as such does not constitute an obligation to give performance to the assignee as long as the latter does not provide evidence of the assignment. In case of uncertainty as to the person of the 'real' creditor, the debtor may be discharged by depositing the amount of his debt with the court (CO Art. 168). On the other hand, if the debtor is informed of the assignment by the assignor and former creditor, he may free himself by payment to the assignee as indicated by the creditor even if, for one reason or another, the assignment should be not valid. The notice of assignment given by the creditor must, in case of a non-existing assignment, be interpreted as an order to pay to a third party which, for obvious reasons, is a sufficient basis for the discharging effect of a payment made to that third party.

Secondly, the debtor must be protected against an alteration in the substance of his debt by effect of the assignment. Therefore, the debtor has all means of defense and exceptions against the assignee he had against the assignor (CO Art. 169 I), such as in the case of assignment of a claim of the seller, the defense that the delivered goods were defective. Compensation (set-off) of a claim of the debtor against the assignor with the claim assigned is permitted after assignment if the debt of the original creditor (assignor) becomes due not later than the claim transferred by assignment (CO Art. 169 II). In addition, the debtor may use all means of defense allowed against the person of the assignee; if e.g. the debtor has a claim against the assignee he may use it for compensation against the assignee.

C. Assumption of Obligations (Art. 175–183 CO) (Schuldübernahme/ Reprisse de Dette)

Articles 175–183 of the CO, introduced in the law reform of 1911, contain provisions with various aspects. The most important may be summarized as follows:

1. Article 175 declares the (obvious) admissibility of a contract of the debtor of an obligation with a third party, the latter assuming the obligation to discharge the debtor, either by an arrangement with the creditor or by fulfillment of the existing obligation. Such a contract does not amount to an assumption of obligation. The assuming third party is obliged against his partner (the debtor) but not against the creditor. An agreement under CO Article 175 is an 'obligation to discharge from an existing obligation'. It does not change the situation of the creditor, who now as before has a claim against his debtor and therefore must not give his consent to said agreement.

2. The CO does not mention the obviously equally existing possibility, that a third party, in the intention of granting a kind of surety, agrees with the creditor to equally be liable for an existing obligation (an agreement possible without the consent of the debtor). Said mechanism of 'accession to an existing debt' has some attraction as it is not submitted to the strict preconditions of the suretyship under CO Articles 492–512. An agreement of the intervening third party with the debtor is equally possible and without the consent of the creditor, who receives a direct claim against the third party if this event corresponds the intention of the latter in the sense of CO Article 112 CO.

3. A transfer of the obligation (debt) from the actual debtor to another person discharging the former is possible but obviously presupposes the consent of the creditor. According to CO Article 176 this consent may be given by ratification of the contract concluded between the debtor and the third party (see point 1 above) by the creditor. The transfer may also be affected by a contract of the creditor with the third party assuming the obligation of the debtor. In both cases the new debtor may 'raise such defenses arising out of the obligation as were open to the original debtor' (Art. 179 I CO).

4. In case that the assumption of the debt should, for whatever reason, be void, the original obligation (i.e. the obligation of the former debtor) 'revives with all accessory rights' (Art. 180 CO). The rules of CO Articles 179 and 180 intend to clarify that by the act of assuming an obligation neither the nature nor the content of the latter is altered in any respect.

D. Transfer of Business-enterprises with Assets and Liabilities (Arts. 181–183 CO) (Übernahme/Cession)

In a very summary regulation Articles 181/182 refer to the problem of transferring a business-enterprise (not constituting a separate legal entity which as such could be transferred) with all assets and liabilities. This transfer (i.e. the contract of the parties) must be followed by publication in official journals; its effect is an immediate liability of the party taking over the business, with a cumulative liability of the former debtor for a period of two years after publication. Under the same conditions a merger (amalgamation, *Vereinigung von Geschäften/fusion*) of two business enterprises and the connected assets and liabilities is possible (Art. 182 CO); in such cases however, each party is, with respect to the liabilities of the other, considered to be the person taking over the business in the sense of CO Article 181. The same scheme is also applied to the transfer of assets and liabilities of a non-merchant.

E. Transfer of the Position as a Party to a Contract to a Third Party

By assignment of claims (Arts. 164–174 CO) and assumption of obligations (Arts. 175–180 CO) not the position as a party to the contract is transferred to a third party, but only claims or obligations resulting from said contract.[31] On the other hand, if the intention is to transfer the position of a party to a contract to a third party, that is, the quality as a seller, a buyer, a contractor, etc., this transfer can only be operated by an agreement including all of the three parties (i.e. the two parties to the original contract and the third party assuming the position of the outgoing party). This type of contract is not mentioned in the Code of Obligations, but there is no doubt as to the admissibility of such a transfer (see I B above).

XI. SET-OFF (*Verrechnung/Compensation*; Arts. 120–126 CO)

If debts of identical objects (practically debts in money) are mutually owed, each of the debtors may be discharged from his obligation by way of set off ('compensation'). This discharge does not, as under the French Civil Code and all codifications following its example, operate automatically but requires a declaration of the party refusing payment on grounds of setting off his counterclaim.[32]

Discharge by set-off is conditional on the mutuality of claim and counterclaim (i.e. if debtor and creditor on both sides are identical). The object of the mutual debts must not be identical in quantity (Art. 120 CO). The set-off operates up to the amount of equality in claims and leaves unaffected the remaining part of the higher claim and debt. On the other hand, the prerequisite of identity of the object of the mutual claims seems to exclude set-off in case of debts in money of different national currency, or debt in money on one side and debt in securities, negotiable instruments etc., on the other. But there is a tendency in the literature to admit set-off in such situations, especially in cases of the possibility to execute the claim of the compensating party being doubtful.

---

31. It is doubtful to what extent the same is true for transfers of business as regulated in Arts. 181–183 CO (above, D).
32. The same mechanism as in the Swiss CO is realized in the German BGB (§ 388), the CC of Japan (Art. 505), China/Taiwan (CC Art. 335), Thailand (CC sec. 342), Portugal (CC Art. 847 f.)

The extinction of the two claims and corresponding debts are connected and interdependent. This extinction becomes effective only upon a declaration to that end by one or the other party (Art. 120 I CO; more explicit BGB § 388). This solution is opposed to that of the French CC,[33] most countries preferring a system of the extinction by compensation being realized *ipso iure* (by rule of law), i.e. automatically at the moment of the coming into existence of the debtor's counterclaim.

The practical importance of the possibility of set-off is most evident in the case of bankruptcy of one party. Set-off under these circumstances is possible even if the debt of the bankrupt is not yet due; special provisions of the Code of Executions and Bankruptcy prevent fraudulent practices, such as assignments by third parties of claims against the bankrupt to his or her debtors.

The mechanism of the set-off can easily be misused, and there must be restrictions to this possibility. The French CC and all codifications following it allow this mechanism for undisputed claims exclusively, a precondition considerably restricting the range of possible applications. Said restriction is missing in the codifications following the system of 'compensation by objection' and requiring, as the Swiss Code, a declaration of the party striving for compensation. Article 125 of the CO does not adequately define the cases which dare not be open for setting off. Compensation should be excluded during court-proceedings if the defendant wants to compensate by a claim which falls neither in the jurisdiction of the court of the main-claim nor can it be ascertained easily and without delaying excessively the decision on the main-claim.[34]

XII. *NEGOTIORUM GESTIO (Geschäftsführung/Gestion d'affaires)* (Arts. 419–424 CO)

This particular type of legal relationship called negotiorum gestio ('acting without authority') is based on the Roman Law tradition and was adopted in one way or an other by all codifications, but is unknown to the laws of the English speaking area. It covers primarily the situation that one person is acting in favor and in the interest of another who is for the time being not in the position to do so. Contrary to the rule 'volunteers have no right' in the continental tradition the relationship between the person acting (the *gestor*, acting person, *Geschäftsführer/gérant*) and the person in who's favor the activity is deployed (*dominus* [*negotii*], *Geschäftsherr/maître*) is submitted to legal rules which are as far as possible following those of mandate: The person acting has to do so according the presumed intention of the *dominus* and to favor and protect his interests (CO Art. 419). All activities being possibly the object of mandate may be covered by the rules of *negotiorum gestio*.

---

33. French CC, Art. 1290.
34. The adequate rule, which should prevail in Switzerland as it does mostly abroad has its origin in the Codex of Justinian (532) 4, 31, 14, 1: *Ita tamen compensationes obici iubemus, si causa ex qua compensatur liquida sit et non multis ambagibus innodata, sed possit iudici facilem exitum sui praestar.* (We order compensations exclusively if the ground of the compensation is indisputable and does not involve in much uncertainty but allows to the judge an easy decision.) See E. Bucher, in *Festschrift für R. Geimer* (Munich 2002), pp. 97–137, (<www.eugenbucher.ch> no. 79).

Does the *dominus* subsequently ratify the intervention of the acting person, the rules of mandate (CO Arts. 394–418) apply altogether (CO Art. 424), therefore restricting the application of CO Articles 419–424 to the event of dissent of the persons involved.

The acting person is responsible for *omnis culpa* (i.e. liable for all *negligence*). This strict liability is alleviated in cases where the intervention was meant to provide protection from imminent danger (i.e. to the *dominus* or his property), but the agent's responsibility is extended to a liability for damages resulting without any fault if the intervention was against the obvious intention of the *dominus* (CO Art. 420). Should the acting person be under age his responsibility is limited to the amount of an eventual profit resulting from the intervention (CO Art. 421).

The *dominus* must reimburse to the acting person all expenses incurred by the latter and in addition also give compensation for losses eventually incurred by accident. Contractual rules apply, if the acting person employs personnel for which he is liable under Article 101 CO. The claim for compensation includes the salaries of employees, but does not comprise any fee or salary of the acting person himself. As under *mandate* the claims for reimbursements are dependent from the (meaningful) activity only.

The *practical importance* of the *negotiorum gestio* is considerable. The set of rules provides the legal bases for compensation of the persons and institutions intervening and helping in cases of natural disasters as earthquakes and inundation, searching for missing persons in case of avalanches or other circumstances etc. The costs caused by searching for missing persons in avalanches etc. may be considerable and include damages incurred accidentally by the helping persons and the salaries of the persons employed by the persons or institutions organizing help in the catastrophe. The argument of *negotiorum gestio* may even help if a person is accepting personal damage in order to save others (a driver driving against a tree in order to avoid hurting a child who runs into the street (decision of the German Bundesgerichtshof, BGHZ 38, p. 274 cons. 2).

In addition to these traditional scenarios the application may be widened to quasi-contractual relations. In a situation comparable to the facts of the well-known decision *Sumpter v. Hedges*[35] the party not delivering the construction due under the contract may, contrary to said English precedent, claim compensation for the value of the work done, if the termination of the project is realized making use of the elements performed by the contractor. The argument to grant (reduced) compensation does apply by analogy the rules of *negotiorum gestio*.[36]

---

35. *Sumpter v Hedges*, Court of Appeal, 1 Q.B. 673: under a lump sum contract for the construction of a work no claim for compensation is given if in case of the abandonment of the work only half done. This rule is still good law in the UK.
36. Had the parties no contract, the termination of the project by the party who ordered the work making use of the work elements granted by the contractor would amount to a ratification of the intervention and constitute 'appropriation of the benefits resulting from the other parties acts', which creates a duty to indemnify the contractor 'to the extent of the benefits received' (Art. 423); the contractor therefore claims for the value of his work (i.e. the reduction of the costs for the ordering party). This is the legal situation in case of absence of a contract between the parties, and the reasoning goes that the existence of a contract cannot do harm to the contractor, who necessarily has the same claims under the contract he had in absence of a contract under the rules of *negotiorum gestio*.

Specific problems:

- *payments made to the account of another person* generally do not qualify as *gestio*. If the person making the payment was in error with respect to the purpose of the payment (he believed erroneously to be obliged to such payment) he may claim the paid sum under the rules of restitution (see VIII above) but has no title under the rules of negotiorum gestio for disbursements against or the third person in who's name payment was made. Exceptions must be admitted to this rule, especially if the payment was meant to execute a third party's duty following directly from legislation or being in public interest; the CO does not include a provision to that end (but the German BGB does; see §§ 679 and 683); it may be assumed that Swiss courts would equally apply the said rule). Nevertheless it is advisable that persons intending to settle the bills of third parties ask for the assignment of the claim they intend to satisfy (i.e. not to perform the respective obligation, but to buy it from the creditor).
- the institution of *negotiorum gestio* is limited to *factual activity* of the *gestor* but does not cover legally relevant declarations. It is not possible without thereto related authorization to accept an offer in the name of the offeree nor is it possible to act in favor of any creditor in order to avoid limitation of his claim. As *gestio* is related to *mandate* it is important to state that it does not provide any authority to act in the name of the *dominus*, because the French Civil Code makes authority to a constituent an element of mandate (see Art. 1984 *et seq.* CC).

XIII. LIMITATIONS OF ACTIONS (*Verjährung/Prescription;* Arts. 127–142)

Actions of claims are limited in time with the exception of claims secured by pawn or real estate mortgage and a few others.[37] The periods of limitation under Swiss law seem short if compared with those of the other Civil Law countries (except the German BGB in its version of 2002 which introduces extremely short periods).

The general time limit for claims not otherwise qualified is ten years (CO Art. 127). A limit of five years applies to claims resulting from rent or hire or from other periodical payments, as to claims for food, board, lodging and similar, for professional services such as legal consulting and for work done by mechanics, etc. (CO Art. 128). A term of limitation of one year is applicable to claims for damages in tort and claims resulting from unjust enrichment (CO Arts. 60, 67). The time-limit of one year is more and more questioned. Claims resulting from tort under the rules of special codes have a longer limit (e.g. two years under the rules for road accidents), and further extension is under consideration. But especially unsatisfactory

---

37. Claims of creditors resulting from losses in bankruptcy proceedings against the debtor are submitted to a time limit of 20 years (and of 1 year as far as directed against the heirs of the debtor); Art. 149 a of the *Schuldbetreibungs- und Konkursgesetz* of 1996.

is the rule of CO Article 67 which establishes a one-year limit for claims for restitution of value and which in most cases was transferred under a presumed contract.

The period commences at the time the obligation becomes due (CO Art. 130). The one-year term regarding tort and enrichment claims starts only when the claim and the person of the debtor is known to the creditor (but an 'absolute' limitation becomes effective ten years after the event causing damage or enrichment, regardless of the knowledge of the creditor; see CO Arts. 60 and 67). Under special circumstances the period does not start or is suspended (CO Art. 134), especially regarding claims between members of the same family, claims of employees against their employers and actions which cannot be brought before a Swiss court (e.g. because the debtor has no legal residence in Switzerland).

The term of limitation is interrupted and a new period commences when the creditor brings an action before a court or arbitral tribunal or when making an application in bankruptcy proceedings. The same effect results from an acknowledgement of the debt by the debtor. By special provision, other acts of the debtor have the effect of interruption, all of them implying an acknowledgement of the debt, such as payment of interest, installments or furnishing a pledge or guarantee (CO Art. 135).

XIV. SPECIAL TYPES OF CONTRACTS

A. *General Remarks*

Swiss law divides the 'Law of Obligations' into a 'general' and a 'special' part. The, general part covers (among other subjects, such as the law of torts and claims arising from unjust enrichment; CO Art. 41 *et seq.* and Art. 62 *et seq.*) the general rules of contract law as exposed above under sections III–VII above; while the special part is mainly reserved for the particulars of special types of contracts, i.e. the following: sale and barter (CO Arts. 184–238); gifts (CO Arts. 239–252); letting and hire, lease (CO Arts. 253–304); loans (CO Arts. 305–318); contract of employment (CO Arts. 319–362); contracts of manufacture (CO Arts. 363–379); publishing contracts (CO Arts. 380–393); the agency contracts, such as ordinary agency (CO Arts. 394–406), letters and orders of credit (CO Arts. 407–411) and brokerage contracts (CO Arts. 412–418); conducting business on behalf of a third party without request (CO Arts. 419–424); commission (CO Arts. 425–439); contracts for transportation (CO Arts. 440–457); procuration and other commercial powers of representation (CO Arts. 458–465); order to pay to third party (CO Arts. 466–471); contracts of deposit (CO Arts. 472–491); contracts of suretyship (guarantee) (CO Arts. 492–512); gambling contracts (CO Arts. 513–515); annuity agreements and contracts for lifelong support (CO Arts. 516–529) and simple partnerships (CO Arts. 530–551).

The lawyer from an English-speaking country may be startled by the fact that this long list of specific types is set out and covered with detailed rules by legislation. In the Common Law areas, the problems related to such contracts are to a great extent solved by recourse to general principles of the law of contracts while under Civil Law many aspects of the law of contract are related to the traditions of the specific types of contract. Their catalogue reflects the Roman Law tradition with its *contractus*, whereby only contracts corresponding to a type in the series of the system were valid in every respect. Thus, the actual contract law of Switzerland is characterized by a double influence:

First, the general rules of contract of any type (described above under sections III–VII) are determined by the legal ideas of the seventeenth and eighteenth centuries of the Enlightenment with its concept of freedom of contract and the *pacta sunt servanda* rule (all contracts, regardless of their content and of the possibility of their attribution to one of the pre-formed types are equally binding).

Secondly, it is influenced by the Roman Law tradition with its list of types of contracts and the specific rules governing each type; however, not adopting the Roman rule that agreements are only fully binding if qualified as a contract, i.e. being in conformity with one of the available types (see I D above).

This combination of two principles has many advantages, and indeed the rules as presented in the context of special types of contracts and developed for specific practical problems in a legal tradition of innumerable centuries are of great help and provide adequate practical solutions not deducible from general principles of contract. On the other hand, it may be added that the combination of the two systems of different historical origin presents an intrinsic contradiction with which jurisprudence and legal literature did not yet fully cope with. Regarding contracts which combine elements of different types, regularly the question is put the way as to whether such a contract is to be qualified as of type A or type B. In resolving the above problem it would be more appropriate to adopt an approach which admits the possibility of an intermediate solution, i.e. a contract which is at the same time partly governed by the provisions of contract type A and partly by those of contract type B. Such a concept is the only way to realize the principle of freedom of contract, which means, *inter alia* that parties are free to depart from the types of contracts offered by the Code.

In the following, only a few remarks with respect to a selected number of types of contracts can be made.

B. Sale *(Arts. 184–236 CO)*

1. The Content of the Contract and Passing of Title

The contract for the sale of any goods creates the obligation of the seller to deliver it and of the purchaser to pay the price agreed, but does not transfer the ownership to the purchaser, a situation corresponding to the *Agreements to Sell* of the English speaking area.[38] The ownership regarding movable goods passes at the moment of their physical transfer (under condition the parties intend the simultaneous transfer of dominium), in case of a sale of land by inscription in the register. Nevertheless, when an individualized object is sold, the risk of loss passes at the moment of the conclusion of the contract, i.e. the buyer must pay the price even if the goods perish

---

38. The opposite solution, i.e. the passing of the title at the moment of the agreement of the parties as in the Sale (or agreement of sale) is established in the French CC (Arts. 711, 938, 1138, 1583) and in many codifications following its example.

or deteriorate before delivery (CO Art. 185). This solution does not reflect adherence to the old Roman principle of *periculum emptoris* (the risk is with the buyer) but was, in the preparation of the Code of Obligations, meant as a step in the direction of the French law which transfers ownership (and, in consequence, the risk) at the moment of the conclusion of the contract.[39]

A contract for the movable goods does not require any specific formalities, i.e. may be agreed orally or even without explicit declaration. Special provisions have been introduced in order to prevent misuse in sales payable by installment and in similar transactions (CO Arts. 226–228). Contracts for the sale of land must be affected by *deed*, i.e. a notarial instrument (CO Art. 216).

Switzerland has adopted the UN convention for the International Sale of Goods of 1980 (CISG, section 4 below).

2. Warranty for Defective Goods

For practical reasons the most important provisions of a sale contract are on the warranty for defects of the delivered goods (CO Art. 197). The general rules of non-performance (as exposed, VII above) apply exclusively in case the goods sold are not delivered in due course. Once delivered, possible defects of the goods are not considered to be a form of non-performance of contractual obligations, but a situation for which the Code is granting specific remedies. This deviating from the general rule is the consequence of the fact, that the contract of sale in its traditional understanding relates to unique objects which as a general rule cannot be influenced with respect to their qualities (a concept which may be called 'technological fatalism'): if the seller has no control over the quality of the sold item, he cannot have a thereto related obligation (*impossibilium nulla obligatio*; no obligation as to impossible things). This is the view of the Roman lawyer. In compensation the buyer has choice between the claim to a reduction of the price (*actio quanti minoris*, *Minderung/action en réduction du prix*) and the request to rescission of the whole transaction (*actio redhibitoria*, *Wandelung/action rédhibitoire*),[40] the latter being possibly combined with a claim for damages (CO Art. 205 I). If the defects are of minor importance, the judge may against the buyer's decision grant only reduction of the price (CO Art. 205 II), a rule which is peculiar to the Swiss code and not existing elsewhere (but in the practical outcome a possible consequence in contracts ruled by the CISG).[41]

The claims of the buyer presuppose that he has upon reception of the goods immediately inspected them and that he has given notice of the defects to the seller

---

39. The French system is mainly inspired by the intention to maintain the Roman *periculum emptoris*-rule but present it in a more modern form and avoid the deviation from the rule *casus sentit dominus* (the risk of a thing is with its owner). See E. Bucher, above footnote 2.
40. This scheme of the sanctions available in cases of the sale of defective goods is common to all codifications of the continental legal tradition and goes back to the remedies offered by the *aediles* who were directing the police of the *forum* (market); the *sale* being legally organized mainly with respect to the practice of the marketplace.
41. CISG Art. 49 (1,lit.a) allows the buyer to avoid the contract in case of fundamental breach (Art. 25) only, excluding thereby to rescind the sale on the ground of minor defects.

(CO Art. 201). If the defects are not perceptible in a normal inspection he may give notice when they have subsequently become apparent. Defects which do not appear within the period of one year from the delivery give no cause of action against the seller if he has not stipulated a contractual warranty of a longer period (CO Art. 201 I).

If the sale is for the delivery of fungible goods the buyer may, instead of rescission or reduction of price, claim the delivery of goods in conformity with the contract (CO Art. 206). If the fungible goods differ substantially from the contract in the sense that they must be regarded as a thing incompatible with the contract (*aliud*, another thing), the delivery is considered as nonperformance (breach) in the sense of section VII above.

3. Warranty for Defective Title

As the seller has no direct responsibility for the quality of the sold item, his obligation does equally not include the obligation to transfer the title; the seller must grant that the buyer enjoys peaceful and undisturbed possession of the purchased good, his responsibility not being engaged by the sole defects of title but becoming effective only in case of eviction, i.e. the threat that the buyer has to surrender it. This realistic and clear position follows the Roman tradition which is prevalent in most codification, the important exception being the German BGB which has created a system of guarantee of title.[42]

4. The Vienna Convention on International Sale

Switzerland adopted the UN Convention on Contracts for the International Sale of Goods of 11 April 1980 (CISG) as per 1 March 1991. It is expected that this codification will in the future influence the understanding of the Sale of Goods contracts in general insofar as its specific concepts deviate from the tradition of this contract in the codifications of the continental tradition. Civil law is deeply rooted in the Roman tradition which is focused on the sale of individualized items, thereby neglecting the sale of goods of a given genus (mass-products from agricultural or industrial origin). The former type of contract still exists and finds perfect regulation in the Roman concept of sale and the thereon based codifications. In modern times such contracts are comparatively few in number; far more important is the type of contract which in the English tradition is called, very much to the point, 'sale by description' (i.e. the sale of all mass products of agriculture and industry, crude, coal etc.). The actual Swiss jurisprudence is characterized by the attempt to find solutions to meet today's needs.

---

42. BGB §§ 433 I, 435. The legal situation is somehow ambivalent and does not exclude the result that the buyer of a stolen object can refuse payment even in the absence of any risk of eviction. For more detail see E. Bucher, *Rechtsgewährleistung in BGB und OR*, *Festgabe für Karl H. Neumayer*, Basel 1997, pp. 171–193 or *recht* 1996, 178–188, (<www.eugenbucher.ch> no. 66).

C. *Letting and Hiring (Rent) (Arts. 253–274g CO)*

The general rules governing the contract of rent (*Miete/bail*) apply both to the rent of movables and immovables. The actual law is characterized by the reform of 1989, in effect since 1 July 1990, which extended largely the protection of housing tenants. Rules allowing control of rentals are established (CO Arts. 269–270e) and the possibility of the owner to terminate the rent are restricted. The renewed text also comprises some rules on how to proceed in disputes developing from rent (CO Arts. 274–274g).

D. *Contract of Manufacture* (Werkvertrag/Contrat d'entreprise) *(Arts. 363–379 CO)*

This type of contract, which follows the Roman law tradition of *locatio conductio operis* has no precise equivalent in the Anglo-American law. Its main characteristics are the obligation of the contractor (*enterpreneur*) to produce a certain effect or result and his strict bearing of risks. If he is not in the position to produce the result as promised, he has no claim for the price, even if the failure is not caused by his fault. The 'result' to be produced by the contractor may vary widely. The construction of a building or other work may be the kind of result mainly contemplated by the CO, but – according to the Swiss Federal Tribunal – even the showing of a film or the staging of a spectacle may be considered to form the object of this type of contract.[43]

E. *Agency (Mandate) and Similar Types of Contracts (CO Art. 394)*

Agency, which is also known as mandate (*Auftrag/mandat*) is the type of contract of the CO influenced by the Roman law tradition more than any other. The main feature of the contract is the rule of loyalty and faithfulness between the parties (see the Latin origin: *mandatum* from *manum dare*, give the hand, *sc.* in order to affirm the mutual intention of good faith). The main duty of the agent is to safeguard the interests of the principal. He has to follow the instructions of the principal but remains responsible for the effects of his own acts. He is obliged to oppose if the principal is giving inadequate instructions. Often the agent is the person with more knowledge or skills than the principal who therefore merely indicated the desired aim, while it is the agent's duty to determine the appropriate means to reach it.

The agent should transfer to the principal the result of his activity (the *actio mandati directa* of Roman law), whereas the principal owes compensation for disbursements, etc. (the *actio mandati contraria*). In the Roman law tradition, still maintained by the German Civil Code, mandate is necessarily gratuitous. Swiss law, however, abandoned this principle, thus safeguarding the practical importance of the mandate in a modern world. In Switzerland, mandate is therefore the traditional type

---

43. See e.g. BGE 109 II 38, 80 II 34, 70 II 218.

of contract governing the activities of lawyers, doctors, etc. but applies in addition to all contracts obliging to whatever activity in favor and interest of the partner.

A basic rule of the Roman mandate, preserved in Switzerland as well as in Germany (BGB § 671 I), France (Fr. CC Art. 2003) and most places of the Civil Law area, is the principle of revocability, i.e. the power of either party to terminate the contract at any time (Art. 404 I CO). This principle is even maintained when an immediate termination of the mandate causes damage to the other party; but in that event compensation is still due by the terminating partner (Art. 404 II CO).

SELECTED BIBLIOGRAPHY

Bucher, E., *Schweizerisches Obligationenrecht; Allgemeiner Teil ohne Deliktsrecht*, 2nd edn., Zurich 1988 (cited 'CO').

Bucher, E., *Obligationenrecht, Besonderer Teil*, 3rd edn., Zurich, 1988.

von Büren, B., *Schweizerisches Obligationenrecht; Allgemeiner Teil*, 1964.

von Büren, B., *Schweizerisches Obligationenrecht; Besonderer Teil*, 1972.

Engel, P., *Traité des obligations en droit Suisse; Dispositions générales du CO*, 2nd edn., 1997.

Engel, P., *Contrats de droit Suisse; Traité des contrats de la partie spéciale du CO etc.*, 1992.

Gauch, Schluep, Schmid and Rey, *Schweizerisches Obligationenrecht; Allgemeiner Teil*, 2 vols., 7th edn., 1998.

Guhl, A. Koller, A.K. Schnyder and Druey, *Schweizerisches Obligationenrecht*, 9th edn., 2002.

Honsell, H., *Schweizerisches Obligationenrecht; Besonderer Teil*, 7th edn., 2003.

Koller, A., *Schweizerisches Obligationenrecht; Allgemeiner Teil*, 1996.

Basler Kommentar zum schweizerischen Privatrecht, ed. by Honsell, Vogt and Wiegand, *Obligationenrecht I; Art. 1–529 OR*, 3rd edn., 2003.

Schwenzer, I., *Schweizerisches Obligationenrecht; Allgemeiner Teil*, 3rd edn., 2003.

Tercier, P., *Les contrats spéciaux*, 3rd edn., 2003.

von Tuhr, A., *Allgemeiner Teil des schweizerischen Obligationenrechts*, 2 vols., 1st edn. 1924/25; 3rd edn. 1974/79.

Chapter 9
Torts

*P. Tercier**

*D. Dreyer***

I. GENERALLY

A. *The Concept*

In a general sense, civil responsibility, or liability, denotes the obligation imposed on a person to repair the tort caused to another party in violation of his legal or contractual obligations. As in French legal terminology, there is little distinction between tortious and contractual liability. This is also true in the insurance context, as civil liability insurance in theory covers all damages caused to others.

In a strict sense, civil liability only relates to obligations resulting from an unlawful act, excluding those arising from contract violation. In this chapter, civil liability will be used in this strict sense.

Civil liability is closely related to insurance, whether public or private. The insurer is, in fact, bound to repair the tort caused to another party based on the contract concluded with the insured. In spite of the close relations which exist in civil liability, this aspect will not be treated in this chapter.

B. *Distinctions*

1. Civil Liability and Penal Responsibility

In Switzerland, criminal responsibility is regulated by the Federal Penal Code. It is usually submitted to judicial authorities named by cantonal law. In principle there is complete independence between criminal responsibility and civil liability: a civil court is consequently not bound by decisions of the criminal court (Art. 53 CO).[1]

As far as their jurisdiction extends, most cantons have implemented this principle in their codes of civil procedure.

---

*Professor, Dr. University of Fribourg, with the assistance of Mr. Lukas Heckendorn
**LL.M. (Berkeley), Dr., Avocat, Prof. tit. University of Fribourg
1. Accepted as a general principle: ATF 125/1999 III 401.

F. Dessemontet and T. Ansay (eds), Introduction to Swiss Law, 145–163.
© 2004 Kluwer Law International. Printed in The Netherlands.

There is, however, a de facto interdependence: the injured party may present a claim for civil damages in the criminal action (joint action).[2] The conditions of such a joint action are determined by the criminal and civil procedures which in Switzerland are governed by cantonal codes. However, in practice, injurers often expect a certain prejudicial effect from penal decisions when their result is an acquittal.

2. Civil Liability and Public Liability

Swiss law attaches considerable importance to the distinction between public and private law. Consequently, civil liability can only concern relations between private individuals. The State (the Confederation or the cantons), the communes and public corporate bodies are therefore not subject to the rules of private law. These rules of private law apply, however, to 'industrial activities' of state servants and officials (Art. 61 CO).[3] The State is also potentially liable and subject to private law for its constructions (roads and others).[4]

The liability of the State is regulated by various provisions of federal and cantonal law. At the federal level, the most important text is the Federal Statute of 14 March 1958, regarding the liability of the Confederation. The liability of the army is dealt with in Article 135 *et seq.* of the Federal Law of 3 February 1995 on the Army and the Military Administration. [5]

3. Civil Liability and Contractual Liability

Civil liability, in its strict sense, is different from contractual liability. Similarities between the two types of liabilities exist, though. The extent of the awarded damages is based on the same rules (referral in Art. 99 III CO). Nonetheless, contractual liability is different in some ways, mainly concerning the conditions, vicarious liability and the statute of limitations.

C. Sources

1. General Sources

The general provisions on civil liability are stated in Articles 41 to 61 CO. They form Chapter Two of Title I of the Code, which is devoted to the origin of obligations.

2. Special Rules

An increasing number of special provisions deal with particular cases of liability. These provisions are found either in the Civil Code (e.g. Arts. 45, 92, 231, 333, 426

---

2. See e.g. ATF 125/1999 III 412.
3. See ATF 126/2000 III 370.
4. ATF 100/1974 II 137, ATF 102 1976 II 343, ATF 103/1977 II 204, ATF 108/1982 II 184.
5. RS 510.10.

CC), in the Code of Obligations (e.g. Art. 752 *et seq.*, 928, 942 CO), or most frequently in special laws. Traditionally these rules merely set forth only the conditions for liability. In contractual claims, the actual damages awarded are determined by the Code of Obligations (Art. 42 *et seq.* CO).

The statute that plays the largest part in practice is unquestionably the Federal Law of 19 December 1958, on Road Traffic; the other relevant statutes will be presented in sections II C and D hereunder.

Conflict of Law rules with respect to civil liability are now regulated in Articles 129 to 142 of the Federal Law of 18 December 1987 on Private International Law (PIL).[6]

3. Revision of Tort Law

Further to a series of parliamentary interventions, the government has set up a group of experts in charge of preparing the revision of tort law. Based on their report, Prof. Pierre Widmer and Prof. Pierre Wessner have prepared a first draft[7] that would replace the Chapter Two of Title I of the Code and harmonize the rules of the different statutes on civil liability. This draft has been submitted to the cantons, political parties, different associations and other interested circles during the consultation procedure. It is expected that the Federal Government will submit its bill to the Parliament in 2002. Some smaller changes are also being prepared. The liability related to genetically modified organisms is being discussed in the Parliament in 2002.[8] A new draft for a Federal Law on Civil Liability of Dam Operators is being prepared by the administration.

II. CONDITIONS OF CIVIL LIABILITY

A. *General Conditions*

Civil liability presupposes in all cases three conditions: (1) that the victim has suffered a tort; (2) that there is a causal link between the loss and the act to which liability is attached, and finally (3) that the elements for a cause of action have been satisfied.

1. Damage

Except for the special cases treated below (section E), in which damages are awarded for immaterial loss (pain and suffering: *tort moral/Genugtuung*), every action in tort requires that the plaintiff suffers financial loss, i.e. damage. Damage is

---

6. RS 291. See below, Ch. 17.
7. Draft on the Revision and the Unification of Civil Liability Law; accompanied by a short and a longer explanatory report; all three documents written by the authors of the draft and issued by the Federal Department of Justice and Police, Berne, 2000.
8. Modification of the Federal Law on the Protection of the Environment, RS 814.01.

defined as the reduction of a person's wealth against his will. Thus, it represents the difference between the state of the patrimony (all assets, liabilities and possible earnings) as it would be if the tort had not occurred and its actual state.[9]

Distinctions have to be made between different types of damages, for practical and for classificatory purposes. Such distinctions are e.g. the one between the actual loss (*damnum emergens*) and the loss of possible earnings (*lucrum cessans*) or the one between bodily damage (resulting from bodily harm), material damage (resulting from damage to property), and other damages sometimes called pure economic loss.[10] Damage is only compensated if the following three conditions are given : the damage must be reasonably certain, which implies that the injured person must be able to establish its existence or at least its probability (cf. Art. 42 II CO); the damage must be personally suffered, which excludes third persons claiming compensation of loss that someone else has experienced (e.g an association claiming damages caused to its members); and finally, it must be direct, that is, it must affect the person who has been the victim of the injury; persons who are only affected by the consequences of an injury (e.g. employer) cannot receive damages unless a statute explicitly provides the contrary (cf. Arts. 45 III and 47 CO).

2. Causation

The defendant is only bound to compensate the damage if there is a causal link between the fact or act, on which the liability is based, and the damage. This question requires a two-step analysis. First, the factual causation deals with the issue of whether the first event is a necessary condition of the second (*conditio sine qua non*): the consequence would not have happened but for the first event. This is a question of fact. Second, the causation needs to be adequate (proximate cause). It would be unequitable to make all the persons who played a role in the causal chain bear the damage. In order to limit liability, it will only be established if it arises from an act which, according to the ordinary course of events and experience, is likely to produce an effect of the kind which has occurred, so that the act in question appears, in general, to have contributed to the effect.[11] This is a question of law that the judge must evaluate in equity in relation to the concrete circumstances and the aim of the liability.

Adequate causation, in particular, is 'interrupted' by any of the following: (1) *force majeure*, an unforeseeable, extraordinary event occuring with irresistible force; (2) the exclusive fault of the person injured; or (3) the exclusive fault of a third party. These intervening acts, however, do not preclude liability unless their seriousness is such that it renders minor the causation linked to the act giving rise to the liability. It should be noted that the theory of adequate causation has recently been criticized in doctrine. Proposed solutions permit, however, wide application of the formula used until now by the courts.

---

9. ATF 127/2001 III 403.
10. ATF 127/2001 III 73.
11. ATF 123/1997 III 110.

3. Cause of Action

A person is only liable for a damage if the liability can be founded on a cause of action. According to this condition, liability can be classified into three categories:

- Aquilian liability (liability for fault), derived from the *lex aquilia* of Roman law, is the general principle of liability. This liability is founded on the fact, that the defendant has committed an unlawful act by fault.
- Simple objective (or simple causal) liability presumes the objective breach of a duty of diligence. The defendant can prove that such a violation did not occur in order to escape liability. This type of liability applies to the employer, the head of a family, the owner of an animal, or the owner of a building.
- Liability for risk (aggravated objective/causal liability) applies to situations in which particular risks are created. Such a risk exists e.g. in the case of the owner of a motor-vehicle, the operator of a transport enterprise, the operator of nuclear installations or the hunter.

B. *Aquilian Liability*

Article 41 of the Code of Obligations states the following:

> Prerequisites for Liability:
> Whoever unlawfully causes damage to another, whether willfully or negligently, shall be liable for damages.
> Equally liable for damages is any person who willfully causes damages to another in violation of *bonae mores*.

This category of liability applies in an extremely vast field, first, because it is not limited to certain injuries, second, because a great number of statutory provisions make references to it, and finally, because the principle is often used in special provisions. In addition to the damage and the causal link, the plaintiff must prove that the defendant committed a fault and acted in an unlawful manner.

1. Unlawfulness

According to case law unlawfulness has two aspects: first, the violation of a rule protecting individual interests of the victim and second, the absence of a legitimate cause to do so.

(a) An act is unlawful whenever it breaches a general legal duty in one of the two following forms. Either it violates the absolute rights of a person (rights operating against everybody, e.g. property, personality, physical, mental and moral integrity) or it infringes a rule which is designed to protect the victim's interest and to prevent the damage that the victim has suffered.[12] Such a

---

12. ATF 123/1997 III 306.

'protective rule' can be written or unwritten, based on cantonal or federal public or on private law.

(b) A breach of the general duty thus described in one way or another may be justified in special circumstances and ceases therefore to be unlawful. Such a justification occurs when the victim has consented to the act (*volenti non fit injuria*: Art. 44 I CO), in so far as the consent was valid. Other special circumstances, justifying even the use of force, are in particular legitimate defense (Art. 52 I CO), cases of necessity (Art. 52 II CO, cf. also Art. 701 CC) and personal defense (Art. 52 III, cf. also Art. 926 II CC and Art. 57 II CO). It is also possible that the law expressly or implicitly places the exercise of a subjective right above some of the protective rights.

According to Article 41 II of the Code of Obligations, liability does not require unlawfulness as defined above, if the tortfeasor intentionally causes damage contrary to good morals. As 'unlawfulness' is interpreted quite broadly, this provision is generally applied restrictively. Its main role is in the field of interference with a contract.

In certain cases, the Swiss Federal Tribunal admits a liability for fault without unlawfulness.[13] This form of liability actually stands between liability in tort and liability in contract. It is called 'liability for the created confidence' and requires a special relation of confidence between the victim and the tortfeasor. In that case, the plaintiff is entitled to claim damages if he suffered a (purely economic) loss because he relied upon a certain information or appearance created by the defendant.

2. Fault

Fault is defined as the reproach that the defendant failed (intentionally or negligently) to fulfill a duty of diligence imposed by the law.

In order to address a reproach to a natural person, it is sufficient that the person has the capacity to make reasonable judgments (Art. 16 CC). It is not necessary that the person be able to exercise his rights (Art. 12 CC). For this reason, minors and persons deprived of exercising rights but able to make reasonable judgments are held responsible for damages caused by their unlawful acts (Art. 19 III CC).

In the case of corporate bodies, fault is determined by the wrong committed by their organs or agents (Art. 55 II CC), i.e. the persons linked to the corporate body who exercise an activity essential to the functioning of the corporation and who occupy management positions. A distinction is made between intentional fault and negligence. In the first case, the tortfeasor desired the unlawful result. In the second he did not act with sufficient diligence to have prevented it. This distinction plays only a secondary role, as the tortfeasor must in principle answer for any fault, including very light fault (cf. Art. 99 I CO for contractual liability). The standard of diligence imposed by law is set in an objective way, by comparison to the 'reasonable person' in similar circumstances.

13. ATF 124/1998 III 297, ATF 121/1995 III 350, ATF 120/1994 II 331.

C. Simple Causal Liability (Simple Objective Liability)

The common element of all liabilities grounded in this category is that implying an objective lack of diligence, liability exists even if the tortfeasor has not committed a fault in the strict sense. This is why he is also liable for the act of a third party or for the consequence of an accident. The law states the following liabilities:

1. Liability of the Employer

Under the terms of Article 55 I CO:

> the principal shall be liable for damages caused by his employees or other auxiliary persons during the performance of their work, unless he proves that he has taken precautions appropriate under the circumstances in order to prevent damages of the kind, or that the damages would have occurred in spite of the application of such precautions.

This provision describes a general standard of liability for the act of another, which applies whenever a person employs an auxiliary to carry on an activity and damage is caused to a third party by this auxiliary. In addition to the general conditions of damage and causation, this liability presupposes that the following four conditions are present:

(a) An employer must have required a subordinate (called an auxiliary) to accomplish a task. The quality of employer supposes personal subordination of the auxiliary, i.e. the employer has the duty to supervise the one who acts.
(b) The auxiliary must have committed an unlawful act (as defined above).
(c) This act must have been committed 'during the performance of the work'. There must consequently exist a direct, functional relation with the accomplishment of the work.
(d) Finally, the employer must have failed to supply the exculpatory proofs offered by the law: he is relieved, if he succeeds to prove that he has chosen his auxiliary with due care (*cura in eligendo*), that he has trained him adequately (*cura in instruendo*), and that he has supervised him adequately (*cura in custodiendo*).

2. Liability of the Head of the Family

Under the terms of Article 333 I CC, the head of the family is liable for any damage caused by minors, by persons deprived of exercising rights, and by persons feeble-minded or suffering mental illness who have been placed under his authority, unless he can prove that he has supervised them in the usual manner and with the attention required by the circumstances.

This cause of action, inserted in the part of the Civil Code concerning family law, assumes that the following conditions are met:

(a) A head of the family must exist, i.e. a person who exerts domestic authority over minors, persons deprived of exercising rights, mentally ill persons and

feebleminded persons living together with him (or her). This may be the father, mother, a third party or even a legal entity, so long as there is a general obligation to supervise the minors or others requiring similar care.
(b) The person placed under the domestic authority of the head(s) of the family must have caused a damage unlawfully.
(c) The head of the family must have failed to establish the exculpatory proof, i.e. having exercised sufficient supervision.

3. Liability of the Keeper of an Animal

Under the terms of Article 56 I CO, 'the keeper of an animal is liable for the damages caused by it unless he proves that he has taken all precautions appropriate under the circumstances as to its custody and supervision, or that the damage would have occurred in spite of the application of such precautions'.

Once again liability is based on insufficient supervision. In addition to the general conditions, the following conditions must be present:

(a) The person whose animal has caused the injury must be a keeper, the person who exerts power (by law or *de facto*) over the animal that put him in a position to take the necessary steps to prevent the injuries which the animal may have caused.
(b) The injury must have been caused by an instinctive act of the animal, which excludes the possibility that the animal served as an instrument in the hands of man.
(c) Finally, the keeper must have failed to establish the exculpatory proofs allowed by the law.

4. Liability of the Owner of a Building

Under the terms of Article 58 I of the Code of Obligations, 'the owner of a building or other constructions shall be liable for the damage which is caused due to its faulty design or construction, or due to inadequate maintenance'.

This general standard of liability for the ownership of an object is limited to things immovable. In addition to the general conditions, the following conditions must exist:

(a) The defendant is the 'owner' at the moment in which the damage occurs. This notion must generally be interpreted within the domain of property rights (Art. 641 CC). The courts admit the liability of the person who has it at his/her disposal only in exceptional cases (e.g. limited property, public property).[14]
(b) There must be a building, that is, any man-made object or group of object, durably fastened to the ground. This concept has also been interpreted broadly. It is sufficient that the object be attached to the ground and that it be

14. ATF 123/1997 III 306, ATF 121/1995 III 448.

created, modified, placed or arranged by human hands. This includes buildings, roads, dams, canals, pools, ski trails, and similar.

(c) Finally, the building must have a defect, i.e. it is not safe enough for the expected use. Thus, the owner did not respect, from an objective point of view, his duty of diligence. The defect may arise from faulty construction or insufficient maintenance.

5. Liability of the Owner of Land

Under the terms of Article 679 CC, 'where damage is caused or threatened by an owner of land who exceeds his rights of ownership, the party injured can apply for a court order providing that the damage shall be made good or for an injunction to restrain the continuance of the wrong and for damages to be paid as compensation'.

This provision has been interpreted as creating a case of objective liability. In addition to the general conditions, the following conditions must be fulfilled:

(a) The defendant must own the land. According to case law, the claim cannot only be directed against the owner in the sense of property rights, but also against the holders of personal rights (tenants farmer, tenant, etc.).[15]

(b) The damage must be caused by an exercise of property rights. As soon as the property rights are exercised in any way (by human action, but no necessarily by the owner)[16] over the limits set by law to property of land (Art. 684 *et seq*. CC), the damage resulting from it must be repaired. In some cases, the courts have even awarded damages if the behavior stayed within the legal limits (e.g. construction works).[17]

6. Liability for Defective Products

The Federal Law on Product Liability of 18 June 1993 (LRFP)[18] takes over the regulation of the European Directive on the same subject. Therefore, many general principles of Swiss tort law do not apply to this special type of liability (e.g. statute of limitations). Liability based on this statute implies the following conditions:

(a) The damage must be caused by a defective product. Only movables (but even electricity!), are considered as products (Art. 3 LRFP). Products are defective, if they are not as safe as one could expect according to the circumstances (Art. 4 LRFP). The nature of the defect does not matter (construction, fabrication, instruction of the user). If it was impossible, at the moment when the product was sold, to detect the defect or if the defect simply did not exist at that moment or if the defect is due to a stature, the defendant is not liable for the damage (Art. 5 LRFP).

15. ATF 104/1978 II 15.
16. ATF 120/1994 II 15.
17. ATF 114/1988 II 230; ATF 91/1965 II 100.
18. RS 221.112.994.

(b) The loss must be due to a personal injury or damage to property. Compensation for purely economic loss cannot be founded on this statute (Art. 1 LRFP). The damage on the product itself is also not compensated.

(c) The Federal Law on Liability for Defective Products establishes the liability of the 'manufacturer' defined as the person who produces the product, the one who presents himself as such, the one who imports the product within his commercial activity or, if no such person can be found, the one who furnished the product (Art. 2 LRFP). The manufacturer can exclude his liability by proving that he has not put the product on the market or that he did not produce or sell the product within his commercial activity (Art. 5 LRFP).

7. Liability of Persons Incapable of Making Reasonable Judgments

Where liability is founded on fault, a person can only be held liable if he/she has the capacity of making a reasonable judgment. An exception to this principle is stated in Article 54 I of the Code of Obligations: 'A judge may determine in equity that a person who has caused an injury shall be liable for partial or full damages even if such person is incapable of making a reasonable judgment'.

The condition of fault, linked to a moral reproach, is replaced by equity. The courts apply this provision whenever it appears reasonable to have the tortfeasor bear all or a part of the loss. This occurs if he has sufficient financial means or if he or she has taken out insurance covering the damage caused.

D. Liability for Risk (Aggravated Objective Liability)

All aggravated objective (strict) liabilities are characterized by the fact that the legislature has attached the duty to remedy the injury due to the exercise of a particular activity, presumably dangerous. Even if such a dangerous activity is allowed because of its utility, those who engage in it in their own interest have to compensate all injuries that the dangerous activity may cause, whether they exercised due diligence to avoid the damage or not. The one who creates the danger should bear the risks. The number of these strict liabilities has been increasing in Swiss law, the legislature responding to the industrial and technical development. Under current legislation, liability for risk is limited to the fields covered by a special statute providing it. The introduction of a general liability for risk is being discussed within the present reform of tort law. In practice, the most important case is the liability of the vehicle owner.

1. Liability of Vehicle Owners

The liability of owners of automobile vehicles is primarily regulated by Articles 58 to 89 of the Federal Law of 19 December 1958, on Road Traffic (LCR) which have been partially revised by a statute of 29 March 1975. The general rule on this liability is stated in Article 58 I: 'If, as a consequence of using an automobile vehicle, a person is killed or injured or material damage is caused, the owner is liable for damage'.

In addition to the general conditions, it is consequently necessary that the following conditions be fulfilled:

(a) The person liable must be the owner, i.e. the person who exercises effective control over the vehicle and employs it for his own use and at his own risk. The law extends this qualification to managers of a business in the automobile field for the vehicles in their charge (Art. 71 I LCR), to organizers of racing events for damages caused to third parties (Art. 72 LCR), as well as to anyone who has unlawfully taken possession of a vehicle (Art. 75 I LCR).
(b) The damage must result from bodily harm or material loss. Recovery of purely economic loss is not possible.
(c) The damage must be caused by the specific risk resulting from the use of the vehicle, i.e. a machine which moves on earth by its own motor-force (Art. 7 LCR). A vehicle is used as soon as the mechanical parts of the vehicle (motor, even lights) are in function.[19] The owner is liable without fault only if the damage is caused by the risk resulting from the use of the vehicle, but not for the damage happening 'at the occasion' of the use (e.g. slamming the door).[20] In the latter case, the owner is only liable if he is at fault or if the damage is due to a defect of the vehicle (Art. 58 II LCR). The fault or the driver is imputed to the owner (Art. 58 IV LCR).

This system of liability is supplemented by an obligation to be insured: 'No automotive vehicle can circulate on public roads before civil liability insurance has been obtained...' (Art. 63 I LCR). This insurance covers the civil liability of the owner and that of persons for whom he is responsible. It shows two characteristics:

(a) The injured party maintains a direct action against the insurer, within the limit of the sums provided for in the insurance policy (Art. 65 I LCR).
(b) The insurer may not defend an action of an injured third party with the exceptions he could assert against the insured (Art. 65 II), which does not prevent him, after he has paid, from claiming against the insured or the policy owner.

2. Other Objective (Strict) Liabilities

There are a large number of special provisions establishing a system of objective (strict) liability for particular risks. It is only possible to list a few of these here:

The liability of railroad enterprises according to the Federal Law of 28 March 1905, on the Civil Liability of Railroad and Steamboat Enterprises and of the Postal Service[21] which includes railroads, boats and other enterprises operating under concessions (cable cars, cable railways, and other means of transport).

---

19. ATF 114/1988 II 376; ATF 107/1981 II 269.
20. ATF 107/1981 II 269; ATF 63 II 67.
21. RS 221.112.742.

The liability of corporations operating electrical installations, under Articles 27 to 41 of the Federal Law of 24 June 1902, concerning Electrical Installations of Low and High Voltage.[22]

The liability of airline companies under Articles 64 to 79 of the Federal Law of 21 December 1948, on Air Transport.[23] This liability only concerns damages caused in flight to persons and property on the ground, which excludes the loss caused to passengers.

The liability of operators of atomic centers is ruled by a Federal Law of 18 March 1983 (=LRCN),[24] which presents the surprising characteristic of imposing upon operators an unlimited liability; obviously, on the other hand, the insurance which completes it is limited, although the Confederation accepts to cover amounts exceeding this coverage, but only up to a maximum amount of CHF 1 billion.

The liability of pipe line enterprises according to Article 33 to 40 of the Federal Law of 4 October 1963, on Installations for Transport of Liquid or Gaseous Combustibles or Motor Fuel through Pipes.

In 1997, the Article 59a of the Federal Law of on the Protection of the Environment[25] of 7 October 1983, as amended on 21 December 1995 (LPE) has replaced previous provisions in special areas (protection of water). It generally establishes that the owners of installations and enterprises, which are dangerous for the environment, are liable for damage caused by 'the realization of this danger', unless the damage is caused by a third person or by *force majeure*. This provision mainly relates to enterprises that treat dangerous substances, the disposal of waste and water-pollution liquids. The law only applies to damages caused by an effect to the environment in the sense of Article 7 I LPE (noise, vibration, pollution), but not to direct damages. Damages to the environment itself are explicitly excluded, only the Federal Law of 21 June 1991[26] on Fishing provides an exception. The LPE reserves all special provisions which are stricter than Article 59a.

The liability for the practice of hunting is ruled by Articles 15 and 16 of the Federal Law of 20 June 1986 on Hunting and on the Protection of Wild Mammals and Birds.

The liability linked to the use of explosives according to Article 27 of the Federal Law of 25 March 1977, on Explosive Substances.

E. *Indemnity for Pain and Suffering* (Tort moral/Genugtuung)

The law does not limit possible remedies to the damage defined above (II A 1). It also provides for reparation of moral damages. This expression is to be understood in its broadest sense and designates all physical or moral sufferings that a person sustains as the result of an unlawful injury to his personal interests. This reparation is, in principle, subject to the same conditions as remedies for material damage, the

22. RS 221.112.734.
23. RS 221.112.748.
24. RS 221.112.732.44.
25. RS 814.01.
26. RS 923.0.

condition of damage being replaced by the condition of moral damage. The following distinctions need, however, to be made.

1. In Case of Bodily Injury or Death

A person who is a victim of an injury to his or her bodily integrity may present a claim for a sum of money as moral compensation for the pain to which he has been subjected, and particularly, for any which he may still suffer because of his injuries (Art. 47 CO). The same provision also recognizes that close relatives of a deceased person are entitled to recover compensation for suffering which they undergo as a result of the death; this right normally extends to the spouse, parents, children, possibly to brothers and sisters, and on rare occasions to others.

The courts now admit, thus completing the legal system, that the next of kin of a person who is severely affected in his physical or mental integrity may also obtain a sum of money as reparation of moral damage.[27]

2. In Case of Other Personal Injury

Any person who suffers an unlawful injury to his personal interests may demand reparation of a moral damage (Art. 49 CO). This concerns mainly cases of injury to one's honor, violation of one's privacy and injury to one's sentiments of affection. Since the revision of the law on individual inherent rights in 1985 (Art. 28 *et seq.* CC), such reparation is subject to the same conditions as the liability for the damage; in any event, it must be established that the victim has suffered a prejudice severe enough to justify a compensation.

III. Effects of Civil Liability

A. *General Principles*

When the conditions of civil liability are fulfilled, the injured party can claim damages (or indemnity for pain and suffering) against the person liable. This action leads to the payment of a sum of money, or, rarely, to reparations in kind.

To determine the damages to be paid by the person liable, the judge starts to establish the damage that the victim has actually suffered. He then sets the amount of the damages owed, taking into consideration different circumstances. In no case the victim can obtain a sum greater than the damage which he has actually suffered.

It should be noted that an action for damages or for reparation of a moral tort only tends to offset the consequences of a past injury. To prevent or put a stop to a present injury there are other means provided for either in Article 28 of the Civil Code, dealing with the protection of the personality, or in the corresponding provisions concerning the protection of property rights (Arts. 641, 679 CC). Anyone who desires to bring suit to prevent or stop the tortious act has to prove only that there is an unlawful injury. He has no need to establish fault or another cause of action against the defendant.

27. ATF 112/1986 II 118, ATF 112/1986 II 258 and 114/1988 II 149.

B. Evaluation of Damage

1. In General

According to the definition given, damages are measured by the difference between the two states of the patrimony which would have existed had the injury not occurred and that which actually exists. This amount is thus determined, not only by the value of the possession damaged, but also by the patrimonial interest which it represented to the victim.

Following this reasoning, the victim must allow the amount from which he has benefited by reason of the injury to be imputed when determining the damage award (*compensation damni cum lucro*). If a person's vehicle has been destroyed, he is entitled to the value of the vehicle less the value of the wreck. Furthermore, he is entitled to damages for the other losses which he may suffer while awaiting the replacement of his car. Similarly, the party sued may deduct from the amount of damages the sums which the victim receives from insurance (if the insurer can exercise the right of recovery against the person liable). The same applies in the field of public insurance (cf. Art. 41 LAA) and property insurance (cf. Art. 72 LCA).

2. Some Special Cases

The Code and court decisions have established a certain number of rules for determining particular damages.

a. Material Damage

Material damage includes not only the value of the object which has been damaged or destroyed, but to a certain extent also the interest which the victim had in using the object. This is why liability includes not only reparation or replacement costs, but also, with exception, other damages linked to the replacement of that object (e.g. costs of renting a replacement).

b. Bodily Injuries

According to Article 46 CO, the victim first has the right to be reimbursed for all medical and hospital expenses connected with his treatment. He then is entitled to reimbursement of lost wages or profits. In case of lengthy invalidity the judge must also award compensation for loss of earning capacity. Consequently, he must estimate the reduction of future earnings that the victim will actually suffer by reason of his physical impairment. The victim should receive this amount allocated in the form of an income. In practice, it is customary to estimate the income due by applying the tables established by M. Schaetzler and S. Weber.[28]

---

28. *Barwerttafeln*, 5th edn. of the tables of W. Stauffer and T. Schaetzle, Zurich 2001.

c. Death

The party who caused the injury in the event of death only has to pay the costs directly linked to the death, particularly the funeral expenses (Art. 45 I CO). The law, however, permits third parties, who received or who would have received support payments from the victim to demand payment of the loss from which they suffer (Art. 45 III CO). In order to determine the amount owed for loss of support, the judge must again estimate the portion of the revenue of the victim that would have been paid to the plaintiff and capitalize the amount on the basis of the Schaetzle/Weber tables.

C. Setting Damages

The maximum amount of the damages awarded by the judge cannot exceed the amount the victim has suffered and the amount he has claimed. It is forbidden under Swiss law to charge the person liable with punitive or exemplary damages. On the contrary, starting with the actual damage suffered, the judge must set the indemnity taking into account all circumstances, especially the fault of the tortfeasor (Art. 43 I CO). In particular, he can reduce the indemnity in consideration of contributory negligence or other circumstances (Art. 44 CO).

1. Circumstances for which the Victim is Responsible

Under the terms of Article 44 I CO, 'The judge may reduce or completely deny any liability for damages if the injured party consented to the act causing the damage, or if circumstances for which he is responsible have caused or aggravated the damage, or have otherwise adversely affected the position of the person liable.'

The most usual case is that in which the victim himself has committed a fault, i.e. contributory negligence. Contributory negligence is evaluated according to the same rules as the fault of the party causing the injury itself and requires especially the capacity of making reasonable judgment. When a fault is so serious as to be exclusive, the judge can refuse all compensation by virtue of the rules of adequate causation.

The victim may also be liable for a personal count of accusation, e.g. the vicarious liability of an (injured) employer or the liability for the risk inherent of the vehicle of the injured owner (Art. 61 LCR, which contains some special provisions on this subject). In those cases, the conjunction of the liabilities is considered as in the case of contributory negligence.

2. Other Factors of Reduction

There are other factors that the judge should consider. He may reduce indemnity if, in the case of aquilian liability, the tortfeasor committed only a very slight fault (Art. 43 I CO), or if the damage has been caused or aggravated by a fortuitous event. The judge may also take into account economic and social considerations: he may decrease the amount of the compensation if the victim had a particularly high income (cf. e.g. Art. 62 II LCR), or reduce the amount when the payment will cause financial distress to the debtor (Art. 44 II CO).

D. Particularities of the Indemnity for Pain and Suffering

A person who had suffered a moral tort (see II E above) can claim for a financial indemnity. To a certain degree, this should permit compensation of the suffering that the plaintiff has experienced. In order to determine this indemnity, the courts base their decisions on amounts awarded in comparable cases. Generally, the amounts awarded for reparation of moral tort are relatively low, even if they are slowly increasing. In case of death, the indemnity varies usually between CHF 10,000 and 40,000,[29] in case of injury they can be higher, but they have not exceeded CHF 120,000.[30]

The law also recognizes other forms of reparation or sanctions (Art. 49 II CO), such as the publication of the judgment (mainly in case of an attack by the media) or the payment of an indemnity to a charitable organization. Such forms of reparation are very rare, though, as in the case of the media other means are available (Art. 28g CC).

E. Concurrent Liabilities

Where several tortfeasors cause the same damage to one plaintiff, they are both liable for the whole damage. In this respect, the law distinguishes the following two situations.

1. Perfect Solidarity (Joint Liability)

In tort law, perfect solidarity between more than one tortfeasor applies only if the law states so (Art. 143 II CO). In that case, the plaintiff can act against any of them and require compensation for the entire injury. The one who has paid the victim can then act against the other persons, who jointly share a part of the liability. There are two main examples in the field of tortious liability:

(a) By virtue of Article 50 CO, joint liability exists between two persons when they have caused damage by joint fault. Consequently, it is necessary that they acted in concert or at least that there was tacit agreement in their behavior (Art. 50 I).
(b) Several other provisions likewise institute liability among several persons even when they have not acted in concert. This is particularly the case for all persons who have together caused damage in an accident involving an automobile vehicle (Art. 60 LCR).

---

29. See e.g. ATF 121/1995 III 252, ATF 123/1997 III 10.
30. See e.g. ATF 125/1999 III 412 (CHF 80,000: AIDS-infection), ATF 125/1999 III 269 (CHF 100,000: sexual abuse), ATF 123 III 306 (CHF 120,000 (as maximum): tetraplegia).

2. Conjunction of Actions

When two persons have caused an accident without having acted in concert and are liable on different grounds, the law applies a somewhat different solution, which is called conjunction of actions or imperfect solidarity (several liabilities Art. 51 CO). Even if that is not a case of joint liability strictly speaking, the victim has an action against each of the responsible persons. The statute of limitations runs separately for each liable person. The other practical differences are very small.

IV. CLAIM FOR DAMAGES

A. *The Rules on the Statute of Limitations*

In the field of tortious liability the legislature has adopted a few particular rules on the statute of limitations. The system is not uniform, and distinctions must be made between general and special rules.

1. The General Rules

They are stated in Article 60 CO, which makes a distinction between three periods:

- The ordinary term is one year running from the date when the damaged person received knowledge of the damage and of the identity of the person liable for it.
- The subsidiary term of ten years runs from the date when the act causing the damage occurred.
- The extraordinary term reserved by Article 60 II CO applies when the claim results from an illegal act which, according to criminal law, is subject to a longer statute of limitations.

2. The Special Rules

There are numerous rules establishing the date at which the statute of limitations will begin to run, and the length of the term. In this respect, two remarks will be sufficient:

(a) In automobile accident cases, the statute of limitations is not one year but two years from the date when the damaged person received knowledge of the damage and the identity of the person liable. It should be noted that this statute of limitations is applicable to any claim related to an automobile accident even if based on civil liability.

(b) There are special rules for the statute of limitations in claims for damages caused by nuclear energy to consider the fact that the damages may not be apparent for some time longer than in cases of ordinary accidents (Art. 10 LRCN).

B. The Rules of Procedure

Neither the Federal Code of Obligations nor the special statutes present a complete set of procedural rules, since each canton has the power to adopt its own statutes on civil procedure. A Federal Law on the civil procedure is in the making. At the moment, the only existing federal rules concern jurisdiction. The Federal Law on Jurisdiction in Civil Matters of 24 March 2000[31] replaces several statutory provisions, and applies Article 30 of the Federal Constitution (adopted in 1998). It establishes the jurisdiction of the courts of the defendant's domicile, of the victim's domicile or of the place where the tortious act happened or showed results (Art. 25). In the case of car- or bicycle- accidents, jurisdiction is limited to the courts of the place where the accident happened or of the defendant's domicile (Art. 26). Similar rules apply to international torts (Arts. 129–131 of the Law on Private International Law).

---

31. RS 272. See Ch. 16 on the Law of Civil Procedure.

SELECTED BIBLIOGRAPHY

A. Treatises on Civil Liability

Deschenaux, H. and P. Tercier, *La responsabilité civile*, 2nd edn., Bern 1982.
Keller, A., *Haftpflicht im Privatrecht*, 6th edn., Bern 2002.
Oftinger, K. and E. Stark, *Schweizerisches Haftpflichtrecht*, 4 vols., Zurich: Besonderer Teil 1, 4th edn., 1987; Besonderer Teil 2, 4th edn., 1989, Besonderer Teil 3, 4th edn., 1991, Allgemeiner Teil, 5th edn., 1995.

B. Treatises on the Code of Obligations

Included are also discussions of civil liability in some general works devoted to the law of obligations or to the relevant portion of the Code of Obligations:

Engel, P., *Traité des obligations en droit suisse*, Neuchâtel 1973, p. 299 *et seq.*
Honsell, H., *Schweizerisches Haftplichtrecht,* 3rd edn., 2000.
Von Bueren, B., *Schweizerisches Obligationenrecht*, Allgemeiner Teil, Zurich 1964.

C. Commentaries on the Code of Obligations

Brehm, R., D*ie Entstehung durch unerlaubte Handlung, Berner Kommentar*, 2nd edn., 1998.
Münch, P. and Th. Geiser, *Schaden-Haftung-Versicherung, als Band V der Handbücher für die Anwaltspraxis*, 1999.
Oser, H. and W. Schoenenberger, *Kommentar zum Obligationenrecht, Teil, Zuercher Kommentar*, Vol. V, 2nd edn., Zurich 1929.
Honsell, Vogt and Wiegand (eds.), *Kommentar zum schweizerischen Privatrecht*, Basel 2003.

Chapter 10
Commercial Law, Competition Law and Intellectual Property

François Dessemontet *

The present chapter is devoted to three areas of the Swiss Commercial Law: corporations and partnerships; competition law; and patents, trademarks and copyrights.

All three areas have experienced considerable legislative changes in the last twelve years. The joint stock corporations are now regulated by the Code of Obligations as amended on 4 October 1991. The anti-trust legislation is the new Law on Cartels and other Restraints of Competition of 6 October 1995 (under revision). The Ordinance on the Register of Commerce of 7 June 1937 has been amended last on 26 June 1996, and on 29 September 1997. The Law against Unfair Competition of 19 December 1986 has superseded the Law on Unfair Competition of 1943. Finally, the Laws on Trademarks and Copyrights have undergone complete revisions on 28 August and 9 October 1992, respectively and the Law on Copyright is again under revision, while the Patent Act of 1954/1976 is being amended. The new Law of the Protection of Designs of 5 October 2001 has superseded the former Law on Industrial Designs and Models of 30 March 1900. As the adaptation of Swiss laws to the European law may proceed at an increased pace in the next few years, utmost care should be taken to assure up-to-date information on the state of the Swiss legislation at the very time a particular question may arise. Ours are no longer the days of the perennial laws of Switzerland.

I. CORPORATIONS AND PARTNERSHIPS

A. Introduction

The Swiss Codes provide for various types of corporations engaged in both profit-oriented and non-profit activities. The non-profit organizations such as associations under Article 60 *et seq.* of the Civil Code, and foundations under Article 80 *et seq.*, as well as Article 335 of the CC, have been discussed in the chapter on the Law of Persons. Therefore, we shall focus on the following legal entities which are suitable for commercial purposes, i.e., the entities which are regulated in the Code of

* Professsor, Universities of Lausanne and Fribourg; President (2000–2003), Swiss Society of Jurists.

F. Dessemontet and T. Ansay (eds), Introduction to Swiss Law, 165–195.
© 2004 Kluwer Law International. Printed in The Netherlands.

Obligations of 30 March 1911: corporations and partnerships. The Code has established four types of corporations:

AG/SA
GmbH/Sa.

- joint stock corporations (*Aktiengesellschaft/société anonyme*);
- corporations with limited liability (*Gesellschaft mit beschränkter Haftung/société à responsabilité limitée*);
- cooperatives (*Genossenschaft/Société cooperative*);
- partnerships limited by shares (*Kommanditaktiengesellschaft/société en commandite par actions*).

The Swiss Code of Obligations also provides for three kinds of partnerships:

- the simple partnership (*Einfache Gesellschaft/société simple*) which cannot be registered but is suitable for commercial purposes as well as non-profit activities;
- the general partnership (*Kollektivgesellschaft/société en nom collectif*);
- the limited partnership (*Kommanditgesellschaft/société en commandite*).

The main difference between corporations and partnerships derive from the emphasis that is usually put in partnerships on the personal confidence, which should unite the partners; whereas corporations are based on their capital, the shares of which provide the measure of each stockholder's rights and duties.

Accordingly, partners should generally have a more active participation in the conduct of the business, while stockholders are supposed to look more for the financial returns on their shares than for their personal influence in the decision-making process. This last proposition really only holds true for some public corporations, while most other companies are owned by the persons who manage them.

Secondly, it is worth mentioning that the commercial legislation of Switzerland does not fully separate public and private corporations, as the laws of some other countries do. Of course, there are corporations whose capital is raised by public subscription, or whose shares may be traded on the stock exchange. Hence, some provisions of the law are designed to ensure the minimal protection for public investors (see Arts. 663c, 685d *et seq.*, 697h, 727b, 729a, 752, 1156 CO). Furthermore, stock exchange regulations provide for some measure of control over the activities of public corporations, especially for corporate governance. Nevertheless, the basic difference between private and public corporations is one that Swiss law does not take into account.

A Federal Law on Stock Exchanges and Security Market has been adopted on 24 March 1995. It also regulates the unfriendly take-over bids, which the Ordinance on the Commission on Take-over Bids of 21 July 1997 subjects to strict constraints.

A federal Law on Mergers and Splits of Corporations and Partnerships has been adopted and will enter into force probably on 1 July 2004. There are ongoing preparatory works for a Bill on the revision of the Law on the Corporations with Limited Liability. An expert committee of three members has prepared a bill for a law on corporate governance during 2003. Finally, a new set of regulations on accounting could be sent to Parliament sometime in 2003–2004.

A practice-oriented view could divide the business associations of Switzerland into two main groups. The modern corporation, which is organized as a joint stock corporation and encompasses almost every kind of important business, ranging from the large conglomerate with a stock of billions of Swiss francs down to the small technology-oriented business primarily based on venture capital, as well as to the drugstore on the corner of the street; the number of joint stock corporations has increased from 18,231 in 1935 to 179,774 in 1998.[1]

All other types of corporations and partnerships, which are to a variable extent sheer remnants of the past, when partnerships and cooperatives were both very much appreciated as legal forms for small or medium-sized businesses. As the figures clearly indicate, these entities are decreasing in number, with the exception of the cooperatives and the general partnership.

B. Joint Stock Corporations

1. Basic Notions

Article 620 of the CO defines the joint stock corporation as follows:

> 'A joint stock corporation is a corporation having its own company name and a predetermined capital which is divided into shares. The liability of the corporation is limited to corporate assets. Shareholders have no duties other than those stated in the articles of incorporation and are not personally liable for the debts of the company'.

Among the features which are required by law for any such company are:

– a company name, which is to be chosen in accordance with Article 944 *et seq.* of the CO on trade names, especially Article 950;
– the capital stock, which is divided into shares;
– the absence of any liability of the shareholders for the debts of the corporation;
– the incorporation of the company by way of registration in the Register of Commerce;
– some degree of organization.

Among the features that are common to many companies limited by shares but not required by law, the plurality of shareholders should be mentioned. Actually, every corporation shall have at least three shareholders at the date of incorporation. However, if at a later date there are only one or two shareholders, any interested party may petition the court for a winding-up order (Art. 625 CO).

This later provision has almost fallen in abeyance, since few creditors have a strong interest in causing the liquidation of a one-man company; moreover, if such a lawsuit were pending, the main shareholder could transfer some of his shares to nominees at any time. As a result, it is estimated that almost half of all Swiss

---

1. This figure includes an indefinite amount, approximately five to ten 'partnerships limited by shares,' a peculiar type of commercial corporation regulated under Arts. 764 through 771 of the Code of Obligations, for which statistics are not kept separately.

corporations limited by shares belong to one or two individuals only. However, there are less tradesmen or manufacturers who are registered under their proper name (172,701 in 1998) than corporations limited by shares (179,774 in 1998). Nevertheless, the whole concept of the law as well as the articles of incorporation of most companies rest on the assumption that more than two shareholders are interested in the corporations' activities. Keeping this in mind, it may be submitted that a plurality of shareholders still remains a typical feature of Swiss corporations.

Another common characteristic of joint stock corporations is the anonymity of the shareholder. Many corporations issue shares to the bearer, which must be fully paid before issue (Art. 683 CO). In such cases, there is no registration of the undivided bearer's interests retained in the corporation, and no one inside or outside the corporation has a right to know who holds the shares (with the obvious exception of the authorities when they assess the income of a given taxpayer who is a shareholder; however, the taxation procedure and relevant data are usually confidential).

In the 1970s and 1980s, many public corporations converted their shares to nominative shares. The existence of such shares entails the registration of the shareholders in the corporation's register, whether they are first holders or assignees of these titles. Nominees may be appointed and mentioned in the company's book instead of the true holders.

Furthermore, some public regulations lift the veil of anonymity that surrounds Swiss corporations; the most notable of these certainly is the Lex Friedrich.[2] The Federal Law on Sea Navigation of 23 September 1953[3] also requires proof of Swiss ownership of a majority of shares if a corporation is to receive the right to fly the Swiss flag on its vessels. A similar requirement will be found for instance in the *intercantonal* concordat on oil prospecting and exploitation of 24 September 1955.[4] The Federal Law on Stock Exchanges and Security Market provides under certain conditions an obligation to announce to the stock exchange and to the involved corporations the equities in the companies that are incorporated in Switzerland and whose shares are traded in the stock market. Federal Laws are taken into account by an important provision on the possible restrictions to transfer of share (Art. 4, Final Provisions of the CO).

A further characteristic of joint stock corporations is the transferability of the shares. The law sets no limit on the free assignment of shares at any time. However, the articles of incorporation may lawfully restrict the transferability of nominative shares, and they often do just that by submitting registration of the assignee to the consent of the company. Nevertheless, the principle of transferability has led the Federal Tribunal to deny any implied relationship of confidentiality between the shareholder as such and the corporation. Actually, the shareholder is free to compete with the company,[5] and buying shares of the company from third persons (prior shareholders, bankers, brokers) does not create any contractual link between buyer

---

2. Federal Law of 16 December 1983, on the acquisition of real estate by persons whose domicile is outside Switzerland; S.R. 211.412.41 and related ordinances, as amended on 14 December 2001.
3. S.R. 747.30.
4. S.R. 931.1; ratified by only six small cantons.
5. RO 91 II 298.

and corporation, which then cannot be held liable for damages if these shares are the object of an invalidation procedure initiated by the company.[6]

As we have seen, the legal mould of the company limited by shares consists of very few legally necessary characteristics and some more typical features. However, a strong doctrine has developed in Switzerland with the goal of making conformity to the type of this corporation the legal test for interpreting ambiguous or obscure provisions of the commercial law. According to the doctrine, the drafting of these legislative provisions was premised on an understanding of the joint stock corporation as being typified by some common features of public companies. Hence, the law should be read with these alleged typical features of that company in mind. The main drawbacks of the typicity doctrine are, first of all, the difficulty of outlining the typical feature of public corporation that the legislature had in mind when enacting the legislation and further, the dangerous neglect of the multifarious sorts of corporations to be encountered in Switzerland, such as a family business, a one-person firm, a real estate holding, a special purpose vehicle, or a smokescreen company, which are by far more frequent than public corporations. The legislative works towards a new law of corporation has abundantly shown that the legislature has no typical corporation in mind when passing a particular provision.

2. Incorporation

There is only one procedure for the incorporation of a Swiss company limited by shares, the simultaneous incorporation, in which the capital being paid, the articles of incorporation are adopted by all the subscribers at once. This procedure culminates in registration by the Register of Commerce, which examines the necessary documents, and incorporates the company if they are formally in order.

One should note the so-called qualified incorporation: there are qualifying circumstances in which specific measures of precaution have to be taken in order to protect the subscribers and the creditors of the corporation from particular perils.

The simultaneous incorporation is performed by some preliminary operations and one founding meeting of the subscribers.

a. Preliminary Operations

Articles of incorporation (*Statuten/statuts*) are prepared, either on the basis of legal forms or by negotiation between the promoters and their advisers; the articles of incorporation necessarily have to define the company's name, purpose, capital and share value, any payment thereof in kind, the procedure for calling shareholders' meetings and their right to vote, corporate organs and powers *vis-à-vis* third parties, and the forms of publication for the corporate notices (Art. 626 CO).

Articles of incorporation will usually include other matters. Provisions on certain items are not valid if they are not included in the articles. Article 627 of the CO lists thirteen such items; for example: amendment of the articles of incorporation, Board members' rights to a share of the profits, intercalary interests, time limits on

6. RO 80 II 267.

the corporation, preferred shares and voting rights, limits to the transferability of shares, delegation of Board powers to some of its members or third parties and auditing, if the auditor's rights and duties go further than required by law.

Furthermore, specific information has to be given on all and any qualifying circumstances (Art. 628 CO).

The founders are free to include all other matters in the articles of incorporation, or, if they are to be regulated at all, to keep them for Regulations, or Board's guidelines, or private covenants between shareholders. This may be the case, for instance, as regards arbitration of the corporations' internal conflicts, accounting methods, depreciation allowances, debentures, and employee participation. Covenants between shareholders can be undertaken in view of the legal regulation of transferability of shares.

Once the promoters have agreed on the articles of incorporation, they have to subscribe to shares and pay their value. Shares shall be issued at par value or above but the law does not require that shares be fully paid at the onset of the corporation's business. On the contrary, the law is premised on the rule that only 20 per cent of each share's value must be paid at the incorporation of the company, provided however that the total amount of the paid capital be at least CHF 50,000 (Art. 632 CO). There used to be a requirement for shares to have at least a CHF 100 face value, which was lowered to CHF 10 in 1991, and a bill is pending to allow for shares without face value.

It is obligatory to transfer capital payments to a bank subject to the Law on Banks and Savings Associations of 1934 (SR 952.0). The consignment office may not transfer these amounts by the order of the board before registration of the corporation in the Register of Commerce. This system has been devised to ensure that the firm actually receives the funds necessary to avoid thin capitalization.

At present, however, there is some degree of concern among interested circles that the system does not circumvent the fraudulent incorporation of companies without even the very low capital required by law (CHF 100,000 for corporations that were founded after 1 January 1985). The 'paper corporation' devoid of any asset is a frequent feature of criminal maneuvers in the underworld of finances.

b. Instrument of Incorporation

The corporation is founded when all subscribers sign the instrument of incorporation (*Gründungsakt/acte constitutif*). They thereby certify that all shares have been validly underwritten; that the assets the conveyance of which has been promised shall meet the total subscription price; that the payment of capital in kind fulfills the requirements under the law or as set out in the articles of incorporation; and that the necessary organs (Board and auditors) are appointed and have accepted.

It is worth mentioning that a public notary has to execute and authenticate the instrument of incorporation. A public notary is mandatory in the incorporation procedure, so that the promoters know about and comply with legal provisions. The public notary bears a special responsibility for fraud or negligence, as do all other founders (Art. 753 CO). Further, it is a criminal offense to obtain a deed authenticated by a notary through false or misleading assertions (Art. 253 Swiss Penal Code). Even the notary public may be indicted under certain circumstances.

c. Registration of the Corporation

The Board members lodge a request for incorporation to the Register of Commerce with the following documents:

- articles of incorporation;
- instrument of incorporation;
- minutes of the board and auditors' appointments, with indication of the domicile and nationality of the board members, the majority of whom must be Swiss citizens;
- notice of the persons in charge of representing the corporation.

The Registrar or his staff will go through the documents with care. They have unlimited competence as regards compliance with formal requirements.

On the other hand, inasmuch as material questions are at stake, the Registrar's office has powers to elicit further information from the founders if needed, especially with regard to qualifying circumstances, but no discovery procedure may help recover information from third parties.

Moreover, unless there is a clear violation of imperative law, the Registrar is not authorized to decide on any legal difficulties which may arise in connection with the nest for incorporation, because the resolution of any controversial point pertains the ordinary courts. In case of doubt, the Registrar shall admit the request. These limitations reduce the effectiveness of the legal measures against fraudulent incorporation of companies.

If the documents are found to be formally in order, and if the name of the corporation is unobjectionable, the corporation is registered. Upon payment of the federal stamp tax on capital, official notice of the registration is published in the Gazette of Commerce (*Schweizerisches Amtliches Handelsblatt/Feuille Officielle Suisse du Commerce*). Registration is conclusive evidence of the incorporation of the company, which is now a legal entity: it may enjoy rights and undertake obligations. All contracts that were concluded by the promoters in the name of the corporation prior to its registration may be ratified by the company, if the board so chooses within three months at their discretion. If not, only the promoters will be bound as parties to the contract.

If the incorporation procedure has not been proper, the registration nevertheless creates a valid corporation, but any legal defect must be removed as soon as possible. If the interests of creditors or shareholders are deeply affected by the violation, one of them may, within three months from the publication of the registration notice, petition the court for an order to wind up the company.

d. Qualified Incorporation

There are three sets of qualifying circumstances that entail accrued measures of protection in the incorporation stage, and increased liability for the promoters.

First is the payment of capital in kind rather than in cash (*Sacheinlage/apport en nature*). There is neither an official valuation of the assets so transferred to the corporation, nor an obligation to obtain consent of the court or an authority. But the valuation of these assets and all other conditions of the covenant shall be disclosed to the subscribers in a special report by the promoters. An auditor must certify in writing that the special report is complete and accurate. Articles of incorporation shall take up the main features of the operation. A special liability is established by law for all those who cooperate in the incorporation of a firm, and contribute either by willful intent or by negligence to some dissimulation of the true facts about the transaction (Art. 753 CO).

If promoters of the corporation intend to invest part of the company's capital in willful fixed assets, either real estate or chattels of all kinds (*Sachübernahme/reprise de biens*), they must disclose such investment as well as the terms of any related agreement. Of course these goods must be of some value in proportion to the starting capital of the corporation, although the law does not state any percentage figure in that connection. All provisions on the payment of capital in kind will then apply.

Finally, if promoters and founders are to be rewarded by certain privileges, the articles of incorporation must set them out. Promoters' privileges currently are not common in Switzerland.

3. Organization

In view of the variety of aims and sizes of the companies limited by shares, the following remarks only sketch out some of the common characteristics of their organization, although there is little in common between the one-man one-office firm and the giant corporation engaged in industry, or in the banking or insurance business. There are always at least three corporate institutions: the general meeting of the shareholders, the Board, and the auditors. By-laws and regulations may establish committees and other offices.

a. *General Meeting* (Generalversammlung/Assemblée générale)

The shareholders convened in a general meeting are the superior authority of the corporation.

(i) Calling of meetings

The general meeting may be called by the Board of directors, the auditors, the liquidators or the representatives of the debenture holders. In any event, there must be an 'ordinary' general meeting once a year, to be held not later than six months after the end of the corporation's financial year. Extraordinary general meetings can be called as often as the Board deems necessary. A general meeting has to be called upon requisition by one or more shareholders who own at least one-tenth of the capital; the requisition must state the objects of the meeting. If the Board does not follow the shareholders may obtain an order of the court. A twenty-day notice of the meeting and an agenda must be served. No decision can be taken on items not on the agenda. Shareholders holding stock of a nominal value of CHF 1 million at least may request that a given point be put on the agenda.

Finally, a general meeting may convene at any time if all shareholders or proxies are present throughout the deliberation. Then no limitations apply in regards to the agenda: all matters falling within the power of a general meeting may be discussed and resolved.

(ii) Powers of the General Meeting

The general meeting of the shareholders has, by law, the following powers:

- To adopt and to amend the articles of incorporation. Absolute majority of the attending shareholders or their proxies is enough, with some exceptions.
- To elect the board of directors and the auditors.
- To approve and accept the yearly accounts and the business reports, to determine the allocation of profits and to fix dividends and profit shares for members of the board.
- To release the members of the Board from any liability which they may have incurred in transacting business for the corporation. The decision precludes individual claims of shareholders against the Board or its members only to the extent that these shareholders consented to the resolution of release, or if they bought their shares afterwards with knowledge of the resolution, of if they did file a suit within six months after the date of the resolution (Art. 758 CO).
- Finally, to decide upon all matters which the law assigns to the general meeting (Arts. 623, 638, 647, 650, 651, 652, 653, 654, 674, 697, 697a, 704 705, 725, 727, 729c, 731, 732, 736 CO), as well as other matters that are made subject to its decision by the articles of incorporation.

The decisions by the general meeting are so important that the Board or any shareholders may take legal action against the corporation to contest any resolution which is defective with regard to the law or the articles of incorporation. Protection of vested rights of shareholders, equality of treatment among them and abuse of rights under Article 2 of the CC are the most common grounds of action, along with procedural flaws. If the resolution is voidable, action must be filed within two months. If the resolution is null and void, there is no such time limit. Are null and void amongst others the decisions that recall or restrict the right to attend the general meeting, the minimal voting right, the right to file a suit or other shareholders' rights that are protected by imperative provisions of the Code, as well as the decisions that restrict the right to obtain information even more than the law permits, and the decisions that run counter to the basic structures of the corporation or the provisions protecting the assets of the company. Resolutions of the Board are null and void in the same conditions. They are not voidable.

b. *The Board of Directors* (Verwaltungsrat/Conseil d'administration)

(i) Appointments

The Board shall be composed of one or more members, all of whom must be physical persons who are shareholders of the corporation. The first members are sometimes named in the articles of incorporation for their initial term of office. Unless otherwise provided in the articles of incorporation, that may set terms of up to six years, the term of office for each member is a period not exceeding three years.

The general meeting may elect members who are proposed by a group of minority shareholders, if the articles of incorporation so provide. The articles shall contain such provisions whenever there are several groups of shareholders with different voting rights or financial rights, which is the case, for example, when a corporation has issued preferred and common stocks.

Furthermore, the articles of incorporation may provide public corporations and entities, such as the municipalities, the cantonal States or the Confederation, with the right to appoint representatives to the Board (and to the auditors), even though the entity is not a shareholder. They may recall these representatives at any time, and have them replaced by other persons. Moreover, the public corporation or entity shall be held liable toward the corporation, the shareholders and the creditors for the acts and omissions of their representatives.

(ii) Powers of the Board

(a) Internal Affairs of the Corporation. First of all, the Board is authorized to decide all matters that are not reserved to the general meeting of the shareholders or to the auditors. Far-reaching contracts may in some cases be presented to the general meeting for approval, contracts with officers and directors in their capacity both of private persons and of representatives of the corporation ('Insichgeschäft', 'contrat avec soi-même') shall be ratified by the general meeting of stockholders or, if concluded by a director or an officer, by a neutral body within the corporation, by the full Board of Directors or by the Chairman of the Board of Directors if the other party is a Director. The grant of extraordinary wages and compensation to a Director who is also an employee of the corporation may harm this corporation and may result in a case for liability of the Director on unjust enrichment (Art. 678 CO), as well as in a defense of misuse of right (Art. 2 II CC). The law, the articles and the by-laws put the Board in charge of many decisions. The Board is responsible for the management and the representation of the corporation. Delegation of powers to one or a few members of the Board is possible, if the articles of incorporation authorize such delegation, which is common practice in the big corporations. In such a case, the other members of the board do no longer remain fully liable *vis-à-vis* shareholders and creditors (Art. 754 II CO). In such a case, a specific organization by-law shall be adopted by the corporation. The Board has to inform third party having a legitimate interest and requesting such information as to the organization of the management.

Among the attributes of the Board, the Code mentions the preparation of the general meetings, the implementation of its resolutions, the duty to control the business of the corporation, to set the necessary instructions, to establish the organization, to set up guidelines for accounting and auditing, to designate and recall the managers and representatives of the corporation, and the power to give instructions to the managers and to supervise them. A financial plan shall be set out by the Board whenever necessary. An annual report on the corporation's financial position and the results of the previous year must be submitted to the general meeting in writing. Furthermore, the Board may remove any delegate, manager, or officer from office at any time.

Finally, the Board has the right and duty to represent the corporation with respect to all administrative procedures, for example with the Register of Commerce, the tax authorities, etc. The Board shall inform the bankruptcy court if the corporation is financially overburdened. If it fails to do so, the auditors shall advise the court. If the Court fails to act and to pronounce the bankruptcy or some other relief, the State can be held liable towards the corporation, but not towards the creditors personally.

(b) Representation of the Company. Generally speaking, the Board shall transact business with all third parties on behalf of the corporation. There is no such rule as the Anglo-American *ultra vires* doctrine; however, the Federal Tribunal has stressed that the powers of the Board members who are authorized to represent the corporation are limited to perform acts which fall within the scope of the corporation business as defined by the articles of incorporation. Moreover, it should be remembered that the shareholder who owns most or all of the stock may be treated in legal proceedings as a Board member authorized to perform legal acts for the company, although no formal appointment to that position has been undertaken in his favor by the general meeting, and even though another person has been nominated by the meeting and is registered as an authorized representative. Any other person exercising in fact the executive power in a corporation may also be held responsible by creditors.

c. Auditors (Revisionsstelle/Organe de révision)

(i) Election
One or several auditors are elected by the general meeting. At least one auditor has to be a resident of Switzerland. All auditors shall have the necessary skills for auditing the corporation. Furthermore, particular skills are required whenever the corporation has emitted debentures, or its shares are listed on the Stock Exchange or on the secondary market, or if its key figures are in excess of two of the three following amounts during the two following years:

- total of the balance sheet: CHF 20 million;
- gross turnover: CHF 40 million;
- labor force: 200 employees.

A governmental ordinance of 15 June 1992 specifies these particular requirements (S.R. 221.302). They might be replaced by different, higher figures in order to define which corporations will be subject to new rules on corporate governance.

The auditors shall be in fact independent from the Board and from any majority shareholder. Furthermore they cannot be hired by the corporation for works not compatible with independent auditing.

A commercial corporation or a cooperative may be appointed as auditor.

The auditors have a term of office of three years, and they are reeligible. If an auditor resigns, his motives have to be disclosed by the Board to the next general meeting of shareholders. The judge may appoint an auditor if the position is vacant. The winding-up of the corporation under the Bankruptcy Act is frequent in such a case. At the request of a shareholder or of a creditor, the court may fire an auditor who does not fulfill the prerequisites of this office.

(ii) Duties

The auditors must determine whether the profit and loss accounts, the balance sheet and the annex match the books, and whether these documents comply with legal terms, as well as with any requirement set down by the articles of incorporation. Proposals for dividends etc. are also subject to their examination.

A short report to the general meeting states in writing the results of the verification and recommends approval or rejection of the accounts. For the big corporations needing particularly skilled auditors, a detailed report to the Board shall add comments and observations.

When the auditors notice violations of the law or of the articles of incorporation, they disclose them to the Board and, if important, to the general meeting of the shareholders.

If the assets no longer cover the company's liabilities, the auditor must inform the bankruptcy court if the Board does not do it.

A special auditing may be ordered by the judge at the request of 10 per cent of all shareholders (or shareholders holding CHF 2 million in shares at nominal value), if they make a prima facie case showing that founders or organs have run afoul of the law or the articles of incorporation, thus causing a damage to the company or the shareholders.

d. Liability of Board Members and Auditors

Swiss law provides for a special action in liability against directors, liquidators or auditors who have caused losses either to the corporation or to its shareholders and creditors. The particular statute of limitations is five years from the day on which the aggrieved party has received knowledge of the damage and of the person responsible, but in no case later than ten years from the day of the last damaging action.

If convicted, all defendants are jointly and severally liable. However, the court can take into account individual circumstances to determine the amount to be paid by each defendant.

Inasmuch as they are not directly damaged themselves, shareholders and creditors may sue for damages to be paid to the corporation. This direct payment should preclude the filing of an action in tort by individual shareholders or creditors whenever the outcome of the litigation is unclear (i.e. most of the time) since, should they lose, plaintiffs would have to pay all legal fees, including those for defendants' counsel, while not cashing in themselves the award of damages if they should win. Therefore, the judge may direct an award for costs and legal fees against the company if the defendant is not ordered to pay them.

If the corporation goes bankrupt, the claims for indirect damages pertaining to the individual shareholders and creditors have to be raised by the administration in bankruptcy. If the administration does not assert such claims, any shareholder or creditor shall be entitled to ask for assignment of the claims. These assignees will be paid first on the proceeds. If there is any surplus, the other creditors first in line, then the other shareholders will be paid for it. The effects of a settlement between parties may vary from case to case.

4. Capital, Reserves, Shares

a. Capital (Aktienkapital/Capital-actions)

Swiss law is premised on the requirement that each and every corporation shall have a fixed capital stock, which is determined by the articles of incorporation and shall remain unaltered, except through the legal procedures to increase or to reduce it.

(i) Preventive Measures
There are several provisions which aim at ensuring such stability of the capital:

- payments in kind for shares are qualifying circumstances in the incorporation;
- shares may not be issued under par value;
- shares may not be paid back to shareholders before winding-up and liquidation of the corporation;
- dividends shall be paid only on profits during the preceding financial year, or on reserves for equalization of the dividends, which entails that net assets of the company have to be greater than its capital for dividends to be authorized;
- the company may not pay interest on its shares, with the exception of one starting period for enterprises in need of large equipment and building facilities;
- as a rule, the company may not purchase more than 10 per cent of its own shares.

If a buy-back system or agreement is in force for restrictedly transferable shares, the amount may reach 20 per cent for a maximum two-year period. These shares enjoy no voting rights as they are owned by the company. A reserve shall be put in the books at their paid-for value. Crossholdings are regulated (Art. 659b). Buy-back transactions on the own shares of the corporation have been common, for flourishing corporations listed on the Stock Market (or corporations wishing to appear to be thriving).

(ii) Emergency Measures
Swiss law provides for some measures that are of importance whenever the survival of the company is endangered by its financial burdens.

If the last annual balance sheet shows that at least half of the capital is no longer covered by the net assets, the Board shall immediately call a general meeting for information.

If there are reasons to believe that the company has become insolvent, an interim balance sheet must be drawn up, on the basis of liquidation value of the assets.

If the assets no longer cover the company's liabilities, the Board must inform the court, which then has the power to declare the corporation bankrupt. However, the court may postpone opening of the bankruptcy if the Board or a creditor files a request to this effect, provided that there are sound prospects for a financial reorganization. In such a case, the court shall order the appropriate measures for safeguarding the assets, i.e. the taking of an inventory or the appointing of a trustee. Publication shall occur only if the interests of third parties require it.

b. Reserves (Reserven/Réserves)

There are four types of reserves:

- the legal or general reserve funds;
- the reserve funds created by the articles of incorporation;
- the reserve funds that are established by the general meeting of shareholders;
- the hidden reserves.

It is within the powers of the Board to accumulate and to utilize these reserves. There is an obligation to disclose decreases in the amount of the hidden reserves if non-disclosure should grossly distort the results of the company. Undervaluation of assets and extremely high provisions for future or non-existent liabilities are among the favorite means to cover up hidden reserves. This topic has been one of the most controversial in the debates surrounding the 1991 revision of Swiss corporate law. Most large corporations are now subject to Stock Exchange requirements that may limit hidden reserves, and some are going over to IAS or US–GAP standards, with the same result.

c. Shares (Aktien/Actions)

There are two kinds of shares: shares to the bearer and shares issued and registered to the names of the shareholders. Both types of stock may be issued at the same time, with equal or different values and voting rights. One type may be converted into the other, with due respect for the vested rights of the interested shareholders.

Shares to the bearer are transferred by delivery of possession of the certificates. Such shares shall not be issued before their full par value has been paid in, because the corporation has no say on the purchase by whoever is willing to buy them.

Shares to the names of shareholders are usually created to their order. Shareholders may then assign their shares by endorsement to the purchaser. Nevertheless, the company has to keep a ledger listing the shareholders, who shall be registered therein with name and place of residence. Entry in the stock ledger is a condition for all dealing with the company by a shareholder. The ledger is confidential.

When a subscriber transfers his shares, he may be held liable for the unpaid amount if the corporation goes bankrupt within two years after its incorporation and if the transferee has not paid upon request. Registered shares which are sold on the stock exchange or over the counter are usually circulated after a blank endorsement, so that only delivery of the possession is required for a valid transfer. In such cases, the registered shareholder is to be considered as a nominee of the actual owner of the stock. Private agreements between bankers' associations and corporations listed on stock exchange regulate the matter. In the last few years, physical transfers of these shares have been greatly reduced, following the expansion of a common-deposit system for all shares listed on the Swiss Exchange (SWX).

Finally, many companies have introduced restrictions on the transferability of shares. Such restrictions do not entirely apply to shares which should be assigned by reason of death, marital property statute or execution of a judgment, unless members of the Board or shareholders already registered in the corporation's ledger commit themselves to purchase the shares at the price quoted on the Stock Exchange or at the actual value of the shares. In all other cases, the transfer shall be agreed to by the Board before entry of the transferee's name in the ledger. In order to refuse their agreement, the Board of directors shall either avail themselves of a good cause or propose on behalf of the company or of third parties to buy back the shares involved, at their real value. The endeavor to pursue the same goal as set forth in the articles of incorporation and the endeavor to maintain the independence of the company are considered as good causes. However, for the companies whose stock is listed on the Stock Exchange, the only good cause for rejecting a shareholder is the fact that a limit which has been set as a per cent of the joint stock by the articles of incorporation for the participation of any one shareholder would be exceeded should the new shareholder be listed in the stock ledger. In all cases, the new shareholder must state explicitly that he is not a nominee, but acts on his own behalf. It is proper for the corporation to request a full identification of the purchaser of the shares.

5. Winding-up and Liquidation

a. *Causes of Dissolution* (Auflösung/Dissolution)

A company may be wound up in accordance with its articles of incorporation; by decision of the general meeting authenticated by a public notary; by a declaration of bankruptcy; by a court order if shareholders representing at least 10 per cent of capital request winding-up on reasonable grounds; and in all other cases provided by law, such as the lack of a sufficient number of shareholders; or serious defects of the incorporation procedure.

Moribund companies can be dissolved following a special procedure with no court order, but an administrative decision that the authority supervising the Register of Commerce will render to the effect that the corporation be struck off.

In fact, many companies devoid of assets and activities are still registered. Through purchase of all shares of such a company, a businessman may avoid paying stamp taxes on the capital of a newly incorporated company. The savings are attractive enough to keep defunct companies in legal life for the sake of selling their shares and their names. Tax authorities may notice these fraudulent transactions, if registrations of Board members and articles of incorporation are both modified to suit the needs of the new owner.

b. *Liquidation* (Liquidation/Liquidation)

Liquidation of the company is carried on by Board members whenever possible, except if the company is bankrupt. In that case, the Bankruptcy Act of 1889, as amended on 16 December 1994, shall apply. A public announcement is directed to all unknown creditors, but they are not foreclosed in their rights if they fail to respond to the announcement. All known creditors are served special notice. Then, balance sheets are made by liquidators at the onset of the liquidation, and each year thereafter until the end of the whole process.

Once the assets are sold, and the creditors paid or guaranteed, the shareholders receive the remaining assets in proportion to their amounts paid in, unless there is preferred stock. After the settlement of all liabilities, the corporation will be struck off the Register, but an interested party may file at any time thereafter a request for reregistration of the wound-up corporation, if he intends to sue it, for example. Therefore, the books of the corporation must be kept for a period of ten years, the general statute of limitations in Switzerland.

6. Groups of Companies and Disclosure of Holdings

The regulations bearing on groups of companies are few. Basically, groups of companies are held to set yearly consolidated accounts, unless there are very small groups with total assets of no more than CHF 10 million, turn-over of no more than CHF 20 million, or yearly average workers of no more than 200. Said exemption does not apply if debentures have been issued, or if stock is listed on the Stock Exchange, further if ten per cent of the shareholders request consolidated accounts, or if this is necessary to disclose as accurately as possible the assets and results of the group.

Equivalent foreign provisions are recognized to the extent that the Swiss company whose accounts are consolidated within a group according to foreign regulations is dispensed of presenting its own group accounts.

The law does not set forth the techniques of consolidation (proportional, etc). Each group shall indicate its guidelines and principles to this effect.

C. Other Companies and Cooperatives

Under Swiss law there are three types of companies other than the corporation limited by shares: the corporation with limited liability, the partnership limited by shares, and the cooperative. Only the first and the last of these corporations are of practical interest.

1. The Corporation with Limited Liability

The corporation with limited liability (*Gesellschaft mit beschränkter Haftung/société à responsabilité limitée*) combines the main features of the joint stock corporation and those of the partnership. Due to its great success in Germany, this form of company was introduced into Swiss law with the amendments of 1936 to the Code of Obligations. It did not fill a real gap in the array of business companies under Swiss law. As a matter of fact, the joint stock corporation generally fulfills the needs of the Swiss businessman, because of its flexibility. Therefore, there have been extremely few corporations with limited liability registered since 1936, 18,485 as of 31 December 1998. Now, a revival of interest has been obvious in the last decade (31,929 in 2001). A general revision of the law of the corporations with limited liability is under way. The responsibility should be further restricted, and the shares more easily transferred to a third party.

At present, the corporation with limited liability is one with a predetermined capital stock and its own corporate name (Art. 772 CO). As is the case for the joint stock corporation, the rights every partner has in the capital are generally speaking apportioned to his share of the capital, the amount of which may vary from associate to associate. However, every associate is jointly and severally liable for the debts of the corporation, but only to the extent that the registered capital has not been actually paid in, or if it has been illegally returned to the associates. As a counterpart of their personal liability, the associates themselves have a right to manage the company's business, unless the articles of incorporation provide for a delegation of these matters to some of the associates, or to a third party who need not be a partner in the company. Finally, as in the general partnership, and unlike the joint stock corporation, the associates enjoy the right to quit the corporation in accordance with the contract or on equitable grounds, with due compensation for their holding interests.

Within this general framework, the drafters of the articles of incorporation may either opt for a general partnership-like formula or utilize the more usual patterns of the joint stock corporation.

Finally, it should be noted that the Code of Obligation, in Article 620 *et seq.* on the joint stock corporation, regulates the following items in the corporation with limited liability:

- reduction of the capital;
- accounting and reserve funds;
- representation of the corporation;
- preventive and emergency measures to maintain the capital;
- auditors, if they are established by the articles of incorporation; if not, the rules on the rights to individual control by each associate as developed in partnership law shall apply;
- winding-up and its consequences, but for some specific grounds of action;
- liability of the promoters and directors.

A thorough revision of the law on corporations with limited liability is under way.

2. Cooperatives

a. Definition

Cooperatives (*Genossenschaft/société cooperative*) are both numerous (2,751 in 1998 and 2,329 in 2001) and important in the fabric of Swiss economic and social life, mainly with regard to small business and agriculture. Some huge insurance and retail corporations used to be organized as cooperatives, even though they were not typical for the particular needs to which the legislature intended to respond while enacting the thorough provisions of Articles 828 to 926 of the CO in 1936.

The cooperative is a 'corporation that physical persons or commercial companies of a variable number shall organize to attain or protect through common action particular economic interests of the cooperators' (Art. 828 CO).

Thus the cooperative is open to all persons whose economic interests and activities fall within the purpose of the cooperative's articles of incorporation. This maxim of the 'open door' prohibits the predetermination of a given amount for the capital, whenever the articles provide for capital to be paid in.

Furthermore, the cooperative's purpose shall consist of the pursuit of some predetermined economic interests of its members. At present, the requirement that these interests be of an economic nature is not stressed. As a result, the registration in the Register of Commerce will not be denied to a cooperative with a non-economic purpose.

Somewhat more stringent is the requirement that the cooperative's purpose is to further the interests of its own associates. Of course, the underlying concept of self-reliance of the cooperators in a given area of their business is difficult legally to enforce, in a society where most economic activities are based on the exchange of goods and services with a variety of producers and retailers. Relationships, sometimes tight business links, must be established with non-cooperators, in order to give the corporate business the desirable extent for a minimal cost-covering capacity. Therefore, there is no objection against the corporation fulfilling orders of or otherwise conducting business with persons other than associates. Nevertheless, it is the opinion of learned scholars that the legal definition still forbids the creation of a cooperative as a profit-oriented trading company.

Finally, there has to be some kind of common effort by all or most cooperatives toward reaching the cooperative's purpose. The scope of individual members' duties depends on the activities of the corporation. Suffice it to say that calls may be directed to members for more than financial contributions.

b. Incorporation and Organization

(i) Incorporation

The incorporation procedure of a cooperative is much simpler than that of the corporation limited by shares. There is no requirement of authentification by a notary public. Nevertheless, the articles of incorporation will be drafted with care, as they shall mention a number of matters important to the cooperative (Arts. 832 and 833 CO).

The articles of incorporation must be signed by all promoters and subscribers. Moreover, if there are qualifying circumstances, such as payment of capital in kind rather than in cash, the promoters have to file a special report, which will be discussed in the incorporation meeting. Finally, registration by the Registrar of Commerce shall be conclusive evidence that the cooperative has been created as a legal entity. By law, the unregistered cooperative is considered not to be a legal entity. In practice, estimations are to the effect that around five thousand unregistered cooperatives are well and active; they are mainly engaged in agricultural production. The rules on partnerships (Art. 530 *et seq.* CO) are applicable to the unregistered companies.

(ii) Organization

There are two types of cooperatives: the single cooperative and the confederation of cooperatives (a confederation may also be open to individual members). This basic difference entails a number of consequences for the organization of the cooperatives, most noticeably as far as the general meeting is concerned. To keep this discussion as short as possible, the organization of the single cooperative is mainly referred to hereafter.

(a) General Meeting. The general meeting of the cooperators is the supreme authority of the cooperative. It has, by law, the following powers, which may not be delegated to another corporate body:

- to adopt and to amend the articles of incorporation;
- to elect the board members and the auditors;
- to approve the accounts and to decide upon the allocation of the new profits; and
- to release board members from any liability with regard to their managerial performances.

The general meeting may further know of all matters which the law or the articles put within its powers. Each cooperator has one vote only.

Cooperatives with more than three hundred members and confederations of cooperatives may hold meetings of delegates, instead of general meetings of cooperators. The same cooperatives may also have the general meeting and members may cast their ballots by correspondence, which of course gives no leeway for lengthy deliberations on the issues on the agenda.

b. Board of Directors. The Board shall include at least three directors. Members of the Board need not be cooperators. A third party (general manager, for example) may receive the right to manage and to represent the cooperative. The liability of Board members is much less stringent that in the joint stock corporation, since they are liable *vis-à-vis* persons other than the cooperative itself only if they fail to act according to their legal duties if the cooperative falls into insolvency.

D. Partnerships

Swiss law regulates three kinds of partnerships:

- the simple partnership (*Einfache Gesellschaft/société simple*) (Art. 530 *et seq.* CO), which is really part of contract law, and may be entered into for all purposes, commercial or otherwise;
- the partnership with a collective name or general partnership (*Kollektivgesellschaft/société en nom collectif*) (Art. 552 *et seq.*CO), which is the proper legal form for two or more businessmen to conduct business without restricting their liability; there were 10,027 such partnerships registered in 2001 willy-nilly, many important law firms are nowadays characterized as general partnerships rather than simple partnership, which may entail effects as to the liability of the partners.
- the limited partnership (*Kommanditgesellschaft/société en commandite*) (Art. 594 *et seq.* CO); there were 1,682 such partnerships registered in 2001.

The partnership contract is a basic element of all three partnerships. This agreement between the associates is not subject to any condition of form. Nevertheless, if some partners want to limit their liability they must register the amount up to which those partners with limited liability shall be held responsible for the debts of the partnership. It is not possible to limit the liability of all partners. Furthermore, registration in the Register of Commerce is compulsory for partnerships with a collective name and limited partnerships, while it is excluded for the simple partnership.

This simple partnership does not constitute a legal entity; it is a sheer contract which binds only the parties thereto, without basically modifying their relationships with outsiders. In contrast, partnerships with a collective name and limited partnerships are legal entities which do not, however, enjoy all the capacities of legal or physical persons. Most noticeably, the assets of the partners' business are owned directly by the partners themselves, under a status of ownership in common (*Gesamthand/propriété en mains communes*) (Ch. 7, IX). This is the reason why the authors refer to partnerships with a collective name and limited partnerships as 'quasi-legal entity.' Due to the partnership capacity to enter into contracts and be held responsible in tort, the partners are only liable for the partnership's debts in case of default of the partnership. Then, partners are jointly and severally liable on all their assets. On the other hand, individual partners' shares in the business may be made subject to lien and attachment. In such a case, partners enjoy the right to expel the partner whose share has been garnished, against payment of his so-called liquidation share. If there is no agreement as to this compensation, creditors of the partner may file a request for a court order to wind up the partnership.

Finally, it is worth mentioning that partnerships concluded for an unlimited period of time, or more than five years, may be terminated at any time by a partner on six months' notice. This rule is sometimes applied to other contracts that are to be performed for long periods of time, such as license agreements. However, a partnership may be validly entered into for the lifetime of one of the partners.

II. COMPETITION LAW

Swiss competition law is divided into two main areas: law against unfair competition and law against restrictive trade practises (antitrust law).

A. *Law against Unfair Competition*

1. In General

Under Article 48 (now repealed) of the Federal Code of Obligations of 1911, it was a tort to distract customers from a competitor through false or misleading advertising, or through other practises which were deemed to be 'contrary to good faith.' This particular provision of the Code was superseded by an act consisting of 22 articles, the Federal Law on Unfair Competition of 30 September 1943, which gave way to the new Law against unfair competition of 19 December 1986 (LCD).

The main objective of the 1943 Act was to guarantee the free interplay of competitors in Switzerland. Faithful to the traditional concept of the market place as a self-regulating mechanism that best serves the interests of merchants and customers alike, the Swiss authorities were nevertheless desirous of taking a firm stand against abuses by unscrupulous competitors. Thus, the concept underlying the unfair competition law is strikingly similar to the basic aim of the regulation against restrictive practices: it is to maintain, or to make free competition possible for everyone who is willing to enjoy the opportunity. The same philosophy prevailed in the 1986 Act. However, more emphasis has been put on the rights and claims of the consumers and their associations, as well as on the right of the Swiss Confederation to act towards condemnation of deceptive practises that put at risk the renown of our country abroad.

Since public interests are at stake, the 1986 Act provides for a broad protection of competitors and customers under criminal provisions (Art. 23 *et seq.* LCD). Nevertheless, the legislature was bound by the rule of 'no offence without statute' (nullum crimen sine lege) so that indictment on unfair competition counts may be pronounced only if the alleged wrong is specifically listed in Articles 23, 24 and 25 LCD. In contrast, protection through civil remedies (Arts. 1 through 11 LCD) may be obtained by an aggrieved competitor, even if the abuse is not explicitly mentioned in the law. It is up to the ordinary courts of law to decide whether the alleged wrongs, when sufficient evidence lies before the court, be deemed an 'abuse of economic competition through deceit or other means contrary to the principles of good faith, and apt to influence on the relationship between competitors or suppliers and customers' (Art. 2 LCD).

This general wording of the law should make clear that not only deceit and frauds are prohibited, but also every practise which in the given case appears to be contrary to good faith.

Currently, there is no clear-cut concept of what good faith requires or precludes. Most of the cases are decided on the assumption that one competitor must refrain from using unfair means in the fight on the market place. The law does not look askance to the goal itself, to enlarge one's own share of the market and, if possible, to get rid of the competitors.

Therefore, it is generally recognized that the law against unfair competition should not protect vested interests or property rights of merchants and producers. Nevertheless, trade secrets and confidential know-how may be conceived of as equitable property rights.

2. Specific Practises which are Prohibited

Of course, no complete list of unfair practises can be spelled out here. It is, however, interesting to outline some of the main counts of unfair competition. The law itself mentions various methods of sale which are per se deceptive:

- disparaging a competitor, his wares, his works, his activities or his business by false of misleading, or uselessly damaging information;
- giving false or misleading information about oneself or about a third party, or about one's or a third party's wares, works, activities or business, to procure oneself or the third party an advantage over the competitors;

- using false titles or professional denominations;
- passing-off one's wares, works, activities or business as somebody else's, or taking measures which may arouse confusion with a competitor's wares, works, activities or business. This is certainly the count under which most actions are filed.

Further, comparisons that are inaccurate, misleading, uselessly disparaging or conducting to passing-off are prohibited. Comparative advertising is not flatly outlawed, but every attempt unfairly to benefit from someone else's fame is to be deemed contrary to the law.

Sale price under cost is prohibited only to the extent advertising therefor is misleading; the theory is that consumers might sometimes be induced to believe that the cost structure of one of the competitors (be it the one who is advertising or the other ones) is different from what it is in fact. Sales with premiums are prohibited if consumers are misled as to the effective value of the offer.

'Aggressive methods of sale' are prohibited.

Misleading information on the quality, quantity, use or utility of wares, works and services in unlawful, as is the fact to conceal their possible harmful effects or inherent danger.

Lack of legally required information on consumer credits or sales on installment plans, or misleading information on the forms used for these contracts is illegal.

Enticing away the customers of one's competitors is prohibited if it entails inducement to a breach of contract. Also prohibited are the bribery of a competitor's employees and the inducement to disclose or spy out its trade secrets. The use of unlawfully acquired trade secrets is ruled out as well.

The misappropriation of another person's work is also prohibited, under qualifying circumstances, for example whenever it occurs in breach of a fiduciary relationship.

Finally, it is unfair competition to use forms spelling out general conditions and terms that are misleading and detrimental to the customers, inasmuch as they depart from the legal regulations or from the sharing of rights and obligation that corresponds to the nature of the contract. It is also prohibited to violate legal rules or those sanctioned by professional or local usage in the employer–employee relationship.

This impressive catalogue of new wrongs as introduced by the Act of 1986 was intended to be the most sophisticated weapon ever given to traditional small businesses against big warehouses, price-cutting and aggressive retailers. It does not appear to have had a great effect on the business practices of the big retailers nor to have slowed down the withering away of the small retailers.

3. Legal Remedies

The Law on Unfair Competition offers a wide array of remedies to the competitors who have been affected.

First of all, there are the penal sanctions against unfair competition: imprisonment or fine, which are measured according to the general provisions of the Swiss Penal Code. A complaint must be filed to start the criminal prosecution. The rules for standing are similar to the rules which are laid down for filing a civil action.

Further, a civil court may issue an injunction against methods that are deemed to be unfair competition, even if the defendants did not act in bad faith. No fault is required for a final injunction. A preliminary injunction *pendente lite* may be obtained against a bond.

Thirdly, the competitors who have suffered losses may sue the wrongdoer for damages. Fault of the defendants is required. As under the patent law, the plaintiffs can now obtain the restitution of the defendant's profits that are derived from his wrongful activities (Art. 423 CO). On the other hand, a special award of damages may compensate a particularly serious disparagement of the plaintiffs (Art. 49 CO). Swiss law does not know punitive or exemplary damages.

All attorney's fees and judicial costs are usually paid by the losing party. Moreover, a court order may be granted:

- to state the unlawfulness of the unfair practises, and to have this statement published or brought to the attention of the customers in an appropriate manner;
- to put an end to the illegal situation of fact which results from the unfair competition acts;
- to search and destroy or auction the products that are obtained through the unfair practises.

This has been applied, for example, to order the seizure of machines that had been built to exploit trade secrets unduly leaked to the defendants.

Finally, individual plaintiffs, such as the affected competitor or the misled consumer, as well as associations of producers, merchants, or consumers have the right to sue, but not as concerns claims for damages. Consumer associations have the standing to sue if they can prove that one of their members has been affected by the unfair practises; these associations have also the right to sue on their own, although they shall not enjoy the possibility of asking for damages.

B. Law on Cartels and Similar Trade Practises

1. The Law on Cartels

The constitutional basis of the Law on Cartels is to be found in Article 96 of the Federal Constitution of 1999. This provision reads:

'Art. 96 Competition policy
The Confederation shall legislate to fight against economically or socially damaging effects of cartels and other restrictions of competition. It shall take measures:
a) to prevent abuses in price fixing by enterprises and organizations
   of private and public law enjoying a dominant position on the market;
b) against unfair competition.'

This provision has two clear meanings: cartels and similar trade practices are not prohibited per se, and their social or economic nocuous side effects must be contained.

The first Law of 20 December 1962 had followed very closely the constitutional mandate. It did not outlaw the cartels, but gave both private parties and public authorities the legal means to restrain excessive interference by cartels and powerful enterprises in Swiss economic life. Nevertheless, the general feeling about that first law and the practise of authorities thereunder was that it was the most ineffective antitrust law in the Western World; indeed it helped maintain the associative and cooperative ways of Swiss businessmen. It should be recalled that Switzerland as such is a small market of slightly more than 7 million inhabitants and prone to compromise both by necessity and by tradition.

Nevertheless mentalities changed by the beginning of the 1980s. It was perceived that private actions are not instrumental to curb the excesses of the cartel, since only one or two private anticartel suits were filed every year. Therefore the Law on Cartels and similar Trade Practises of 29 December 1985 was enacted to strengthen the administrative remedies and to extend the field of application of the Law. This revision has been made within 9 months in 1995. Three new Federal Acts now purport to enliven the competition within Switzerland:

(a) The (new) Law on Cartels and other Restraints of Competition of 6 October 1995, entered into force 1 July 1996 (S.R. 251);
(b) The Law on Technical Trade Barriers of 6 October 1995, entered into force 1 July 1996 (S.R. 946.51);
(c) The Law on the Internal Market of 6 October 1995, entered into force 1 July 1996 (S.R. 943.02).

A further important text should be mentioned:

(d) The intercantonal treaty on public procurements of 25 November 1994, entered into force on 21 May 1996 (S.R. 172.056.4) with federal guidelines and cantonal regulations relating to them.

Even this act was thought to be ineffective in view of the GATT requirements and the general liberalization of world trade. Therefore, Parliament enacted a new Law on Cartels and other restraints of Trade on 6 October 1995. This Act strengthened the powers of the cartel commission, streamlined the procedure and introduced a merger control *ex ante*. There is now a Bill pending before Parliament proposing the introduction of direct sanctions and a leniency program. Direct sanctions could be immediately pronounced, without having to state a violation of a cartel commission decision. The revised Law will enter into force in 2004.

The law applies to cartels and all agreements restrictive of competition. It also outlaws the misuse of a dominant position. Thus the law encompasses all contracts and agreements or gentlemen's agreements that may influence the market of certain wares and services through a collective limitation of competition, especially by means of regulating the output, the sale or the purchase of wares and of prices and other terms and conditions. Further, businesses which, on their own or through tacitly coordinated action, dominate a given market or decisively influence it are to be considered as organizations similar to cartels. Market influence must be nonetheless stronger for the law to apply, if only one enterprise is involved.

The newly christened Commission on Competition (the former 'Commission of Cartels') shall publish guidelines or regulations for various provisions that, although anticompetitive to a point, may be allowed in some areas where it is desirable to further co-operation between competitors (so-called 'exemption regulations').

Labor unions and agreements relating to labor conditions do not fall within the scope of the Law. The territorial scope of the legislation is Switzerland, the test being influence exerted on the Swiss market. Thus, foreign cartels or merging firms which exert some influence on the Swiss market may be brought to bar within Switzerland. Conversely, export cartels that are active only on foreign markets without exerting influence in Switzerland fall outside the Swiss jurisdiction. The same holds true for foreign cartels.

2. Unlawful Restraints of Competition

The Law on Cartels aims at furthering an 'efficient competition', that is a competition allowing the consumers or buyers to have recourse to a different provider if they so wish, with no or little additional costs. Three standards are applied: behaviour of the competitors at issue; structures of the industry; results of the restraints of competition.

The vertical agreements (between entities of different phases of production and marketing) fall under the Law on Cartels as well as the horizontal agreements (binding entities that are active on the same level of production or marketing). On 18 February 2002, the Commission on cartels handed down a Communication on vertical agreements which parallels the relevant European Union texts, with some minor differences.

According to the law, are unlawful all agreements that notably restrict the competition unless they are justified by economic efficiency, and all agreements that eliminate the competitors. The law itself defines the justifying grounds based on economic efficiency, e.g. the possibility to lower the costs of production or of marketing, to improve the products or the processes of manufacture, to promote R&D or the diffusion of technical or professional skills and knowledge and to exploit resources more rationally.

In exceptional circumstances, the government can authorize an agreement in restraint of competition when the cartel commission has stated that it is unlawful, if prevailing public interests so require.

3. Administrative Authorities and Procedures

The Law establishes a Commission of Cartels. A key provision, Article 23, mandates this authority to help maintain competition through specific inquiries on a given cartel or similar organization. Such an inquiry may be preceded by preliminary researches (Art. 26). The secretariat and/or the Cartel commission can launch an enquiry. If acting alone, the secretariat must seek the agreement of one of the members of the presidency of the Cartel commission (i.e. its president or vice-president). In the same way the secretariat will render the necessary procedural ordinances during the enquiry. The Federal Law on Administrative Procedure is applicable. If the Cartel commission finds a given restriction unlawful, it will render a decision. An appeal may be lodged to the Appeal Commission for Competition and, further, to the Federal Tribunal. There is no specific limitation as to the facts or legal grounds that can be invoked in the appeal before both these review authorities.

The secretariat can also launch a preliminary research. The main difference from a procedural point of view is that the parties have no right of access to the file in preliminary researches.

4. Civil Remedies

Cartels or dominant entities may unduly restrict the competition by third parties, either by prohibiting or making more difficult their entry onto the market, or by restricting their competition, once these third parties are active on the market. Civil actions can be brought against the responsible entities to obtain cease and desist orders, or damages, or accounting for profits. Non pecuniary harm can be compensated. The court may order a party to conclude a contract with the aggrieved party, to the conditions that are usual on this market.

III. PATENTS, TRADEMARKS AND COPYRIGHTS

The field of intellectual property covers various distinct areas: protection of inventions, trademarks and geographical denominations, copyrights, ornamental models, plant varieties and software.

A. *Protection of Inventions*

1. Patent Law

The Swiss law on patents is comparatively recent. Although Switzerland was one of the founders of the Paris Union of 1883 and always ratified the latest versions of this international convention, a full-fledged patent system has existed only since 1907. This belated acknowledgment of the value of the patents for invention in the industrial development process has been used of late as an argument by the proponents of a special system of industrial property, which would be tailored to the needs of developing countries, in derogation from the international conventions. It is obviously impossible here fully to assess the merits of such an argument: suffice it to say that no convincing parallels can be drawn between Switzerland at the turn of this century and the less developed countries of today, because of the considerable differences between national traditions, as well as the changed patterns of world trade and industry.

The present Patent Act of 25 June 1954 was revised on 17 December 1976 to incorporate into Swiss law the European Patent Treaty of 1973 and the Patent Cooperation Treaty of 1970. Hence, new procedures for filing or continuing patent applications under the Munich and PCT conventions have been established. The 1976 Patent Act has also modified the legal definition of inventions that may be patented. The test of non-obviousness shall be applied in lieu of the test of so-called 'inventive level', to determine whether an invention deserves protection. The test of novelty with respect to the state of the art has been remodeled, to keep it in line with recent developments: no objection founded on a disclosure to the public within six months before the filing or priority date may be opposed, if the disclosure results from an 'obvious abuse' to the detriment of the inventor. This will be the case, for example, whenever disclosure has been made possible through breach of confidence.

Patent protection lasts twenty years from the date of filing. The condition of the continued validity of the patent is the payment of annuities, which increase with time.

Further, the Patent Act has been revised in 1994, 1995 and 1998. A Bill for the protection of biotechnology through patents for inventions is pending. This Bill is patterned after the European Directive on the same topic. It meets with some scepticism. Still, for national patents, the main features of the Patent Act of 1954 have been left unchanged. All inventions are subject to a formal examination only.

An interesting feature of Swiss patent law is the right for bona fide third parties to continue using the patented invention without even taking a license from the patentee, provided that the third party had already put the invention to work in his business located in Switzerland, or taken special preparatory steps towards this aim before the filing or priority date.

Remedies against patent infringements are:

– an injunction to cease all acts of infringement;
– a court order to seize and destroy infringing apparatus and to auction counterfeited wares, to estimate damages, or to account of defendants' profits.

Punitive damages or treble damages are unknown to Swiss law; nevertheless, if the plaintiffs cannot prove the amount of their losses, the court may award a sum equal to reasonable royalties for a license under the infringed patent. An injunction *pendente lite* may be issued against a bond filed by plaintiffs, if there appears to be sufficient grounds for the action.

2. Protection of Know-how and Trade Secrets

Switzerland's industries often protect their inventions as trade secrets. There is a long-standing tradition of secrecy, for example, in the chemical and pharmaceutical industry. Therefore, with respect to trade secrets, the following provisions of the Swiss Penal Code are worth mentioning: Article 162 of the Penal Code provides that the person who discloses an industrial or commercial trade secret which he has a duty to keep confidential, and the person who benefits from this disclosure shall be punished by a fine or imprisonment, both of which are determined according to the general provisions of the Code. The action stands and falls with the filing and the withdrawal of a private complaint by the injured businessman.

Articles 4 lilt. c and 6 of the Law on Unfair Competition make it an offense for a competitor to entice employers or agents to let him know secrets or to search for these within the competitor's business, and a second offense to use or further disclose trade secrets that have been otherwise unveiled against good faith.

Finally, Article 273 of the Penal Code makes it a felony to disclose a trade secret to a foreign authority, private enterprise or to their agents; even the attempt to uncover a trade secret with such an aim is a felony. In serious cases, the wrongdoer may be sentenced to confinement of up to twenty years. In any event, the convict may be sentenced additionally to a fine of up to CHF 40,000. This stringent protection of trade secrets against foreign states and businesses should be seen as aiming to protect Switzerland's public interests rather than the industry's private equity in its know-how. Nevertheless, the end result thereof is a splendid legal armor against all spies and pirates preying upon other people's secret innovations.

B. Trademarks

1. Trademark Law

The former Law on Trademarks, Geographic Denominations, and Mentions of Industrial Awards dated back to 26 September 1890. The main characteristics of the New Trademark Law passed on 28 August 1992 are as follows. Protections exist for trademarks that are affixed on products or packaging of all sorts and for service marks, as well as for three-dimensional marks. Registration is open to individual persons or legal entities. Further, Swiss and foreign public corporations that conduct trade of industrial activities may have their marks registered.

Registration is equally possible for so-called 'collective trademarks', that is, certification marks which manufacturers' or dealers' associations may allow their members to affix to their wares, so as to evidence the origin or quality of the products, in compliance with industry regulations, or other specifications of production controlled by association.

Registration is a prerequisite for protection under the relevant sections of the Trademark Law. The right to a particular mark in case of conflict between two businesses shall rest upon priority of registration. The new Law is premised on the constitutive effect of filing (first-to-file system). A transitory period of two years (until 1 April 1995) had been open to register trademarks acquired through use.

No defensive mark may be registered. If a mark is not in use during five consecutive years, a court can order that the mark be struck from the Register at the request of any interested party.

Protection of the mark extends only to its use on products identical or similar to the wares for which it has been registered. There is now enlarged protection for the world-renowned marks outside specific categories of merchandises that are indicated in the Register.

Trademarks can be freely assigned, even without the business which uses them. Licenses are possible as well, to the extent that the consumers shall not be deceived in any manner on the quality or origin of the wares.

2. Company Names

The company names, firm's marks and other signs which help identify the enterprise as such (rather than its products) can be protected under the special provisions of

Article 956 of the Code of Obligations against abuse of company name, as well as under the provisions of Articles 28 and 29 of the Civil Code on protection of the name and the economic personality. Remedies under competition law also lie against competitors.

3. Geographic Denominations

The protection of geographic denominations rests upon the general provisions of Article 46 *et seq.* of the Trademark Law, and upon the more specific provisions of various acts concerning food products, cheese and wine labels, watches, public coats of arms, emblems of international organizations, etc. Switzerland is a party to the Madrid Agreement of the repression of false indications of source on wares, and to the Stresa Convention on the use of denominations for cheese, but not to the Lisbon Treaty on Appellations of Origin. To date, six bilateral treaties of similar content ensure protection of geographic denomination (the Federal Republic of Germany, France, Spain, Czechoslovakia, Portugal and Hungary).

Marks and Names have been protected against cybersquatting by a few individual decisions of the courts, as well as under the UDRP procedure.

C. Copyright Law

The Swiss Law on Copyrights of 1922 was amended in 1955 to ensure conformity between the national law and the Berne Convention of 1886, as revised in Rome (1928) and Brussels (1948). There have been five drafts for a new Law (1971, 1974, 1984, 1987 and 1989), and preparatory works have continued for thirty years. A new law was adopted by Parliament on 9 October 1992. Swiss law now provides satisfactory solutions to most of the legal questions raised by new technologies. However, in order to apply the WIPO Copyright Treaty and the Performers' Rights Treaty of 1996, Switzerland is preparing a revision of the 1992 law.

The works that are protected encompass all the traditional works of literature, music and fine arts, as well as photographic and scientific works, geographical maps, choreography, architecture, and computer programs.

There is a modest requirement of originality for the legal protection. Many theories have been submitted to circumscribe this requisite of originality. In practise, it may be difficult to obtain protection for sheer compilations of scientific or commercial data, as well as for architectonic drawings devoid of any individuality. On the whole, nonetheless, the condition of originality seldom constitutes a bar to protection.

Protection is warranted in two different areas. The financial rewards obtained through utilization of the works shall be equitably shared by the authors, but their ideal interests also deserve proper consideration. Thus, the copyright always belongs to the author within the meaning of the law, so that employers organized as corporations never acquire original title to the works of their employees; they may, however, receive derivative title on the financial side of the copyrights. Generally, a complete assignment of copyrights in a given work is excluded by law, since the author must retain his moral privileges: the right to integral reproduction or publication of his work; the right to amend his work (if there are no contractual commitments to the contrary); the right to be named as author; the rights of access to the work in order to make a copy thereof; the right to obtain restitution of his work free of charge, if the owner thereof wants to destroy or otherwise dispose of it.

This impressive listing of so-called 'moral' privileges is by no means exhaustive, since the courts and the authors may further develop the protection of authors' ideal interests on the grounds of Articles 27 and 28 of the Civil Code (protection of personality) or of Article 9 para. 1 Copyright Act of 1992. On the other hand, financial rights may be freely assigned to another physical or legal person. The protection lasts seventy years after the death of the author, unless the work is either anonymous or published under a pseudonym, in which case the protection ceases seventy years after publication. If there are two or several authors, the time limit is counted since the last collaborator's death. The new Law introduces full protection for interpreters and for radio, television and phonogram producers, so as to enable Switzerland to ratify the Rome Convention. Five collecting right societies administer the financial rights of the authors, under supervision of the government. Their tariffs are freely negotiated with the users' representatives. If no agreement is reached, there is a decision by a standing Arbitration committee, then appeal to the Federal Tribunal.

D. Designs and Models

Parliament has passed on 5 October 2001 a new Law on the Protection of Designs. The protection is patterned after the European Parliament and Council Directive on the Legal Protection of Designs of 1998. Both novelty and a quantum of originality are required. A grace period of 12 months is granted for the novelty. A design which is purely dictated by the technical function of the product is not protectable.

A register of design is kept. The design can be registered for 25 years at most, by periods of 5 years. The first-to-file system is applied to determine who has the right onto the design.

The right of exclusivity applies as against any industrial personal or industrial use. There is a defense of personal use in given circumstances, against the payment of a reasonable royalty. This privilege can be transferred only with the entity using the design.

The law also provides for stiff criminal penalties and for the assistance by the Customs in order to seize counterfeiting wares. The exclusive licensee can file a suit for infringement.

E. The Semi-conductor Topography ('Chips')

A special law has been passed on 9 October 1992. There have been 16 valid registrations under this scheme in 10 years, two of which were stricken off. The paucity of precedents implies that the system is not really of any use to the industry.

SELECTED BIBLIOGRAPHY

A. Commercial Law

1. Partnerships and corporations

Böckli, P. *Schweizerisches Aktienrecht*, 2nd edn., Zurich 1996.
Forstmoser, P., A. Meier–Hayoz and P. Nobel, *Schweizerisches Aktienrecht*, Bern 1996.
Meier–Hayoz, A. and P. Forstmoser, *Schweizerisches Gesellschaftsrecht*, 9th edn., Bern 2004.

2. Securities

Boemle, M., *Wertpapier des Zahlungs- und Kreditverkehrs sowie der Kapitalanlage*, 8th edn., Zurich 1991.
Meier–Hayoz, A. and H.C. von der Crone, *Wertpapierrecht*, 2nd edn., Bern 2000.

B. Unfair Competition

Von Büren, R. and L. David (eds.), *Schweizerisches Immaterialgüter- und Wettbewerbsrecht V/1: Wettbewerbsrecht*, Basle/Frankurt am Main 1994.
Romy, I., E. Wollmann Gautier and M. Wemli (ed. F. Dessemontet), *Concurrence déloyale: textes législatifs et répertoire des arrêts fédéraux et cantonaux*, Lausanne 1989.

C. Cartels

Von Büren, R. and L. David (eds.), *Schweizerisches Immaterialgüter- und Wettbewerbsrecht V/2: Kartellrecht*, Basle/Frankurt am Main 2000.
Drolshammer, J.I., *Wettbewerbsrecht*, Bern 1997.
Homburger, E., *Kommentar zum schweizerischen Kartellgesetz*, Zurich 1996.

D. Intellectual Property

Dessemontet, F., *Intellectual Property Law in Switzerland*, The Hague/London/Boston 2000.
Pedrazzini, M.M., *Patent- und Lizenzvertragsrecht*, 2nd edn., Bern 1987.
Troller, A., *Immaterialgüterrecht*, 3rd edn., Basel 1983–1985.
Troller, K., *Précis du droit suisse des biens immatériels : droit des brevets, droit des dessins et modèles, droit d'auteur, droit de l'infomatique, droit des marques, droit de la concurrence déloyale*, Basel 2001.

Chapter 11
Banking Law

Rolf H. Weber*

I. PUBLIC BANKING LAW

A. Constitutional Basis

Switzerland is a federal state composed of 26 cantons, and has a constitutional division of legislative authority between the federal government and the cantons. In principle, the federal government is authorized to enact laws only in areas specifically enumerated in the Constitution.

Banks, insurance companies and stock exchanges fall within the competence of the federal legislative authority (Art. 98 of the Swiss Constitution of 2000). In the past (until 1997), as long as the federal government had not exercised its authority in the field of securities law, the cantons were free to regulate the stock exchanges. Now, however, cantonal laws no longer play a role in the banking, insurance, and securities markets.

Furthermore, the federal government is responsible for regulating monetary and foreign exchange policy (Art. 99 Cons.), and implementing appropriate measures to maintain a well-balanced economic environment (Art. 100 Cons.). It is also responsible for the legal framework related to cross-border business activities (Art. 101 Cons.).

The freedom of individuals and enterprises to start a business and to enter into commercial relationships is guaranteed (Art. 27 Cons.). Governmental regulation is only possible to the extent that a specific provision is stipulated in the Constitution (Art. 94 IV) for this, as is the case for the banking, insurance, and stock exchange sectors (Art. 98).

B. Legal Sources

The Swiss regulatory system is based on two pillars, namely the laws and ordinances enacted by the legislature, constituting the legal framework, and self-regulation by private organizations. The second pillar is of major importance particularly

---

* Dr. iur., Professor of International Commercial Law at the University of Zurich and practicing attorney in Zurich.

F. Dessemontet and T. Ansay (eds), Introduction to Swiss Law, 197–216.

with regard to stock exchanges, which are required to ensure that their operations, administration, and supervision are established in a manner that is adequate for their business activities. The most important laws in the banking sector are the following:

1. National Bank Law

According to Article 99, paragraph 2 of the Constitution, an independent central bank must be established in Switzerland, to be responsible for the execution of monetary and foreign exchange policy. The Swiss central bank is called the Swiss National Bank. Details are set forth in the National Bank Act of 1953/78, which regulates the issuing of banknotes on behalf of the federal government, the organization of the National Bank, its fields of activity and the instruments to be used to fulfill its functions and purposes.

The National Bank, founded in 1905, is a joint-stock company with a share capital of CHF 50 million. The majority of the shares are held by public entities (particularly by the cantons), although shares may also be acquired by private persons. The Bank Council consists of forty members; twenty-five members, including the chairman, are appointed by the Federal Council, and fifteen members are elected at the general meeting of shareholders. At the organizational level, three directors appointed by the Federal Council conduct the business. Aspects of private law do not play a major role in the National Bank's structure and organization since the National Bank is obligated to serve public interests. For example, the dividend is limited to 6 per cent. Additional amounts, depending on the profit, are paid out to the cantons.

The National Bank issues the country's banknotes (Art. 1 of the National Bank Act; further details are set forth in the Federal Act on Currency and Legal Tender of 1999) and strives for stable monetary and foreign exchange policies for the benefit of the country (Art. 2 of the National Bank Act). Significantly, the National Bank is involved in monitoring the liquidity of the commercial banking system, and collects statistical data to be used by government agencies in general (Art. 7 of the National Bank Act).

The main instruments available to the National Bank in connection with the implementation of its policies consist in (1) the discount and collateral loan policy which influences lending rates and the money supply through the official discount rate, and (2) the open market policy through which it influences the money supply by restricting or extending purchases of commercial paper on the capital market, foreign currencies or gold. Further instruments are used in extraordinary situations. In particular, these situations are concerned with problems with regarding trade or monetary balance. This includes the minimum reserve policy, regulation of bond issues on the capital markets, control of interest rates, and possible credit restrictions. However, these instruments have not played a significant role in recent decades. The National Bank may also restrict capital imports or exports in order to stabilize the economy, but the current monetary situation does not require the use of such instruments.

The National Bank also exercises clearing functions for the private banking system in Switzerland, and established Swiss Interbank Clearing (SIC) – operated by Telekurs AG, a subsidiary of the major Swiss banks – as a money transfer system for the banks. Since Switzerland is not an EU member state and the National Bank is not connected to TARGET (Trans-European Automated Real-time Gross Settlement

Express Transfer), Swiss banks founded Swiss Euro Clearing Bank GmbH in Frankfurt, charging Telekurs with operating the euro/SIC system.

The National Bank also acts as banker to the federal government. It may further enter into any banking business which it thinks fit to support the pursuit of its functions.

2. Banking Law

The legal basis of the banking business is the Banking Act of 1934, which has been constantly amended and adapted to new requirements. Since banking is a rather 'technical' business, a substantial part of the relevant regulations is contained in the implementing Banking Ordinance and the Foreign Banks Ordinance issued by the Federal Council, as well as in many other ordinances and regulations dealing with specific topics. Furthermore, the numerous circulars of the Federal Banking Commission are another important legal source for the conduct of business activities.

According to Article 1 of the Banking Act, any person, partnership or legal entity, borrowing and lending money, i.e. any party operating on the basis of the difference in interest rates, as well any similar enterprise (such as finance companies) is subject to this Act.

3. Stock Exchange Law

The main legal source in the field of securities regulation is the Federal Act on Stock Exchanges and Securities Trading (Stock Exchange Act) of 1995, in force since 1 February 1997, and 1 January 1998 (takeover rules), respectively. The Stock Exchange Act reflects three developments, namely (1) replacement of previous stock exchange laws of the cantons, (2) establishment of the world's first fully electronic stock exchange, and (3) most importantly, the move from a mainly organizational to a more transactional regulatory regime.

4. Investment Fund Law

The Federal Investment Fund Act, enacted in 1993, regulates the activities of Swiss investment funds (i.e. funds whose management is domiciled in Switzerland). The scope of the Investment Fund Act is more restrictive than regulations in other countries. Indeed it only covers the promotion of open-end funds that are organized as unincorporated collective investment agreements and are publicly advertised). However, investment funds cannot be established in the form of corporations (with variable capital). And a corporation with a similar statutory purpose is subject to specific stock exchange listing rules. Moreover, foreign investment funds organized in any form (including corporations) in accordance with their respective legislation may be authorized to distribute their certificates in Switzerland.

The Investment Fund Act distinguishes – apart from special in-house bank funds – between the most common securities funds, other funds (e.g. funds with higher risks that are therefore obligated to demonstrate greater transparency), real estate funds, and mortgage funds. According to the Investment Fund Act, the fund management must be legally independent of the custodian bank. In contrast to former legal regulations, the new concept of the Act no longer greatly restricts the fund management in its investment decisions, but it does require the fund's policy to be more transparent, for example obliging the fund management company to publish a prospectus for each fund and to regularly inform investors about the fund's financial situation.

5. Other Legal Sources

Private insurance business in Switzerland is regulated by the Federal Act on the Supervision of Private Insurance Companies of 1978, as amended (currently being completely revised). The main purpose of this Act is to protect insured persons. Combining banking and insurance activities in the same group of companies has raised new questions, particularly given that a special supervisory system is in place for the insurance industry. A group of experts has recommended integrating insurance supervision into banking supervision, but the future of this proposal is still unclear.

Another Federal Act of 1930 regulates the so-called central mortgage bond banks, special institutions that issue long-term bonds for the financing of mortgages by mortgage banks. This Act is now only of minor economic importance.

Furthermore, the Swiss Penal Code contains a number of provisions which are relevant for the banking business, such as:

- Price manipulation: The Stock Exchange Act has introduced a specific criminal provision regarding price manipulation. It makes illegal any practises on financial markets undertaken with the intent of influencing the price of securities listed in Switzerland, i.e. traded on a Swiss exchange market, in order to obtain an illegitimate profit. The crime may be committed by securities dealers or their customers who knowingly disseminate false or misleading information or forecasts relating to listed securities.
- Insider trading: Since 1988, the use or transfer of confidential information by a member of the board of directors, management or auditing entity, by the agent of a company or any affiliate (parent/subsidiary) thereof, member of an authority or governmental agency or an auxiliary person to the aforementioned persons, with the intention of realizing an unjustified gain, is considered as a criminal market misconduct (Art. 161 Penal Code). In this context, confidential information means information whose publication may materially affect the price of securities of a company listed on a Swiss stock exchange market. The person receiving such confidential information and misusing it to procure unjustified enrichment to himself or a third party is also considered to be committing a criminal offense.
- Money laundering and lack of vigilance in financial operations: From August 1990, the Swiss Penal Code (Art. 305bis and Art. 305ter) made money laundering a criminal offense. One who performs an act that may serve to prevent determining the origin of, tracing or confiscating funds that, as the offender knows, or should presume, have a criminal origin, is punishable by imprisonment or a

fine. Furthermore, in order to strengthen vigilance in the financial sector, the law stipulates that one who accepts, deposits, invests or assists in the transfer of funds from third parties on a professional basis and fails to ascertain the identity of the beneficial owner with the due diligence required under the given circumstances is punishable for lack of due diligence in finance operations.

6. International Harmonization

For many decades Switzerland has been actively participating in efforts aimed at international harmonization in banking and securities law. The following deserves especial mention:

- Switzerland is a member of the Basle Committee under the auspices of the Bank for International Settlement (BIS). This Committee released the Basle Capital Accord in 1988 (amended and now again in revision) and the Market Risk Accord in 1995. Furthermore, Switzerland has adhered to the Core Principles of the Basle Committee of 1997 for the Surveillance of Banking and Financial Systems. In general, Switzerland is incorporating international principles in its own legislation.
- Switzerland is actively engaged in the preparation of harmonization principles in the securities markets under the auspices of the International Organization of Securities Commissions (IOSCO). The guidelines concern the trading of securities and the establishment of collective investment schemes being transferred into the national legislation.
- Switzerland is a member of the Financial Action Task Force on Money Laundering (FATF). With its substantial financial and banking market, Switzerland has a major interest in avoiding money laundering and criminal activities in the financial markets.

Under the General Agreement on Trade in Services (GATS), each WTO member, including Switzerland, is required to accord most-favored nation treatment to services and service suppliers of other WTO members (Art. II para. 1). The GATS specifically applies to financial services. Moreover, the member states of the WTO have negotiated additional protocols to the GATS with respect to financial services; the key document is the Fifth Protocol on Financial Services of 12 December 1997, together with the annexed Schedules of Specific Commitments and Exemption Lists, which came into force in Switzerland on 1 March 1999. Switzerland has adjusted its national legislation as necessary. Previous policies applying the approach of measured reciprocity and thereby introducing limited access to home markets for foreign financial products and financial institutions have now been overruled by the Fifth Protocol. Apart from specific restrictions on trading services, the reciprocal approach has lost its importance.

According to Article 23[quinquies] of the Banking Act and Article 37 of the Stock Exchange Act, authorization of a foreign stock exchange or of a stock exchange controlled by foreign persons may be refused if the country in which the foreign stock exchange has its registered office, or where the controlling foreign persons are domiciled, does not provide Swiss stock exchanges genuine access to their markets and does not offer the same competitive opportunities as it does to local stock exchanges. This reciprocity requirement is no longer applied in respect of enterprises originating from countries that are members of the WTO that have ratified the Fifth Protocol on Financial Services. With regard to other countries, the practise of the Federal Banking Commission is quite liberal.

The same rules also apply in respect of the authorization and supervision of securities dealers.

However, since Switzerland is not a member of the European Union, the single passport principle does not directly apply, and foreign businesses must make the appropriate application.

C. Market Participants

1. Federal Banking Commission

Both the Swiss banking business and the Swiss securities markets are supervised by the Federal Banking Commission (FBC). This Commission is composed of seven to eleven members, all experts in their fields and independent of the banks they supervise. However, the chairman is the only to be employed full-time. The FBC is supported by a permanent secretariat staffed by qualified professionals. The FBC is an independent regulatory agency and is not part of the general administration of the federal government.

The powers of the FBC, as laid down in the Banking Act and Stock Exchange Act, are quite broad. The FBC is entitled to request comprehensive information from private market participants about business activities and financial data. However, the FBC does not supervise all details through its own secretariat. Each bank must have external auditors, approved by the FBC, who collect information and report their findings to the FBC. This two-pillar approach may occasionally create conflicts of interest for an external auditor (loyalty to the client, i.e. the bank, or compliance with the request of the FBC). Nevertheless, the system has functioned properly during recent decades.

In particular, the FBC has a duty to judge whether the banks conduct their business in a sound and prudent way and whether the bank officers deserve a good reputation. The FBC can take numerous measures, such as issuing a specific warning or fine, requesting replacement of a director, revocation of the license or even closing down of the business.

2. Banks

By legal definition, the business of a bank consists in accepting deposits from the public and extending loans on its own account and at its own risk to third parties/entities in order to earn its income from the spread between the interest paid to the depositors and the interest received from the debtors. The Banking Act partly distinguishes between savings banks, private banks, cantonal banks and banks under foreign control. Despite the fact that banks have been pursuing activities for a long time in many other areas of the financial sector (i.e. asset management, private equity, investment banking), no separation exists under Swiss law between commercial banking and investment banking businesses. Consequently, most securities dealers in Switzerland are banks.

(1) The conduct of banking activities is subject to authorization and supervision by the Federal Banking Commission. A license is granted if the conditions set forth in the Banking Act are met, in particular:

(a) Organizational requirements. Swiss banks must have a place of business in Switzerland, fully paid-in capital of at least CHF 10 million, a clearly defined scope of business in the articles of incorporation and the by-laws, adequate internal organization, appropriate risk management procedures and an effective internal control system (Art. 3 of the Banking Act). An important aspect is the precise scope of business operations. Nevertheless, a bank is free to establish several entities with specific purposes, whereby the business is supervised on a consolidated basis. The Federal Banking Commission does not consider electronic banking or internet banking a special field of business but rather as part of the general banking business. Banks are therefore not required to ask for a special license in this regard. Recent rules, established in a circular of the FBC, only request banks to observe particular care in creating an electronic banking relationship. This implies that Switzerland is not planning to follow the EU directive of 2000 on e-money institutions.

(b) Directors, managers and qualifying shareholders. The Banking Act explicitly requires that the directors and managing officers of a Swiss bank must have good reputations and offer assurance of proper business conduct. In interpreting the term 'proper business conduct' (Art. 3 II, Banking Act), the Banking Commission makes extensive use of its discretion.

Likewise, qualifying shareholders of a bank who hold 10 per cent or more of the bank's capital or voting rights, are – similar to the regulations of the European Union – also subject to the test of 'proper business conduct'.

The Banking Act relies on the principle of strict separation between the management and board of directors, thus aiming at a supervision of management within the organization.

(c) Particularities for banks controlled by foreign shareholders. A bank domiciled in Switzerland is considered to be under foreign control if one or more foreigners directly or indirectly hold qualifying shareholdings exceeding 50 per cent of the voting rights, or if foreigners otherwise exercise a controlling influence on the bank. The Banking Act makes it clear that a foreign bank incorporating a subsidiary in Switzerland should be aware that this subsidiary will be subject to Swiss banking supervisory rules. In particular, the license will be granted to a foreign-controlled subsidiary if (i) the home country of the foreign bank grants reciprocal treatment to Swiss banks establishing banking operations under its jurisdiction, (ii) the foreign-controlled bank does not choose a corporate name suggesting that the bank is controlled by Swiss persons, (iii) the foreign-controlled bank complies with the information requirements of the Swiss National Bank, and (iv) in the case of a financial conglomerate, adequate supervision on a consolidated basis is ensured.

Special rules apply if a foreign bank plans to establish a branch or representative office in Switzerland. In particular, the Federal Banking Commission will look at the supervision of the bank in its home country and the existence of reasonable internal rules and regulations defining the organization and the scope of its business in Switzerland.

It is also important to note that the Banking Act has been recently amended with regard to international cooperation in respect of consolidated supervision and now allows foreign supervisory agencies to operate controls in loco over Swiss subsidiaries of foreign banks subject to their jurisdiction (Art. 23^{sexies}). The Banking Act also allows foreign-controlled banks in Switzerland to make data available to the foreign parent company without violating Swiss banking secrecy rules, to the extent that such disclosure is strictly necessary for the purposes of a consolidated supervision.

(2) The conditions of the original license must be fulfilled during the entire lifetime of the bank. Specific aspects are:

(a) Proper business: With regard to the personnel, the key elements are the good reputation of directors and management and the proper conduct of business by the bank.

(b) Risk management and liquidity: From a financial perspective, Article 4 of the Banking Act requests that Swiss banks provide for an adequate relationship between (i) their equity (own resources such as capital and certain reserves) and total liabilities (capital fund ratio), and (ii) their liquid assets and easily marketable assets on the one hand and their short-term liabilities (cash liquidity ratio) on the other. In this respect, the Banking Ordinance provides for (i) detailed capital adequacy requirements which largely correspond to those of the Basle Committee on Banking Regulations and Supervisory Practices, as well as (ii) detailed accounting and consolidation rules which apply in addition to the accounting and consolidation rules set forth under Swiss corporate law. Furthermore, the Banking Act imposes restrictions on the extent of the liabilities of any one customer (cluster risk) and prohibits the granting of unduly favorable loans to directors, members of management and important shareholders.

(c) Accounting: The financial statements of a bank are subject to specific reviews by qualified external auditors who are requested by law to assist the Federal Banking Commission in its supervisory activity. The auditors' reports for banks are therefore generally much more detailed than those for other corporations. However, it must be acknowledged that this system could lead to potential conflicts of interest, the auditors having a duty to their client to faithfully and carefully perform their mandate.

(3) The Banking Act also contains rules relating to moratorium, bankruptcy and reorganization; in a partial revision of the Act, adjustments have been made in line with international trends. The Act does not yet require the establishment of a special 'guarantee fund' in favor of small depositors. Nevertheless, this disadvantage is not too serious since the Swiss Bankers Association, together with the Swiss banks, have established a private fund structure which guarantees depositors quick repayment of deposits not exceeding CHF 30,000. Furthermore, the Banking Act deals with the civil responsibility of founders, directors, managers, auditors, liquidators, etc. of a Swiss bank, as well as with the consequences of banking secrecy violations.

3. Securities Dealers

The Ordinance to the Stock Exchange Act defines five categories of securities dealers: (1) underwriters (making primary offerings of securities to the public on a professional basis), (2) derivatives houses (creating and offering derivatives to the public on a professional basis) and (3) broker-dealers constituting three sub-categories, namely (i) dealers trading on their own account, (ii) market makers and (iii) brokers buying and selling in their own name but for the account of third parties.

In order to achieve equal treatment of all market participants, the requirements for obtaining the securities dealer's license are similar to those for a banking license. However, the law includes for some specific requierements. The minimum capital requirement for securities dealers is CHF 1.5 million (compared with CHF 10 million for banks). In addition, securities dealers must observe the rules of conduct issued by the Swiss Bankers Association with regard to the duties of information, due diligence and loyalty towards the customer. Even though the Stock Exchange Act does not specifically require strict separation between the board of directors and management, the FBC has established a practice making this separation necessary, unless the organization is so small that such separation is not feasible.

4. Stock Exchanges

The main stock exchange activities are conducted by an association which operates the SWX Swiss Exchange in Zurich and is also a partner in international joint ventures (Eurex Zurich/Frankfurt, Virt-X Zurich/London). A small telephone trading system exists in Berne.

The SWX Swiss Exchange is incorporated as an association constituted in accordance with Articles 60–79 of the Civil Code; management and supervision are in accordance with civil law. The members of this association are banks and securities dealers. A special supervisory authority dealing with reporting obligations under the disclosure rules for shareholdings has been established.

Based upon the principle of the Stock Exchange Act, this organization of securities trading should remain the responsibility of the market participants concerned. Several ordinances and regulations have been enacted by the competent bodies, namely:

- Ordinance of the Federal Council on Stock Exchanges and Securities Trading
- Ordinance of the Federal Banking Commission on Stock Exchanges and Securities Trading
- Ordinance of the Takeover Board on Public Takeover Offers
- Regulations of the Takeover Board on its organization and competencies
- Several Circulars ('Rundschreiben') of the Federal Banking Commission (92/1, 96/3, 96/6, 97/2, 98/2)
- Guidelines of the Swiss Bankers Association on certain rules of conduct for securities dealers.

In particular, the SWX Swiss Exchange has the following functions:

(a) Admission of securities dealers: The Swiss Exchange has issued regulations regarding the admission, duties and exclusion of securities dealers. According to Article 7 of the Stock Exchange Act, these regulations shall reflect the principle of equal treatment of market participants. The SWX Swiss Exchange must inform the FBC before admitting foreign securities dealers. Since Switzerland ratified the Fifth Protocol to the GATS (General Agreement on Trade in Services) in 1998, admission of foreign securities dealers has been simplified. The SWX Swiss Exchange has established an internal supervisory and controlling body for complaints raised by securities dealers.

(b) Listing of securities: In 1996, the Swiss Exchange issued regulations on the listing of securities which contain provisions relating to (i) the admission and negotiability of securities, (ii) the information to be provided by listed companies to investors and (iii) the internationally recognized accounting standards which must be complied with by listed companies. These listing rules have been amended several times, particularly in 2000, to be in line with prevailing European standards.

(c) Organization and trade: The Swiss Exchange has issued regulations designed to organize the market to achieve efficiency and transparency. The extremely detailed rules on the disclosure of acquisition or sale of important participations are particularly noteworthy.

D. Transaction Rules

1. Securities Offerings

(1) An offering of shares can be a primary offering or a secondary offering. Primary offerings involve the creation and distribution of newly-issued shares, whereas secondary offerings involve the sale of existing shares. Unless the shares are placed among a specified, small circle of investors (private placement) a prospectus must be made available to investors in both cases. Often, the issuing of new shares and their distribution to the public is accompanied by the sales of already existing shares in the market.

The law does not specifically define the concept of private placement. However, under the Banking Act and the Federal Investment Fund Act, offerings made to a circle of a maximum of twenty persons are considered to qualify as a private offering. If more than twenty persons are approached in the context of a promotional action, the offering is likely to be deemed public.

In the context of a public offering outside the SWX Swiss Exchange, a prospectus pursuant to Article 652a of the Swiss Code of Obligations must be issued. However, the information to be contained in this prospectus is quite limited (contents of the entry in the commercial register, existing amount and structure of the share capital, provisions in the articles of incorporation concerning an authorized or conditional increase of capital, number of benefit certificates and specification of the rights associated therewith, the last annual financial statements and consolidated financial statements together with the auditors' report, dividends paid within the last five years or since the date of incorporation, any resolution concerning the issuance of new shares). If the shares are offered on the SWX Swiss Exchange, then the stricter listing and disclosure requirements of the listing rules apply.

Usually, the share offering involves investment banks subscribing securities on a firm commitment basis, thus assuming the risk of the distribution. The main point to be agreed in the underwriting agreement between the issuer (or selling shareholder) and the investment banks is the subscription price, which is not determined until just before the offering takes place since it must be in relation to current market conditions. Therefore, the underwriting agreement is usually finalized and signed on the day before the effective date of the offering. Until this point, the relationship between the parties is usually governed by a letter of intent or engagement letter that is for the most part a non-binding agreement. However, parties have started to sometimes attach a standard underwriting agreement to the engagement letter according to which the final agreement will be substantially in line with the attachment.

(2) Public offerings of bonds require publication of a prospectus pursuant to Article 1156 of the Code of Obligations. If the bonds are listed, additional information must be provided in the listing prospectus as required by the listing rules. Notes are usually medium-term paper with a maturity of five to seven years and privately placed, in most cases with clients of the syndicate banks. In recent years, medium-term note programs have become quite common, allowing an issuer to issue medium-term paper with a maturity of up to five years in several tranches and on several stock exchanges. Unless the listing rules of the SWX Swiss Exchange apply, the issue and placement of notes is regulated by Convention XIX of the Swiss Bankers Association, which provides for particular prospectus information.

Likewise, offerings of bonds and notes are usually purchased by a syndicate of banks which will place them either on the stock exchange or with a closed circle of investors, thus bearing the risk of distribution.

(3) Derivatives may be listed on the SWX Swiss Exchange, provided the issuer is a licensed Swiss bank subject to the Banking Act, a licensed Swiss securities dealer subject to the Stock Exchange Act, or the issuer is subject to comparable foreign supervision. The same concept applies to derivative securities entitling purchases of shares or bonds issued by the issuer of such derivatives. Even though the contents and the documentation of OTC derivative securities may vary from product to product, the use of international market standards in Switzerland has become increasingly common; in particular, the ISDA Master Agreements together with their schedules are increasingly popular. The main purpose of these agreements is to reduce capital adequacy requirements for the banks on the one hand and to balance risks on the other hand with far-reaching netting clauses. With respect to the enforceability of such clauses in the event of a bankruptcy, the recently revised Federal Act on Debt Enforcement and Bankruptcy now provides for automatic termination of all transactions involving financial futures, swaps and options, which can be valued based on market or stock exchange prices as at the time of the opening of the bankruptcy, thus preventing any cherry-picking by bankruptcy administrators in enforcing individual rights of the bankrupt debtor. However, since the aforementioned Master Agreements are generally subject to English or New York law, the enforceability of their clauses, in particular their netting clauses, under Swiss law must always be checked.

2. Disclosure of Holdings

According to Artcile 20 of the Stock Exchange Act, shareholders must report the acquisition and/or disposal of equity participations in a legal entity if certain thresholds are met. Disclosure is required if a title owner or a group of title owners acquires or disposes of equity participations and thereby reaches, exceeds or falls below the limits of 5 per cent, 10 per cent, $33\frac{1}{3}$ per cent, 50 per cent or $66\frac{2}{3}$ per cent of the voting rights of the company in question. Some thresholds correspond to specific minority rights (in particular, 10 per cent of capital stock gives the right to call for a shareholders' meeting, the right to initiate a special audit, the right to file for dissolution of the company) or majority quorums ($66\frac{2}{3}$ per cent of the votes and absolute majority of the par value present at the shareholders meeting allow important decisions to be taken as described in Art. 704 CO) under Swiss stock corporation law. The term 'acquisition and disposal' includes all types of equity transfers including share exchanges, donations, inheritances, conversions of shares and usufructuary rights.

The disclosure obligation concerns equity participations. Since most legal entities listed on the Swiss Exchange are stock corporations, in practise all substantial share transactions must be disclosed. The key element is the voting right, not the capital amount; therefore, all transactions which have the effect of conferring voting rights relating to equity securities (for example in the business of securities lending and repurchase agreements) are subject to the disclosure obligation.

Furthermore, after long discussions, the legislator has decided that the acquisition of call options and conversion rights are subject to the disclosure obligation, provided the terms of the options give a right to physical delivery of the underlying equity securities. However, a de minimis exception exists: The thresholds mentioned apply separately for equity securities and derivative instruments, meaning that a person may own 4.9 per cent of the shares of a stock corporation, as well as options granting the right to have physical delivery of another 4.9 per cent of shares of the same corporation without being forced to disclose such holdings until the time of the actual conversion of the options.

The disclosure obligation for an acquisition of equity securities for own account is obvious. However, the financing of an indirect acquisition must also be reported, meaning that a beneficial owner of equity securities remains as fully responsible for notification as does the formal owner. For example, in the framework of a fiduciary arrangement, the principal (beneficial owner) and the trustee (formal owner) must disclose if either of them exceeds a relevant threshold. Special rules apply in respect of investment funds, trusts, and pension funds; in such cases, their management is responsible for delivering notification since that is the only body with proper control of the investments.

Special disclosure is called for if a company increases, restructures or reduces its capital, if a company buys or sells its own equity securities, or if in-house funds of financial intermediaries buy or sell equity securities.

Organized groups of holders of equity securities and such holders acting in concert have the privilege of complying with the disclosure obligation as a whole (Art. 20 III of the Stock Exchange Act). The privilege applies to groups of companies and companies under common control, and to holders of equity securities who establish or terminate agreements relating to the exercise of voting rights and/or relationships in order to acquire or dispose of equity securities. In specific cases, however, it might be debatable whether an 'agreement' or only a loose (not directly discussed) understanding between holders of securities exists; the supervisory authority has established some guidelines in the meantime. The group must report the grand total of its securities' holdings, the identity of its members, the nature of the arrangement, and the representation of the group. Securities transactions within the group, however, are not subject to the disclosure obligation.

Further (partial) disclosure rules also exist in other laws: (1) Article 663c of the Code of Obligations requires corporations having their shares listed on a stock exchange to disclose in the notes to the balance sheet the significant shareholders (those who own more than 5 per cent equity in the corporation), provided the management knows or ought to know of such shareholders; the effects of this provision, however, are limited due to many disadvantages, namely (i) it is difficult to identify the shareholders in the case of bearer shares, (ii) the corporation is charged with an inquiry duty not related to company matters, and (iii) balance sheets are issued only once a year, and thus do not provide sufficient transparency for the capital market. Further, Article 663b of the Code of Obligations provides for disclosure of material participations in other companies. (2) The Investment Fund Act and the Banking Act contain similar provisions as to the disclosure of significant shareholders.

3. Public Takeover Bids

Articles 22–33 of the Stock Exchange Act provide a number of general principles governing takeover bids; much of the legal basis, however, is contained in ordinances. The recommendations of the Takeover Board are also of great importance (available at <www.takeover.ch>).

The provisions on tender offers apply in respect of equity securities in companies of which at least one class of equity securities is listed on a Swiss exchange. Under special circumstances, a deviation from this rule can take place. Domicile and nationality of the offeror (bidder) are not of importance.

The Stock Exchange Act covers any kind of public tender offers including self-tenders (public offers by a company to repurchase its own equity securities), unless the transaction does not exceed 2 per cent of the equity capital of the company and the holders of the securities are treated equally. The Stock Exchange Act does not exempt restructurings from the scope of application, although the Takeover Board may recommend exemption for good reasons subject to the particular circumstances.

An offeror is obliged to extend equal treatment to all holders of equity securities of the same class. Furthermore, the best price rule applies and requires from the offeror that the highest price paid from the date of the pre-announcement of the tender offer to any holder of securities is offered to all holders. The offeror is obliged to publish a preliminary announcement containing the substance of the subsequent tender offer, upon its decision to plan a takeover. The details of the tender offer must later be published in a prospectus that is correct and complete, containing all relevant information appropriate and necessary for investors to adequately evaluate the tender offer. The offeror may make an offer conditional, but only such conditions can be imposed in the offering documentation which cannot be influenced to a significant extent by the offeror.

To achieve full transparency, transactions involving securities of the company concerned must be reported. Furthermore a cooling off period needs to be observed in order to give shareholders and the target company time to consider their positions. In the case of competing offers, it is imperative that holders of the securities of the target company are able to choose freely among them and to withdraw from any prior acceptance of a previous tender offer.

The board of directors of the target company is obliged to issue a report on the tender offer containing all information necessary to allow shareholders to make an informed decision. This report should also contain information about the intentions of significant holders of securities of the target company and about potential conflicts of interest involving board members and directors. Moreover, the target company must treat all competing offerors equally.

The board of directors of the target company is restricted in its ability to introduce defensive measures against tender offers (Art. 29 II of the Stock Exchange Act). In particular, the company may not engage in any transactions that would alter, to a significant extent, the assets or liabilities of the company. The main examples in practise are the (conditional) sale of important parts of the business ('scorched earth' approach, 'crown jewel defence' or 'lock-up agreements'), the conclusion of special agreements in favor of management and directors ('golden parachutes'), the conditional increase of capital with a unilateral allocation of subscription rights ('poison pills'), and the issuance of new shares or convertible debts with exclusion of subscription rights of existing holders of securities. Within the legal framework, the pac-man defense and white knight defense are possible. Notwithstanding the intensive discussion, these legal provisions have not yet gained practical importance with the exception of some preventive effects. After the tender offer has been launched, only the shareholders' meeting of the target company may decide on any relevant defensive measures.

Holders of equity securities with a large investment in a company (more than $33\frac{1}{3}$ per cent) are legally forced to make an offer to the remaining shareholders (Art. 32 of the Stock Exchange Act). A company in Switzerland, however, has the legal possibility to agree on an opting-out or an opting-up to 49 per cent in the articles of association (by qualified majority decision of the shareholders). The mandatory offer obligation is triggered whenever a holder of securities or an allied group of holders directly or indirectly acquires equity securities exceeding the threshold of $33\frac{1}{3}$ per cent of the voting rights of the target company, if this company has not introduced an opting-out or an opting-up clause. A number of exceptions from the mandatory offer obligation exist, such as the acquisition of voting rights as a result of a donation, foreclosure sale, or corporate reorganization.

The offeror is obliged to buy all outstanding equity securities of the target company at no less than the stock exchange price. This price is defined as the average opening price on a Swiss stock exchange for the thirty exchange trading days before the publication of the offer document. Additionally, if the offeror has purchased equity securities at a premium prior to the tender offer, the minimum price for the tendered equity securities must be the higher of the stock exchange price or 75 per cent of the highest price paid by the offeror for equity securities of the target company in the twelve months preceding the announcement of the offer. The price for the tendered equity securities may vary if the target company has issued several classes of equity securities. Under certain specific circumstances, exceptions from the minimum price rule may apply.

II. PRIVATE BANKING LAW

In the field of private banking law, considerably fewer legal developments have occurred during the last years. In Switzerland, private banking law is traditionally a legal area without specific legal sources, but the respective transactions are governed by civil law, mainly laid down in the Civil Code (CC) and in the Code of Obligations (CO).

A. *Basis of the Contractual Banking Relationship*

1. Legal Qualification

The contractual relationship between the customer and the bank is usually based on certain documents. Although one specifically entitled 'agreement' may not be among them, the bank does give customers a signature card and the general banking conditions. If the customer is interested in having the bank carry out certain transactions, other documents are available (administration of assets, fiduciary agreements, foreign exchange transactions). The signature card, traditionally the key document, contains the specimen signature of the customer and the signatures of any representatives (power of attorney). If the customer does not want the account in his or her own name, the bank can open a so-called numbered account, which is only designated by a number; however, the identity of the customer must be known to the bank and be filed separately.

In entering into a contractual relationship, the bank is obliged to check the identity of the customer. Furthermore, it is imperative that the bank knows the beneficial ownership in respect of the deposited assets. The details of the identification process are laid down in the Agreement on the Swiss Banks' Code of Conduct with Regard to the Exercise of Due Diligence, issued under the auspices of the Swiss Bankers Association (1998).

The General Banking Conditions, which are quite standardized in Switzerland, contain rules relating to checking the legitimacy of the customer, the responsibility for wrong or misleading instructions, handling of correspondence, details of power of attorney, the ranking of several banking documents, the applicable law and jurisdiction, etc.

The contractual relationship is governed by banking secrecy rules. The duty of confidentiality to be observed by the bank extends not only to the details of any transactions, but also to the fact that the customer maintains an account with the bank.

No clear legal opinion exists as to the legal qualification appropriate for the opening of a banking relationship. Some argue that signing the signature card and the general banking conditions would 'only' constitute a current account agreement for the operation of transactions and a so-called giro agreement for paying agency functions, both of which are basically governed by the laws of the mandate (Arts. 394–406 CO). Other authors contend that the conclusion of a general banking contract is a contractual 'model' not regulated by Swiss law, which makes it necessary to go back to the general rules of the Code of Obligations. However, the practical difference between the two approaches is fairly insignificant. If the law of the mandate applies, the bank is also obliged to observe the duty of care, the duty of loyalty, and the duty of information, even in a pre-contractual context. So far, case law has not made any relevant difference in connection with the description of the corresponding rights and obligations to be assumed by the bank and the customer.

2. Representation

If the customer is a legal entity or consists of a group of several persons, the decision must be taken whether an individual or collective signature should apply. Depending on the agreed system, the bank can act on sole or joint instruction. In case of a so-called joint account, the bank fulfills its obligations towards all contracting partners by acting on the instructions of one contracting partner if the individual signature principle applies (Art. 150 CO). Otherwise, at least two persons must act severally or jointly, notwithstanding the fact that all partners in a joint account have their own legal position. The execution of banking transactions can be facilitated by issuing a power of attorney (Art. 32 CO).

The power to act on behalf of a legal entity, a collective partnership or a single firm, being registered in the commercial register, is derived from the respective entry. Internal resolutions which deviate from that entry are not decisive for the other contracting partner as long as such partner is acting in good faith.

In Switzerland, the ultra vires concept only applies in a very restricted way. Any business activity which can be justified within the scope of a legal entity reflected in the commercial register is considered as valid business.

B. *Types of Banking Relations*

1. Payment Transactions

The execution of payment transactions is part of the giro agreement or the general banking agreement. The rules of the mandate apply for incoming and outgoing money transfers. A payment instruction must be seen as specific direction under the mandate.

The actual transfer of a payment to a specific addressee is considered a so-called three-party transaction: the customer instructs his or her bank to make a payment to a beneficiary (assignation, Art. 466 CO). Such instruction may be revoked until the other party has 'accepted' the instruction by confirming the execution of the trans-action to the beneficiary.

A standardized form of money transfer transaction is documentary credits, which usually involve the parties of the substantive transaction and two banks. Particularly in cases of the cross-border delivery of goods, payment must be made upon presen-tation of the appropriate documentation of the goods' delivery to a specific person accepting and confirming the due performance by the seller. Thereafter, the payment can be executed through the established banking channels. Refusal of payments may only be made if the documents substantially deviate from the contractual arrangement or if manifest fraud has occurred. In Switzerland, the 'Uniform Customs and Practices for Documentary Credits' of the International Chamber of Commerce (ICC, Paris) are regularly applied. The underlying Swiss law is consistent with these international standards.

2. Deposits

If a customer deposits money or securities with the bank, a savings account is opened; the contractual relation constitutes a deposit contract (Art. 472 CO) or as a loan contract (Art. 312 CO). Under Swiss law, the relevant provisions of these two contractual types are fairly similar. Therefore, the exact qualification does not have major legal consequences. The bank can produce a savings book in document form or as a negotiable instrument issued in the name of the owner or in the bearer's name. This practice is no longer common.

Another banking operation is the collection of moneys in the form of time deposits, as short-term money or medium-term notes. Functionally, all forms of time deposits are liabilities of the bank and must be considered as 'incoming' loans.

Usually the banks are also prepared to make safe deposit boxes available. These contracts are considered as special kinds of lease agreements.

In connection with operating and maintaining a current account for the customer, the bank may offer services relating to asset administration. For such contracts, the law of the mandate applies (Art. 394 CO).

3. Loans

Another typical kind of banking business is quite the opposite, the granting of loans (Art. 312 CO). Loans can have different forms, namely (1) money credits, such as fixed loans or credit lines to be drawn by the beneficiary and borrower at his or her request, or (2) commitment credits which oblige a bank to commit itself to third parties within the agreed limit. Specific rules for commitment credits do not exist in Swiss law.

Banks can grant loans and credits on a secured or on an unsecured basis. Securities are expressed *in personam* or *in rem*.

4. Securities Trading

Securities dealers, in most cases banks which act as brokers, can sell and buy securities of any kind (shares, bonds, derivatives, etc.), for the account of customers and for their own account. Securities dealers usually act in their own name even if a transaction is made for the account of a customer. Securities trading constitutes a contract of commission according to Articles 425 and 436 of the Code of Obligations. The bank as commissioner sells on its account the goods purchased for the customer and purchases on its account the goods sold for the customer.

The opening of securities accounts for customers constitutes a deposit agreement (Art. 472 CO) to the extent that the obligation consists in the safeguarding of the securities, and as a mandate (Art. 394 CO) to the extent that the bank is obliged to administer the securities. The bank is obliged to return the deposited securities to the customer even if a third partly has claimed ownership, unless the securities are judicially seized or an action for restitution has been initiated (Art. 479 CO).

In recent years, listed companies have begun to stop issuing securities in paper form. Legitimation is only based on a book entry with the company. If negotiable securities are issued, the actual documents are usually deposited with a collective depository. In such cases, the customer is awarded co-ownership in proportion to the number of securities deposited with the depository organization. If the securities are listed on a foreign stock exchange, a foreign correspondent or depository acts for the account and at the risk of the customer.

Securities trading is often combined with the advance of a loan, granted by the bank to allow the customer to trade in higher volumes. A special kind of transaction is the lending and borrowing of securities. Instead of a sum of money, the customer forwards to or receives from the bank certain securities for a specified period allowing him or her to take advantage of their fluctuations on the stock market. This kind of transaction is basically governed by the provisions of the loan contract (Art. 312 CO).

5. Foreign Exchange Business

Foreign exchange contracts (spot and forward) play a major role in the banking business. Such contracts can be concluded between banks, or between a bank and a customer. The discharge of an obligation is made by paying the amount due in the agreed currencies. With the introduction of the euro and the establishment of a special clearing center for the Swiss banks in Frankfurt, business transactions are now concentrated in only a few currencies (euro, US dollar, pound sterling, yen).

Swiss law does not have specific legal provisions governing the exchange of interest rates and currencies (swap contracts). In principle, the rules of the general part of the Code of Obligations apply, supplemented by an analogous application of the purchase contract law. Foreign currencies are not legal tender in Switzerland. Therefore, the debtor can fulfill his or her obligation by converting the foreign currency into Swiss currency as local currency, unless the agreement explicitly requires the delivery of foreign currency.

A Swiss bank is not obliged to hold foreign currency available at all times in favor of a customer who has an account for foreign currency. The bank must only maintain in the countries of the respective currency a balance equivalent to the balance shown in the account and make such balance available at the request of the customer.

For new types of foreign exchange and similar transactions, such as spot agreements, the Swiss banks apply internationally accepted rules, i.e. the model agreements applicable to the contractual relationship with the customer.

6. Precious Metals Business

Swiss banks also engage in precious metals business, partly for their own account and partly for the account of customers. If a customer instructs the bank to buy gold or silver, the metals are placed in a corresponding bullion account without direct ownership of the customer, or in a safe custody account with ownership or co-ownership of the customer.

7. Secured Transactions

In order to minimize risks for the banks, many transactions executed by banks are done on a secured basis. The following forms of secured transactions are common in Switzerland:

- The customer may assign in an individual or general way certain rights and claims (Art. 164 CO). The assignment agreements of the Swiss banks are standardized and usually include future claims or accounts receivable. Furthermore, in most cases the bank is entitled to collect any account receivable on behalf of the customer, at least until the customer's debt has been repaid.
- The customer may pledge movable goods (securities etc.) and claims to the bank (Art. 884 CC). Pledge agreements (deeds) of Swiss banks are also standardized and have quite a broad scope. In the case of collateral loans (lending on securities), the contract usually contains a margin and reserves the right to sell the securities if the margin is no longer maintained.
- The customer may secure a loan or credit with real estate assets, particularly with mortgages. In most cases, the customer pledges a mortgage note as movable goods to the bank (Art. 793 CC). However, it is also possible to register the bank directly in the land register.
- Swiss law provides for a specific reservation of ownership (Art. 715 CC). However, the disadvantage of this instrument consists in the fact that the movable goods concerned must be registered with a specific municipal registrar or at least kept separate from other goods of the debtor, which is often not easy or even possible in practice.
- The customer may issue an irrevocable and independent guarantee in favor of the bank (Art. 112 CO). In such cases, the means of defence for the customer if the guarantee is drawn down are rather remote.
- The customer may issue a special surety (Art. 492 CO), which then will be accessory to the main debt (loan or credit) and can only be drawn if and to the extent that the main debt is due and payable.

SELECTED BIBLIOGRAPHY

Bodmer, Kleiner and Lutz, *Kommentar zum Bankengesetz*, Zurich 1971–2001.

Daeniker, D., *Swiss Securities Regulation, An Introduction to the Regulation of the Swiss Financial Market*, Zurich 1998.

Malacrida, R. and R. Watter, *Swiss Corporate Finance and Capital Markets – Legal Aspects*, Basle 2001.

Nobel, P., *Swiss Finance Law and International Standards*, Berne 2002.

Schürmann, L., *Nationalbankgesetz und Ausführungserlasse*, Berne 1980.

Weber, R. H., 'Securities Law – Structuring of a Modern Capital Market: The Swiss Example', in: J. Norton, S. Goo and D. Arner (eds.), *International Financial Sector Reform: Standard Setting and Infrastructure Development*, London 2002.

Weber, R. H. and L. Cereghetti, 'International Securities Regulation Switzerland', in: Center for International Legal Studies (ed.), *International Securities Regulation*, The Hague/London/Boston 2002.

Chapter 12
Law of Taxation

*Isabelle Althaus–Houriet**

I. INTRODUCTION

A. *The Tax System*

The Swiss tax system is not centralized and is therefore somewhat complicated. Each taxpayer is subject to federal, cantonal and communal tax authorities. The Federal Constitution grants specific tax powers to the central government, and the 26 cantons are autonomous and sovereign in all other tax matters. Besides levying their own taxes, the cantonal tax authorities assess and gather some federal taxes at the Confederation's request. Finally, the municipalities exercise the tax powers delegated by the cantons.

The Confederation can only levy the taxes it is expressly empowered to by the Federal Constitution. The central government has the exclusive power (the cantons cannot levy similar taxes) to levy a withholding tax on income from capital investment and certain insurance payments (federal anticipatory tax), a compensatory tax for the exemption of civil and military service, customs duties, federal stamp duties, taxes on commodities such as alcohol (not wine), beer and tobacco, and a value-added tax and, since 1998, a special tax on gambling houses.

Together with the cantons, the Confederation has the concurrent power to levy taxes on income of individuals and on income of corporations (federal direct tax). There are neither federal taxes on net worth for individuals and corporations, nor on inheritance and gifts.

The federal direct tax is levied in addition to similar taxes levied by the cantons and the communes. Some formal uniformity has been brought into force regarding income taxes in Switzerland by the federal law on harmonization, based on Article 129 of the Constitution, which is compulsory since 2001. However, the 26 cantonal tax laws differ in many respects from canton to canton and from the federal law. The definition of taxable income, the deductions and amortizations allowed, the tax periods are uniform since 2003, but differences still remain in the interpretation of certain concepts, between cantons and with the federal administration. Formally, there are many similarities and the general rules are often identical.

The tax rates and the tax periods are not comprised within the scope of harmonization, but since 2003 almost all cantons levy their income taxes on a yearly basis,

* Lic. jur., lawyer, chartered tax expert, president of the Tax Court of the Canton of Neuchâtel.

F. Dessemontet and T. Ansay (eds), Introduction to Swiss Law, 217-232.
© Kluwer Law International. Printed in The Netherlands.

for individuals as well as for companies, as the Confederation does, and this method will probably prevail as harmonization in the future.

Besides taxes on income, the cantons may levy:

- a capital and wealth tax;
- special taxes on certain items of income, such as capital gains; gains from the sale of real estate, which are now compulsory according to the federal harmonization law; and taxes on inheritance and gifts;
- special taxes on certain items of capital such as a tax on motor vehicles, a complementary tax on real property, etc;
- miscellaneous taxes such as stamp duties, registration duties, church tax, tax on entertainment or admissions, tax on advertising posters, holiday tax on tourists, etc.

Numerous taxes which transfer on consumer the cost of consumption of certain goods as water, electricity, elimination of waste, etc. are based on federal legislation by the cantons or the communes.

The communes levy their own income and wealth taxes. They are generally a percentage of cantonal taxes. Each commune independently determines its own rates, but the actual trend in the cantons is to set up special equalization funds for redistributing part of communal taxes among them. Communes sometimes levy specific taxes such as land tax, entertainment or admission tax, dog tax, fire exemption tax, etc.

The cantons are entitled to a part of the revenue from the federal taxes. Communes are also entitled to a part of the cantonal taxes, especially from the inheritance and gift taxes.[1] This chapter does not describe the tax system of each canton. Only a short survey of the principal cantonal taxes is given in addition to the more detailed analysis of the federal taxes. As the federal law on harmonization has, in several matters, the same wording as the federal direct tax law, the general income tax rules are similar in almost all cantons. The tax rates, however, still vary from canton to canton and, although less significantly, within the cantons from municipality to municipality. The choice of location is therefore important for special purpose companies, such as holding or domicile companies, which are theoretically eligible for preferential treatment in all cantons, but benefit of particularities of certain local legislations. The liberty of the cantons is restricted by the new harmonization law.

B. Administration

Most federal taxes are administered by the Federal Tax Administration in Berne. Stamp duties, the anticipatory tax and the value added tax are within the exclusive jurisdiction of the Federal Tax Administration.

---

1. 30% of the net revenue from the federal direct tax (one-quarter is attributed to a special intercantonal equalization fund); 20% of the net revenue for the federal stamp duties; 20% of the net revenue from the military service exemption tax; 50% of the net revenue from the taxes on alcohol (10% of the cantonal share must be used to combat alcoholism).

The federal direct tax, on the other hand, is assessed and collected by the cantons for the federal government. Thus, the Federal Tax Administration supervises the cantonal authorities' administration of the tax.

The cantonal authorities administer their own taxes. They have immediate responsibility for the administration of federal and municipal taxes on income and net worth.

II. Federal Direct Tax[2] (*Direkte Bundessteuer/Impôt federal direct*)

A. Introduction

The current federal direct tax was introduced during World War II. It replaced the old federal crisis contribution and increased government revenues. The tax is authorized since 1995 by a formal law, which was discussed in Parliament together with the harmonization law, so that most articles have a similar wording. Differences still remain, for items reserved to the originally competence of the cantons, but also in the interpretation of the law.

The federal direct tax was first (until 1983) called the federal defense tax. That name came from its first application during the war. Since the tax does not apply specially to military expenses any more, the name has been changed.

The federal direct tax is levied on individual income and profits of corporations or other legal entities in addition to the similar taxes levied by the cantons and the communes. It is assessed based on tax returns filed by the taxpayers.

The assessment and the collection of the tax are decentralized in the hands of the cantons. The cantons are entitled to a 30 per cent share of the tax collected from their residents, 13 per cent being paid to the equalization fund. The Federal Tax Administration supervises and only intervenes to ensure uniform application of the tax.

B. Tax Liability

1. Unlimited Tax Liability

Individuals, whether Swiss or of foreign nationality, have tax liability without restriction on their total income (with the exception of income from real estate abroad, income from a personally-owned business abroad, or from a permanent establishment abroad) if they are:

- domiciled in Switzerland;
- residing in Switzerland while gainfully employed in Switzerland;
- not gainfully employed in Switzerland, but residing there for more than 30 days when gainfully occupied and 90 days without being gainfully occupied;

---

2. Fed. Cons. Arts. 127 and 128; Law of 14 December 1990, regarding the federal direct tax as well as the harmonization.

– employed by the Swiss government, residing abroad, and exempted from direct taxes in their country of residence as a result of a treaty or of international agreement (diplomatic agents).

Foreign nationals working in Switzerland and deriving employment income only are subject to income tax at source. The tax rates vary from canton to canton and from municipality to municipality, and include federal, cantonal and communal taxes.

Corporations whose registered office or place of effective management is in Switzerland are subject to unlimited tax liability. Income from real estate abroad or from a permanent establishment abroad, however, is exempted.

2. Limited Tax Liability

Individuals and corporations, even if not residents of or incorporated in Switzerland, may be subject to a limited tax liability on certain items of income from Swiss sources. This liability applies when:

– they own or have a beneficial interest (usufruct) in real property situated in Switzerland.
– they own or have a beneficial interest (usufruct) in debt-claims secured by real estate in Switzerland;
– they are owners of, or partners in, business enterprises in Switzerland;
– they have a permanent establishment in Switzerland;
– they work in Switzerland;
– they receive fees or other remuneration as directors or managers of Swiss corporations;
– they receive from Swiss sources a retirement, old-age, or disability pension due to previous employment;
– they trade in real estate in Switzerland or act as agents in such trade;
– as employees of a Swiss company engaged in international traffic on a ship, aircraft or road transport, they receive a salary from an employer having its registered office or a permanent establishment in Switzerland.

C. Taxable Income

Resident individuals and corporations are subject to the federal direct tax on their total income regardless of source. An exception is made for real estate situated abroad and the income derived therefore, as well as for income derived through capital invested in foreign permanent establishments (or in foreign enterprises). Such income has to be reported (for determining the tax rate), but is non-taxable. Taxable incomes are:

– Income from the performance of professional services (dependent or self-employment, including the income of partnerships or limited partnerships, because such associations are not taxed as such).

- Income from Swiss estates (the rental value of a self-occupied house is included in taxable income).
- Income from capital (interest, dividends, royalties, rents; all payments subject to the federal anticipatory tax are to be treated as income; gross income (net income + anticipatory tax) has to be declared).
- Capital gains obtained by an enterprise on the increase in value of assets recorded in their books of accounts (according to Swiss law, all enterprises engaged in trading, manufacturing, or commerce are obliged to keep books, providing that their gross receipts exceed CHF 100,000); capital gains realized on the sale of goods which formed part of the private fortune of a taxpayer (providing that the seller is not professionally engaged in the trade of such goods) are not subject to the federal direct tax.
- Lottery prizes, but not gains realized in a gambling saloon.

Individuals pay the federal direct tax on their net income as listed above less fixed deductions and allowances.

For the purposes of the federal direct tax, legal entities are classified into two categories:

- corporations (stock companies, limited liability companies, cooperatives, limited partnerships with shares) pay taxes at a flat tax rate of 8.5 per cent;
- other legal entities (associations, foundations, public and ecclesiastical bodies and institutions) pay a flat tax of 4.25 per cent as soon as their net profit exceeds CHF 5,000).

D. *Federal Tax on Profit of Corporations*

For the computation of the taxable profits of corporations, the following items are considered:

- the profits as shown by the corporation's profit and loss account after eliminating the profit reported from the previous year;
- all deductions which cannot be considered normal business charges;
- depreciation or provisions in excess of normal business requirements (they normally may not exceed the maximums set by the Federal Tax Administration, unless the taxpayer can justify application of a higher rate).

E. *Tax Period*

The federal direct tax is assessed every year since 1995 for corporations and other legal entities, and since 2001 for individuals (before, the tax was levied at the federal level bases on a two years period, and calculated based on the preceding two years period). The cantons are theoretically still free to use for the taxation of individuals the calculation on two years period, but only 3 out of 26 had kept this procedure on 1 January 2001, so that the harmonization should be effective as regards tax periods in 2005, although tax periods are not compulsorily fixed in the new federal law on harmonization.

Income of the tax period (period for which the tax is due) is now levied for the corresponding year, and the tax is determined on the basis of the effective income. The tax form must be filled each year for the preceding year, and the taxpayer pays provisory installments until the final assessment is made.

For the computation of the income tax, the personal situation of the taxpayer at the end of the year is relevant, even if some changes have happened shortly before. Example: marriage, divorce or separation effective by 31 December are presumed having been existing during the whole year.

Losses suffered during the seven years preceding the tax period may be deducted from the taxable income.

F. Computation of the Tax and Tax Rates

To calculate the income of an individual, one must aggregate his, his spouse's and his minor children's incomes.

To determine the applicable tax rate, the total income of fully or partially liable taxpayers is established including income not subject to the federal direct tax, such as income from immovable property or from a permanent establishment abroad.

Foreign corporations carrying on activities in Switzerland through a permanent establishment will be subject to tax on the profits realized by this permanent establishment.

The following table shows the amounts of federal direct tax payable by an unmarried individual on his net income.

Net Income (CHF)	Tax
0–12,800	0
12,800	0.77
27,900	116.25
36,500	191.90
48,600	511.30
63,800	962.70
68,800	1,259.70
91,100	2,731.50
118,400	5,133.90
154,700	9,126.90
664,300	76,394.10
664,000	76,406
onwards	flat tax rate of 11.5 per cent

Corporations pay tax on profit at the rate of 8.5 per cent.

Since 1998, Tax on capital is not yet withheld on corporations, but most cantons do levy such taxes.

G. Special Cases

1. Assessment of Individual on a Lump-sum Basis

Foreign nationals residing in Switzerland who have exercised any activity in Switzerland may replace the federal direct tax with a lump-sum payment. The tax is assessed at the normal tax rate on the basis of expenditure, i.e. the amount paid by the taxpayer for his living expenses. This amount should not, however, be less than five times the rental value of the house the taxpayer lives in. The tax must also be equivalent to the ordinary income tax which would be due on income arising from Swiss sources, or on income for which the taxpayer takes advantage of double-tax treaties.

2. Holding Companies, Domicile and Service Companies

For corporations, income from participations in other companies is subject to a tax reduction of the federal direct tax, provided that the participation exceeds 20 per cent of the capital of the other company or that its market value exceeds CHF 2,000,000. The corporation may claim a reduction of its income tax in the proportion that the net profit from this participation bears to the overall net profit as well as, fully effective as per 1 January 2007, on capital gains realized on the sale of substantial participation. As a rule, no tax is due if the corporation derives income only from participations. The treatment of holding companies for the purpose of the cantonal and communal taxes varies from canton to canton, as cantons are not obliged, according to the harmonization law, to follow strictly the rules valid for the federal direct tax for this type of companies.

Domicile and service companies are liable to the federal direct tax similar to ordinary corporations. In most cantons, however, they are subject to special taxes which, compared with the normal taxation of corporations, grants considerable tax relief.

III. Federal Anticipatory Tax[3] (*Verrechnungssteuer/ Impôt anticipe*)

A. Introduction

The federal anticipatory tax was introduced in 1944 with the dual purpose of fighting internal tax fraud by requiring taxpayers to declare their investments and the income they obtain from them, and of taxing the income from capital invested in Switzerland by persons living abroad. It is now controlled by a law passed in 1965.

---

3. Fed. Cons. Arts.127 and 132; Fed. Law regarding the Anticipatory Tax of 13 October 1965; Ordinance of the Fed. Council of 19 December 1966, for carrying out the above-mentioned law.

The anticipatory tax is withheld at source. In exceptional cases, for example in case a company transfers its place of effective management abroad, the payment may be replaced by a declaration of the income to the Federal Tax Administration. The tax rate is 35 per cent, levied on income from capital investment, money prizes paid by Swiss lotteries, and with a reduced rate of 15 and 8 per cent on certain insurance payments.

Beneficiaries of such income who are resident of domiciled in Switzerland can claim a refund of the tax, provided that they have accurately declared the value of the investment and the income in their tax returns. The main purpose of the antici- patory tax collection system is not so much to obtain immediate revenue for the State, but to encourage people earning capital income to fulfill their tax obligations correctly. In case of non-declaration, the tax is a final burden. But non-declaration is no substitute for regular taxation for Swiss residents. When a beneficiary has concealed his investments and his income derived there from, the tax administration will bring an action against him to recover the income tax avoided, impose a fine, and, to increase the penalty, refuse to refund the anticipatory tax deducted at source.

For beneficiaries residing abroad, the tax is final, unless they can reclaim the anticipatory tax except within the frame of a double taxation convention concluded by Switzerland with their country of domicile.

B. Income Subject to Tax

1. Interest and other income from bonds and debentures issued by Swiss debtors. Any monetary benefit received by a creditor through payment, transfer, crediting, setting off, or other means, based on the indebtedness and which does not consti- tute repayment of the capital is taxable. Interest on private loan is not subject to the anticipatory tax.

2. Dividends and equivalent distributions on shares from participation certificates of Swiss corporations. In principle, taxes must be paid on any distribution made by the corporation to the shareholder, or to persons closely related to him, which do not appear as the repayment of the capital invested. The following types of income are subject to the anticipatory tax dividends, the allotment of bonus shares, the distribu- tion of a bonus related to a participation, the payment of liquidation surpluses (only in the case of the dissolution of a corporation), and the grant to shareholders of dividend right certificates as well as distributions equivalent to dividends (so-called hidden profits distributions). A company buying its own shares from its sharehold- ers has to pay the anticipatory tax on the difference between the price paid and the nominal value of the shares, unless it sells them within six years. Special tax treat- ment is granted for actions acquired for setting employee's remuneration schemes.

Amounts granted by a company to a shareholder which do not represent genuine repayment of capital, and all payments for transactions with shareholders and their relatives (parent companies or individual) at conditions which differ from market prices and which the company would not have considered in dealing with independ- ent third parties are considered as hidden profit distributions for the purpose of the anticipatory tax. In such cases, the gross amount of the hidden profit distribution is subject to the anticipatory tax as well as to the ordinary income tax.

Examples of hidden profit distributions are:

- corporation loans to shareholders with exceptionally low or no interest rate;
- shareholder grants of credit to the corporation at exceptionally high interest rates;
- corporation payments of excessive salaries to a shareholder employed by his own company;
- corporation services rendered free of charge or below market prices to a shareholder or close relatives;
- corporation payments of excessive or unjustified royalties to a shareholder.

3. Income from shares in an investment fund issued by a Swiss resident, or by a Swiss resident together with a person resident abroad.

4. Interest on deposits with Swiss banks and savings banks.
The terms bank and savings bank not only cover institutions falling under the Federal Law on Banking of 8 November 1934, but also any person who advertises in public to accept capital for payment of interest, or continuously accepts interest-carrying funds. Enterprises that accept interest-bearing deposits from their employees or shareholders are considered as banks for anticipatory tax purposes when deposits exceed a certain number (12 to 20). They do not qualify as banks, however, when the funds are solely invested in assets the income of which is subject to the anticipatory tax.
Interest on registered deposits with a Swiss bank (a bank under the Federal Law on Banking) are, however, free from anticipatory tax if the interest does not exceed CHF 50 a year.

5. Lottery winnings issued from Switzerland and exceeding CHF 50, but not gains realized in gambling houses.

6. Certain insurance payments made to beneficiaries residing in Switzerland.
Capital payments from life insurances exceeding CHF 5,000, annuities, and pensions (from any insurance contract) over CHF 500 a year are taxable. Several categories of insurance payments, however, are not subject to the anticipatory tax. Payments from the federal old age and survivors insurance, and federal disability insurance plans, for instance, are completely tax-free as regards the anticipatory tax.
Income not subject to the anticipatory tax includes:

- interest from debt claims of every kind not mentioned under 1, 3 or 4 above such as loans granted by a private creditor, inter-company loans, etc,
- royalties and license fees.

C. Tax Rates

The anticipatory tax is withheld at the rate of 35 per cent on capital income and on lottery prizes, 15 per cent on annuities and pensions paid by Swiss insurers, and 8 per cent on other insurance payments.

D. Procedure

1. Tax Collection

The debtor of the taxable income must withhold the tax, and remit it to the tax administration with a special return. Switzerland is negotiating at present time with the European Community for replacing the present system of withholding at source by the debtor by a tax levied by the paying agent. This negotiation is linked with the Swiss treaty policy on the exchange of information.

2. Recovery of the Tax

Individuals and corporations residing in Switzerland can claim a refund of the anticipatory tax provided that:

– they resided in Switzerland at the time the income subject to tax became due;
– they are the beneficial owners of the income; and
– their investment and income accrued there from have been correctly declared in their income tax return.

Beneficiaries residing abroad can reclaim the anticipatory tax within the frame of a double taxation convention. Switzerland has concluded such conventions with numerous countries. Ordinarily, the beneficiary of Swiss income subject to the anticipatory tax must prove through official certification given by the tax authorities of his country of residence that he is a resident of a State with which Switzerland has concluded a double taxation convention, the beneficial owner of the income, and that the income and the investment have been declared there. Such conventions, however, do not apply to the anticipatory tax withheld on lottery prizes.

Foreign owners of shares in an investment fund may claim a refund of the tax deducted from the income of these shares if at least 80 per cent of this income comes from foreign sources.

Individuals claim a refund of the anticipatory tax by filing a special supplemental form with their tax return. This form must be sent to the cantonal authorities of the canton of domicile. The refund is generally granted in the form of a deduction on ordinary cantonal and communal taxes on income and on capital. Thus, for individuals, the anticipatory tax has the character of a prepayment for taxes subsequently assessed.

Beneficiaries of insurance payments must submit their claim directly to the Federal Tax Administration. They must remit the certificate of deduction given by the insurer, together with all information needed by the tax authorities. The amount of tax withheld is refunded in cash. Corporations claim the refund directly from the Federal Tax Administration. Their refunds are made by cash payments.

The refund may be claimed on or after the date of 1 January following the due date of the income, but not later than 31 December of the third year following the calendar year in which the income became due.

IV. FEDERAL STAMP TAX[4] (*Stempelabgaben/Droits de timbre*)

The federal stamp duties are imposed on certain legal and economic transactions. The term 'stamp' is misleading because the payment of the tax does not involve affixing of fiscal stamps. The tax is levied on:

- The issue of Swiss shares, limited liability and cooperative companies' certificates; the tax is not levied if the capital does not exceed CHF 250,000; are also subject to stamp tax the issue of enjoyment and participation shares, bond and money market certificates. The rate of the tax is generally 1 per cent on the issue of securities.
- The payment of certain insurance premiums, although life, sickness, and accident insurance, as well as insurance for natural damage concerning agriculture (hail insurance, cattle insurance, etc.), reinsurance, ship and aircraft insurance are exempt. The tax is withheld at a rate of 5 per cent for all insurances but life insurance, and at a rate of 2.5 per cent on life insurance premiums.

V. VALUE ADDED TAX[5] (*Mehrwertsteuer/Taxe sur la valeur ajoutée*)

Switzerland has accepted the introduction of a value added tax to replace the former Swiss turnover tax, as the one, which operates in most European countries after having refused twice the government's proposal. The value-added tax has been introduced in Switzerland since 1 January 1995.

The value-added tax is levied on imports and deliveries of merchandise and services. Goods that are exported are entirely exempt from duty. A difference is made between items exempt of tax, which are not considered in the calculation of the taxable turnover, but allow the deduction of tax paid previously, and items excluded from the scope of tax, which are not subject to tax, but do not allow any deduction of tax paid previously. Exported goods are exempt of tax, health care is excluded from the scope of tax. Prepaid tax will be refunded on the first, not on the second, although both are not considered as taxable turnover.

This tax is collected from anybody who has an independent business activity with yearly turnover exceeding CHF 75,000. This amount is increased up to CHF 150,000 for companies acting in sport, non-profit organizations and charitable institutions.

The value-added tax is normally levied at a rate of 7.6 per cent. It is withheld at a rate of 2.4 per cent on some basic products, like water, foodstuffs, and non-alcoholic drinks which are not delivered in restaurants, cattle, poultry, fish, cereals, seeds, flowers, pharmaceuticals, newspapers, magazines and books. The tax rate for hotel and similar items amounts to 3.6 per cent.

4. Fed. Cons., Art. 132, I; Fed. Law on Stamp Taxes of 27 June 1973.
5. Fed. Cons., Art. 130; Fed. Law on Value Added Tax of 2 September 1999.

The persons who have to pay the tax must declare spontaneously their transactions normally every three months, on an official form. Taxpayers whose turnover does not exceed CHF 3 million and whose tax debt does not exceed CHF 60,000 may replace the exact calculation of the tax by a tax calculated on the turnover at a special tax rate determined according to the kind of business they are acting in.

VI. Federal Tax on Gambling Houses[6]

Since 1998, the Confederation is entitled to levy a special tax on gambling houses, the so-called 'casinos'. For casinos, the tax rate is of 40 per cent on the gross income from gambling, and increases up to 80 per cent. Gambling houses must be officially registered and benefit of special licenses, the number of which is strongly restricted. At the end of 2001, the Federal Government decided to allow less than 25 concessions, so that several existing casinos had to close in 2002. This new tax is meant to sustain the Swiss system of social security.

VII. Miscellaneous Cantonal Taxes

A. *Inheritance and Gift Taxes*

All cantons but one, plus a few municipalities, levy taxes on estates or inheritances. Their respective tax laws differ widely, but there are some general principles.

The canton in which the deceased was residing at the time of death has the right to tax the whole estate, irrespective of the domicile of the heirs. The right to tax real property, however, belongs to the canton in which the real estate is situated. The rates are progressive, based on the relationship between deceased and heir, and depending on the value of the estate.

Taxes on inheritance are generally coupled with taxes on gifts because a transfer between living persons could avoid the former.

Where property is abroad or persons are residing in a foreign country, double taxation conventions on inheritance and gifts may be involved.

B. *Taxes on Transfer of Real Property*

In all cantons, all forms of transfers of ownership of real property (including, in most cantons, transfer of most of the shares in a real estate company) are subject to transfer tax. The tax is generally payable on the purchase price, or, if that cannot be determined, on the market value.

C. *Property Taxes*

Many cantons impose taxes on the taxable value of real estate.

6. Fed. Cons. Art. 106; Fed. Law of 18 December 1998 on gambling and gambling houses.

VIII. CONVENTIONS FOR THE AVOIDANCE OF DOUBLE TAXATION

A. *Common Principles*

Internal double taxation may often arise in Switzerland, since taxpayers are subject to three different tax jurisdictions (federal, cantonal and communal). Article 127, paragraph 3 of the Federal Constitution prohibits intercantonal double taxation and gives the federal legislator authority to enact rules to prevent this. This authority was never exercised, and the Federal Tribunal, by way of decisions in specific cases, created an extensive network of rules to avoid double taxation. These rules, however, do not apply at the international level so that, except for a few internal rules (e.g. exemption for real estate or permanent establishment situated abroad), the only way to prevent international double taxation is the application of international conventions. Switzerland has an extensive system of international tax treaties regarding taxes on income, capital, and inheritance as well as several specific agreements for the avoidance of double taxation of shipping and aviation companies. The conventions concluded by Switzerland are largely based on the OECD rules, especially the Model Double Taxation Conventions on Income and Capital and the Model Double Taxation Convention on Estates of Deceased Persons and Inheritances.

The tax conventions may restrict the taxing powers of the Confederation, the cantons and communes, but they cannot enable the tax authorities to levy new taxes that are not anticipated in the internal laws. The tax conventions normally cover all Swiss federal, cantonal and communal taxes.

Bilateral double taxation conventions apply to residents of each contracting State, regardless of nationality. Residents are individuals and corporations who, under the laws of one of the contracting States, are fully liable to tax therein. A few treaties enforced by Switzerland do not recognize as residents of Switzerland – and consequently deny them the benefits of the treaty unless they fulfill certain requirements – individuals who are taxed on a lump sum basis, especially if they do not fully tax their income, having taken advantage of the treaty.

In case of a conflict of residence, the conventions establish special mechanisms to determine which of the two residences is to be given preference.

Double residence (or double domicile) may arise, for example, when an individual, having his home in France where his family lives and where he works, spends more than 90 days a year in Switzerland. Following their internal laws, both States may claim the right to tax this person on his total income. In such cases, the conventions set the following rules (the criteria apply in turn). An individual must be considered a resident of the State in which he has a permanent home and has his closest personal and economic relations (center of vital interest), or in which he has a habitual abode, or of which he is a national.

If none of the above criteria allows the contracting States to attribute that person to one or the other's sovereignty, the question must be solved by agreement between the administrations of both States.

A corporation that both States can consider as a resident under their internal law is deemed under a double tax convention to be a resident of the State in which its place of effective management is situated.

Under the Swiss conventions, foreign enterprises are taxed in Switzerland only if they carry on their activities within the country through a permanent establishment. 'Permanent establishment' is defined in each treaty. It generally covers a branch, an office, a factory, a place of exploitation of natural resources or any other fixed place of business. It does not include the casual and temporary use of storage facilities, nor the existence of a warehouse for the purpose of delivery, processing, storage or display of goods in the other country.

The conventions attribute to one or the other of the two contracting States the right to tax certain items of income:

- Income from real estate, including capital gains from the sale of such property, is taxable by the State in which the property is located.
- Salaries and compensation for dependent professional services are taxed in the country where the services are performed except in cases of very short displacement abroad.
- Income from independent activities is taxable in the State of residence, unless the activities are exercised through a fixed base (office, practice) situated in the other State.
- Directors' fees are taxable in the State in which the company is a resident.
- Pensions are generally attributable to the State of residence except for public pensions (which are normally like any income from government services taxable in the country of source).

Dividends, interest and royalties are as a rule taxable in the State of residence of the beneficiary. In most countries, however, some or all of these forms of income are subject to taxation at source. To avoid double taxation, the conventions provide for partial or complete relief of tax at source. In its more recently concluded treaties, Switzerland had to concede to its partner State a limited tax at source. In order to avoid double taxation, Switzerland grants to the beneficiary of dividends, interest and royalties that are taxed at source a credit against his own taxes on that income for the portion of taxes that cannot be reclaimed in the country of source. This is the only instance where a credit of foreign taxes against Swiss taxes is available. The general method for the avoidance of double taxation is exemption.

Tax conventions also provide for cooperation between the administrative authorities of both States through:

- the mutual agreement procedure which provides that the competent authorities of both States shall endeavor by mutual agreement to resolve the situation of taxpayers subject to double taxation, and enables the administrations of both States to consult when difficulties arise regarding the interpretation or application of the convention or in cases of double taxation not provided for by the treaty;
- the exchange of information clause which allows the two contracting States to exchange the information necessary for carrying out the provisions of the convention and the prevention of abuses of the treaty and, for the USA, for preventing fraud or similar crimes.

B. The Swiss Legislation to Counteract Abuses of Tax Conventions[7]

In the 1960's, since income tax rates were often lower than in other European countries, and because of the favorable tax climate, a number of foreign-owned corporations were established in Switzerland. These entities could take advantage not only of the low rates of Swiss taxes, but also of the double taxation conventions.

In order to avoid foreign-controlled companies unconditionally making use of the combined effects of these tax benefits, the Swiss Federal Council has passed legislation to combat abusive claims for relief of foreign taxes under double taxation conventions. Besides the Decree of 1962, which applies to all conventions, Switzerland has also inserted in some treaties additional provisions aimed at avoiding abuses of the convention. The Decree of 1962 does not apply to the double tax treaty with the USA, as this convention contains specific rules to counteract the abuse of the treaty.

The 1962 Decree and its executory regulations provide measures against the granting of relief or deduction under a convention when the claimant does not fulfill the requirements specified in the tax convention (the use of the convention is then obviously unjustified), and when the granting of a tax relief constitutes an abuse, even though the taxpayer is technically entitled to the benefits of the tax treaty.

A person claiming a tax relief has to prove that he satisfies the material and personal requirements specified in the tax conventions. Such requirements are: residence (domicile or registered office) for tax purposes in which the income in question is derived, and any other conditions specified in the tax conventions or in the relevant regulations. If those conditions are not met, the claim for relief of double taxation is obviously unjustified.

Not only the obviously unjustified but also the abusive claim of tax relief is improper. This exists if a tax relief, claimed by an individual, a legal person or a partnership residing in Switzerland, would substantially benefit, directly or indirectly, persons not entitled to benefit by the tax convention. The 1962 Decree stresses four situations where a tax relief claim is always abusive in the sense of the preceding general clause.

- If it relates to any income of which an essential part (50 per cent) is used, directly or indirectly, to satisfy the rights or claims of persons not entitled to benefit from a tax convention.
- If it relates to any income which benefits a corporation residing in Switzerland in which persons not entitled to the benefits of a tax convention have, directly or indirectly, a substantial interest by way of participation in the financial structure or otherwise, and do not make appropriate profit distributions (at least 25 per cent of double taxation protected income must be distributed, unless bona fide deficits prohibit such distribution).
- If it relates to any income which benefits, by virtue of a fiduciary relationship, a person not entitled to benefit from a tax convention.
- If it relates to any income which benefits a family foundation or a partnership residing in Switzerland, but not carrying on business in Switzerland, in

---

7. Decree of the Fed. Council of 14 December 1962; Executory Regulations to the 1962 Decree/Circular Letter of 31 December 1962 and 17 December 1998.

which persons not entitled to benefit from a tax convention are substantially
involved.

In case of abuse, the Federal Tax Administration may:

- refuse to certify claims for the refund of foreign taxes;
- refuse to forward certified claims for the refund of foreign taxes to the relevant
foreign authority;
- revoke or cancel certifications;
- collect, for account of the relevant authorities of the other country, the
withholding taxes for which relief has been granted under the double taxation
convention, and/or
- advise the relevant authorities of the foreign country of the abusive utilization
of the relief clauses in the double taxation treaty.

The 1962 Decree is still applicable, although most conventions contain specific anti-
abuse clauses. Some of them have included the wording of the 1962 Decree in the
tax treaty, making it international law, others, such as Luxembourg and the USA
contain specific clauses to counter-act the abuse of the treaty.

Chapter 13
Labor Law

*Rémy Wyler**

I. Short Introduction**

This chapter only deals with the labor relationships concerning private law. Therefore, it does not include the rules covering the magistrates and other public servants who work for public offices or public authorities.

II. Swiss Rules Concerning Private International Law and Place of Jurisdiction

A. *Private International Law*

According to the Federal Law on Private International Law (PIL), an employment contract is governed by the law of the country where the worker habitually performs his or her work. If the worker habitually performs his or her work in several states, the employment contract is governed by the law of the country of the employer's business establishment or, if there is none, of the employer's domicile or habitual residence. The parties may submit the employment contract to the law of the country in which the worker has his or her habitual residence or to the law of the employer's business establishment, domicile, or habitual residence (Art. 121 PIL).

As to the competent jurisdiction, Article 115 PIL provides that, the Swiss courts at the defendant's domicile or at the place where the worker habitually performs his or her work have jurisdiction to entertain actions relating to employment contracts. An action initiated by a worker may also be brought before the court of the employee's domicile or habitual residence in Switzerland.

According to the Lugano Convention on Jurisdiction and the Enforcement of Judgments in Civil and Commercial Matters, in matters relating to individual employment contracts, an agreement conferring jurisdiction shall be enforceable only if it is entered into after a dispute has arisen (Art. 17 § 5 LugC). For this reason, parties must be aware that a contractual prorogation of jurisdiction may be void.

*Dr. jur., attorney, lecturer, Faculty of Law, University of Lausanne.
**I would like to thank Mrs. Jacquie Lutz and Professor François Dessemontet for their valuable help with the editing of the English text.

F. Dessemontet and T. Ansay (eds), Introduction to Swiss Law, 233–244.

B. *Place of Jurisdiction*

The person seeking employment or the worker cannot waive his rights in advance, either by entering into an agreement or by appearance before a court pursuant to the Swiss Federal Act on Civil Jurisdiction (PJA). The freedom to choose the place of jurisdiction exists only after the beginning of a dispute. Consequently the freedom of the parties to choose jurisdiction is restricted by this law.

According to Article 24 PJA, the court of the domicile or seat of the defendant or at the place where the worker habitually carries out his work, shall have jurisdiction over actions relating to employment law.

III. INDIVIDUAL EMPLOYMENT RELATIONSHIP

A. *In General*

In Switzerland, individual employment relationships may be governed by:

- An individual employment contract (*contrat individuel de travail/ Einzelarbeitsvertrag*). Such a contract is governed by Articles 319–343 of the Swiss Code of Obligations. These provisions contain some restrictions to the freedom of the parties, principally to insure protection to the worker, who is generally considered to be the weaker party, the one in need of protection.
- A collective employment contract (*convention collective de travail/ Gesamtarbeitsvertrag*) is a contract whereby employers or associations thereof and workers' unions jointly establish provisions concerning the conclusion, content and termination of individual employment relationships of the partici- pating employers and workers. Such provisions are mandatory as soon as an individual employment contract is concluded between an employer and a worker who are either both members of the contracting associations or if the employer is directly party to a collective employment contract. The rules con- tained in collective employment contracts are different. Such contracts are widespread in Switzerland. Some of these collective employment contracts may be mandatory, based on official decisions which extend their scope of application to employers and workers who are not bound by the agreement. Consequently, an employer must verify whether or not his scope of activity is submitted to a collective employment contract before entering into a relationship with a worker.
- Standard employment contract (*contrat-type de travail/Normalarbeitsvertrag*) is a contract that establishes provisions concerning the conclusion, content and termination of specific kinds of employment relationships. In the absence of an agreement to the contrary, the provisions of the standard employment contract apply directly to the employment relationships covered thereby. Once again, an employer must verify whether or not his activity is submitted to a standard employment contract. If this is the case, the employer must include specific provision to override the application of the standard employment contract.

– Moreover, the Swiss Labor Act (*loi sur le travail/Arbeitsgesetz*) contains a number of mandatory provisions concerning health protection, hours of work, the protection of women who are pregnant or who have recently given birth.

B. *Individual Employment Contract*

1. Definition and Form

The individual employment contract is a contract whereby the worker has the obligation to perform work in the employer's service for either a fixed or an indefinite period of time, during which the employer owes him a wage.

No special form is required for the validity of an individual employment contract. Nevertheless, many provisions of the Code of Obligations (Arts. 319–343) contain a requirement of written agreement in order to derogate to the legal provisions. Further, if nothing else is agreed upon, the provisions of the Code of Obligations will apply. Thus, the Code of Obligations has a general and subsidiary scope of application.

2. Duration of the Employment Contract

The employment contract may be concluded either for a fixed or for an indefinite period of time. In the case of a fixed period of time, the contract shall be terminated without notice upon the expiration of the period, unless otherwise agreed.

If the employment contract is not concluded for a definite period of time, the termination notice must be given by either of the contracting parties. The contract may fix a period for giving notice of termination, but the period shall not differ for the employer and the worker. Even if there is an agreement to the contrary, the longer period shall be valid for both parties. The notice period shall not be reduced to less than one month by a written agreement. When nothing else has been agreed upon, if the employment relationship has lasted more than one year it may be terminated with a notice period of one month in the first year of work, of two months from the second to the ninth year of work and with a notice period of three months as of the tenth year of work. If nothing else has been agreed upon, the first month of the contract concluded for an indefinite period is considered as a probationary period.

The probationary period can be removed or extended to three months by written agreement. During the probationary period, the employment relationship may be terminated at any time on seven days' notice effective at the end of a working week unless otherwise determined by agreement. If the contract is concluded for a definite period, it is presumed without any probationary period; such a period shall be introduced and agreed upon by written agreement and cannot exceed three months.

3. Worker's Duties

The worker must personally perform the work contractually undertaken, unless otherwise agreed upon, or unless circumstances indicate otherwise (Art. 321 CO).

The worker must carefully perform the work assigned to him, and loyally safeguard the employer's legitimate interests. In the course of an employment relationship, the worker shall not make use of or inform others of any facts to be kept secret, such as, in particular, manufacturing or trade secrets that come to his knowledge while in the employer's service. Moreover, after termination of the employment relationship, he shall continue to be bound to secrecy to the extent required to safeguard the employer's legitimate interests (Art. 321a CO). The worker shall render an accounting to the employer for everything he receives for the employer from third parties in the course of his contractual activity, such as, in particular, amounts of money, and he shall immediately remit all of the same to the employer. He shall also immediately remit to the employer everything he produces in the course of his contractual activity (Art. 321b CO).

The employer may establish general directives and give specific instructions about the execution of the work and the conduct of workers in his employ. The worker must in good faith observe such general directives and specific instructions.

The worker shall be liable for any damage he causes to the employer, whether willfully or negligently. The degree of care for which the worker is liable is determined by the individual employment relationship with due regard to the occupational hazards of the work, the educational level or professional skills required for the work, and by the worker's abilities and qualities, which the employer knew or should have known when the worker was offered employment (Art. 321e CO). Consequently, in most cases, the liability of the worker is reduced to a portion of all the damage incurred by the employer according to all circumstances. The remaining portion of the damage is payable by the employer.

4. Wages

In Switzerland, the determination of the wage level does not require any particular form. Usually, the wage is fixed by a written agreement. Under Swiss law, there is no fixed minimum wage. A collective employment contract may, however, fix a minimum wage. Similarly, some special acts require certain other limits to be respected. These include the application of the principal of equal pay for men and women, for the same work or for work to which equal value is attributed; the elimination of all kinds of discriminations on grounds of sex with regard to all aspects and conditions of remuneration. For foreign workers who are subject to an official authorization to work in Switzerland, wages will be controlled and approved by the authorities. The approved wage is mandatory and cannot be reduced without the authorization of the public authority which has delivered the work permit. This is so even after the entering into force of the Bilateral Agreement between the European Union and Switzerland on the free movement of workers on 1 June 2002.

In some cases, the wage shall be paid even if the worker does not perform his or her work. If the work cannot be performed due to the employer's fault, or if, for other reasons, the employer defaults in accepting the performance, he shall remain liable to pay the wage without an obligation of the worker to engage in subsequent performance as long as the default is remaining. In particular, the employer shall be liable for all economic risks (Art. 324 CO). If the worker, for reasons inherent to his or her person, such as sickness, accident, compliance with legal obligations, or exercise of public office, is by no fault of his or her own prevented from performing his work, the employer shall pay for a limited period of time the corresponding wage normally due, provided that the employment relationship has existed for more than three months, or was concluded for more than three months. If longer periods of time have not been fixed by agreement, or standard employment contract, or collective employment contract during the first year of employment, the employer shall pay the wage for three weeks, and afterwards for an appropriately longer period depending on the duration of the employment relationship and the particular circumstances involved. Usually, tables are used by courts to fix the duration of the period of time for which the employer shall pay the wage. Such a table can be included in the agreement under the condition that it will not deprive the worker of his rights:

First year of employment	three weeks
Second year of employment	one month
Third and fourth year of employment	two months
Fifth to ninth year of employment	three months
Tenth to fourteenth year of employment	four months
Every additional five years	one more month

The employer also has the possibility of concluding an insurance policy to cover the loss of wages due to sickness or pregnancy. Usually such an insurance will cover 80 per cent of the wage for a period of 720 days in the case of inability to perform the work. The employer shall pay at least half of the insurance premium. By a written agreement, parties may decide that the insurance will release the employer from his obligation to pay wages in cases of illness or pregnancy, according to the conditions by which the insurance is covering the corresponding risks.

5. Holidays

The employer shall grant the worker a minimum of four weeks holiday period every year and a minimum of five weeks period in the case of juvenile workers until completion of the 20th year of age. The employer shall pay the worker his or her full wage during the holiday. As long as the employement contract remains valid and in effect, payments or other benefits shall not be substituted for holidays.

6. Rights to Inventions and Designs

Inventions and designs, regardless of their protectability, belong to the employer, if the worker, in whole or in part, invents or creates them or participates in their creation while performing his employment activity and contractual duties. The employer may, by written agreement, reserve his or her rights to acquire any inventions or designs that are invented or created by the worker while performing his or her employment activity, but not during the performance of his or her contractual duties. The worker who creates an invention or a design and is subject to such a written agreement shall inform the employer in writing about his or her invention or design. The employer shall then inform the worker in writing within six months whether he wishes to acquire the rights to the invention or design or whether he releases them to the worker. If the invention or the design is not released to the worker, the employer shall pay him special and appropriate compensation which shall be determined by taking into account all circumstances, such as the economic value of the invention or the design, the employer's participation, the use of employer's staff and operational facilities, as well as the worker's expenses and his position in the enterprise.

Concerning author's rights, the only legal provision contains a similar rule concerning software (Art. 17 Copyright Act). According to this rule, only the employer is authorized to use the exclusive rights in software which has been created by the worker while performing his or her employment activity and contractual duties. In particular, the employer has no rights in software which has been created by the worker while performing his or her employment activity, but not during the performance of his contractual duties, unless otherwise agreed. The whole regime of the employee's authors' rights may be revised in a not too distant future.

7. Protection of Worker's Individuality and Equal Treatment
   for Men and Women

In the course of the employment relationship, the employer shall respect and protect the worker's individuality, give due regard to the worker's health, and care for the preservation of morality. In particular, the employer has the obligation to prevent any sexual harassment and to ensure that the worker will not suffer any disadvantage if subjected to such harassment. For the protection of the worker's life and health, the employer shall take the necessary measures according to experience, applicable under the current state of technology, and adequate under the circumstances of his business enterprise, to the extent that may reasonably be expected, taking into consideration the individual employment relationship and the nature of the work.

According to the Swiss Equal Treatment Act of 24 March 1995, it is forbidden to discriminate against workers on grounds of sex. The principle of equal treatment means that there shall be no discrimination whatsoever on grounds of sex directly or indirectly in access to employment, promotion, working conditions, level of pay and termination of the employment contract. The Equal Treatment Act ensures wide protection against such discrimination. In particular, the Act protects workers against dismissal by the employer as a reaction to a complaint regarding the application of the principle of equal treatment or to any legal proceedings undertaken aimed at enforcing compliance with such a principle. In some cases, when the dismissal results from a claim, the worker's dismissal can be invalidated by the judge.

The civil liability of the employer can be engaged when all measures to protect the worker's individuality, or to protect the employee against any sexual harassment or discrimination have not been taken.

8. Prohibition against Competition

It is possible to introduce into the employment contract a specific provision regarding prohibition against competition, subject to limits which are mandatory (Arts. 340–340c). The worker who has full legal capacity may bind himself in writing to the employer to refrain from engaging in any competitive activity after termination of the employment relationship, in particular neither to operate a business for his own account which competes with the employer's business, nor to work for nor participate in such a business. The prohibition against competition is only binding if the employment relationship gives the worker access to the customers or to manufacturing or trade secrets, and if the use of such knowledge could significantly damage the employer. The prohibition shall be reasonably limited in terms of place, time, and subject, in order to preclude an unreasonable impairment of the worker's economic prospects. It may normally not exceed three years, except in very special circumstances. The judge may, at his or her discretion, limit excessive prohibition against competition taking into account all circumstances, and he or she shall give due consideration to the worker's contributions, if any.

9. Impossibility of Waiver and Statute of Limitations

During the course of an employment relationship, and for one month after its termination, the worker may not waive any claims resulting from mandatory provisions of law, or of a collective employment contract. In particular, this means that the worker is protected against pressure from the employer, who is not entitled to ask the worker to sign a disclaimer; such a disclaimer is not valid if it does not respect the conditions of Article 341 CO.

IV. END OF THE EMPLOYMENT CONTRACT

A. *Different Forms of Termination*

A contract of definite period comes to an end by its own terms at the expiration of the agreed period.

As previously mentioned, a formal notice of termination is necessary to end a contract of indefinite period. The notice period is the agreed period of time between the day of reception of the termination notice by the worker and the end of the contract.

For just cause, the employer, as well as the worker, may at any time terminate with immediate effect the employment relationship. A just cause is considered to be, in particular, any circumstance under which, if existing, the terminating party can in good faith not be expected to continue the employment relationship. The judge shall decide at his or her own discretion on the existence of such circumstances. In no event shall he or she consider the fact that the worker is prevented from performing work through no fault of his or her own to be a just cause.

The immediate termination of the employment contract constitutes an ultima ratio. Termination without notice is not permitted when other less dramatic measures can be taken, such as a warning or an ordinary termination of the contract while respecting the notice period.

If the just cause for the termination of the employment relationship without notice is one party's conduct contrary to the agreement, this party shall fully compensate for damages, taking into account all claims arising from the employment relationship. In all other cases, the judge shall decide at his discretion on the financial consequences of a case of termination without notice, taking into account all the circumstances (Art. 337b CO).

If the employer dismisses the worker without notice in the absence of a valid reason, the latter shall have a claim for the wages for the fixed agreement period, or for the period until the expiration of notice. Moreover, the judge shall define compensation to be paid by the employer to the worker, which may not exceed the amount of six months' remuneration of the worker. This compensation is a penalty and it is defined based on all circumstances. In case of misuse of termination without notice, the dismissal will stay valid (the only exception being in the case of dismissal as a reaction to a claim concerning sexual discrimination). However, the employer must pay full compensation to the worker, on top of the penalty which may not exceed an amount corresponding to six months' wage.

B. *Protection against Termination and at an Improper Time*

Upon expiration of the probationary period, the employer shall not terminate the employment relationship:

a) during compulsory Swiss military or civil defense service by the worker and, should such service last more than eleven days, during the four weeks prior to and after the service.
b) if the employee is unable to work as the result of illness or accident, by no fault of the worker, within thirty days during the first year of service, within ninety days during the second through the fifth year of service and within one hundred and eighty days from the sixth year of service and beyond.
c) during pregnancy and during the sixteen weeks that follow childbirth.
d) while the worker participates, with the employer's consent, in a voluntary foreign-aid service organized by federal authorities.

Any notice of termination given during one of the forbidden periods shall be void. If notice is given prior to the beginning of a period, however, and if the notice period has not expired prior to such a period, the expiration shall be suspended and shall continue only after termination of the forbidden period. If, for the termination of the employment relationship, a final date is fixed, such as the end of a month or of a working week, and if such date does not coincide with the continued notice period, the notice period shall be extended until the next following final date.

Protection against termination at an improper time does not prevent the worker from handing in his or her resignation during that time.

C. Collective Redundancies

Collective redundancies mean dismissals effected by an employer for one or more reasons not related to the individual workers concerned, where the number of redundancies is, over a period of thirty days,

- at least 10 in companies normally employing more than 20 and less than 100 workers;
- at least 10 per cent of the number of workers in companies normally employing at least 100 but less than 300 workers;
- at least 30 in companies normally employing 300 workers or more (Art. 335d CO).

Where an employer is contemplating collective redundancies, he shall begin consultations with the workers' representatives, or, in the absence of such representatives, directly with the workers, with a view to reaching an agreement. These consultations shall, at least, cover ways and means of avoiding collective redundancies or reducing the number of workers affected, and mitigating the consequences. To enable the workers' representatives, or in the absence of representatives, the workers, to make constructive proposals, the employer shall supply them with all relevant information and shall in any event give in writing the reasons for the redundancies, the number of workers to be made redundant, the number of workers normally employed and the period over which the redundancies are to be effected. The employer shall forward to the competent public authority a copy of all the aforementionned written communications. The Act specifies a procedure for collective redundancies (Art. 335g CO). Employers shall notify the competent public authority in writing of any projected collective redundancies. These redundancies shall take effect not earlier than 30 days after the notification. Moreover, if the employer does not respect the proceedings and the workers' rights, he may be condemned to pay a compensatory sum to every worker, which may not exceed two months' wage.

D. Transfer of the Employment Relationship

When the employer transfers his or her business or a part of it to a third party, the transferor's rights and obligations arising from a contract of employment or from an employment relationship existing on the date of the transfer shall, by reason of such transfer, automatically be transfered to the transferee. In addition to the transferee, the transferor shall continue to be liable in respect of obligations which arose from a contract of employment or an employment relationship. The transferor shall inform the representatives of the workers affected by a transfer, or, if there is no representative, the workers themselves, of the following:

- the reasons for the transfer;
- the legal, economic and social implications of the transfer for the workers;
- measures envisaged in relation to the workers.

V. Consequences of Termination of the Employment Relationship

All claims arising from the employment relationship shall become due upon its termination (Art. 339 CO). Upon the date of termination of the employment relationship, each party shall make restitution for everything he has received during the period of the employment relationship from the other party, or from third parties, for their account. The rights of retention of the contracting parties are not affected thereby (Art. 339a CO).

VI. Strike

A. Definition

According to Article 28 of the 1999 Federal Constitution of the Swiss Confederation, workers, employers, and their organizations have the right to unionize to protect their interests, to form unions and to join them or to keep out of them. Conflicts shall be resolved to the extent possible through negotiation and mediation. Strike and lockout are permitted when they relate to labor relations, and when they are not contrary to obligations to keep labor peace or to resort to conciliation. Legislation may prohibit certain categories of persons from striking.

The strike is defined as a collective stoppage of work for one limited period of time.

B. Conditions for a Legal Strike

The right to strike is subordinated to the following conditions:

a) The rights to strike and to lockout employees are only permitted if they are supported by organizations of employers or employees.

b) The strike must relate to the employment relationship. As a consequence, the political or secondary 'strike', which attempts to put pressure on third parties or the government and not directly on the employer, is prohibited. With respect to the working relationship itself, the strike must not have for its object to enforce legal protection, because the courts of law guarantee such rights. The strike can only attempt to be conducive to new conditions of work, which will be negotiated through a collective bargaining agreement.

Finally, strikes of solidarity (so-called 'secondary' strikes or boycotts), when they pursue the interests of third parties or interests outside the working relationship, are also prohibited.

c) The strike must not interfere with the obligation to maintain peace in the work place. There is a distinction between relative and absolute peace. Relative peace means the obligation of every party to a collective bargaining agreement, association or union, to abstain from all forms of violence (therefore also including the strike) over matters covered in the collective bargaining agreement. This obligation is imposed by the law, from the moment the parties sign a collective bargaining agreement. Absolute peace goes further, covering matters that are not addressed in the collective bargaining agreement. But absolute peace is not imposed by the law. It only exists if the collective bargaining agreement itself imposes it through an express provision.

d) The strike must be proportional to the particular labor dispute. Thus, Article 28 of the Federal Constitution imposes the precondition discussed above of an attempt to negotiate a mutually agreeable solution at the time a work conflict arises. As a consequence, if the informal resolution measures are not successful, according to this principle of proportionality, successively more formal steps can be taken. The strike is a means to be used only as a last resort when negotiation and conciliation have failed.

e) Finally, the law can prohibit recourse to the right to strike for some categories of employees. For example, there is a limitation on the right to strike for employees in an essential public service, to maintain public order, and for the protection of goods and people, such as firefighters, police or hospital workers.

C. Civil Consequences of the Strike

1. The Legal Strike

With regard to the employment contract, it will not be terminated, but only suspended with respect to the essential reciprocal obligations of the parties, including the performance of work and the payment of wages for the corresponding time period. However, it is not possible to stop paying wages beyond the duration of the strike. In other words, a legal strike does not end the employment relationship and the reinstatement of the strikers in their professional activity is in principle guaranteed. In addition, it is established that the employer cannot use the legal strike as grounds to terminate the employment contract with immediate effect.

2. The Illegal Strike

With regard to an employment contract, the illegal strike constitutes a breach of this contract. If the employee was able to recognize the illegal character of the strike, the employer can determine if the employee's behavior justifies only a warning or, in the most serious cases, is grounds for immediate termination of employment. In any case, termination of the contract following the illegal strike and with respect to the notice period will not constitute a wrongful termination.

With regard to liability for the illegal strike, the employee can be held liable to reimburse the damage caused to the employer due to the employee's failure to honor his contractual obligations. However, the employee will be absolved of all responsibility where the mistake is not attributable to him, such as where he could not lawfully avoid the strike.

In conclusion, Switzerland is a country which only recognizes the right to strike as a last resort when negotiations and other less conflicting means to resolve labor disputes have failed.

SELECTED BIBLIOGRAPHY

Berenstein, A. and P. Mahon, *Labour Law in Switzerland*, Kluwer Law International and Berne 2001.

Brühwiler, J., *Einzelarbeitsvertrag*, 2nd edn., Berne/Stuttgart/Vienna 1996.

Brunner, C., J.-M. Bühler and J.-B. Waeber, *Commentaire du contrat de travail*, 2nd edn., Lausanne 1996.

Duc, J.-L. and O. Subilia, *Commentaire du contrat individuel de travail*, Lausanne 1998.

Portmann, W., *Individualarbeitsrecht*, Zurich 2000.

Rehbinder, M., *Schweizerisches Arbeitsrecht*, 15th edn., Berne 2001.

Streiff, U. and A. von Kaenel, *Leitfaden zum Arbeitsvertragsrecht*, 5th edn., Zurich 1993.

Wyler, R., *Droit du travail*, Staempfli 2002.

Chapter 14
Criminal Law

S. Trechsel*
M. Killias**

I. Sources of Swiss Criminal Law

A. Preliminary Note

This chapter is intended to be an introduction to Swiss criminal law for Anglo-Saxon readers.[1] Several comparisons will therefore be made with American and English law in order to highlight the characteristics of Swiss criminal law. The present introduction shall deal primarily with the principles set out in the General Part of the Swiss Penal Code (PC), whereas the Special Part, comprising definitions of offenses, will be only briefly dealt with. Indeed, finding definitions of offenses is not difficult, whereas putting them into context may be less straightforward for foreign readers. A particular challenge has been the revision of the General Part of the Swiss Penal Code, adopted by Parliament on 13 December 2002. The revised Penal Code (revPC) is likely to come into force by January 2005. The reform mostly concerns the system of sanctions, whereas the general rules about offenses, intent, justification etc. have only been slightly changed. In the following text reference will be made to:

- the existing PC for sections which have not changed and have not been renumbered,
- the revised PC (revPC) for rules which are substantially new,
- both the existing and the revised PC wherever sections have been renumbered, but not fundamentally changed.

*Professor, University of Zurich Law School. Former President of the European Commission of Human Rights.

**Professor, University of Lausanne School of Criminal Justice. Part-time judge at the Federal Supreme Court of Switzerland.

1. For this reason, sources will be given only if they are in English, or if they are highly specific. Otherwise, readers will find a list of introductory texts to Swiss criminal law at the end of this chapter.

F. Dessemontet and T. Ansay (eds), Introduction to Swiss Law, 245–268.

B. *Constitutional Level*

The Federal Constitution[2] contains a few fundamental rules with respect to criminal law and procedure. According to Article 123 I, the Confederation is competent to pass legislation in the field of substantive criminal law. In section 10 (first and third paras.), capital punishment, cruel, inhuman or degrading treatment and torture are without exception prohibited. Article 31 I guarantees the principle that no one should be deprived of his or her liberty except in cases provided by the law. The *nullum crimen nulla poena sine lege* rule is also set forth in section 1 of the PC. It is furthermore guaranteed by Article 7 of the European Convention on Human Rights (ECHR) which has been ratified by Switzerland in 1974. In practice, the ECHR is dealt with as a source of constitutional law.[3]

C. *The Swiss Penal Code*

1. Historical Background of the Swiss Criminal Law

Over many centuries, Switzerland's penal law was heavily influenced by the so-called continental *common law* which prevailed in vast parts of Europe at that time.[4] The first national penal code was passed in 1799 during the *Helvetic Republic* (1798–1802) when the country became a type of French protectorate. This code had been significantly influenced by the French Penal Code of 1791.[5] Although the *code pénal helvétique* was only in force for a short period of time, the influence of French criminal legislation (i.e. the *code Napoléon* of 1810) retained its importance long into the 20th century. When the country changed from a loose Alliance into a Confederation in 1848, criminal legislation was left to the cantons. The only federal criminal law passed in 1853 dealt with offenses against federal institutions, including high treason or assault against officers of the Federal Government. Military criminal law was another matter of federal legislation and models from the Swiss Regiments in the foreign service of the early 1800s survived until the 1920s.

The initiative to unify criminal law came originally from the Swiss Lawyers Association, at a period when other European countries had enacted major criminal codes (Germany 1871, Italy 1889, the Netherlands 1882) and when civil law underwent the same process of codification at national level (Switzerland 1881/1907, Germany 1900). After an unsuccessful first attempt, the Constitution (of 1874) was amended in 1898 to make criminal legislation a federal matter. Preparatory work had started in 1889 when the Federal Government entrusted Professor Carl Stooss of the University of Berne, with an inventory of the existing criminal law of the 25 cantons. Based on this comparative study of cantonal criminal legislation, the first draft of a

---

2. Adopted on 18 April 1999. It replaced the Constitution of 1874.
3. See S. Trechsel, 'Der Einfluss der Europäischen Menschenrechtskonvention auf das Strafrecht und Strafverfahrensrecht der Schweiz', *ZStW* 100 (1988), 673.
4. M. Killias, *Précis de droit pénal général*, 2nd edn., Berne: Staempfli 2001, pp. 4–12.
5. M. Alkalay, *Das materielle Strafrecht der französischen Revolution und sein Einfluss auf Rechtsetzung und Rechtsprechung der Helvetischen Republik*, Zurich: Schultess 1984.

Federal Code was submitted by Stooss in 1893–94. In 1918 the Federal Government finally submitted the official draft to Parliament. However, due to the World War I experience with a military criminal code heavily influenced by early 19th century models (and harsh penalties), the Parliament gave first priority to the reform of military penal legislation, and it only resumed debates on the PC in 1928 (after the final approval of the military penal code in 1927). After almost 9 years of debates, the code was submitted to a referendum where it was passed by a rather narrow majority on 21 December 1937. It came into force on 1 January 1942.

The Swiss Penal Code followed a rather independent line, integrating French, German, and Austrian models. In the great debates of the late 19th century among continental (and especially German) criminal law professors, the Swiss Code often opted for innovative (though mostly intermediate) solutions, which gave it some prestige and international recognition. Even before its official enactment in Switzerland, it was adopted in Peru – a fact which explains the links between Peruvian and Swiss universities.[6]

2. Amendments to the Definitions of Offenses since 1942

Since 1942, the Penal Code has been amended many times. These amendments have usually concerned the definition of offenses (in the Special Part of the PC), such as political offenses and libel (1950), the protection of private communication against undue intrusion, such as wire-tapping etc. (1968), the reshaping of offenses against the person, particularly in connection with kidnapping (1989) and the introduction of offenses of insider trading (1987) and money laundering (1990 and subsequently amended in 1994). In 1992, the chapter on sex offenses was considerably revised, extending the concept of rape (making, among other things, marital rape a crime) and offering more protection to vulnerable persons on the one hand, and, on the other hand, decriminalizing certain forms of sexual acts as well as consensual sexual relations between minors of a similar age. In 1994, all forms of criminal organizations were outlawed, and in 2000, statutes on corruption (even abroad) were considerably extended. In 1995, property offenses and other offenses against economic interests, such as fraud, computer offenses and forgery were subject to amendements. Concern about racism and xenophobia led to the adoption of a section (261-bis) in 1993 making racist propaganda, racist attacks on human dignity and the refusal of a publicly offered service on the grounds of racial discrimination an offense. Switzerland also ratified the International Convention on the Elimination of All Forms of Racial Discrimination. All in all, the impact of all these new offenses was rather limited. Whereas the revision of traditional (violent or property) offenses had little practical consequences, the rarity of convictions for money laundering, international corruption and for supporting criminal organizations[7] came as a surprise to many observers who used to see Switzerland as a safe haven for dirty money

---

6. J. Hurtado Pozo, *Droit pénal*, 2 vols., Zurich: Schultess 1997/2002. This influence of Swiss criminal law on Peruvian legislation has resulted in many students from Peru coming to Swiss universities. José Hurtado Pozo even became professor of criminal law at the University of Fribourg.

7. C. Besozzi, *Organisierte Kriminalität und empirische Forschung*, Chur/Zurich: Ruegger 1997.

and dubious practises in international business.[8] These results are, however, rather consistent with international indicators on corruption and the shadow economy which consistently show Switzerland to be at the lower end of the scale.[9] The new statutes on illegal financial transactions (including insider trading) have had, however, a substantial effect on international legal co-operation.

3. Changes Affecting the General Part

Beyond these changes affecting the definitions of specific offenses, a few general principles and rules regulating sentencing were also amended over the decades. In 1971, the possibility of suspending custodial sanctions was extended in several respects, and a few embarrassing accessory penalties (such as depriving convicts of civil rights) were repealed. In connection with outlawing criminal organizations, the rules on the confiscation of assets were also considerably altered (1994). The law regulating criminal attempts had already been extended in 1982 to cover so-called preparatory acts; fearing uncontrollable side-effects. However, it was decided to criminalize such acts in connection with certain serious crimes (such as murder, robbery, or hostage taking) by creating a new offense (Art. 260bis), rather than by making all preliminary acts punishable (in the general part of the PC).

Beyond these limited changes, the Federal Government entrusted a former Professor of the University of Berne, Hans Schultz, with the task of preparing a draft for a new 'General Part' of the Swiss Penal Code. First presented in 1984, this draft was then debated for several years by an Expert Committee. It was submitted to the Parliament in 1999 and the two Chambers adopted the revised draft in a final vote on 31 December 2002. It mainly relates to sentencing issues which will be subject to a radical overhaul (see IV below).

4. The Interpretation of the Swiss Penal Code

As a basic rule it may be stated that the PC is to be interpreted just like any other law. There is, however, one fundamental exception to this rule: The principle of legality. Punishment may not be pronounced unless the person concerned has committed an offense which is expressly provided for by law. While analogy is quite indispensable as a technique of interpretative thinking, it may not be applied with a view to creating offenses not provided for by law.

In practice, the application of this rule creates considerable problems as it is hardly possible to draw a clear distinction between extensive interpretation and the creation of a new offense. In practise, interpretation is often made easier thanks to the equality of three official languages used in federal legislation (German, French, and Italian). With three texts, it is likely that ambiguities in one language can be removed by looking at the other two versions. One may also suspect that legislation enacted simultaneously in three languages is likely to be more thoroughly checked by parliamentary committees.

8. M.B. Clinard, *Cities with Little Crime: The Case of Switzerland*, Cambridge University Press 1978.
9. See the data in M. Killias, *Grundriss der Kriminologie – Eine europäische Perspektive*, Berne: Staempfli 2002, pp. 139–141.

D. *Other Penal Legislation*

In addition to the PC, numerous federal statutes contain criminal law provisions. Two of them are of a general nature, the others deal with specific matters, and list only certain accessory offenses.

1. The Military Penal Code (MPC)

The MPC of 1927 was drafted on the basis of preparatory work to the PC and has since been amended to maintain parallel wording throughout most of the General and a large portion of the Special Part. It applies primarily to persons doing service in the army, but also to civilians for certain offenses. Its scope of application, *ratione personae*, is widened in times of war. It is applied by military courts, a system which is likely to become the exception in today's Europe (where military courts were abolished in most continental countries). Among the specifically 'military' offenses, refusal to do military service (Art. 81 MPC) is often applied. Over many decades, several hundred young men were convicted of this offense every year. After the end of the cold war and following a certain loss of prestige of Switzerland's traditional army, it became possible to decriminalize conscientious objection. Conscientious objectors are now eligible for community service, although this is 50 per cent longer than an ordinary soldier's overall military training time.

2. The Administrative Penal Code

In 1974, the Confederation passed an Administrative Penal Code which sets out general rules for administrative offenses (e.g. against customs law and federal tax laws). As an exception in Swiss criminal law, it provides for the punishment of a judicial person if a fine of not more than CHF 5,000 is at stake and if investigating the individual responsible would require disproportionate efforts and costs.

3. Offenses set out in other Federal Laws

The list of offenses dealt with in the PC is determined by tradition rather than principle. Thus, a considerable number of offenses are to be found in other federal laws. Some of them are of considerable quantitative and substantive importance. Examples are traffic offenses, such as driving under the influence of alcohol and other substances, which are contained in the Road Traffic Act of 1958, and trafficking in illegal drugs according to the Narcotics Act of 1951. Overall, some 250 federal laws contain criminal offenses. The general principles, as codified in the General Part of the PC, also apply to offenses defined in other federal laws (Art. 333 PC).

E. *Cantonal Legislation*

Cantonal criminal legislation continues to exist alongside federal penal law (Art. 335 PC), although only in areas of marginal importance, such as petty offenses, violations of administrative law, offenses in the context of civil proceedings (comparable roughly to 'contempt of court'), breaches of public order, hunting offenses and tax violations. In these areas, custodial sentences are imposed in exceptional cases only. As a rule, the General Part of the Swiss Penal Code also applies to cantonal criminal law.

F. Case Law

By far the most important case law on federal criminal law consists of the rulings of the Criminal Law Chamber (*Cour de cassation*) of the Federal Supreme Court (see Ch. 15, VIII B). As a rule, the PC is applied by cantonal courts in the first place, and the Federal Supreme Court acts only as a last court of appeal. Some cantonal courts of appeal also publish highlights of their case law. The case law is available on the internet.

G. Legal Doctrine

Finally, legal doctrine is also considered as a source of law in Switzerland. Judgments of the Federal Supreme Court often refer to scientific publications including textbooks and doctoral dissertations. The Federal Supreme Court also often refers to the legal doctrine of neighboring countries, especially Germany.

II. THE SCOPE OF APPLICATION OF THE PENAL CODE

A. As to Time

According to the *nullum crimen* principle, the retroactive application of legislation in criminal matters is strictly forbidden. It follows that, as a rule, the PC only applies to offenses which were committed after it came into force (Art. 2 I PC). The only exception is changes which are favorable to the defendant (Art. 2 II PC). The question, of course, remains as to what measures can be regarded as 'favorable' or 'more lenient'. As a general rule, this principle applies only to punishments, not to therapeutic measures which relate to the offender's rehabilitation.

B. Regarding the Place of the Offense

1. The Principle of Territoriality

In the first place, the Penal Code is applicable to all offenses committed on Swiss territory (Art. 3 PC). This includes, under certain circumstances, aircraft and vessels under the Swiss flag. The place where an offense is committed is determined by the place where the offender performed the act, but also the place where the criminal result was obtained (*Ubiquitätsprinzip/principe de l'ubiquité*, Art. 7 SPC/8 rev PC). If, for example, a German citizen sent a letter-bomb from Germany to Switzerland where it exploded causing bodily harm, the crime will fall under both the Swiss and the German Penal Code. This may lead to double jeopardy, since a foreign conviction concerning such an offense will not bar prosecution in Switzerland, unless the foreign authorities acted at the request of Switzerland. However, any punishment served abroad will be taken into account at the sentencing stage.

2. The Protection of the State principle

All offenses against the Swiss State, wherever and by whomever they are committed, fall under the PC, and a judgment by a foreign court will never be recognized (Art. 4), but the penalty served in a foreign country will be discounted.

3. The Passive and the Active Personality Principle

Offenses committed abroad against a Swiss national fall under the PC, if they are also punishable in the country where they were committed, and if the offender is arrested or handed over to Swiss authorities (Art. 5). If the offender has been convicted and the sentence has been completely served abroad, no second prosecution will take place in Switzerland.

The Penal Code is applicable to offenses committed by Swiss nationals abroad, if they are punishable in the country where they were committed (Art. 6). There will be no second prosecution in Switzerland if the offender has been put on trial and acquitted abroad, or if he has served a foreign sentence.

In the revised Penal Code, the active and the passive personality principle will be dealt with together (Art. 7). The offender will be punished in Switzerland according to Swiss penal law whenever the offense has been committed abroad, but extradition is not feasible.

4. Universal Jurisdiction

Finally, a limited number of offenses fall under the Swiss Penal Code wherever and by whomever they were committed. Examples are counterfeiting of money and trafficking in illegal drugs. Upon ratification of the European Convention on the Suppression of Terrorism, Article 6bis PC (Art. 6 rev PC) was adopted, providing for the applicability of Swiss penal law in cases where Switzerland is obliged to prosecute under international law. According to Article 5 of the revised PC, the universality principle will apply also to cases of sexual abuse of minors younger than 14 years, and to violent sexual acts against minors younger than 18 years.

C. Regarding the Offender

The Swiss Penal Code (Art. 8/9 revPC) is not applicable *ratione personae* to offenders falling under the Military Penal Code, nor to members of (national and cantonal) parliaments and governments for statements made in the course of parliamentary debate (for which these persons are immune to prosecution). Other cases of immunity, concerning diplomats, parliamentarians, members of governments (outside parliamentary debate) and civil servants are only of a procedural character. The immunity can be lifted in which case the PC would apply.

III. GENERAL RULES ON OFFENSES

The General Part of the Penal Code sets out the rules applicable to all offenses. Basically, they also apply to offenses set out in other federal and cantonal laws. These rules can be divided into two groups. The first group contains general elements of crime, such as criminal responsibility, illegality and justification, criminal attempt and participation in crimes. The second part deals with criminal sanctions.

A. *Classification of Offenses*

The Penal Code (Arts. 10, 103 revPC) follows the classical French system in that it distinguishes three categories of offenses. The relevant criterion is their gravity as expressed by the maximum penalty they carry. Thus, 'felonies' (*Verbrechen/crime*) are offenses carrying a custodial sentence of more than 3 years, 'misdemeanours' (*Vergehen/délit*) are offenses whose maximum penalty is no more than 3 years of custody, and 'contraventions' (*Uebertretung/contravention*) are petty offenses carrying detention of up to 3 months or a fine.

Originally, this division was also meant to reflect three degrees of first-instance-courts: jury, district court and single judge. In practice, however, the competence of the court is determined by the expected sentence rather than the theoretical maximum sentence.

While a set of special rules apply to contraventions (Arts. 103–109 revPC), the distinction between crimes and misdemeanours is of very little importance (see III I 3). Hereafter, the term custody will be used in a broad sense, and will include several categories of confinement.

B. *Crimes of Omission*

Two categories of crimes of omission are to be distinguished. Crimes of omission (strictly speaking) are offenses which consist of the omission of an act called for by law (*echte Unterlassungsdelikte/délits d'omission proprement dit*). Examples include the failure of the perpetrator to assist a person whom he or she has injured, the failure to act to help someone whose life is in mortal danger (Art. 128), or the unjustified omission to pay alimony (Art. 217 PC). Conduct of commission by omission (*unechtes Unterlassungsdelikt/délit d'omission improprement dit, délit de commission par omission*) is the omission to avert a criminal result. This category of offenses has been developed by doctrine and case law; it will be defined, but not changed, in the revised PC (Art. 11). The difficulty arises in defining the situations in which a person is under a special duty to actively intervene in order to avert the result (*Garantenstellung/position de garant*). Such a duty must, as a rule, originate in law, in a contract or from the fact that the defendant has himself provoked a dangerous situation.

C. Self-defense and Similar Defenses

As a rule, acts which constitute an offense under the Penal Code are unlawful. In some cases, however, a conflict of social interests may justify or, at least, excuse the defendant's behaviour.

1. Acts Required or Authorized by Law, Official Duty or Professional Duty

Law ought to be free of contradictions. Acts which are lawful by any statute cannot be punishable. Article 32 PC (Art. 14 revPC) expresses this principle by stating that acts which are required or declared lawful by law, do not constitute an offense. Professional organizations, such as the Bar Associations or Medical Associations, often adopt guidelines on good practise in critical areas, such as on the definition of death and the limits of medical duties. Although such guidelines adopted by private bodies cannot change the law, they usually reflect unwritten principles underlying legal thinking in the areas in question.

Article 32 (Art. 14 revPC) is also the legal basis for all kinds of interventions by the police and courts. Examples of practical importance are the laws authorizing arrest, detention and searches.

2. Self-defense

Article 33 PC (Art. 15 revPC) (*Notwehr/légitime défense*) declares any act of self-defense against an unlawful attack by any third party which is ongoing or immediate to be lawful. An act committed in self-defense may be directed against the body or any other interest of the aggressor, but must be proportionate to the seriousness of the attack (Art. 16 revPC). Unlike English law,[10] Swiss legislation provides for mitigating circumstances if an act of self-defense exceeds what might reasonably be considered as a proportionate response to the attack. This provides some explanation for the fact that 3 per cent of sentences for manslaughter are below one year of custody in Switzerland.[11] This relatively high proportion of exceptionally lenient sentences reflects the wide recognition of mitigating circumstances in cases where the use of force in self-defense may not have been entirely justified.

The rules of self-defense also apply to situations in which an act is aimed at defending a third party who happens to be threatened by an illegitimate attack. Self-defense is a general principle which, along with the duress defense, applies to

---

10. A. Ashworth, *Principles of Criminal Law*, 3d edn., Oxford University Press 1999, pp. 138–151.
11. *European Sourcebook of Crime and Criminal Justice Statistics 1999*, Strasbourg: Council of Europe, p. 152.

all areas of law. Swiss civil law also expressly recognizes the right of any person to infringe on the rights of other parties in cases of self-defense or in an emergency.[12]

3. Acts Committed in Situations of Necessity or Duress

According to Article 34 PC (Art. 17 revPC) acts performed in a situation of necessity *(Notstand/état de necessité)* are lawful (i.e. 'not punishable'). The duress defense is open whenever there is an immediate risk to life, safety, or any other interests of the acting person or a third party, if this risk has not been self-induced, if it cannot be prevented in any other way, and if one could not reasonably expect the defendant to abandon the interest at stake. Unlike self-defense which is justified by the unlawful attack of an offender, the necessity defense concerns situations where the risk to be prevented may not have been provoked by any third party fault. Therefore, the limits – particularly in terms of proportionality of the response – must be more carefully evaluated. The necessity defense is unavailable if the protected interests are of lesser value than those sacrificed. If the two conflicting interests are of comparable value, as in cases where one life is saved whereas another person's life is sacrificed, the duress defense does not, strictly speaking, apply, but the judge may consider the moral dilemma as a mitigating circumstance which might even justify the decision not to impose a punishment (Art.18 II revPC).

Although the necessity defense can also be invoked in cases where the act was committed to protect the interests of a third party, it never may serve as a justification for acts committed in the public interest. Under continental law, public agents (including police officers) have to respect civil rights of defendants and citizens. Were they entitled to invoke the necessity defense in situations where they tried to protect public interests, the limits resulting from laws on procedure and on the exercise of public force might easily be avoided. Therefore, bounty hunting or similar practises common in America would be considered criminal under Swiss law (see Ch. 15 VI B 4). Private citizens only have the right to stop and detain offenders (i.e. to enact a citizen's arrest) if they catch the offender in *flagrante delicto* (i.e. in the act of committing the offense) and only if they immediately call the police.

4. Defenses not Codified in the Penal Code

Article 1 PC *(nullum crimen sine lege)* does not prevent the admission defenses which are not expressly set out in the PC. Therefore, Swiss courts have always recognized several defenses which are not codified in any written law. The most important one in practise is the defense that the victim had given his/her consent to the act which might otherwise constitute an offense. The most prominent example is medical intervention which, without consent, constitutes an illegal bodily injury. Consent has to be given after due information on all relevant facts and risks. It can be revoked, or given under conditions (as in sports) which are to be respected. Nobody can legally consent to give away his or her life or freedom. Consent to

---

12. Art. 52 Swiss CO.

serious bodily harm must serve some social value, as in the case of donating a kidney. Article 114 PC makes killing at the victim's request (euthanasia) an offense.

D. *Criminal Responsibility*

1. Age

In Swiss law children under the age of 7 are deemed to have no criminal responsibility and thus cannot be prosecuted. Moreover, special sentencing (and procedural) rules apply to children (7–14) and juveniles (15–18). Before the age of 15, the only available sentencing options are: cautioning, community work or disciplinary sanctions executed by the school, or education measures, such as educational supervision (probation), placement in a foster family or in an appropriate home. Between the ages of 15 and 18, custodial sentences can be imposed up to a maximum of one year.[13] Juveniles can also be placed in borstal-type homes for longer periods. When sanctions available for minors in Switzerland are examined in an international context, they appear to be among the most lenient in the Western World. This is particularly true since there are no exceptions allowing for juveniles to be treated as adults. Nowhere else does the fact of having committed an offense just before or just after reaching 18 have such dramatic implications. Even some special rules applying to offenders between the ages of 19 and 24 years (e.g., provision for committal to a borstal home) do not much mitigate the effects of the age-limit of 18 years. Based on a draft by Professor Martin Stettler of the University of Geneva, Parliament has adopted a new penal law for minors which may come into force in early 2005. It provides for a maximum custodial penalty of 4 years for offenders who are 16 or over at the time of the offence, thus reducing somewhat the importance of the 18 years age-limit.

2. The Insanity Defense

Article 10 PC makes insanity (*Unzurechnungsfähigkeit/irresponsabilité*) an absolute defense, and Article 11 provides for a mitigating circumstance if the defendant was not fully responsible for his act. (In the revised Penal Code, both situations will be treated together in Art. 19 revPC.) Insanity is defined as the temporary or permanent lack of capacity to understand the criminal nature of an act, or the inability to control one's behavior in accordance with one's mind. The criminal responsibility of the defendant is diminished if his capacity to understand or control his behavior was – at the time of the act – temporarily or permanently impaired. Several mental troubles have been recognized as causes of insanity, such as mental illness, feeble-mindedness and serious intoxication through alcohol or drugs. In practise, alcohol intoxication is presumed (though not necessarily assumed, since individual differences in tolerance are being recognized) beyond a blood-alcohol concentration of 0.30 per cent; between 0.20 and 0.30 per cent, partial insanity may be admitted by the court,

13. See M. Boehlen, *Kommentar zum Schweizerischen Jugendstrafrecht*, Berne: Staempfli 1975.

whereas lower levels of blood-alcohol concentration will not usually be considered to be a mitigating circumstance.[14]

Whenever the judge has some doubt about the (full) responsibility of the offender, he must call for a medical expert (in general, a psychiatrist) to examine the defendant (Art. 13 PC/Art. 20 rev PC). Although the judge is not legally bound by the expert's opinion, he or she may not reject his conclusions without good reason, for instance on the basis that the report is contradictory or otherwise flawed (see Ch. 15 V B 3). In such cases, he or she usually will ask for another expert's opinion.

The rules on insanity and diminished responsibility (Art.10–11 PC/Art.19 revPC) do not apply if the defendant had himself induced his condition in order to facilitate the commission of the offence, or while he could foresee committing an offence in this state (according to the *libera actio in causa* rule, Art. 12 PC). In practice, this means that a driver who, before starting to drink, might have been able to foresee that he would drive later that evening has no defense for insanity or reduced responsibility. In cases where the defendant had committed an offense after having induced his full insanity (through intoxication), he will be guilty of a minor offense (Art. 263) even if he did not anticipate committing an offense in that state. In comparison to the legislation in other European countries – such as Italy or France – which never consider alcohol or drug intoxication to be a mitigating factor and sometimes even consider it to be an aggravating circumstance, Swiss criminal law recognizes relatively widely mitigating circumstances for offenders whose responsibility was temporarily impaired due to excessive drinking or drug abuse.

E. Mens Rea

Swiss criminal law is based on the principle *nulla poena sine culpa*, also recognized in the European Convention of Human Rights (ECHR, Art. 6 II). This means that anyone who did not act with *mens rea*, i.e. with 'fault', either intentionally or negligently cannot be found guilty of an offense. Swiss criminal law distinguishes only two forms of guilt: criminal intent (*dolus, Vorsatz/intention*) and criminal negligence (*Fahrlässigkeit/négligence*). As a rule, unless the law expressly says otherwise, offenses are punishable only if committed intentionally (18 I PC). Offenses without fault (or strict liability) are unknown in Swiss criminal law. Strict liability is limited to tort where it plays an important role in traffic accidents.

1. Criminal Intent (*Dolus*)

A person acts intentionally when he or she commits an offense with full knowledge of all relevant facts and with intent. Knowledge must include all objective elements of the offense as defined by the PC. Intent is independent of the offender's motive and may include the so-called *dolus eventualis*, i.e. situations where the offender accepts the result of his act as inevitable although he does not really desire it (Art. 12 II revPC). This form of quasi-intent facilitates the proof of intent in situations where the

---

14. See Ch. 4.

offender acted and simply ignored the inevitable consequences of his behavior. If the risk was relatively high, the conclusion would be that he had 'accepted' (and, thus, willingly induced) the outcome.

2. Criminal Negligence

Criminal negligence is defined in Article 18 III (Art. 12 III revPC) under two alternative forms. Conscious negligence (*luxuria*) is the form of guilt where the perpetrator is aware of the risk, but nevertheless acts hoping that the danger will not materialize. It is this hope which distinguishes *luxuria* from *dolus eventualis*. Unconscious negligence (*negligentia*) is the form of guilt where a person is not even aware of the risks his or her behavior might carry for third parties. In both cases, criminal negligence will be assumed only if the defendant could have foreseen, using reasonable precautions, the harmful consequences of the risks he created, and if he did not take the steps required to prevent the outcome. In assessing whether or not the measures taken were sufficient, reference will be made to general standards of precaution as well as to the defendant's personal circumstances. As a rule, the degree of required precaution will be determined by special legislation (such as the Road Traffic Act), *leges artis* (e.g. in cases of medical malpractice), as well as by general standards resulting from previous (bad) experience. Although courts are always at risk of considering risks as 'unreasonable' whenever the results are dramatic, it should be kept in mind that the concept of required reasonable precaution is ultimately dynamic, i.e. developing alongside the increasing standards of technology and accident prevention. Unlike Swiss civil law, criminal law does not distinguish between serious and ordinary negligence, although the sentence will, of course, reflect the degree of the defendant's fault. Similarly, the concept of *recklessness* is unknown in Swiss criminal law.

3. Error of Fact

As knowledge of all relevant facts is required in order to assume criminal intent or criminal negligence, a mistake as to the facts is of great practical importance in criminal proceedings. If a person commits an offense because he or she is ill-informed or has misinterpreted certain facts, he or she will be judged as if the facts were such as he or she had imagined (Art. 19 I PC/Art. 13 I revPC). However, ignoring or misinterpreting relevant facts may be considered to be negligent if the error might have been avoided by taking reasonable precautions. In this case, the defendant might be found guilty of an offense committed by negligence, if any such offense exists under the law (Art.19 II PC/Art.13 II revPC). As a general rule, all errors which are of an essentially *cognitive* nature will fall under Article 19 PC (13 § 2 revPC).

4. Error or Ignorance of the Law

Errors which are essentially of a *normative* nature will fall under Article 20 PC which deals with situations where the defendant ignored or misinterpreted the legal (criminal) nature of the act. Unlike French, English and American law, which all start from the principle that no one should ignore the law, the Swiss criminal law (following the German model) has traditionally made allowances for such errors. However, this does not mean that anybody could easily invoke an error of this kind. In order to successfully invoke this defense, the defendant has to establish that the error resulted from good reason, such as being given incorrect information from a competent authority, or from the fact that the behavior in question had previously been tolerated by the authorities for some time. In addition, the defendant has to establish that he or she thought of acting lawfully, and not just of avoiding the risk of conviction on technical grounds. If the error was fully justified, the defendant will be fully excused, if not, the error may be considered as a mitigating factor. In practise, Article 20 is relatively often invoked by police officers who, e.g., fired at suspects in situations where the limits of legal police action are blurred, or whenever courts change the interpretation of the law in a sense which is unfavorable to the defendant who thought he or she was acting in accordance with legal practise and thinking. Given the limited discretion Swiss prosecutors have to drop prosecutions (see Chapter 15 IV B 3), many conflicts of this kind have to be settled through defenses based on substantive criminal law.

F. Specific Preconditions of Punishment

Normally an offense is punishable if the requirements as described by law (*actus reus*) have been met by the perpetrator, including the element of fault (*mens rea*). In some exceptional cases, however, further prerequisites must be fulfilled, which are independent of the behavior of the defendant. Thus, offenses in connection with bankruptcy are not punishable unless the perpetrator has been declared bankrupt (Arts. 163–167). Similarly, participation in acts of collective violence (Arts. 133–134) is only punishable if a participant has been wounded or killed, irrespective of whether the defendant himself contributed to that result.

By far the most important example of such a prerequisite is a formal complaint (*Strafantrag/plainte*) from the victim. Offenses only punishable on complaint (e.g. libel, simple assault and property offenses involving damage of less than CHF 300 or USD 230 (EUR 200), Art. 172ter PC) cannot be prosecuted unless the victim files a complaint within three months from the time that he or she learns about the offense and the identity of the suspect. Since prosecution is, as a rule, compulsory (see Ch. 15 IV C 1), making certain offenses, where personal interests are at stake, punishable only after a formal complaint is a way of taking the victim's priorities into account.

G. Periods of Limitation (Prescription)

Unlike Anglo-Saxon law, continental criminal law has only allowed, since the French Revolution, criminal prosecution within certain time-limits (*Verjährung/ prescription*). These limits vary according to the seriousness of the offense. Under the influence of Anglo-Saxon legal thinking, these time-limits have been abolished for crimes against humanity such as genocide (Art.101 revPC). For ordinary crimes (felonies) for which the maximum penalty is more than three years, such as theft (Art. 139), fraud (Art. 146), rape (Art. 190 PC) or forgery of documents (Art. 251), prosecution is possible, according to a new amendment which came into force on 1 October 2002, if a conviction (before appeal) is secured within fifteen years following the commission of the offense (Art. 97 revPC). For offenses carrying a maximum penalty of no more than three years, the period of limitation is seven years, and for crimes for which a life sentence can be imposed, thirty years.

Similar rules apply with respect to the execution of sentences (Art. 99 revPC). Here, the time-limits range from a minimum of five years to thirty years for life sentences.

H. Criminal Attempt

Swiss criminal law distinguishes between two degrees of attempts: Completed attempts where the offender has completed the activity, and uncompleted ones where the line of action was interrupted before all steps were accomplished. In all cases of attempts, the judge has discretion to mitigate the sentence. In addition, there is also the category of impossible attempt. In the revised PC, all attemps will be regulated in the same Article 22.

1. Incomplete Attempts

An attempt is considered to be incomplete (*unvollendeter Versuch/tentative simple*) if the offender has started the criminal activity, but ceased before the offense had been completed (Art. 21). The main difficulty is in drawing the line between mere preliminary acts which, in general, are not punishable, and the beginning of the execution of the criminal act as such which constitutes a punishable attempt. According to doctrine and court practise, an attempt is assumed whenever, according to the offender's plan, he has reached the point of no return. In 1982, preparatory acts for some particularly serious crimes have been made punishable under the form of a special offense (see above I C 3). In cases where the offender abandoned the criminal project on his or her own initiative, the judge has unlimited discretion to mitigate the sentence, including abstaining from imposing any punishment.

2. Complete Attempts

An attempt is considered to be complete (*vollendeter Versuch/délit manqué*) whenever the offender has done everything he or she had planned to do in order to commit the offense, although the result which characterizes the offense may not have been achieved (Art. 22). If the perpetrator actively contributed to prevent the criminal result (*tätige Reue/repentir actif*), the judge has discretion to mitigate the sentence.

3. Impossible Attempts

An attempt is considered to be impossible (*untauglicher Versuch/délit impossible*) whenever the offense could technically not be committed against the object in question, or with the means chosen by the offender (Art. 23 PC). This allows to punish offenders who thought committing the offense, without being able to achieve their criminal project because they acted while mistaking certain facts. In this sense, impossible attempts are a sort of inverse mistake of facts (Art. 19, see above). The judge has discretion to mitigate the sentence or, in special cases, may even abstain from imposing any punishment.

I. Participation

Of the several possible forms of participation in an offense (*Teilnahme/participation*) only two are expressly dealt with in the PC, namely incitement and aiding and abetting. There is no equivalent to 'conspiracy' in Swiss criminal law, although participation in a criminal organization or supporting organized crime became a special offense in 1994 (Art. 260ter). In certain cases, it is an aggravating circumstance to have acted as a member of a gang, e.g. in connection with theft or robbery (Art. 139 § 3.1, or Art. 140 § 3.1 PC). Participation is accessory to the principal offense. It is completed as soon as the principal offense has at least been attempted. In cases where the sentence will be aggravated or mitigated according to specific personal qualities or circumstances of the author, each participant will be punished according to his own acts and circumstances (Art. 26 PC/Art. 27 rev PC).

1. Co-offenders

Several persons committing an offense together, in such a way that each of them takes an equally important part in planning or performing the criminal act, are considered co-offenders (*Mittäter/coauteurs*). This is not dealt with in the PC, but has been developed by legal doctrine and case-law.

2. Indirect Offenders

An indirect offender (*mittelbarer Täter/auteur médiat*) is a person who compels another person to commit an offense or who, through deception, causes another person to commit an offense. The person subject to the deception will typically have no knowledge of or misconceive the relevant facts and thus act without *mens rea*. Examples include cases where a police officer arrested a person on the basis of suspicion which was fabricated by another party, or where an accountant enters false data into a company's books because he or she does not understand the true nature of certain operations. This is not codified in Swiss law, but has been developed by doctrine and case law.

3. Incitement

Instigation (*Anstiftung/instigation*) consists of any form of persuasion by which another person is led to commit an intentional offense (Art. 24 PC). The instigator is

Criminal Law   261

subject to the same punishment as the principal offender (*Haupttäter/auteur principal*). Attempted instigation is punishable if the offense which the instigator tries to suggest is a felony.

4. Aiding and Abetting

Complicity (*Gehilfenschaft/complicité*) is any form of assistance, including psychological support, of a principal offender before or while he or she is committing the offense (Art. 25 PC). The sentence for an accomplice will be the same as that for the principal offender, but with some mitigation. Assistance after the offense has been achieved is generally no longer punishable as complicity, but the offender may be punishable as an accessory after the fact, either for receiving stolen goods (Art. 160, *Hehlerei/recel*), for 'obstruction of justice' (Art. 305, *Begünstigung/entrave à l'action pénale*), or for money laundering (Art. 305bis).

5. Companies

Companies and other legal persons were traditionally not punishable under continental criminal law, since punishing an artificial construct was considered to be contrary to the principle *nulla poena sine culpa*, given that only individuals can act with fault. Under heavy international pressure, particularly from Anglo-Saxon countries where strict liability is not uncommon,[15] Switzerland and other continental countries have widened the possibilities to hold companies criminally liable. In an amendment to the PC which will become legally effective in 2004, companies may be held criminally liable if their internal organization did not allow determination of individual responsibilities in the decision-making process (Art. 102 revPC). Since cases like these may not be too frequent, things will probably not change very much. It should be noted, however, that the PC (in Art. 59) offers very wide possibilities to confiscate criminal profits regardless of the fault of the person or company who owns them (see below IV C). Therefore, the principle that criminal profits should not be left in the hands of criminals or their proxies is almost completely achieved under continental criminal law, although companies are not as widely punishable as under Anglo-Saxon law. It should also be noted that making shareholders (indirectly) criminally liable for offenses committed by the management may be unfair, particularly if they were unable to influence the internal decision-making process.

6. Offenses Committed by the Press

In order to preserve the freedom of the press, Article 27 PC/Article 28 revPC establishes specific rules as to the responsibility of participants. As a rule, the author of a text is solely responsible. However, the PC also protects the anonymity of an author. The editor's premises may not be searched in order to discover the identity. Instead, the editor or, if there is no editor, the printer may be held responsible. Nor can the

---

15. A. Ashworth, *op. cit.* (fn. 10), pp. 183–191.

media be compelled to disclose the identities of their sources, except in cases involving very serious offenses (Art. 27bis PC, Art. 28a revPC).

IV. CRIMINAL SANCTIONS

The Penal Code, although based upon ideas which date from the end of the nineteenth century (see above C 1) provides for a large variety of criminal sanctions. The following information will be limited to sanctions against adult offenders (for minors, see above III D 1). The revised PC, which will probably come into force in 2005, will substantially change the system of sanctions. The main categories will remain custodial and financial penalties on one hand, and measures of security or rehabilitation on the other. In addition, community service may become one of the more frequently imposed sanctions.

A. Sanctions

According to the revised PC, sanctions will be day-fines, community service, and custodial sanctions.

Capital punishment is prohibited by the Constitution (Art.10 I) and by Protocol No. 6 to the European Convention of Human Rights, ratified by Switzerland in 1987. Although the death penalty was removed from the PC in 1942, executions were nevertheless allowed until 1992 under the Military Penal Code for a number of offenses committed in wartime; seventeen death sentences were executed during the Second World War.[16] In practise, the death penalty had already vanished under the former cantonal codes, although rare executions continued until 1940. This is perhaps one of the reasons why public opinion is, compared to other countries, very unfavorable towards capital punishment, as a series of surveys conducted over 20 years have shown.[17]

1. Custodial Sanctions

Traditionally, the Penal Code provided for three degrees of custodial sanctions: penal servitude (*Zuchthaus/réclusion*), imprisonment (*Gefängnis/emprisonnement*) and detention (*Haft/arrêts*). However the differences between these three degrees have gradually vanishd over the last 50 years. Therefore, the revised PC will only provide for one type of custodial sanction. The important innovation will be that its duration is to be of at least six months. This will dramatically change Switzerland's sentencing structure. Until now, short custodial sentences were the favored mechanism of disposal, contributing to one of the most lenient sentencing structures

---

16. P. Noll, *Landsverräter, 17 Lebensläufe und Todesurteile, 1942–1944*, Frauenfeld/ Stuttgart: Huber 1980.
17. M. Killias, *Grundriss der Kriminologie – Eine europäische Perspektive*, Berne: Staempfli 2002, p. 423.

in Europe.[18] According to proponents of the reform (inspired largely by late 19th century debates), short custodial sentences are responsible for damaging the prospects of rehabilitation and therefore should be avoided whenever possible. Although the revised PC makes it possible to impose custodial sentences of less than six months, whenever the prospects that an 'alternative' sanction (fine or community service) will be successfully served are too slim, judges will, in the future, have to impose a fine on first-time offenders (except, of course, in the case of serious crimes carrying a custodial sentence of more than 6 months), followed by community service (in the case of repeat offenders), and, finally, custodial sanctions as a last resort. So far, custodial sanctions of up to 18 months were suspended in about 3 out of 4 cases. In the future it will be possible to suspend sentences of up to two years (Art. 42 revPC) whenever the risk of defendant re-offending seems reasonably moderate. This is, according to current practise, usually assumed if a defendant has no more than two previous convictions. In the future, it will also be possible (contrary to the current system) to suspend sentences *partially* (Art. 43 revPC). According to this system, the convict will have to serve one part of his term in custody, while another part will be suspended.

In the past, immediate short custodial sentences were often executed under the form of 'half-detention', meaning that the convict had to stay in prison overnight and at the weekend, but continued doing his usual job or community service during the day. These alternative ways of executing custodial sentences have reduced entries into institutions from approximately 12,000 per year in the 1980s to about 7,000 after 1995. Since sentences have become increasingly longer over the years, this drop has not translated into lower incarceration rates. Indeed, Switzerland's incarceration rate has remained around or below 90 per 100,000 population over the last 20 years. However, the drop of entries into institutions may have contributed to reducing the proportion of Swiss nationals in prisons, since they disproportionately used to serve short sentences for drunken-driving, drug abuse and other minor offenses. The proportion of foreign nationals in Swiss prison has increased, since 1988, from 33 per cent to 59 per cent in 2001.[19]

Prisoners having served two thirds of their custodial sentence have until now been eligible for conditional release or parole (Art. 38 para. 1.1 PC, *bedingte Entlassung/libération conditionnelle*). In the future, parole will be maintained and will be – 'exceptionally' – available after one half of the sentence has been served (Art. 86 I and Art. 4 revPC). This reform will certainly produce a short-term drop in the number of persons detained in institutions, at least if the 'exception' becomes more or less the rule. If this happens, however, judges are likely to react by taking earlier release into account when determining sentences.[20] It is, therefore, rather difficult to anticipate the precise effects of this reform on the size of the future prison

18. *European Sourcebook* (*op. cit*, note 10), pp. 149–166. Sentences have remained remarkably stable over the last twenty years (M. Killias, M. Aebi, A. Kuhn and S. Rônez, 'Sentencing in Switzerland in 2000', *Overcrowded Times* 10/6–1999, pp. 1–20), as well as the (moderate) incarceration rate of approximately 90 per 100,000 (A. Kuhn, *Détenus: Combien? Pourquoi? Que faire?*, Berne: Haupt 2000).
19. M. Killias, *Grundriss, op. cit.* (note 17), p. 529.
20. A. Kuhn, *op. cit.* (note 18), p. 160; M. Killias, *op. cit.* (note 17), pp. 526–528.

population. Parolees can be put under the supervision of the Parole Board, although in practise this measure seldom restrains freedom of movement, usually taking the form of support from social workers. Unlike America where re-incarceration mostly occurs for parole violations, former prisoners hardly ever re-enter institutions unless they have been responsible for the commission of a new offense. Over a five year follow-up period, approximately 40 per cent of former inmates were sent back to prison for having committed a new offense.[21]

2. Fines

Until now, fines have been imposed in the form of fixed amounts and, depending on the judge's discretion, could vary between CHF 1 and 40,000 (approximately USD 30,000). According to the revised PC, the imposition of fines will be a two stage process (Art. 34 revPC): First, the judge will have to determine, according to the seriousness of the offense, the number of days to be 'served'; then, he or she will have to establish the defendant's daily net income. By multiplying the daily income by the number of days, he will determine the sum to be paid by the defendant. According to the new system, the minimum daily income may range from 1 cent to CHF 3,000 (approximately USD 2,300).

This new system is designed to bring the amount of the fine more in line with the defendant's financial situation (as in Finland, Germany, Austria and some other countries). Parliament was careful to set the maximum daily income high enough to include very wealthy defendants. Despite this, however, there is still the risk that many offenders who have no (known) income, may receive either ridiculously low or ridiculously high fines. In Germany, Austria and other countries which rely on this system, the number of defendants who end up 'paying' their fine by going to prison has reached embarrassing proportions. The effect has been to socially redistribute rather than to abolish short custodial sentences. It remains to be seen how the new Swiss system will be able to deal with these possible dilemmas.

Unpaid fines will continue to be converted into other sanctions. Under the new system, fines are first to be converted into community work, if the defendant can reasonably be expected to serve the sanction under this form. As a last resort, the fine will be converted into a confinement order, where the defendant will pay one day in prison per day-fine. In practise, however, judges will be able to avoid these complications by imposing custodial sentences of more than 6 months at the outset. Since virtually all offenses provide for a maximum penalty far beyond that limit (see IV D 1 below), there might be few technical obstacles to such a shift in the sentencing structure, as has been observed in Portugal, Greece,[22] and Spain after short custodial sentences were substituted with 'alternative' sanctions.

In the future, day-fines can be suspended under the same conditions as custodial sentences (Art. 42 revPC). The main condition will be that the offender's predicted risk of future offending is low. In practise, this is likely to be assumed whenever the offender has no more than two previous convictions.

---

21. R. Storz, *Rückfall nach Strafvollzug*, Berne: Federal Office of Statistics 1997.
22. A. Kuhn, *op. cit.* (note 18), pp. 45–49.

3. Community Service

Community service was introduced as an experimental form of executing short immediate custodial sentences in 1991. In one cantonal experiment (Vaud), offenders who had been sentenced to short custodial sanctions were even randomly assigned to either community service or imprisonment.[23] According to Article 37 revPC, community service will become the main sanction which judges will be able to impose whenever they feel that a penalty of less than 180 days (under the day-fine scheme or in custody) will be appropriate. In that case, four hours of community work will correspond to one day (in custody or to one day-fine). If the defendant does not serve his community work within two years, the sentence will be converted into a fine (calculated according to the day-fine system) or into an immediate custodial sentence. Community work is unpaid. It is to be performed under the supervision of the correctional service, whenever feasible in a hospital or any other institution serving the public interest. Community service can be suspended under the same conditions as custodial sentences or fines (Art. 42 revPC).

4. Electronic Monitoring

Electronic monitoring is currently only available in a few cantons as an experimental form of executing short immediate custodial sentences. This is likely to remain the case under the new system, since the revPC will continue to allow cantons to experiment with innovative sanctions (Art. 387 IV revPC). Currently, a controlled experiment (comparing electronic monitoring and community service) is ongoing in the French-speaking part of Switzerland.[24]

B. Measures against Persons

1. Therapeutic Measures and Incapacitation (Internment)

For adults of all ages, the Penal Code created special measures with a view to rehabilitating mentally ill or mentally impaired offenders (Art. 59 revPC), alcoholics and drug addicts (Art. 60 revPC) and young offenders who were under 25 years at the time they committed the offense (Art. 61 revPC). Some of these measures are non-custodial (Art. 63 revPC). The others will be pronounced in addition to a term of imprisonment; however, this term does not determine the time the offender spends in custody. The person must be interned in a specialized instiution (Art. 58

23. M. Killias, M. Aebi and D. Ribeaud, 'Does Community Service Rehabilitate better than Short-term Imprisonment? Results of a Controlled Experiment', *The Howard Journal of Criminal Justice* 39/1 (2000), 40–57.
24. M. Killias, M. Aebi and D. Ribeaud, 'Learning Through Controlled Experiments', *Crime & Delinquency* 46/2 (2000), 233–251.

revPC). The duration of confinement is five years for adults, four years for young adults below 25, and three years for alcohol or drug addicts (Arts. 59 IV, 60 IV, 61 IV revPC). However, this period can be extended to 6 years for young adults and alcohol or drug addicts, and indefinitely for adults. The precise duration of confinement will be largely determined by the (psychiatric) experts (Art. 62d revPC). In the event that it is shorter than the duration of the custodial sentence imposed, the defendant will have to serve the surplus before being eligible for parole (Arts. 57, 62b III revPC). Interestingly, the judge can impose a therapeutic measure (in custody, Art. 59 revPC) later, i.e. during the execution of a custodial sentence; this hardly seems compatible with the maxim of *res iudicata*, i.e. the principle according to which definitive decisions (including sentences) should not be reviewed later. If the defendant is found guilty of a violent or particularly serious crime (for which he might be sentenced to a maximum penalty of at least 10 years), and if it is likely that he might commit more similarly serious offenses in future, the judge can impose a measure of incapacitation (internment, Art. 64 revPC). The duration of this measure of confinement is not time limited; it just depends on the risks of future re-offending (Art. 64a revPC).

The recent reform has considerably reshaped therapeutic and incapacitative measures. It seems likely that such measures, which are, under the narrower conditions of existing law, only rarely used, will become quantitatively more important. It is also highly probable that these measures will result in an increase in the prison population.

2. Other Measures (Arts. 66–68 revPC)

If the offender has committed an offense in connection with his or her professional activities or his or her business, the judge may bar him or her from exercising this job or business for a period of up to five years, starting from the time he or she is released on parole (in the case of a custodial sentence). If the offense had been committed while the defendant was driving a car, the judge may revoke his or her driver's license for a period of up to five years. These measures can only be imposed in addition to an ordinary sanction (custody, day-fines, community service, or any of the incapacitative or therapeutic measures).

C. Measures against Objects

Objects which are the product of a criminal activity (for example, counterfeit money) which were used during the commission of an offense or which were designed for the purpose of committing an offense, may be confiscated if they constitute a danger to the safety of persons or to public security (Art. 58 PC/Art. 69 revPC, *Einziehung/confiscation d'objets*). According to Article 59 PC (70 revPC), the same rule applies to valuables. They can also be confiscated from third parties. This rule tries to make sure that neither an offender nor a third party will benefit from the commission of a crime.

D. Sentencing Rules

1. General Rules

As a rule, the Swiss Penal Code allows judges discretion in determining sentences. In some extreme cases, such as the making of false accusations (Art. 303), the sentence may vary from three days to twenty years of custody. Aggravating and mitigating circumstances merely serve to widen the frame. Under both the current and the revised PC, several simultaneous verdicts will not lead to separate sentences, but to one sentence which will be determined by the most serious offense. Irrespective of the number of additional offenses which the defendant has been found guilty of, the maximum penalty will be no more than 50 per cent higher than the ordinary maximum for the most serious offense (Art. 68 PC/Art. 49 I revPC). Sentencing decisions are not structured by guidelines, although some informal standards exist at local level for common offenses. By increasing the requirements concerning the reasons for the sentences, the Federal Supreme Court has, in recent years, tried to steer lower courts into being more consistent in their sentencing decisions. Article 50 revPC will even oblige judges to indicate not only the aggravating and mitigating circumstances that they considered, but also to indicate the weight given to each factor. This might lead, in the long term, to greater standardization of sentencing decisions.

2. Fault, Mitigating and Aggravating Circumstances

According to Article 47 revPC (formerly Art. 63), the sentence should reflect the seriousness of the defendant's motive, his past and his personal circumstances. The revPC abolishes the rules on aggravating circumstances (with the exception of the rule on plurality of verdicts, Art. 49 revPC), concentrating instead on mitigating factors (Art. 48 revPC). Whenever the judge finds that some mitigating factor should be considered, he will be free to set a sentence below the minimum provided by the SPC for the offense at stake (Art. 48a revPC).

E. The Execution of Custodial Sentences

Each canton is responsible for the execution of custodial sentences. The revPC merely imposes a limited number of general rules (Arts. 74–92 revPC). In general, both sentences and prison regimes are rather liberal in Switzerland – even in high security prisons.

SELECTED BIBLIOGRAPHY

Corboz, B., *Les infractions en droit suisse*, Berne: Staempfli 2002.

Graven, P. and B. Sträuli, *L'infraction pénale punissable*, 2nd edn., Berne: Staempfli 1995.

Hurtado Poso, P., *Droit penal: Partie générale*, 2 vols., Zurich: Schultess 1997/2002.

Killias, M., *Précis de droit pénal général*, 2nd edn., Berne: Staempfli 2001.

Niggli, M. and H. Wiprächtiger (eds.), *Strafgesetzbuch (Basler Kommentar)*, Basel: Helbing and Lichtenhahn 2003.

Rehberg, J., *Strafrecht*, 3 vols. (with several co-authors), 8th edn., Zurich: Schultess 2003.

Stratenwerth, G., *Schweizerisches Strafrecht: Allgemeiner Teil*, Berne: Staempfli, Vol. I, 2nd edn. 1996, Vol. II 1989.

Trechsel, S., *Schweizerisches Strafgesetzbuch: Kurzkommentar*, 2nd edn., Zurich: Schultess 1997.

Trechsel, S. and P. Noll, *Schweizerisches Strafrecht: Allgemeiner Teil*, 2 vols., 5th edn., Zurich: Schultess 1998.

Chapter 15
Law of Criminal Procedure*

S. Trechsel**
M. Killias***

I. Laws on Criminal Procedure

A. General Remarks

The former Federal Constitution, while vesting the competence to legislate in the field of substantive criminal law in the Confederation, left the competence with respect to criminal procedure with the cantons (Art. 64bis). The new constitution which came into force on 1 January 2000, gives the Confederation powers to unify the law on criminal procedure (Art. 123 para. 3). Since this new federal law on criminal procedure has not yet been adopted,[1] all 26 Swiss Cantons and half-cantons continue to use their own codes of criminal procedure. Although these codes share many common features, particularly in light of the growing influence of the European Convention of Human Rights, they vary according to their principle source of inspiration, with the French, German and old Austrian laws being the most influential models over the last two centuries. On the federal level, a Federal Code of Criminal Procedure (FCCrP), a Federal Code of Military Criminal Procedure and a Federal Administrative Penal Code regulate procedures before federal courts and authorities.

Over the decades, cantonal legislation in the field of criminal procedure has been considerably reshaped by federal laws passed in order to standardize the application

---

* This chapter is intended to be an introduction to Swiss criminal law for Anglo-Saxon readers. Therefore, several comparisons will be made with American and English due process rules in order to highlight the characteristics of Swiss criminal procedure. Sources will only be given if they are in English, or if they are highly specific. A list of introductory texts to Swiss criminal procedure will be given at the end of this chapter. The authors wish to thank Sarah Summer, LLB, assistant at the University of Zurich Law School, and Cynthia Tavares, Home Office Research, Development and Statistics Directorate, for their invaluable help with English.

** Professor, University of Zurich Law School, former President of the European Commission on Human Rights.

*** Professor, University of Lausanne School of Criminal Justice. Part-time judge at the Federal Supreme Court of Switzerland.

1. A draft has been drawn up by Niklaus Schmid, Emeritus Professor of Law at the University of Zurich Law School. It has been submitted to all interested parties for comments, and it is currently being redrafted by the Federal Office of Justice.

F. Dessemontet and T. Ansay (eds), Introduction to Swiss Law, 269–286.

of the Swiss Penal Code (PC), as well as by principles developed by the Federal Supreme Court. Examples are the rules on the administration of evidence (Art. 249 FCCrP, *freie Beweiswürdigung/principe de la libre appréciation des preuves*) which oblige judges to give due consideration to all evidence which may be relevant (including, e.g. hearsay evidence) without any limitations resulting from formal rules (e.g. requiring witnesses to give evidence under oath). Also important is the principle that any cause might be subject to a re-trial in the event that new evidence is discovered which was not available at the first trial (Art. 397 PC/385 revPC), and the rule, developed by the Federal Supreme Court, according to which prosecutors (and the police) may not use their discretion in a way which might *de facto* 'decriminalize' conduct which constitutes an offense under federal criminal law (i.e. mainly the PC).[2]

The most important area of *de facto* unification of the law of criminal procedure is, without doubt, the protection of human rights. While the former Federal Constitution contained a very limited list of fundamental rights, the Federal Supreme Court created an impressive series of case law extending the protection of human rights. The European Convention on Human Rights, which sets out important procedural guarantees, particularly in Articles 5 and 6, and which Switzerland ratified in 1974, has further contributed to the unification of the rules on criminal procedure.[3]

B. Constitutional Level

1. The Federal Constitution

The new federal constitution contains due process guarantees which are almost identical to those set out in the European Convention on Human Rights. These include the guarantee of fair, speedy decision by independent judges in all procedures, a right to have all convictions reviewed on appeal, a right to counsel (including those persons deprived of financial resources), a right to a prompt hearing by a judge in case of pre-trial detention, and the presumption of innocence (Arts. 9, 29–32). Given this extensive catalogue of human rights, the cantonal constitutions (which contained most of these guarantees as cantonal principles for more than a century) are no longer of great relevance in this domain.

---

2. Readers should be aware that Swiss prosecutors have, even beyond this rule and compared to countries with the expediency principle (England, France, the Netherlands, the USA), very little powers to drop proceedings (for details, see IV B 3 below).
3. S. Trechsel, *Die europäische Menschenrechtskonvention, ihr Schutz der persönlichen Freiheit und die schweizerischen Strafprozessrechte*, Bern: Staempfli 1974; S. Trechsel, 'Der Einfluss der Europäischen Menschenrechtskonvention auf das Strafrecht und Strafverfahrensrecht der Schweiz', *Zeitschrift für die Gesamte Strafrechtswissenschaft* (German Criminal Law Review) 100 (1988), 673; R. Levi, 'Der Einfluss der Europäischen Menschenrechtskonvention auf das kantonale Prozessrecht, Erwartungen und Ergebnisse, *Zeitschrift für Strafrecht* (Swiss Criminal Law Review) 106 (1989), 225; L. Rouiller, 'L'effet dynamique de la Convention Européenne des droits de l'homme', *Zeitschrift für Strafrecht* (Swiss Criminal Law Review) 109 (1992), 233.

2. The European Convention on Human Rights (ECHR)

The ECHR is directly applicable by Swiss courts and may be considered to be a source of constitutional law. As a rule, it may be said that the Convention's guarantees coincide with those in Swiss constitutional law. As Switzerland has accepted the individual's right of petition (Art. 34 ECHR), issues of federal and cantonal criminal procedure may finally be brought before the Court in Strasbourg. In recent years, this has occurred quite frequently.

C. *Statutes on Criminal Procedure*

1. Federal Statutes

On the federal level, there are four statutes of major importance in the field of criminal procedure. The Federal Law on the Judicial System (FLJS, *Bundesgesetz über die Organisation der Bundesrechtspflege/loi fédérale d'organisation judiciaire*) contains basic rules of procedure for the Federal Supreme Court. The Federal Code of Criminal Procedure applies to offenses prosecuted by federal authorities, such as crimes directed against the Confederation, its institutions or a major national interest (Art. 340–340bis PC), as well as to appeals brought before the Federal Supreme Court in criminal matters (Arts. 268–278 FCCrP). The Federal Code of Military Criminal Procedure applies to cases dealt with by the military criminal justice system. The Administrative Penal Code deals with the prosecution of 'administrative offenses', such as offenses against customs laws and federal tax laws. It establishes an elaborate system of co-operation between administrative and judicial authorities with the defendant retaining the right to have his or her case reviewed in court (Art. 21 para. 2).

2. Cantonal Codes of Criminal Procedure

Cantonal codes of criminal procedure present a large variety both in form and content. While some of the smaller cantons (e.g. Zug) have codes of fewer than one hundred articles, some of the major cantons (e.g. Zurich, Vaud, Geneva) have very elaborate codes of over five hundred articles. As a rule, the codes tend to set out general rules in order to avoid repetition, thus attaining a volume of some three to four hundred articles. Unfortunately, there is no central edition of these texts, and it is quite difficult to keep track of the frequent amendments.

D. *Case Law and Legal Doctrine*

1. Case Law

Since the Swiss law of criminal procedure is so scattered, case law, with the exception of leading cases ruled by two sections of the Federal Supreme Court, is difficult to locate. At this level, issues of interpretation of substantial criminal law are dealt with by the Criminal Law Chamber (*Kassationshof/Cour de cassation*), whereas issues of procedural law (related to due process and human rights) are dealt with by the Constitutional Law Chamber.

2. Legal Doctrine

Despite the lack of uniform legislation on criminal procedure, issues of criminal procedure and due process have found considerable interest among scholars over the last three decades. There are several excellent introductions to the law of criminal procedure, often written from a comparative perspective. In this sense, a large variety of rules and the necessity to develop a comparative perspective may have been a stimulating element. Variety also offers the opportunity of learning from the experiences of other cantons.

II. THE CRIMINAL JUSTICE SYSTEM

A. *Prosecuting Authorities*

The term 'prosecuting authorities' (*Strafverfolgungsbehörde/autorité de poursuite*) is used here in a broad sense: it includes the police (*Gerichtliche Polizei/police judiciaire*), investigating authorities (*Untersuchungsbehörde/autorité d'instruction*), prosecuting authorities in the narrow sense (*Anklagebehörde, Staatsanwaltschaft/ ministère public*) and authorities of indictment (*Ueberweisungsbehörde, Anklagezulassungsbehörde/autorité de renvoi, autorité de mise en accusation*).

1. The Police

The police are generally the first authority to deal with an offence. It is their task to ascertain whether an offense was committed, to secure evidence and to discover the whereabouts of a suspect. Whereas, according to theoretical positions, they generally should not lead the investigation, in practise they do so because they are often in a much better position to conduct these operations.

2. The Investigating Authorities

In most cantons before 1950, the investigation used to be handled by a district governor (*Statthalter/préfet*), i.e. an executive authority whose origins date back to the *Ancien Régime*. Over the 19th century the French (and Austrian) system(s) of the investigating judge (*Untersuchungsrichter/juge d'instruction*) became more and more popular, particularly in the French-speaking cantons. At the same time, the cantons of Zurich and Basel adopted the German system of the *Staatsanwalt* (prosecutor) with one or more district prosecutors (*Bezirksanwalt/district attorney*). In many respects, these magistrates (often elected by the voters of the district) are comparable to American district attorneys, although they act under the authority of a cantonal prosecutor who is ultimately employed by the cantonal government. Since these investigating magistrates have powers to issue arrest and search warrants, the question came up whether they can be considered to be independent judges (in the sense of Art. 5 (3) ECHR). The European Court of Human Rights initially answered affirmatively,[4] but subsequently reversed this ruling in 1990.[5] Over the following years, all cantons changed their systems in order to comply with the requirements of the ECHR. In cantons with a French system (having independent investigating judges), no change was needed, whereas those with the District Attorney system had to provide for the possibility of an appeal to a court in all matters of arrest and warrants. The draft of the future federal code of criminal procedure will probably opt for the German *Staatsanwalt* model.

3. Cantonal Prosecutors

The institution of a public prosecutor originated in France and was introduced in Switzerland in the early nineteenth century. The organization and function of this authority varies across cantons. In every jurisdiction the public prosecutor (*Staatsanwalt/procureur district*), although appointed by the cantonal government, is expected to exercise his or her functions objectively and with due independence. In most cantons, the cantonal prosecutor (often called *Generalstaatsanwalt/procureur général*) supervises the activities of district attorneys. Usually, this magistrate has the ultimate power to drop prosecutions (*Einstellungsbeschluss/ordonnance de classement*). Once the investigation has been completed, he will present the case for the prosecution before courts.

4. The Authority of Indictment

With regard to the authority of indictment, a wide variety of solutions can be found. In several cantons (e.g. Berne, Thurgau, Neuchatel, Geneva), a special Bench of justices (*Anklagekammer/chambre d'accusation*) acts as the authority of indictment. Its powers are comparable to those of the American Grand Jury.

B. Trial Courts

During the 19th century, many cantons adopted the jury system which, at that time, was seen as a prerequisite to democracy. Over the 20th century, this optimistic view has widely faded away, and jury trials are increasingly seen as an unpredictable element in the criminal procedure. Therefore, today, in most cantons trials are conducted in district courts where between one and three professional judges sit with two to four lay judges. At the trial (*Hauptverhandlung/débats*), preliminary questions are dealt with first. Then the indictment is read out and the evidence is

4. ECtHR, *Schiesser v. Switzerland,* judgment of 4 December 1979, Series A, no. 34.
5. ECtHR, *Huber v. Switzerland*, judgment of 23 October 1990, Series A, no. 188.

heard – questions will at least be put to the defendant in order to ascertain the facts and his personal background. The file is made available to the judges and often constitutes the main piece of evidence. After the pleadings, the defendant has the right to make a final statement. The court then deliberates *in camera*. Finally, the verdict and the sentence (which is set during the same hearing) will be communicated, along with a summary of the court's considerations. The ruling with the full reasons, usually drafted by the court clerk and the presiding judge, will later be communicated in writing.

III. THE PARTIES TO THE CRIMINAL PROCEEDINGS

A. *Preliminary Observation*

The notion of 'parties to the proceedings' usually refers to two or more participants opposing each other in the pursuit of their individual interests. In Swiss criminal procedure, this term is regarded as inappropriate with regard to the public prosecution. In fact, the public prosecutor does not actually 'oppose' the defense, but his role is, not unlike an *amicus curiae*, to intervene in the sole interest of preserving law and justice. Prosecutors and the police all have the duty to also investigate facts which might be favorable to the defendant. If they fail to do so, they may be punishable under Article 312 PC ('abuse of powers'/*Amtsmissbrauch/abus d'autorité*).[6] Therefore, it is not unusual for prosecutors to file an appeal in the interest of the defendant, or to call for a new trial of a person who they later conclude (on the basis of new evidence) was indeed innocent. As a further consequence, the court will not be presented with files from the prosecutor and the defense counsel. Instead, all relevant documents collected during the investigation – no matter who introduced them into the case – will be presented to the court. In practise, however, the prosecution will generally be more sympathetic to the victim than to the defendant.

B. *The Defense*

By 'defense', we refer to both the defendant (*Beschuldigter, Angeschuldigter, Angeklagter/prévenu, inculpé, accusé*) and counsel (*Verteidiger/défenseur*).

1. The Defendant

The defendant's position in criminal proceedings is twofold. On the one hand, he or she is to be regarded as an active subject who benefits from the presumption of innocence. He or she has the right to be heard, but also the right to present evidence, to put questions to witnesses and to appeal. On the other hand, the defendant is also subject to investigatory measures, such as finger-printing, DNA analysis, and blood

---

6. There were several cases where prosecutors themselves were prosecuted and convicted for not having disclosed evidence which might have been favorable to the defendant (including mitigating circumstances).

test, and may also have to accept coercive measures such as arrest, pre-trial detention, searches or wire-tapping. Such interferences with fundamental rights must be based on the law and respect the limits of proportionality. The defendant is under no obligation to contribute to the prosecution, and no pressure may be applied in order to obtain statements. Devices such as the lie detector or methods like drug analysis are inadmissible irrespective of whether or not the defendant consents (see also VI, below). The defendant is neither obliged to answer questions nor to tell the truth.

2. Counsel

According to Article 6(3)(c) ECHR everyone subject to a criminal charge has the right to legal assistance by a counsel of his own choice. This right is generally granted in Switzerland, although not necessarily before the first police interrogation (on Miranda warnings, see V B 1). On the other hand, the defendant has no discretion to refuse legal assistance. In some cases, counsel may be imposed, for example if the prosecutor pleads orally before the court in person.[7] If the case is sufficiently complex or serious, e.g. if there is the likelihood that the defendant will receive an immediate custodial sentence, the accused person may be granted legal aid, i.e. he or she will be awarded a counsel, if possible of his or her own choice. These possibilities have been extended after a ruling of the European Commission and the Court of Human Rights which found the Swiss rules to be too restrictive.[8] It is the task of counsel to act solely in the legitimate interest of the client by watching over the legality of the proceedings and taking all lawful steps with a view to obtaining the best possible result. Ethical guidelines of bar associations will further define counsel's role; for example, telling a lie or presenting facts which a lawyer knows to be false is considered unethical. The defendant ought, at all times, to be in a position to consult his or her counsel in private. Swiss law is still not entirely satisfactory in this respect, as many cantons provide for limitations on this right immediately following arrest, a practise which has been found to be in violation of the Convention by the Strasbourg organs.[9]

Unlike American defense lawyers, Swiss lawyers usually do not conduct their own investigation, but they may request that the police (or the investigating judge or district attorney) examine hypothetical facts which might be favorable to the defense. Since the police and all magistrates (including courts) are in any case obliged to investigate evidence which might potentially be favorable to the defense, the role of defense lawyers is not as crucial in Swiss (and generally continental) criminal procedure as under Anglo-Saxon law, or in European civil proceedings. There are no rules of disclosure, since defense counsel have full access to the prosecutor's file from the early stages of the investigation;[10] on the other hand, defense lawyers are

---

7. In routine cases, prosecutors send the complete file to the court, but do not attend court hearings. It will then be the presiding judge's role to hear witnesses and the defendant.
8. ECtHR, *Quaranta v. Switzerland*, judgment of 24 May 1991, Series A, no. 205.
9. ECtHR, *S. v. Switzerland*, judgment of 28 November 1991, Series A, no. 220; see also ECtHR, *Schönenberger and Dumaz v. Switzerland*, judgment of 29 June 1988, Series A, no. 137.
10. The right to see all relevant documents and to be present at all hearings of witnesses, experts and other parties during the pre-trial investigation has always been considered as part of the right to be heard or, more generally, as a prerequisite of *due process*.

expected to draw the prosecutor's attention to possibly favorable (or mitigating) circumstances in order to allow such facts to be investigated before trial. For this reason, the trial is not so controversial as it is under the Anglo-Saxon system. The only surprise may come from a witness who does not relate the expected story.

C. The Victim

While everyone has the right to report (*anzeigen/dénoncer*) an offense to the prosecuting authorities, only persons who have personally been victims of an offense have *locus standi* in criminal proceedings. In 1993, a law on the protection of victims came into force, considerably extending the position of victims of violence (in a broad sense) in all kinds of procedures. In particular, it offers victims wide legal remedies to press for the prosecution of suspects (and to oppose decisions not to prosecute). It protects victims in their role as witnesses (from undue interrogation in court or during a confrontation with the alleged offender), and it obliges criminal courts to hear related civil claims for damages.[11] Victims of offenses against the person are to be informed about all relevant steps of the procedure, and they are entitled to act as a party at the trial (this includes the right to appeal against any decision which might interfere with their right to civil compensation).[12]

IV. GOVERNING PRINCIPLES OF CRIMINAL PROCEEDINGS

A. Preliminary Observation

In criminal procedure, legal doctrine has identified a certain number of governing principles. In the present chapter, general principles governing procedure (B), and principles concerning trial hearings (C) will be presented.

B. General Principles

1. The 'Principle of Instruction'

The 'principle of instruction' (*Instruktionsmaxime, Ermittlunsgrundsatz/principe d'instruction*) – as opposed to the 'principle of negotiation'[13] – applies in criminal matters and imposes a duty on all authorities involved in criminal proceedings to search for the truth. As a result, even courts are not bound by the evidence brought

---

11. In the event that the offender is unable to pay compensation, a comparatively generous compensation scheme has been set up in order to award all victims of violence reasonable amounts of damages.
12. For details, see M.E.I. Brienen and E.H. Hoegen, *Victims of Crime in 22 European Criminal Justice Systems*, Nijmegen 2000. According to this excellent overview of all European victim protection schemes, Switzerland's law seems to be among the most favorable to victims.
13. Called *Verhandlungsmaxime* or *Dispositionsmaxime*, or *principe des débats* in French (*quod non est in actis non est in mundo*) which prevails in civil procedure.

before them by the 'parties'. Plea-bargaining is thus, with very few exceptions, excluded (see VII B below).

2. The Right to be Heard

No disadvantageous decision may be taken unless the person concerned has been offered an opportunity to explain his or her point of view (*rechtliches Gehör/droit d'être entendu*).

3. The Principles of 'Legality', 'Opportunity' and '*Ex-officio*'

As has been explained above (I A), offenses will be prosecuted as soon as the prosecuting authority reaches the conclusion that an offense might have been committed and irrespective of the victim's wishes. This is the German-style principle of 'legality' (or of compulsory prosecution) which is related to the '*ex officio*' principle. This principle implies that prosecution takes place without the consent of the victim or any other party. There are some exceptions to the '*ex officio*' principle, since a number of offenses directed against private interests are prosecuted upon complaint only (see Ch. 14 III F), and prosecution of certain political offenses requires the consent of the Federal Government (Art. 105 CCrP).

In the vast majority of Swiss cantons, prosecuting authorities are required by law to bring a charge whenever there are sufficient grounds to suspect a person of having committed an offense (*Legalitätsprinzip/système de la légalité des poursuites*). A prosecutor (or police officer) who drops proceedings despite the existence of sufficient ground to suspect a person of having committed an offense, will be punishable (as a kind of accessory after the fact) under Article 305 PC ('obstruction of justice'/*Begünstigung/entrave à l'action pénale*). Several convictions over the last years show that this is not a merely theoretical risk. The opposite principle of 'expediency' (*Opportunitätsprinzip/système de l'opportunité des poursuites*) which is to be found in Geneva (as well as in neighboring France) leaves the public prosecutor wide discretion to drop a charge (classement). Currently, the expediency principle is becoming increasingly popular, particularly within the revised PC, where Article 53 will permit the prosecution to drop charges after reparation and in connection with drug offenses (following the Dutch model, Switzerland is considering adopting a system of de-facto-decriminalization of the production, trade, and consumption of cannabis).

4. Accusatorial and Inquisitorial Elements in Swiss Procedure

In an accusatorial system, the tasks of prosecuting and of determining a case on the merits are strictly separated, while in the inquisitorial system the judge also investigates the facts. In Switzerland, pre-trial proceedings mostly follow the inquisitorial system, whereas the accusatorial model prevails at the trial stage. In practise, however, prosecutors do not usually appear at hearings (see III B 2 above), and the defendant as well as witnesses are primarily examined by the presiding judge.

C. Trial Procedures

1. The 'Principle of Immediacy'

The 'principle of immediacy' (*Unmittelbarkeitsprinzip/principe de l'immédiateté*) requires evidence to be taken 'live' by the court (e.g. witnesses must be heard in person and no statements made during preliminary investigation may be read out). This principle prevails in jury trials, which, however, are rather exceptional in modern Swiss procedure. Other courts rely widely on evidence taken during the pre-trial stage of criminal proceedings. While, at first sight, this practise appears questionable,[14] it must be borne in mind that it applies mostly in cases where the defendant pleads guilty,[15] and that contested evidence (e.g. testimony which is challenged by the defendant) is usually presented again at trial. Furthermore, the defendant and his counsel have the right to be present whenever witnesses or experts are heard during the pre-trial investigation, and they can ask them any relevant questions.

Written proceedings are common in appeals, particularly if the higher court only has the power to review issues related to the interpretation of the law.

2. The Principle of Publicity

Whereas the preliminary investigation is not accessible to the public (with special rules governing the information of the media), the trial, according also to Article 6(1) ECHR, must be held in public. However, television and radio are not admitted to the court room. Under certain conditions, especially at the request of the victim, trials will not be public.

V. THE LAW ON EVIDENCE

A. General Rules

1. Iura Novit Curia

Evidence is required to convince the court of relevant facts and empirical principles. The law itself is not subject to proof (*iura novit curia*).

2. The Principle of Free Evaluation of Evidence

One of the binding federal rules of criminal procedure is the principle of the free evaluation of evidence (Art. 249 CCrP). This principle is a logical consequence of

---

14. The case law of the European Court of Human Rights leads to the conclusion that this principle is in fact a requirement of 'fair trial,' see e.g. ECtHR, *Lüdi v. Switzerland*, judgment of 15 June 1992, Series A, no. 238.
15. In such cases, American defendants will be directly sentenced without any hearing in court.

the focus on substantive truth (IV B 1). It means that the court should give due consideration to all sorts of evidence presented, and that no evidence should be barred on the grounds of formal rules, such as the rule that two concurring witnesses cannot lie, or that the defendant's wife cannot be heard as a witness. According to this principle, the reasonable conclusion reached by the court will be the base of its decision. In particular, the judge is in no way bound by a guilty plea, and defendants admitting to having committed an offense will have a full trial just as any other defendant. Evidence obtained unlawfully is not automatically barred at the trial, i.e. there is no general exclusionary rule under Swiss law. Illegally obtained evidence may indeed be taken into account if excluding it seems disproportionate in view of the interests at stake. For example, the European Court of Human Rights found no violation of Article 6 ECHR in a murder trial where the prosecution had presented a tape recorded in violation of privacy laws.[16] On the other hand, confessions brought about by torture or other unlawful means of pressure would definitely not be admitted. The 'fruit of the poisonous tree doctrine', although discussed in legal doctrine, is not applied by Swiss courts. One reason may be that police behavior, which the American Supreme Court tried to control through a wide interpretation of the exclusionary rule,[17] is kept in line through the risks of criminal prosecution of police officers who make illegal searches and arrests. Since such acts, if not justified by duty, are offenses (punishable under Arts. 183, 186 and 312 PC), police officers face a risk of criminal prosecution under the system of compulsory prosecution (legality maxim, see IV C 1 above).

3. The Presumption of Innocence

Article 6(2) ECHR (and Art. 32 I Federal Cons.) establishes the rule that 'everyone charged with a criminal offence shall be presumed innocent until proven guilty according to law' (*Unschuldsvermutung/présomption d'innocence*). In practise, the principle of free evaluation of evidence serves the same purpose, since no defendant should be found guilty on the grounds of formal rules unless the evidence available suggests he or she is guilty.

B. Individuals as a Source of Information and Evidence

1. The Defendant

The right to be heard gives the defendant the opportunity to comment on all factual or legal aspects of his case. While defendants have an absolute right to remain silent, they can never take the oath and be a witness on their own behalf. As a consequence, they are allowed to lie and they cannot be punished for perjury. Given the rule that evidence is to be evaluated independently of formal rules, it is not unlikely that a court finds the defendant not guilty because of his/her own plausible explanations.

16. ECtHR, *Schenk v. Switzerland*, judgment of 12 July 1988, Series A, no. 140.
17. This is well illustrated in the opinions of the majority justices in *Miranda v. Arizona* (384 U.S. 436).

Miranda warnings are not required by the statutes of all cantons but the right can largely be deduced from the new Constitution (Arts. 31 II, 29 III).

2. Witnesses

Witnesses (*Zeugen/témoins*) are obliged to testify honestly or to face prosecution for perjury (Art. 307 PC) (i.e. intentionally lying in court), although the obligation to testify under oath is only imposed in a few cantons. The victim (even if he/she intervenes in the procedure as a party) can be compelled to testify in some cantons. Again, the rule on the free evaluation of evidence presented to the court eases the difference between the defendant (who cannot testify) and the victim as a witness. Any person (except those with close family ties to the defendant, doctors and other holders of professional secrets) can be compelled to testify; in the event that they refuse, they may be held liable for contempt of court. Bankers' secrecy is not a ground for refusing to testify. No one is obliged to disclose facts which might expose him to criminal liability. There are no 'crown witnesses' under Swiss law. The testimony is void if a witness was not warned, in advance, of his or her privileges, rights and duties.

As a rule, witnesses are questioned by the presiding judge while the parties only have a right to propose questions. Only in jury trials are witnesses cross-examined, but the presiding judges will only allow questions which are relevant to the case. Neither psychological pressure or rigorous 'Anglo-Saxon style' questioning nor the interruptions of the witness through objections are permitted. Victims of violence who have to appear in court as witnesses are entitled to the assistance of counsel. As a corollary of the 'soft' treatment of witnesses in court, preparation of their statement (in rehearsals) by attorneys or parties is unusual. Although not an offense, misbehavior of this kind would lead the court to award little credit to the witness' version of the facts.

3. Experts

In some cases, an expert is required in order to ascertain certain facts (e.g. the insanity of the defendant, Ch. 14 III D 2). As the expert must be impartial, he or she is usually appointed by the examining magistrate, normally after having consulted the parties. Experts usually present a written report. The court is not bound by their findings, but must give reasons if it does not follow their conclusions. In such cases, a second expert is usually called in. If the report is challenged by the prosecution or the defense, the expert might eventually be required to appear in court to answer relevant questions. Experts who knowingly present inaccurate conclusions may be punished for perjury (Art. 307 PC).

C. Technical Evidence

Scene of the crime inspections (*Augenschein/inspection locale*), analysis of fingerprints, DNA tests, blood tests and all other technical evidence (including ballistic evidence or examination of documents) is widely used in more complex cases. Usually, technical reports will be prepared in writing by police experts or specialized forensic science units.[18]

VI. COERCIVE MEASURES

A. *Preliminary Observations*

As suspects often see it in their own interest to frustrate the course of justice, coercive measures are necessary to secure evidence and to prevent the defendant from avoiding trial and eventually serving a sentence. Such coercive measures (*Zwangsmassnahmen/mesures de contrainte*) must be based on law, they must respect the principle of proportionality and they must not violate fundamental rights.

B. *Arrest and Detention*

1. Types of Deprivation of Liberty in Criminal Proceedings

Persons who, although summoned, do not appear at a judicial hearing can be arrested and brought to court by the police. Persons caught in the course of committing a crime or immediately after having committed a crime (*flagrant délit*) may be arrested without a warrant either by the police or by an individual (citizens' arrest). They must, however, be brought promptly before a judge (Art. 5 para. 3 ECHR, see Ch. 14). While those executing a citizens arrest must bring such an arrestee immediately to a magistrate (or the police), the police have to do so within an average period of 48 hours. Detention on remand (*Untersuchungshaft/détention preventive*) is usually ordered by an examining magistrate, after having been reviewed by a judge.

2. The Prerequisites of Detention on Remand

A person, against whom criminal prosecution is initiated, is not automatically arrested, nor automatically detained on remand. Exceptionally, pre-trial detention is ordered if there is reasonable suspicion, as well as a high risk, that the defendant might escape before trial (e.g. if he/she has no legal residence within the country), or that he or she might destroy relevant evidence (e.g. by influencing witnesses). A high risk of re-offending may, if there is strong suspicion, also justify pre-trial detention.

3. Limits on the Duration of Detention on Remand

According to Article 5(3) ECHR, detention on remand may not exceed a 'reasonable time'. In order to control the duration of detention on remand, the cantons have

18. In particular, the Forensic Science Unit of the Zurich City Police, and the Forensic Science Institute at the Lausanne University School of Criminal Justice.

instituted a variety of control systems. The Federal Supreme Court has ruled that pre-trial detention never should exceed the time to which an offender might reasonable be expected to be sentenced (if convicted).

4. Release on Bail

Although release on bail is generally provided for in Swiss legislation on criminal procedure, it is not really popular, except in Geneva. There is a general tendency to regard release on bail as the privilege of the wealthy. It should be kept in mind that arrests and pre-trial detention are exceptional in Switzerland, and that defendants who might otherwise be seen as eligible for bail may rather be released from pre-trial detention on substantial grounds. Bounty hunting is unknown and would be illegal under Swiss law (see Ch. 14 III C 3).

5. Judicial Control of Pre-trial Detention

Persons detained on remand have the right to have their detention reviewed by a judge (Art. 5(4) ECHR). In the last resort, such appeals can be brought before the Federal Supreme Court (see VIII B below).

6. The Right to Compensation

Time spent in detention on remand is usually deducted from the sentence (Arts. 69, 375 PC). If a defendant has been detained illegally, if he or she is acquitted or if the suspicion on which the detention was based eventually proves to have been ill-founded, he or she is eligible for compensation. In this respect, Swiss law clearly goes beyond the requirements of Article 5(5) ECHR.

C. Search and Seizure

Suspects and their home or office or any other place where relevant wanted objects or persons are presumably to be found may be searched. Objects of proof including loot may be seized wherever they are found. If the seizure concerns papers containing professional secrets, they may be sealed until the court decides whether and to what extent the interests of the prosecution prevail over the preservation of secrets.

D. Examination of Body and Mind

The defendant must submit to an examination of his or her body, including fingerprints, blood and DNA tests. In order to facilitate mental examination – with a view to ascertaining insanity, or assessing the need for security measures or treatment (see Ch. 14 IV B 1) – a defendant may be committed to a mental hospital.

E. *Interference with the Right to Privacy*

At times, efficient investigation requires secret surveillance of a suspect's private life. Prosecuting authorities are authorized by law to intercept postal and telecommunications to and from a defendant. Since defendants are not usually informed of such measures, they will need to be automatically reviewed by a higher ranking judicial authority (usually the authority of indictment, see above II A 4).

VII. SPECIAL FORMS OF PROCEDURE

A. *Private Prosecution*

Actions for libel and slander, although based on criminal law (Arts. 173–177 PC), are sometimes dealt with under the form of civil proceedings, or by a special criminal procedure in which the prosecuting authorities do not take part.

B. *The Penal Order: A Swiss Form of Plea Bargaining?*

The penal order (*Strafbefehl/ordonnance de condamnation*) is the most common form of summary criminal procedure. The examining magistrate (investigative judge, or district attorney) or, in some cantons, the prosecutor, writes out a form on which the offense is summarily described, and a sentence (usually a fine, sometimes a short custodial sentence of up 6 months) is imposed. If the defendant does not agree, either with the verdict, with the legal interpretation adopted by the magistrate, or the sentence, he or she can insist on a full trial by completing a simple declaration at the bottom of the form. This system (which exists in many continental countries) has been described as the continental form of guilty plea.[19] Indeed, in common with guilty pleas, the defendant admits the facts as described in the penal order, he or she agrees with their legal qualification, and accepts the sentence. Unlike American defendants, Swiss defendants insisting on a full trial (usually before a lower court) do not run the risk of receiving a bigger sentence. It should also be kept in mind that this procedure is available only for routine minor offenses (often traffic violations) for which the prosecutor considers a minimal sanction appropriate. Penal orders are popular especially in countries where prosecution is compulsory; in France or in the Netherlands, where the expediency principle (see IV B 3 above) is widely used, prosecutors usually drop proceedings in such cases, sometimes after 'negotiating' with the defendant the payment of a 'fine' to the treasury or to a charity.

C. *Proceedings in the Absence of the Defendant*

If a defendant is absent without justification, a warrant will, in the first place, be issued for his or her arrest. If he or she cannot be brought to trial, judgment may be

---

19. J.H. Langbein, 'Controlling Prosecutorial Discretion in Germany', *The University of Chicago Law Review* 41 (1974), 439–467.

passed in his or her absence (*Kontumatialverfahren/procédure par défaut*) if the person had been heard at least once by the authorities. However, if the defendant is later arrested, he or she has the right to ask for a new trial (*Wiederherstellung/demande de relief*).

D. *Proceedings against Children and Juveniles*

Children and juveniles are prosecuted in different proceedings which have more to do with welfare and youth protection principles, than with general due process rules.

VIII. REMEDIES

A. *Types of Legal Remedies in Criminal Proceedings*

A full-fledged appeal (*Berufung/appel*) is the most comprehensive ordinary remedy. It means that the higher court (usually at the cantonal level) will fully review the case (in fact and in law). In practise, appeals are often limited to certain issues, such as the type and severity of the sentence. Usually, appeals are not possible if the trial has been before a jury or a higher (cantonal or federal) court.

Wherever a full appeal is not available, both the prosecutor and the defendant have the right to file a limited appeal where the higher court will only review certain legal issues (either of procedural or substantive law).

Before a verdict has been reached, the defendant and the prosecutor (and possibly also the victim and other interested parties) may file a petition limited to a specific issue, such as the decision to allow pre-trial detention, not to call certain witnesses, to confiscate an object (or document), or to drop the charges.

Legal remedies in criminal matters are subject to the prohibition of *reformatio in peius*. This means that in cases where only the defendant has filed an appeal, the previous decision may not be altered to his or her disadvantage. However, this rule does not apply when both parties appeal.

B. *Appeals before the Federal Supreme Court*

There are two different types of remedies by which final decisions of cantonal courts can be brought before the Federal Supreme Court.

One is called plea of nullity (*Nichtigkeitsbeschwerde/pourvoi en nullité*). It allows the Criminal Law Chamber of the Federal Supreme Court to review the interpretation of substantive criminal law, i.e. mainly of the PC. Through this form of appeal, the Federal Supreme Court has succeeded in overseeing the uniform interpretation of criminal law. It is open to the defendant, the prosecutor, and sometimes also to the victim.

The other remedy is called constitutional law appeal (*staatsrechtliche Beschwerde/recours de droit public*) which allows all issues of alleged violations of the Constitution (or the ECHR) to be brought before the Federal Supreme Court.

In criminal proceedings, it allows the defendant to seek redress against any violations of due process, including the garantee of *in dubio pro reo*. It is only open to defendants and (sometimes) victims, but never to government agencies (such as prosecutors).

C. The Individual Application to the European Court of Human Rights

Once remedies are exhausted, particularly after an unsuccessful constitutional law appeal to the Federal Supreme Court, any person claiming that a decision violates his or her fundamental rights under the ECHR, may file an application to the European Court of Human Rights.

D. The Petition for Re-trial

While all the remedies mentioned above are subject to certain time limits, a petition for re-trial (*Wiederaufnahme/révision*) can be filed after a judgment has become final.

A petition for retrial can either be filed in favor of the (convicted) defendant, or against an acquitted person. Thus, Switzerland (as continental countries in general) does not proscribe double jeopardy (with the exception of Geneva). A new trial may be required if new evidence (which was not available at the first trial) may lead to a different conclusion, if the former trial was tainted by illegal means (e.g. perjury, bribery etc.) which, at that time, could not be brought to the attention of a higher court, or if a later ruling in the same case (e.g. on civil damages) contradicts the verdict (or an acquittal). Usually, a petition for a new trial must be filed within certain time limits once the relevant new facts have become known to the interested party.

SELECTED BIBLIOGRAPHY

Hauser, R. and E. Schweri, *Schweizerisches Strafprozessrecht*, 5th edn., Basel: Helbing and Lichtenhahn 2002.

Piquerez, G., *Procédure penale suisse. Traité théorique et pratique*, Zurich: Schultess 2000.

Oberholzer, N., *Grundzüge des Strafprozessrechts*, Berne: Staempfli 1994.

Schmid, N., *Strafprozessrecht*, 3rd edn., Zurich: Schultess 1997.

Chapter 16
Law of Civil Procedure

*Hans Ulrich Walder–Richli**

I. SOURCES OF CIVIL PROCEDURE LAW

Swiss civil procedure law is mainly cantonal. Each of the twenty six cantons and 'half cantons' institutes a Code of Civil Procedure (*Zivilprozessordnung/Code de procédure civile*) and a Code of Judicial Organization (*Organisationsgesetz, Gerichtsverfassungsgesetz/loi d'organisation judiciaire*). A new federal act on the jurisdiction in civil matters, however, has entered into force as of 2000 (see below VI.B). This is made possible through the Article 30 II of the Federal Constitution (accepted by referendum on 18 April 1999), which says that a person against whom a civil action is brought, has the right to have the case heard before the court of his domicile, if the federal law does not provide a different jurisdiction.[1]

The Swiss Code of Civil Procedure too applies to cases before the Swiss Federal Tribunal with primary jurisdiction only. The conditions under which this may happen are determined by Articles 41 and 42 of the Federal Statute on the Organization of the Federal Judiciary. The number of such cases is newly reduced in order to enable the Swiss Federal Tribunal to deal within a proper time with the great number of cases that are brought before it by means of appeal from the cantonal courts.

Important rules on procedure are also found in the Swiss Civil Code (CC), in the Code of Obligations (CO) and in other fundamental acts of civil law. Professor Wildhaber points out that 'in a very bold series of decisions the Federal Tribunal has declared that any application or interpretation of cantonal law which is so manifestly wrong as to be arbitrary or capricious amounts to an inequality before the law',[2] and therefore is a violation of Article 9 of the Federal Constitution. Additionally, the Federal Tribunal has found on several occasions that there are certain rules of law which at first sight might belong to the law of civil procedure, but that they find their sources in substantive law and therefore are to be followed by any cantonal jurisdiction. This problem might come to vanish in a few years time. On the basis of the

---

* Prof. Dr., University of Zurich; former judge at Zurich Kassationsgericht.
1. See R.A. Surber, 'Art. 30 Abs. 2 BV', in: *Basler Kommentar (BSK) Gerichtsstandsgesetz*, 2001, 11–25.
2. L. Wildhaber, 'The Swiss Judicial System' in: *Modern Switzerland*, 1978, p. 318.

F. Dessemontet and T. Ansay (eds), Introduction to Swiss Law, 287–299.

Article 122 I of the Constitution,[3] a committee of experts prepares the draft for a federal code of procedure, which will be applied to all cases before cantonal courts in the future. This draft that later has to be dealt with by government and National Assembly, will first be presented to the public and be discussed by all interested persons before it is enacted. Probably, however, it will not come into force before 2008.

Finally, the Federal Law on Private International Law (PIL) contains numerous procedural rules, and its twelfth chapter is concerned with international arbitration.

II. MAIN PRINCIPLES OF SWISS CIVIL PROCEDURE

The following six principles dominate civil procedure in Switzerland:

1. The principle of free disposal of each party to the matter in dispute. A judge may not award more than a party claims or less than the other party recognizes. Nor may his judgment be different from that sought for (*Dispositionsmaxime/maxime de disposition*).
2. Each party bears the burden to assert relevant facts, to state defenses and to submit evidence to be relied on (*Verhandlungsmaxime, maxime des débats*). On the other hand, the court's duty is to question insufficient or unclear allegations made by the parties (*richterliche Fragepflicht/interpellation des parties*).
3. In order to settle disputes in due time, the parties may submit briefs only within a certain time limit (*Konzentrationsmaxime, Eventualmaxime/maxime éventuelle*).
4. Each party is granted the right to be heard.
5. The judge is responsible for the administration of procedure.
6. The judge has to take the initiative in finding the applicable law. However, in certain cases the assistance of the parties may be required (Art. 16 I PIL). Swiss law shall apply if the content of the foreign law cannot clearly get established (Art. 16 II PIL).

Principles one and two are limited by the investigation principle (*Untersuchungsmaxime/maxime inquisitoire*). In cases where this happens (e.g. labor and rent disputes) there is a duty of the judge to help the parties in eliciting the facts.

III. COURT STRUCTURE

Swiss courts are normally not divided into civil and criminal courts. Administrative courts may form a chamber of the court of appeals or, as in the canton of Zurich, a special court of their own (*Verwaltungsgericht/tribunal administratif*).

---

3. This provision was introduced on 12 March 2000.

In larger cantons there are several courts of primary jurisdiction, each normally consisting of five or three members (*Bezirksgericht, Amtsgericht/tribunal de première instance*). Their jurisdiction covers civil and criminal cases not specially assigned to other tribunals. If the amount of dispute does not exceed a certain sum of money and where summary or accelerated procedure is applied (see below VIII) disputes are settled by the president or a vice-president of the tribunal as a single judge or by a commission of three (instead of five) of its members.

Justices of the peace or mediators (*Friedensrichter, Vermittler/juges de paix*) try to settle the disputes between parties by working out a draft settlement. Most mediators have no legal education, but are appointed in view of their general experience. Should the conciliation prove unsuccessful, the mediator has to issue a document (*Weisung, Leitschein/acte de non conciliation*) that entitles the plaintiff to introduce action before the competent tribunal. In disputes involving extremely small claims, mediators act as judges.

There are four cantons (Zurich, Berne, Aargau and St. Gallen) where civil matters are heard in commercial courts (*Handelsgericht/Tribunal de commerce*) if they involve commercial transactions of a certain importance and if both parties and at least the defendant are listed as firms in the Swiss commercial register. Commercial courts are normally composed of two judges and three assessors. Assessors are drawn from the local chambers of commerce. In many commercial court trials, no expert is heard (see below VII E) since the court considers itself as expert.

Other specialized courts are those for labor disputes (*Arbeitsgerichte/tribunaux de travail, tribunaux des prud'hommes*). They consist of one employer representative and one employee representative, and a member of the primary jurisdiction court acting as chairman. A similar system is applied for rent tribunals (*Mietgerichte/ tribunaux des baux*).

Appeals and pleas for nullity go from the first court to the cantonal court of appeal (*Obergericht, Kantonsgericht/tribunal cantonal, cour de justice*). Notwithstanding the decisions of these courts, parties may file an appeal to the Federal Tribunal claiming that rules of Swiss federal civil law have been violated by the cantonal court. The cantons of Zurich and St. Gallen have stipulated that a motion to set aside the judgment or plea for nullity (*Nichtigkeitsbeschwerde/recours en nullité*) may be brought before a court of cassation (*Kassationsgericht/cour de cassation*) in cases where important rules of procedure are alleged to be violated. In addition, the Federal Tribunal acts upon 'constitutional reviews' (*Staatsrechtliche Beschwerde/recours de droit public*)[4] in civil cases as well (see above I and below VI).

The independence of courts is safeguarded by Article 30 I of the Federal Constitution. Any party to a law suit may demand the replacement of a judge whom she suspects to be biased.

---

4. See Ch. 2, VI, B on the Swiss Federal Constitution.

IV. Persons Participating in the Administration of Justice

A. *Judges* (Richter/Juges) *and Court Reporters or Clerks* (Gerichtsschreiber, Gerichtssekretäre/Greffiers)

A law school graduate intending to become a judge usually starts to work in a court of primary jurisdiction. At the end of this training period he may be appointed as a full-fledged clerk. In order to become a judge he must join a political party because judges get elected by political authorities. A formal legal education is not required but in a few cantons; present practise, however, is not to appoint as a professional judge an individual who has not obtained a law school degree. On the other hand, judges with different and non-legal professional backgrounds are still found in primary courts and even in cantonal tribunals of appeal. Judges are elected for periods of between two and ten years and get generally re-elected until they retire.

Clerks usually have to be lawyers as well; they keep the minutes of the proceedings and are responsible for the formulation of decisions. Usually they have a consultative function.

B. *Attorneys* (Rechtsanwälte, Fürsprecher, Advokaten/Avocats)

There is no distinction between solicitors and barristers in Switzerland. A young lawyer who wants to become an attorney must spend a training period of one or two years at a court or with a law firm. He then has to undergo an additional examination before a committee of judges, attorneys and law professors. Such committees are appointed by the court of appeal of each canton. Until now, after having passed such examination in one canton, a lawyer, upon request, was given permission to exercise his profession in any other canton. This system is going to be changed and there will be a federal admission for attorneys.

In order to pratice at the court there is no need to join the local bar association. Disciplinary proceedings against an attorney are administered by the cantonal court of appeal or by a special committee formed by judges and attorneys.

C. *Notaries*

Notaries (*Notare/notaires*) are authorized to authenticate legal transactions. One need not be a law school graduate to become a notary; a special training, however, is required. In some cantons notaries are officials, in others they are freelance.

V. Parties

The capacity of an individual to sue or be sued (*Parteifähigkeit/capacité d'être partie*) depends on his capacity to be subjects of rights (*Rechtsfähigkeit/jouissance des droits civils*). Under Article 11 of the Swiss Civil Code every real person is subject of rights. The capacity of a legal person to sue or be sued is determined by the law under which it was organized. According to Article 54 of the Civil Code corporate bodies acquire legal capacity as soon as their official organs have been established in accordance with the requirements of the law and their by-laws.[5]

Upon reaching the age of majority, which is 18 years, a person may conduct civil proceedings (*Prozessfähigkeit/capacité d'ester en justice*) if he has full discretion to make rational decisions (*Urteilsfähigkeit/capacité de discernement*). An infant or incompetent person is represented in court by his parents or guardian. When reasons putting a person under the total control of a legal guardian are insufficient but where his own interests require that his legal capacity be appropriately restricted, a legal adviser can be appointed for court proceedings whose concurrence will be required to bring or settle an action (Art. 395 I, no. 1 CC).

An action may be brought or defended by a person who is not the real party in interest. The sources of such regulation (*Prozessführungsbefugnis, Prozessstandschaft/qualité pour agir et pour défendre*) are found in substantive law. For example an executor may sue in his own name without joining the community of heirs for whose benefit the action is brought.

Parties to a law suit need not be represented by counsel. A party may bring or defend actions personally, even before the Federal Tribunal (*Postulationsfähigkeit/capacité de revendiquer*). However, courts may decide that a person is unable to plead properly and require the appointment of an attorney at the party's own expense. Persons of limited financial resources and with a chance of winning their case may demand legal assistance. This means that they have not to pay any proceeding costs and that, if necessary, they are given an attorney at the expense of the public treasury. This right is granted by Article 29 I of the Federal Constitution.

The substantive law determines whether a joinder of persons is needed for just adjudication (*notwendige Streitgenossenschaft/consorité nécessaire*). For example all individual members of a community of heirs must agree to sue before they commence an action. Separate parties who appear before a court with claims arising from the same facts may be considered a joinder of persons (*einfache Streitgenossen schaft/consorité simple*).

At any time after the commencement of an action, a defendant may cause a summons and complaint to be served upon a person not a party to the original suit, but who is or may be liable to him for all or a part of the plaintiff's claim. Furthermore, a plaintiff may cause a summons and complaint to be served upon a person who is not a party but who is or may be liable if a favorable judgment is not forthcoming (*Streitverkündung/appel en cause, dénonciation du litige*). If this happens within the time allowed, the said person will be unable in further litigation to make the assertion that the judgment rendered in the original proceeding was not correct.

A person who fears that his rights might be affected by a judgment to be rendered in a law suit of other persons may demand to be admitted to the assistance of one of the parties if a sufficient legal interest can be substantiated (*Nebenintervention/intervention*).

There is still no legal basis for class actions. Although Article 27 of the Federal Act on the Place of Jurisdiction in Civil Matters (PJA, see VI B below) states that in

5. See Ch. 4 on the Law of Persons.

cases of damage involving a multitude of injured persons the court of the place where the act was committed shall have mandatory jurisdiction, there is still no legal basis for class actions. It must be possible, however, to get recognition and enforcement for a foreign class action settlement if the conditions of PIL are fulfilled (see below XI).

VI. COMMENCING AN ACTION

A. *Competence* (Sachliche Zuständigkeit/Compétence matérielle)

The manner in which an action is commenced depends mainly on the amount in controversy. The amount also makes a difference for the question whether a special kind of procedure (e.g. accelerated procedure, see below VIII) is requested. In most cases, with the exception of minor disputes, the plaintiff must draft a petition and file it in the appropriate court.

Claims may be brought, as mentioned above, in district courts, commercial courts, labor courts etc. Parties to a law suit may agree to submit their claims to a court other than specified by statute. Such agreement is binding upon the judge only if ordered by statute; otherwise the judge will refuse to hear the case by declaring himself not competent to review the matter.

B. *Territorial Jurisdiction* (Örtliche Zuständigkeit/Compétence locale)

The general rule in Switzerland is that claims must be brought in the courts of defendant's domicile. This is granted to any individual in Article 30 paragraph 2 of the Federal Constitution. The said provision allows, however, exceptions from the general rule if they are stated by a federal act. The Federal Act on the Place of Jurisdiction in Civil Matters of 24 March 2000 brings such exceptions.

Additionally the Federal Statute on Private International Law states the possibility of suing a person with no domicile in Switzerland for certain claims before a Swiss judge and it recognizes, on the other hand, judgments from abroad which can get enforcement in Switzerland under certain conditions (section XII below).

Finally, Switzerland is a Contracting State to the Lugano Convention on Jurisdiction and the Enforcement of Judgments in Civil and Commercial Matters, signed on 16 September 1988, by the EC and EFTA countries (LugC). This convention offers special venues in a member state for claims against residents of another member state to the Convention.

According to Article 113 of the PIL a law suit related to a contract may be brought before the Swiss court at the place of its performance if the defendant has neither his or her domicile nor a business establishment in Switzerland and Article 5 no. 1 of LugC says that a person domiciled in a Contracting State may, in another Contracting State, be brought to the courts of the place of performance of the obligation in question; but there is no corresponding rule in PJA.

As to PIL, it might be interesting that in a case where the statute does not provide for jurisdiction in Switzerland and proceedings abroad are impossible or highly impracticable, a jurisdiction of last resort is given by its Article 3 (*Notzuständigkeit/ for de nécessité*). This jurisdiction lies with the Swiss judicial or administrative authorities at the place with which the facts of the law suit have a sufficient connection (Art. 3).

If a case is not heard due to lack of competence of venue and there exists another court which seems to be competent, some cantons, in their statutes allow the case to get transferred directly to that court upon the plaintiff's request. Anyhow, if an action that was withdrawn or dismissed for lack of jurisdiction is filed with the competent court within 30 days, commencement of the action shall be deemed to be effected on the date of the first filing (Art. 34 II PJA).

C. Pleadings

A written petition of a plaintiff must state the following:

(a) the names of the parties;
(b) the claim;
(c) the facts the claim is based upon;
(d) a summary of the legal basis which is not indispensable because of the sixth principle mentioned in section II above.

In most cantons an action is deemed to be commenced when the document issued by the mediator is presented to the court. In international cases, to determine when an action has been filed in Switzerland, the date of the first act necessary to institute the action shall be decisive and the initiation of conciliation proceedings shall be sufficient for that purpose (Art. 9 II PIL). After filing the plaintiff's petition a summons is sent to the defendant together with a copy of the petition. The defendant's time limit to answer is 20 or 30 days and may be extended upon his request by court decree or by order of a single judge concerned with the administration of the case.

The defendant has to raise the defense of an improper venue at the beginning. Lack of competence defenses (section A above) may be raised at any stage of the trial if there is no contrary statutory provision.

In his brief the defendant may deny the facts as stated by the plaintiff. He may also assert new facts and include in his own petition a counterclaim (*Widerklage/action reconventionnelle*).

After the filing of the defendant's answer each party is heard once more, either by filing a second written statement or through a statement made in the trial proceedings.

If the defendant fails to file his first answer he is granted additional time, but the court does warn him that if his second filing will not be timely he will be foreclosed from submitting any defense whatsoever. In such a case the judgment must be rendered upon the plaintiff's plea (*Säumnisurteil/jugement par défaut*).

VII. Evidence

A. *Burden of Proof*

As to the burden of proof, the general rule is stated in Article 8 of the CC: In the absence of a special provision to the contrary the burden of proving an alleged fact rests on the party who bases its claim on that fact. Among the special provisions to mention are those regulating presumptions, such as Article 3 I of the CC, which reads as follows: 'Bona fides is presumed whenever the existence of a right has been expressly declared to depend on the observance of good faith.'

B. *Admissibility*

Admissibility of instruments of proof is left to the discretion of the judge, and thus no instrument is binding upon him. In addition, no cantonal law may stipulate that a written instrument be necessary to prove a legal transaction, for the validity of which Federal substantive law does not require any such form (Art. 10 CC).

C. *Documents* (Urkunden/Preuve par titre)

There are two kinds of documents: those which are issued to conclude a legal transaction and those bearing witness to a fact observed by the author of the document.

Parties and third persons in possession of documents necessary to prove a fact may be compelled to produce them upon the request of a party. If the party in possession of the documents fails to exhibit them, the court may take such refusal into consideration when rendering its final decision. A third party refusing to produce documents may be fined unless he is entitled to refuse to give testimony (*Zeugnisverweigerungsrecht/refurs justifié de témoigner*).

D. *Witnesses* (Zeugen/Témoignage)

A witness must testify orally. The judge cautions him as to the necessity of telling the truth (warning him that he might otherwise be punished according to Art. 307 of the Penal Code) and informs him of possible reasons for refusing to testify. Then he questions the witness as to the merits of the case. The questioning is carried out by the judge himself; but the parties may suggest further questions. The Canton of Glarus, however, recently has introduced a sort of cross-examination by the parties or their representatives.

The attendance of a witness is secured by subpoena served by mail. A witness gets fined if he does not appear or if he refuses to answer the questions without being entitled to do so. The persons entitled to refuse include relatives of a party or persons who must keep a professional secret. There are no more cantons where a witness might be excluded by a party due to his close relation to the opposing party or for another special reason.

E. *Experts* (Sachverständige/Expertise)

If the judge does not have special knowledge needed for rendering the decision, the parties may prove their case through the use of an expert who submits a written or oral opinion (*Gutachten/expertise*) with respect to certain aspects of the case. Experts are retained by the court. The parties, however, may question them about their opinion and request the opinion to be completed or that a second expert be appointed by the court.

F. *Questioning of Parties* (Parteibefragung, Beweisaussage/ Interrogatoire des parties)

The court may on its own initiative or upon the request of a party order either or both parties to be questioned about the alleged facts (*Persönliche Befragung/ interrogatoire des parties*). If the court finds the proof offered by one party almost but not completely satisfactory certain cantons allow that party to be questioned once more. In that case he is punishable under Article 306 PC if he does not tell the truth.

VIII. SPECIAL PROCEDURES

Summary proceedings (*Summarisches Verfahren/procedure sommaire*) take place if the defendant's liability is not denied or can be proven immediately by written instrument. They also take place for the enforcements of judicial decisions or when a party requests a court order to prevent any action which might prejudice a future court decision or interfere with the carrying out of such a decision.

An accelerated proceeding (*beschleunigtes Verfahren, rasches Verfahren/ procédure accélérée*) is followed when the nature of the case demands that a decision must be rendered without delay, such as in labor disputes and disputes connected with the enforcement of debts.

IX. RENDITION OF JUDGMENT

The parties have the opportunity to argue their case based on the evidence prior to the court's verdict. The superior courts of a few cantons and the Federal Tribunal deliberate in public.[6] The grounds on which the decision is rendered must be in writing. The court minority, disagreeing with the majority decision or with the grounds upon which it is based, may draw up a dissenting opinion.[7]

---

6. Some chambers of the Federal Tribunal, a few years ago, have begun to decide about their cases without any deliberation, circulating the file among their members in order to reach unanimity.
7. At the Federal Tribunal dissenting opinions never published, whereas sometimes it does happen at the Zurich Obergericht and Kassationsgericht.

Final judgment has to be distinguished from the interlocutory decision. The latter is rendered throughout the course of a law suit on issues such as the taking of evidence. The former is a decision based on the merits of the case. Interlocutory decisions may be reconsidered by the court at any time during the trial, whereas a final judgment may be changed by appeal or another means of redress only.

X. APPEAL *(Berufung/Appel)* AND OTHER MEANS OF REDRESS

Each canton has a court of appeal which is in some cantons divided into chambers. An appeal (the admission of which depends, *inter alia*, on the amount in litigation) goes from the district court or other court of primary jurisdiction to the chamber of the court of appeal that handles the type of subject-matter involved. Interlocutory decisions are open to appeal or reversible by action of nullity in exceptional cases only.

As far as federal private law is concerned and if the amount of litigation reaches the sum of CHF 8,000 a further appeal may be brought before the Swiss Federal Tribunal (see also section III, above). In cases of civil disputes of non-financial matters and on the application of foreign law the Federal Tribunal has to decide.[8]

As to the motions to set aside *(Nichtigkeitsbeschwerde, staatsrechtliche Beschwerde/recours de droit public)* see section III above.

XI. COURT COSTS, ATTORNEY'S FEES AND LEGAL AID

Court costs and the attorney's fees of the other party are normally borne in advance by claimants with no residence in Switzerland or in a contracting state to the respective international convention, and by bankrupt claimants. The same rule is applied to a party (both claimant and defendant) who wants to attack a judgment by appeal. As to the action of nullity, the costs and fees are borne in advance by any party attacking the judgment.

After the decision is rendered, the loser pays both the court costs and the attorney fees of the other party. In special cases, however, the court may depart from that system. If a party does not lose totally, it has to pay a reduced amount and the remainder gets paid by the other party.

Contingency fees for attorneys are not allowed in Switzerland.

As to the legal assistance provided by the Federal Constitution see section V above.

XII. ENFORCEMENT *(Vollstreckung/Exécution)*

Any person claiming an award of money outstanding may apply to the execution officer *(Betreibungsbeamter/préposé aux poursuites)* who then orders the defendant to pay his debt within twenty days *(Zahlungsbefehl/commandement de payer)* or to

---

8. Art. 43a II of the Federal Statute on the Organization of the Federal Judiciary.

deny the claim within ten days (*Rechtsvorshlag/opposition*). In the latter case the plaintiff must initiate an action through ordinary or summary proceeding in order to get a court decision. If the defendant fails to deny the debt within the ten day time limit, the creditor may ask for seizure of a debtor's assets (*Pfändung/saisie*) or, if the debtor is a merchant, that he be declared bankrupt. In the case of seizure, creditors may also secure payment from a third person owing money to the debtor, especially from his employer. In a bankruptcy case, all assets of the debtor will be collected and sold. The procedural fees will be deducted from the proceeds; the remainder will be distributed among all the creditors in the order of three classes (Art. 219 of the Swiss Debt Enforcement and Bankruptcy Law [SDEBL]). Creditors of the same class are equal among themselves, but creditors of a class only receive proceeds once the creditors of the class or the classes above have been satisfied (Art. 220 SDEBL). All items, however, that are indispensable for the debtor and his family, must be left at the debtor's free disposal (Art. 220 SDEBL). If there are no assets at all, the bankruptcy will be suspended (Art. 230 I SDEBL).

According to Article 166 I of the Federal Law on Privatec International Law (PIL) a foreign bankruptcy decree rendered in the state of the debtor's domicile is to be recognized if it is enforceable in the country where it was made and if that country would reciprocally recognize a Swiss bankruptcy decree. It shall, however, not be recognized if such recognition would be manifestly incompatible with Swiss public policy (Art. 27 PIL).

If a judgment for the recovery of movable property is rendered, the defendant is ordered by the judge to deliver it to the plaintiff. The property will forcibly be removed from the defendant's premises by the execution officer. If the defendant has been ordered to leave an apartment, he may be physically and forcibly removed from it.

If a judgment orders the defendant to carry out some work and he does not comply with this order, a third person may be asked to do the said work at the defendant's expense, and the corresponding sum of money must be deposited at the court by the plaintiff.

If a judgment orders the defendant to refrain from doing an act, disobedience is punishable by a disciplinary fine or in more severe cases criminal sanctions are applied.

Federal Law on Private International Law provides in its Article 25 that any foreign decision against which there is no further appeal can be lodged shall be recognized in Switzerland if the judicial or administrative authorities of the state in which the decision was rendered had jurisdiction and if there are no grounds of refusal such as the manifest incompatibility with Swiss law (Art. 27 PIL). The question whether the foreign authorities have jurisdiction is ruled by the PIL that provides the conditions for each case and similar rules are to be found in the Lugano Convention (see section VI B above).

XIII. ARBITRATION

Arbitration in Switzerland is governed, on the one hand, by the Intercantonal Arbitration Convention (IAC) that has established a uniform law applicable to all cantons. Chapter 12 of the PIL, on the other hand, shall be applied to arbitrations if at least one of the parties at the time when the arbitration agreement was concluded, had neither its domicile nor its habitual residence in Switzerland (Art. 176 PIL).

The arbitral rules of procedure may be determined by agreement between the parties (Art. 24 I IAC; Art. 182 I PIL), but the selected rules of procedure must in any case accord due respect to the principle of equality and the rules must permit both parties to exercise their rights to be heard (Art. 25 lit. A IAC; Art. 182 II PIL).

In cases governed by the IAC, a motion to set aside the arbitral award (*Nichtigkeitsbeschwerde/recours en nullité*) may be brought before the court of appeal of the canton in which the arbitration has taken place, where a special reason determined by a provision of the law is alleged. Such reasons are (Art. 36 IAC):

- that the arbitral tribunal was not properly appointed;
- that there was a breach of one of the mandatory rules mentioned above;
- that the award is arbitrary in that it was based on findings that were manifestly contrary to facts appearing on the file, or in that it constitutes a clear violation of law or equity.[9]

In international cases, a motion to set aside the award (*staatsrechtliche Beschwerde/recours de droit public*) may only be brought to the Swiss Federal Tribunal.[10]

Switzerland is a Contracting State to several international arbitration conventions, including the Geneva Protocol of 24 September 1923, relating to Arbitration Clauses; the Geneva Convention of 26 September 1927 on the Enforcement of Foreign Arbitral Awards, the New York Convention of 10 June 1958 on the Recognition and Enforcement of Foreign Arbitral Awards. Switzerland has not ratified the European Convention of 21 April 1961 on International Commercial Arbitration ('Geneva Convention of 1961').

9. The award according to equity is that rendered by an '*amiable compositeur*', who is a person vested by the parties with the power to settle the dispute without being bound by the substantive rules of law or by non mandatory rules of procedure as to its form. 'Equity' is used here to mean general concepts of justice, rather than the technical concept of the Common Law' (Translator's note in: Lalive, Poudret and Raymond, *Le droit de l'arbitrage interne et international Suisse*, 1989, p. 168).
10. See Ch. 17 on Private International Law, section V E.

SELECTED BIBLIOGRAPHY

Amonn, K. and D. Gasser, *Grundriss des Schuldbetreibungs- und Konkursrechts*, 6th edn., Berne 1997.

Berti, S.V., *Swiss Debt Enforcement and Bankruptcy Law: English translation of the Amended Federal Statute on Debt Enforcement and Bankruptcy (SchKG) with an Introduction to Swiss Debt Enforcement and Bankruptcy Law*, Zurich 1997.

Donzallar, Y., *Commentaire de la loi fédérale sur les fors en matière civile*, Berne 2001.

Fritzsche, H. and H.U. Walder, *Schuldbetreibungs- und Konkursrecht*, 2 vols., 3rd edn., Zurich 1984/1993.

Frank, R., H. Sträuli and G. Messmer, *Kommentar zur zürcherischen Zivilprozessordnung*, 3rd edn., Zurich 1997; Ergänzungsband, Zurich 2000.

Jaeger, C., H.U. Walder, T. Kull and M. Kottmann, *Das Bundesgesetz über Schuldbetreibung und Konkurs. Erläutert für den praktischen Gebrauch*, 4th edn., Zurich 1997/2001.

Kellerhals, F. and N. von Werdt (eds.), *Gerichtsstandsgesetz. Kommentar zum Bundesgesetz über den Gerichtsstand in Zivilsachen*, Berne 2001.

Müller, T. and M. Wirth (eds.), *Gerichtsstandsgesetz. Kommentar zum Bundesgesetz über den Gerichtsstand in Zivilsachen*, Zurich 2001.

Spühler, K., L. Tenchio and D. Infanger (eds.), *Bundesgesetz über den Gerichtsstand in Zivilsachen (GestG) mit Kommentierung von Art. 30 Abs. 2 BV*, Bâle 2001.

Staehelin, A., T. Bauer and D. Staehelin (eds.), *Kommentar zum Bundesgesetz über Schuldbetreibung und Konkurs unter Einbezug der Nebenerlasse*, 3 vols., Basel 1998.

Vogel, O. and K. Spühler, *Grundriss des Zivilprozessrechts und des internationalen Zivilprozessrechts der Schweiz*, 7th edn., Berne 2001.

Chapter 17
Private International Law

François Dessemontet*
Walter Stoffel**

I. INTRODUCTION

A. Characteristics

1. Sources

a. National Legislation

Swiss private international law was a body of case law for more than a hundred years. The principles were developed by the Federal Tribunal by way of analogy with an old statute, enacted in the days before the Civil Code and designed primarily to govern inter-cantonal conflicts of law.

Since 1 January 1989, the Swiss private international law has been governed by the Federal Law on Private International Law of 18 December 1987 (PIL). The PIL governs, in some 200 articles, all aspects of the international application of private law. It regulates not only the applicable law (conflicts of law) but also the jurisdiction of Swiss courts and authorities in international matters and the recognition of foreign judgments and decisions. These three questions as well as the definition of domicile and nationality are dealt with generally in the first chapter. They are taken up again, but in a specific form, in each of the other ten chapters, which all treat successively jurisdiction, application law and enforcement. These chapters follow the structure of the Civil Code and of the Code of Obligations: Natural persons (Ch. 2), marriage law (Ch. 3), children and adoption (Ch. 4), guardianship (Ch. 5), succession (Ch. 6), property law (Ch. 7), intellectual property rights (Ch. 8), law of obligations (Ch. 9) and corporations (Ch. 10). The Law on Private International Law concludes with a chapter on international bankruptcy (Ch. 11) and one on international arbitration (Ch. 12).

The Act partly codified the principles developed by the Federal Tribunal and partly introduced new solutions. However, the fundamentals have not been changed (below, section 2).

* Professor, Universities of Lausanne and Fribourg.
** Professor, University of Fribourg.

F. Dessemontet and T. Ansay (eds), Introduction to Swiss Law, 301–318.
© 2004 Kluwer Law International. Printed in The Netherlands.

b. International Conventions

Switzerland is a party to numerous multilateral conventions. International conventions are applicable in Switzerland, without transformation. In the field of private international law, they can be invoked directly before the courts and override the internal law including the PIL.

The most important multilateral convention for Switzerland is the 'Lugano Convention' of 1988 on jurisdiction and enforcement of judgments in civil and commercial matters. This Convention paralleled the Brussels Convention of 1968 and it extended it, almost word by word, to the international relations between the members States of the EU and the EFTA countries. It is still in force, but shall soon be adapted to incorporate the amendments of the Regulation (EC) No 44/2001 which succeeded to the Brussels convention as of 1 March 2002. The 'Brussels II' Regulation (EC) No 1347/2000 on matrimonial decisions and custody, however, is not applicable to Switzerland and will not be introduced into the new Lugano Convention within the foreseeable future.

In addition Switzerland has concluded bilateral treaties on applicable law, jurisdiction and enforcement with the following countries: Austria, Belgium, Czechoslovakia, Federal Republic of Germany, Greece, Iran, Italy, Liechtenstein, Spain, Sweden and the United States of America.

2. Principles

Swiss private international law is characterized by the principles of habitual residence, party autonomy, a favorable attitude towards recognition, and a regard for the judge.

a. The Principle of the Habitual Residence (Gewöhnlicher Aufenthalt/Résidence habituelle)

Swiss private international law traditionally used the habitual residence as the main connecting factor. The PIL confirms this option. The habitual residence is the principal connecting factor for the status of persons and corporations in the relationship between spouses, for divorce, in family law in general, in the law of succession, and even to some extent in torts. The nationality, especially if common to both parties, plays a subsidiary role in some cases (e.g. Arts. 44 II, 54 II, 61 II).[1]

Consequently to the basic option in favor of the habitual residence, the PIL is generally hostile to the *renvoi*.

b. Party Autonomy

The PIL expresses high regard for the autonomy of the parties. The parties are free to elect the applicable law in contracts and corporations, by a choice of law clause

---

1. Articles referred to in this chapter indicate the Federal Law on Private International Law.

or by incorporation. In addition, a limited choice of law is possible in the law of matrimonial property regimes (Art. 52), of succession (Arts. 90 II, 91 II) and torts (Art. 130 II).

The autonomy of the parties is limited mainly by the public order (Art. 17) as well as by two articles that give effect to mandatory applications of Swiss and foreign law (Arts. 18 and 19), much like in the Rome Convention of 1980 on the Law Applicable to Contractual Relationships.

c. Favorable Attitude towards Recognition

The PIL liberally recognizes foreign judgments and decisions. Reciprocity is never required, except for the recognition of foreign bankruptcy decrees. Foreign international jurisdiction is very broadly admitted, often to a larger extent than the one to which the PIL claims international jurisdiction for Swiss courts. Frequently, recognition is possible if a foreign decision is recognized in another foreign state (e.g. Arts. 58, 65 I, 70, 78 II, 96 I).

The PIL claims exclusive jurisdiction only for actions concerning interest in real property (Art. 97) and for actions based on an agreed venue (Art. 5).

d. Discretionary Power

Quite a few conflicts of law rules of the PIL constitute an answer to the American 'conflicts revolution' of the post war era, by incorporating result oriented considerations in their solutions (e.g. maintenance claims, form of contracts, torts, limitations for treble damages, etc.). They give to the judge who feels that she should favor a certain result, considerable latitude to do so. In addition, general provisions like the exception clause (Art. 14) and the taking into account of mandatory provisions of Swiss and foreign law (Arts. 18 and 19) give the judge an important power of discretion.

B. General Provisions

The first chapter of the PIL contains the general provisions on the jurisdiction of Swiss courts and authorities, on the applicable law and on recognition and enforcement of foreign judgments.

1. Jurisdiction

The international jurisdiction of Swiss courts and authorities is regulated mainly in the special part of the PIL. Each section begins with provisions on jurisdiction, continues with rules on the applicable law, and ends with provisions on recognition. The general provisions of the first part, therefore, deal only with common features; they regulate the principles of jurisdiction, prorogation and jurisdiction for provisional orders.

The main and subsidiary venue is the habitual residence of the defendant. The additional venues (of the special part) generally constitute additional possibilities. If the defendant does not have his habitual residence in Switzerland, the PIL provides a venue at the place of performance of a contractual obligation as well as at the place of the assets and allows for the validation of an attachment order there, it being understood that these matters are governed by the Lugano Convention in the European context.

Concerning pecuniary claims, the parties can choose a Swiss forum (Art. 5). The prorogation clause must be made in writing or by any other means of communication that evidences the terms of the agreement by text. The Swiss court that has been agreed upon must accept its jurisdiction if one party has his habitual residence or place of business in the canton of the court or if Swiss law is applicable to the case by virtue of the conflict rules of the PIL or by virtue of a choice of Swiss law by the parties.

Regarding provisional orders, Swiss courts have jurisdiction even if they do not have jurisdiction on the merits (Art. 10).

2. Applicable Law

Generally speaking, the applicable law is the one that presents the closest relationship with the case. Normally, this relationship is defined by the detailed and numerous conflicts rules of the special part. If, for some reason and in a particular case, these rules fail to designate the law with which the case really presents a close relationship, but instead refer to one with only limited connections, the judge can apply another law that has closer connection, on the basis of the famous exception clause of Article 15.

An example of the functioning of the exception clause can be found in divorce judgment concerning spouses who lived for two years in Texas and the following 17 years in five countries and three continents, before settling for five years in Switzerland. The conflict of law rules would have called for the application of the law of their common nationality (Texas), but the Federal Tribunal applied Swiss law, considering that none of the factual connections reflected the real situation and that the closest ties existed with Switzerland.[2]

The law designated by the conflict of law rules of the PIL include all provisions applicable to the case under that law, be they private or public in character (Art. 13), except where the application of the foreign law would produce a result which is incompatible with Swiss public policy (Art. 17).

As indicated above, the PIL is hostile to the *renvoi*. The *renvoi* (of first and second degree, *Rück-und Weiterverweisung*) is accepted only in two specific cases, regarding the name (below II, A), some aspects of the law of inheritance (below II C 3), and more generally in matters of status (Art. 14).

As does the Rome Convention of 1980, the PIL regulates the application of mandatory provisions of Swiss and foreign law (*Loi d'application immédiate*). Mandatory provisions of another law than the one designated by the conflict rules

---

2. ATF/BGE 188/1991 II 79.

may be applied under limited circumstances. The provisions must be closely connected with the case and has to be legitimate; manifestly preponderant interests of a party must require their application and the result must be adequate under Swiss concepts of law (Art. 19).

Mandatory provisions of Swiss law that have the character of *loi d'application immédiate* must be applied regardless of the law designated by the PIL (Art. 17).

The content of the foreign law must be established *ex officio* by the judge, who can require the parties to furnish assistance. This rule applies without restrictions in family law. For pecuniary claims, the judge may impose the burden of proof on the parties (Art. 16).

3. Recognition (*Anerkennung/Reconnaissance*)

The PIL defines the jurisdiction of foreign courts and authorities. The general provisions state the principles according to which a foreign judgment must be recognized in Switzerland if the defendant has his habitual residence in the State in which the judgment was rendered or if he has submitted to the jurisdiction of this State either by a prorogation agreement or tacitly (Art. 26).

As a rule, recognition does not depend upon reciprocity, except for the recognition of foreign bankruptcy decrees. Recognition may be refused if a party establishes that he was not duly notified of the proceedings or that the decisions was rendered in violation of fundamental principles of Swiss procedural law, especially in violation of due process of law, or if, in a general way, recognition would be manifestly incompatible with material Swiss public policy (Art. 27).

II. NATURAL PERSON

A. *The Status of Natural Persons*

The short first chapter of the PIL deals with legal capacity, the capacity to act in the name of natural persons.

Swiss law regards legal capacity as a matter of public policy. The principle of legal capacity is therefore always governed by Swiss law (Art. 34 I). The questions of the beginning and the termination of legal personality, however, are governed by the law applicable to the main legal relationship (Art. 34 II).

The capacity to act is governed by the law of the habitual residence (Art. 35). But for the security of transactions, a person who lacks capacity under the law of his habitual residence is regarded as having capacity if the other party was entitled to rely on it under the law of the State where the transaction took place.

The name of a person having his habitual residence in Switzerland is governed by Swiss law. The name of a person having his habitual residence abroad is governed by the law of his habitual residence, but Swiss law accepts a *renvoi* of first and second degree (Art. 37 I). In both cases, the person can request that his name be governed by the state of which he is a national (Art. 37 II).

B. *Marriage and Relationship between Parent and Child*

1. Conclusion of Marriage

Jurisdiction to perform marriage is granted very broadly to Swiss authorities. Swiss authorities have jurisdiction when either one of the future spouses has his habitual residence in Switzerland or is a Swiss citizen. Even nationals without habitual residence in Switzerland can perform marriage in Switzerland if the marriage is recognized in the State of citizenship or habitual residence of both spouses (Art. 43).

The legislature tried to avoid marriages that are valid in a foreign country but not in Switzerland. Therefore, the PIL is very generous with respect to recognition. Any marriage validly performed abroad is recognized in Switzerland, except if a Swiss spouse or spouses having their habitual residence in Switzerland have tried to defraud Swiss law (Art. 45). Marriages between persons of the same sex[3] or marriages with several spouses, however, are not recognized, according to present state of the law (which may change with respect to relationships between persons of the same sex).

2. Divorce

The Swiss court of the habitual residence of the defendant always has jurisdiction for actions on divorce (Art. 59/a). In addition, a Swiss citizen or a foreigner residing in Switzerland for more than one year can sue for divorce at the habitual residence of the plaintiff, or, under restrictive circumstances, at the place of Swiss citizenship.

Divorce and separation are governed by Swiss law or by the law of the State of a common foreign citizenship, if only one of the spouses has his habitual residence in Switzerland and if this law does not impose extraordinarily severe conditions on divorce (Art. 61). Waiting periods of three years after separation, as foreseen by Italian law, are not considered to be extraordinary severe.[4] The applicable law on ancillary effects, especially on the matrimonial property regime and the effects of paternity, as well as the protection of minors, is designated by the special provisions applicable for these matters (Art. 63).

Foreign decisions on divorce or separation are recognized very generously in Switzerland if they were rendered in the State of the habitual residence or of the citizenship of one of the spouses, or if they are recognized in one of these States. 'Private' or 'customary' divorces, not decided before a State authority, can be recognized, but only if they are made in a proceeding which is not unilateral.[5] Restrictions to recognition may apply if none of the spouses or only the plaintiff had his habitual residence in the State in which the decision was rendered (Art. 65).

3. Matrimonial Property Regimes

The matrimonial property regime is governed by the law of the State in which both spouses are domiciled simultaneously (Art. 54 I a). If the spouses are not domiciled

---

3. ATF/BGE 199/1993 II 264.
4. ATF/BGE 121/1995 III 246.
5. ATF/BGE 122/1996 III 344.

in the same state, the law of the State in which they were last domiciled simultaneously applies (Art. 54 I b). If the spouses were never domiciled in the same State and if they do not have a common state of citizenship, the PIL subjects their matrimonial property regime to the Swiss regime of separate property.

A choice of law is possible for the matrimonial property regime. The choice of law must be made in writing or be implied in a marriage contract, and it can be changed at any time. The spouses may choose the law of the state in which they are domiciled, or will be domiciled, or the law of the state of one spouse's citizenship (Arts. 52 and 53).

The law applicable to matrimonial property regime changes when the spouses change their domicile or their choice of law. Unless the spouses were subjected to a marriage contract or decided in writing to maintain the former law, the new law applies with retroactive effect from the date of the marriage (Art. 55).

4. Relationship between Parent and Child

The relationship between parent and child is governed by the principle of the habitual residence of the child. The habitual residence of the child determines the jurisdiction and the applicable law (Arts. 66, 68). Nevertheless, actions to ascertain or contest paternity can be brought before the court at the habitual residence of the mother or the father, and the law of the state of a common citizenship is applicable when neither the father nor the mother has the habitual residence in the same state as the child.

Maintenance claims are brought before the Swiss courts at the place of the habitual residence of the child or, in the absence of such residence in Switzerland, before the courts of the habitual residence of the defendant parent (Art. 79). The maintenance obligations are governed by the Hague Convention of 1973 on the Law Applicable to Maintenance Obligations.

C. Inheritance

1. Principle

The PIL is based upon the principle of the unity of the succession. It applies the same law for the whole succession, and Swiss authorities have jurisdiction over movables as well as immovables unless exclusive jurisdiction claimed by the state in which real property is located takes precedence.

The PIL distinguishes between persons whose last domicile was within Switzerland and persons whose last domicile was abroad. The PIL considers that Switzerland is mainly concerned with the first situation and with the second only in a subsidiary way.

2. The Decedent having been Domiciled in Switzerland

If the decedent had his last domicile in Switzerland, Swiss courts have jurisdiction for inheritance disputes as well as for probate proceedings (Art. 86). The Swiss court and authorities apply Swiss law as the law of the state of the last domicile (Art. 90 I).

However, a foreigner can make a choice of law. He may submit his estate by will or by testamentary contract to the law of one of the states of his citizenship. The choice of law is valid if he conserves this citizenship until his death and if he has not acquired Swiss citizenship (Art. 90 II).

3. The Decedent having been Domiciled Abroad

If the decedent had his last domicile abroad, the Swiss authorities do not normally have jurisdiction. Switzerland considers that such successions should not be dealt with by Swiss courts, but by the courts of the foreign residences of the decedent. Exceptions apply only if a Swiss citizen has submitted his estate or the parts of it located in Switzerland to Swiss jurisdiction, or if the authorities of the place of his last domicile do not deal with his estate (Art. 87). An additional exception, limited to the property located in Switzerland, exists over the estate of a foreigner who has been domiciled abroad, if the authorities of his domicile do not deal with these properties (Art. 88).

For these – exceptional – situations, the PIL designates, as a rule, the law of the state of the last domicile of the decedent, but it recognizes a *renvoi* of the first and second degree (Art. 91 I). Yet if the decedent was a Swiss citizen and had submitted his estate to Swiss jurisdiction by will or by testamentary contract, Swiss law shall apply unless the decedent has expressly reserved the law of his last domicile (Art. 91 II). In this case, an election of Swiss jurisdiction is deemed to be an election of Swiss law, and vice versa (Art. 87 II).

4. Recognition

Foreign decision, measures and documents are recognized in Switzerland if they were rendered in the state of the last domicile of the decedent or were made pursuant to the law chosen by him, or if they are recognized in one of these states. If the decisions concern real property, they are recognized in Switzerland if they are established in the state where the property is located or recognized (Art. 96).

III. PROPERTY

A. *In General*

Real and movable property is subject to the jurisdiction and the law of the place where it is located. This holds generally for real property (Arts. 97, 99).

Acquisition and loss of an interest in movable property is governed by the law of the place where it was located at the time when the decisive facts occurred (Art. 100 I); but the extent and the exercise of these interests are governed by the law of the place where the properties are located at that time (Art. 100 II). If the movable property is in transit, the acquisition and the loss of interest based on a legal transaction is governed by the state of destination (Art. 101).

B. Pledge of Movable Property and Retention of Title

Normally, the general rules extend to the pledge of movable property and retention of title: the law of the place where the property is located applies. For the pledge of claims, securities and other rights, the PIL designates the law of the state of the habitual residence of the secured creditor (Art. 105).

Retention of title over property is a complicated matter under present substantive law in Switzerland. The same is true for international relations: property imported into Switzerland must be modified in order to comply with the requirements of Swiss law. However, title remains valid for three months, but only amongst the parties, not against a bona fide third person (Art. 102). Retention of title over exported property is subjected to the law of the state of destination (Art. 103).

A choice of law for the acquisition and loss of an interest in movable property is possible. A party may elect either the law of the state of shipment or of the state of destination or the law applicable to the underlying legal transaction (Art. 104 I). Here again, the bona fide third party is protected; such a choice of law cannot be applied against him (Art. 104 II).

C. Intellectual Property

Switzerland follows the territoriality doctrine for the whole of intellectual property. As a matter of principle, intellectual property rights are governed by the law of the country for which protection of these rights is sought (Art. 110 I). This system is rooted in the multilateral conventions to which Switzerland is party: the Paris Convention on Industrial Property, the Berne Convention of Copyright, the GATT–TRIPS Agreement and a number of conventions of lesser importance (the Rome and Geneva Conventions on neighboring rights, for example). Interestingly, bilateral conventions on geographic denominations may depart from the territoriality doctrine, resulting, for example, in foreign law circumscribing the conditions of use of a given denomination.[6]

Swiss case law is mostly to the effect that the law of the country where protection is sought also applies to the acquisition of the right, be it through registration or through conveyance of title. In a case where a business had been transferred in Germany between two German entities, all trademark rights passing along, the Federal Tribunal nonetheless considered that the expectancies for protection of these marks in Switzerland when registered at a later date were transferred under Swiss law.[7] However, there are cases to the effect that conflicts between trade may be settled taking into account the law or the facts at the common place of business of the parties.[8] The PIL now provides that the law governing the corporation applies to its name or trade name (Art. 155 lit. d). Nonetheless, the protection of the business name remains subject to the law of the country where protection is sought (Art. 157 I). Contracts involving intellectual property rights are subject to the law of the transferor's or the licensor's place of business or domicile (Art. 122 I).

---

6. See case Turron de Alicante, decided by the EC Court of Justice 10 November 1992, GRUR Int. 1993 76 *et seq.*
7. RSPI 1992, at 252.
8. ATF 91 II 125; RSPI 1976, at 64.

Finally, the exhaustion of rights is not subject to express rules, so that case law shall decide whether the exhaustion of rights follows from marketing abroad or only from marketing within Switzerland. For patents, case law accepts national exhaustion, while it admits international exhaustion for copyrights and trademarks.

IV. CONTRACTS, TORTS AND CORPORATIONS

A. *Law of Obligations*

The provisions of the PIL on the conflicts of laws in the area of the law of obligations are based on a rich case law.

1. Contractual Obligations

There is no legal definition of 'international contract.' Some or all of the following points of contacts shall exist with two or more states in order for the rules on jurisdiction and applicable law of the PIL to come into action:

- habitual residence
- place of business or domicile of the parties
- in addition to other elements, place of performance.

a. *Jurisdiction*

Lawsuits in contract are subject to the jurisdiction of the Swiss courts at the defendant's domicile, or, if there is none, at his habitual residence. Lawsuits arising out of the activity of a business establishment in Switzerland are also subject to the jurisdiction of the courts at the place of business thereof.

According to the Lugano Convention (Art. 5 I), Switzerland has recognized, after a transitory period ending 31 December 1999 (Art. 1bis, Protocol no. 1), the jurisdiction of the place of performance of the contract, in cases involving both Swiss residents and residents of other countries having ratified the Lugano Convention.

A consumer may not waive in advance his right of venue at his own domicile or residence in Switzerland. Lawsuits arising out of employment contracts are to be brought either at the general forum of the defendant's domicile or at the place where the employee performs his work; further, at the employee's domicile or habitual residence in Switzerland if he files the suit.

b. *Applicable Law*

(i) Scope of Applicable Law
The law deemed to be applicable to the contract shall govern most questions of law, with the following general exceptions:

- the capacity to act, which is subject to the law of domicile, with some safeguard if the act has been executed in a country where the incapable person would enjoy the capacity to act (Art. 35 *et seq.* PIL);

- the commercial law of agency, which is subject to the law of the country in which the agent has his business establishment or in which the agent mainly acts in the particular case;
- the modality of the performance and the formalities for inspection, subject to the law of the country where they in fact take place or should take place;
- the form of the contract, subject to the law of the country where it is executed.

Some other restrictions on the application of the law of contract may derive from the public policy provisions of the PIL (Swiss public policy; Swiss laws of direct application such as the regulation on the sale of real estate to foreigners; labor protection law; human rights; mandatory provisions of foreign laws, if legitimate and clearly overriding interests of a party so require). As the case may dictate, further restrictions on the scope of applicable law shall be based on the particular nature of the rights involved in the transaction, e.g. patent or trademark rights, the validity of which may not be submitted by the parties to a law other than the law of the country where they are registered.

(ii) Applicable Law

As a rule, contracts are governed by the law chosen by the parties. This choice is a contract in itself, validity of which is subject to the law chosen. Under Swiss law, it can be made at any moment, even during litigation. It may be implied in fact. It is totally free, no requirement as to a necessary point of contact being made by the new Swiss law (contrary to the former case law). It seems to be lawful to make a partial choice, bearing only on some matters. A change of choice is possible, but rights of third parties are reserved. Choice of law is excluded for contracts with consumers, and restricted for employment contracts.

If there is no choice of law, the contract is governed by the law of the country most closely connected with it. Switzerland follows the doctrine of the characteristic obligation, as developed by A. Schnitzer and adopted by case law as in the Rome Convention of 1980, i.e. the closest connection is assumed to exist with the country where the party that must discharge the characteristic obligation has his habitual residence or place of business. A few statutory examples may suffice to illustrate that this is not necessarily the place where the performance of the characteristic obligation is due to take place:

- in contracts to convey title, the transferor's law shall apply;
- in rental, lending and loan, the renter, lender or creditor's law shall apply
- in service contracts, the contractor's law shall apply;
- in deposit contracts, the keeper's law shall apply;
- in guarantee contracts, the guarantor or surety's law shall apply;
- in license agreements, the licensor's law shall apply.

Contracts on immovable property are subject to the law of the place of location of the property involved.

2. Unjust Enrichment

Claims based on unjust enrichment are governed by the law applicable to the (apparent) legal relationship on which the enrichment is grounded, or if none is found to exist, by the law of the country in which the enrichment took place. This provision applies if accounting of the profits for unlawful use of a trademark, copyright or patent is sought. It may also apply where the monies deposited in a bank are credited on another customer's account.

3. Torts

The PIL constitutes a pioneering work in the field of conflict of laws for torts. The basic rule is that when the wrongdoer and the injured party are habitually resident in the same country, liability in tort shall be governed by the law of that country.[9]

If the two parties do not have a common country of residence, the law of the country where the tort has been committed is applicable. If the result does not occur in the same country, the law of the country where the result occurs is applicable if the wrongdoer could have expected the result to take place in that country.

If the tort is connected to an existing legal relationship between the parties, the law governing that relationship shall apply.

The parties may agree after the damaging event that the law of the forum shall apply. This may be the first step towards a settlement. Lawsuits based on torts are subject to the jurisdiction of the Swiss courts at the domicile, habitual residence or business establishment of the defendant. If the defendant is not a Swiss resident, the suit can be introduced at the place where the act occurred or where its result took place. If several defendants are subject to Swiss jurisdiction for the same facts, each judge has jurisdiction over all defendants; the court before which proceedings are first instituted shall have exclusive jurisdiction over all of the defendants.

There are a number of special rules on jurisdiction and applicable law. For example, in a case of damages that are caused by a nuclear plant or shipment, in a case of a direct claim against an insurer, a claim arising out of traffic accidents (where the Hague Convention of 4 May 1971 shall apply), for product liability, for unfair competition and restraint of competition, for nuisance caused by or from an immovable property, and for violation of the right of personality, as well as for claims in personal liability against the (former) directors of a corporation.

4. Common Provisions

The PIL deals separately with a few questions arising out of a plurality of debtors, whatever the source of their obligation, be it a contract, a tort or unjust enrichment. It provides that contractual assignment of a claim is governed by the law of the claim, if no law has been chosen by the parties. The currency in which payment must be made is determined by the law of the country where payment must be made. The statute of limitations is governed by the law applicable to the claim.

The rules of conflicts for Bills of Exchange and Notes are to be found in the Swiss Code of Obligations (Arts. 1086 to 1095 and 1138 to 1142); they embody the Geneva Conventions on the Law Applicable to Drafts and to Checks of 1930.

---

9. Compare ATF 99 II 315: where two Swiss residents bought a car in Switzerland and caused a car accident in France, the liability of the driver is subject to Swiss law.

B. Corporations

1. Recognition of Foreign Entities

The PIL defines 'corporations' as organized entities of persons and organized units of assets. All legal entities are recognized in Switzerland, even if some of them as the trust, are unknown under Swiss municipal law. Switzerland is not party to the Hague Convention of 1 July 1985 on the law applicable to trust.

Besides that very liberal recognition of foreign legal entities, the PIL is based upon the principle of incorporation. The applicable law is the law of the country according to which they are incorporated.

According to the most recent case law, the PIL does not allow the courts to push aside a so-called 'fictitious seat' or place of incorporation. There would be no application of the *fraus legis* argumentation against, say, recognition of a Panama company that is in fact active in Switzerland and administered in Geneva, or against the recognition of a Lichtenstein establishment (*Anstalt*) which may well purport to escape the rigorous provisions of Swiss law on family foundations.[10] However, the public policy exception of Article 17 PIL may apply, as could the special provision on responsibility for foreign companies of Article 159 PIL.

The partnership (*einfache Gesellschaft/société simple*) is subject to the law determined by the PIL provisions on contracts, as they are not recognized as legal entities.

2. Scope of Applicable Law and Jurisdiction

As a rule, the law of the country of incorporation governs the legal nature of the company, its formation and dissolution, its capacity to act, its organization, the relationship between the corporation and its members, liability for its debts, the power of representation of the persons acting on its behalf according to its organization (as opposed to general rules on agency), and their liability arising from the violation of corporation law.

As to liability, if the business of a corporation organized under foreign law is executed in or managed from Switzerland, the liability of the directors or managers shall be governed by Swiss law. Lawsuits against a person liable under the law of corporation may be entertained before the Swiss courts at the defendant's domicile or his habitual residence. Further, all litigation under the law of corporations may be brought also to the Swiss court at the seat of the corporation. This jurisdiction cannot be waived for lawsuits arising from the public issue of shares and bonds. Claims therefore may be filed under either the law governing the company or the law of the place of performance.

Finally, it should be noted that a company may not invoke the limitations of the power of representation of an officer or an agent that are unknown to the law of the country where the other party has its place of business or habitual residence, unless the other party knew or had reason to know of the limitations.

The PIL further regulates Swiss branch offices of foreign corporations, the transfer of corporation from abroad to Switzerland or from Switzerland to a foreign

---

10. Compare ATF 117 II 494 with ATF 102 Ia 410, ATF 108 II 122 and 108 II 398.

country, the protection of debtors if the corporation is to be stricken out of the Swiss Register of Commerce, and recognition of foreign court decisions regarding the corporation.

C. Bankruptcy

A foreign bankruptcy decree issued at the domicile or the habitual residence of the debtor may be recognized in Switzerland upon a motion by the foreign receiver in bankruptcy or by one of the creditors. Recognition depends upon the usual conditions (above I B 3) as well as upon reciprocity.

Recognition poses an obstacle to all special enforcement measures in Switzerland and invalidates such measures – including attachments – if they exist already. It leads instead to an ancillary bankruptcy proceeding at the place where the Swiss assets are located. The recognition procedure is simplified. Neither an assembly of creditors nor a committee of creditors is formed. The competent bankruptcy office draws up an inventory of assets, issues a call to the creditors in the Official Gazette of Commerce and prepares a schedule of claims. In this schedule are entered only claims secured by pledge and claim by creditors who enjoy one of the privileges mentioned in Article 219 IV of the Federal Law on Execution of Debts and Bankruptcy (presently undergoing revision) and who are domiciled in Switzerland. If a creditor has been paid in foreign proceedings, that amount shall be deducted from his dividends in the Swiss proceedings.

After payment of the privileged creditors in Switzerland, but before the handing out of the surplus, the foreign schedule of claims is examined by the Swiss court that recognized the foreign bankruptcy decree. That court shall recognize the schedule, when the claims of creditors domiciled in Switzerland have been properly taken into account in the foreign schedule. Then the monies will be paid to the foreign receiver. If the foreign schedule is not recognized or not submitted for recognition within the period set by the judge, the balance shall be awarded to the common creditors domiciled in Switzerland.

V. INTERNATIONAL ARBITRATION

Switzerland plays an important role in the field of international arbitration, whether between states, between private parties to international commercial transactions, or between private parties and a foreign state or state agency. Switzerland is the seat of many arbitral tribunals that are appointed *inter alia* by the International Chamber of Commerce, the London Committee for International Arbitration or the International Center for Settlement of Investments Disputes (ICSID).

A. Scope of the PIL

The only codification bearing on arbitration proceedings used to be the 1969 Intercantonal Concordat of Arbitration adopted in all but one canton, Lucerne (SR 279). Since 1989, the Concordat governs only Swiss arbitration proceedings, while

Chapter 12 of the PIL applies to international arbitration. Nevertheless, the parties to an international arbitration may validly submit their dispute to the rules of the Concordat; they have to agree in writing that the provisions of the PIL are excluded and that the Concordat shall apply. Thus, existing arbitration clauses providing for arbitration in Switzerland are subject to the PIL.

For a case to be international, at least one of the parties has to have neither domicile nor habitual residence in Switzerland at the time of the conclusion of the arbitration agreement.

For a litigation to be submitted to the PIL, the seat of the arbitral tribunal, as determined by the parties or by the arbitration institution or by the arbitrators must be in Switzerland. Meetings of the arbitrators or hearings of the arbitral tribunal outside of Switzerland do not affect the seat.

B. *Arbitrability*

Arbitrability is defined in broad terms. Any dispute relating to patrimonial interest may be submitted to arbitration. The legislature wanted to open up the arbitrability much farther than had been accepted a few decades ago. Corporation law, validity of patents, trademarks, designs and copyrights, even antitrust claims may be brought before an arbitral tribunal.

A state or a state agency that is party to an arbitration agreement cannot invoke its own municipal law in order to contest the arbitrability of a dispute or its capacity to arbitrate within, of course, the limits of the arbitration agreement.

C. *The Arbitration Agreement*

The arbitration agreement shall be in writing, which for the purpose of the PIL includes telefax and any other means of communications that can establish the agreement by a text. A more liberal foreign law may lend it validity, if the agreement conforms to the law chosen by the parties either for this agreement or for their contractual relationship, or if it conforms to the law governing the litigation in the absence of choice of the applicable law.

If the arbitration agreement appears to be valid prima facie, the Swiss courts shall decline jurisdiction (Art. 7). Validity and scope of the arbitration agreement are to be determined by the arbitrators. The arbitral proceedings are deemed to be pending from the time one of the parties starts the procedure for appointment of the tribunal.

The arbitrators are appointed according to the arbitration agreement and the procedures of the institution they have selected for resolution of the dispute. Failing such an agreement, the Swiss courts at the seat of the tribunal shall appoint the arbitrators. A judge cannot reject a request to this effect unless a summary examination shows that no arbitration agreement exists at all between the parties.

An arbitrator might be challenged if he does not meet the qualifications agreed upon by the parties (i.e. as to his nationality), or if he does not appear to be independent of both parties, or if the procedural rules of a given institution (e.g. ICC rules) allow for a challenge.

D. Procedure

The PIL does not lay down procedural rules except for the very basic principles. The parties may determine the rules freely, either directly or by reference to institutional arbitrations. If they did not determine the procedure in advance, the arbitrators can lay down the procedural framework, in a procedural order or in terms of reference if they choose to do so.

The arbitrators can issue interlocutory orders or injunction pendente lite. If a party does not willingly comply, the arbitrator may request the assistance of the competent state court, that shall apply its own law.

As Switzerland has made a pioneering attempt to grant interlocutory powers to the arbitrators, it seems that few other jurisdictions may enforce such provisional measures abroad. For these jurisdictions, some sort of procedure of *référé* (provisional orders, interlocutory orders, etc.) before the local courts shall in practise be preferred to an exequatur procedure of the arbitrator's order.

The arbitrators may order measures of a procedural nature (sealing offices, possible discovery) or measures aiming at safeguarding assets (freezing bank accounts, stopping a liquidation of the defendant corporation). Enforcing these measures abroad may require the assistance of the local courts.

The Swiss courts shall assist the arbitrators in the taking of evidence. The system of deposition as known in the United States is not practiced in Switzerland.

The arbitral tribunal may decide on its jurisdiction in a preliminary or in the definitive award if there is a dispute in this regard. For example, a first set of terms of reference may be adopted towards the resolution of that issue, the parties being however under a duty faithfully to cooperate later for the establishment of a second set of terms of reference if the arbitral tribunal finds itself competent on some or all claims.

Unless otherwise agreed upon by the parties, the arbitrators may issue partial awards.

The arbitral tribunal shall apply for its decision on the merits the rules of law most closely connected to the case at bar; it is not necessarily bound by the conflict rules of the PIL. This provision means that the arbitrators might consider applying more than one municipal law, since it does not refer to a single body of law but to 'rules of law' (*Billigkeit/equité*).[11]

E. Appeal

The former system of dual challenge, first before the cantonal court of the seat, then before the Federal Tribunal, was deemed to be cumbersome and lengthy, especially if other proceedings for an exequatur were necessary abroad.

There is now only one appeal, as a rule to the Federal Tribunal or to the cantonal tribunal of the seat if the parties have explicitly agreed not to go to the Federal Tribunal.

---

11. In the French text of Art. 187 PIL.

The nature of this appeal is *sui generis*; but some of the rules on the appeal towards annulment are applicable, and the Federal Tribunal may only invalidate the sentence, without power to modify it. In case of invalidation, the arbitral tribunal originally competent is again competent, unless some specific grounds for challenging it may be asserted in view of the appeal proceedings. As a rule, the appeal does not entail a suspension of the effects of the award, but the president of the competent court may order a suspensive effect. Therefore, the disbursement of monies or conveyance of title that are based on an invalidated award are valid at the time they are made – but might be deemed to constitute an unjust enrichment in case of annulment of the award later on.

The five grounds for challenging the award are mentioned in an exhaustive way by the PIL:

1. when the arbitrator(s) were not properly appointed;
2. when the arbitral tribunal has made an erroneous ruling on its jurisdiction;
3. when the award went beyond the questions submitted to it or failed to decide on one of the claims;
4. when the principle of equal treatment or the right to be heard was breached;
5. when the award is contrary to (international) public policy as understood in Switzerland.

Very few awards have been invalidated since enactment of the PIL. The following cases are representative:

1. An arbitral tribunal should not decide an award when only two of its three members are present.
2. An arbitral tribunal should not reject for lack of jurisdiction a plea contending that a contract is null and void under Article 85 of the Rome Treaty if the validity of the contract is an item subject to the arbitration agreement.
3. The right to be heard encompasses the right to obtain an expertise whenever the arbitrators or one of them is not technically knowledgeable.

If none of the parties have their domicile, habitual residence or business establishment in Switzerland, they may waive the right to appeal for invalidation of the award. The usual statement that 'the award shall be definitive' is not deemed to be a waiver. On the other hand, a clause stating that the award shall not be appealable should be construed as a waiver.

Finally, it is to be noted that Switzerland is a party to the New York Convention of 1958 on the Recognition and Enforcement of Foreign Arbitral Awards, but not yet to the 1961 Geneva Convention.

SELECTED BIBLIOGRAPY

Bucher, A., *Droit international privé suisse. Vol. II – Personnes, Famille, Successions,* Bale 1992.

Dessemontet, F. (ed.), *Le nouveau droit international privé suisse*, publication CEDIDAC Vol. 9, Lausanne 1988.

Gillieron, P.-R., *Les dispositions de la nouvelle loi fédérale de droit international privé sur la faillite internationale,* Lausanne 1991.

Heini, Keller, Siehr, Vischer and Volken, *IPRG Kommentar,* Zurich 1993.

Honsell, Vogt and Schnyder (eds.), *International Arbitration in Switzerland,* Basel 2000.

Keller, M. and K. Siehr, *Allgemeine Lehren des internationalen Privatrechts,* Zurich, 1986.

Knoepfler, F. and P. Schweizer, *Précis de droit international privé suisse,* Bern 1990.

Lalive P., J. F. Poudret and C. Reymond, *Le droit de l'arbitrage interne et international en Suisse,* Lausanne 1989.

Schnyder, A. K., *Das neue IPR-Gesetz,* 2nd edn., Zurich 1990.

Schwandler, I., *Einführung in das Internationale Privatrecht: Allgemeiner Teil,* 2nd edn., St. Gallen 1990.

Vischner, F. and A. von Planta, *Internationales Privatrecht,* 2nd edn., Basel/Stuttgart 1982.

Chapter 18
Bibliography on Swiss Law (in English)

*Compiled by Alain Thevenaz**

I. GENERAL

Linder, W., 'Switzerland' in: H. Schaeffer, and A. Racz (eds.), *Quantitative Analyses of Law. A Comparative Empirical Study. Sources of Law in Eastern and Western Europe*, Budapest 1990, pp. 339–352.

Pestalozzi and Gmuer, 'Switzerland Law Digest' in: *Law Digest*, Vol. 6, *Martindale–Hubbel Law Directory*, New York 1975.

Schlesinger, R.B., *Comparative Law. Cases–Text–Materials*, 4th. edn., Mineola, New York 1980.

Soloveytchik, G., *Switzerland in Perspective*, London/New York/Oxford: University Press 1954.

Stoffel, W.A., 'Switzerland' in: *International Encyclopedia of Comparative Law*, Vol. 1: *National Reports*, 1987, pp. 177–204.

Szladits, C., *Guide to Foreign Legal Materials. French–German–Swiss*, New York: Oceana Publ. 1951.

Walther, F.M.R., 'The Swiss Legal System. A Guide for Foreign Researchers', Int'l J of Legal Information 1–24 (2001).

II. CONSTITUTIONAL LAW AND ADMINISTRATIVE LAW

After 1982:

Darrel, A.H., 'Killing the Rhine: Immoral, but is it Illegal?', 29 *Virginia Journal of International Law* 421–472 (1989).

Fleiner–Gerster, T., 'The Concept of Constitution (Switzerland)' in: T. Fleiner–Gerster and S. Hutter (eds.), *Federalism and Decentralizaition. Constitutional Problems of Territorial Decentralization in Federal and Centralized States*, Fribourg: Editions Universitaires Fribourg, Suisse 1987, pp. 139–154.

Meiss, F. von, 'Government Procurement in Switzerland', 21 *George Washington Journal of International Law and Economics*, 1987, 151–163.

*Dr. jur., master-assistant at the University of Lausanne.

F. Dessemontet and T. Ansay (eds), Introduction to Swiss Law, 319–344.

Schwietzke, J., 'Constitutional Courts of Germany, Austria and Switzerland' in: I.I. Kavass (ed.), *Supranational and Constitutional Courts in Europe: Functions and Sources*. Papers presented at the 30th Anniversary Meeting of the International Association of Law Libraries, Bibliotheque Cujas, Paris, August 1989, 1992, pp. 147–209.

Thürer, D., 'The judicial control over the discretionary power to expel and extradite foreigners from Switzerland', in: *Swiss Reports Presented at the XIIth International Congress of Comparative Law* (Sydney/Melbourne, 18–27 August 1986), Zurich: Schultess 1987, pp. 159–177.

Wildhaber, L., 'Switzerland' in: H.J. Michelmann and P. Soldatos (eds.), *Federalism and International Relations: The Role of Subnational Units*, Oxford: Clarendon Press 1990, pp. 245–275.

——, 'Conclusion and Implementation of Treaties in Switzerland' in: *Swiss Reports Presented at the XIIth International Congress of Comparative Law* (Sydney/Melbourne, 18–27 August 1986), Zurich: Schultess 1990, pp. 173–194.

——, 'Limitations on Human Rights in Times of Peace, War and Emergency, a Report on Swiss Law' in: A. de Mestral *et al.* (eds.), *The Limitation of Human Rights in Comparative Constitutional Law*, Cowansvill (Y. Blais) 1986, pp. 41–62.

Before 1982:

Bassand, M., 'The Jura Problem', *Journal of Peace Research* 139–150 (1975).

Bufford, S., 'Aesthetic Legislation in Vaud: A Swiss Model adaptable for American use', 24 *American Journal of Comparative Law*, 391–446 (1976).

Cahannes, M., 'Swiss alcohol policy: The emergence of a compromise', 10 *Contemporary Drug Problems*, Spring 1981, New York, 37–53.

Codding, G.A. Jr., *The Federal Government of Switzerland*, Boston: Houghton Mifflin 1961.

Duft, E., 'Political and Parliamentary Tradition in Switzerland', 41 *Interparliamentary Bulletin* 5–12 (1961).

Dunn, J.A. Jr., *Social Cleavage, Party Systems and Political Integration: A Comparison of the Belgian and Swiss Experiences*. Ph.D. Thesis 1970, University of Pennsylvania, 31/10–A.

Friedrich, C.J. and C. Taylor, *Responsible Bureaucrat: A Study of the Swiss Civil Service*, Cambridge 1932.

Haller, W., 'The ombudsman idea in Switzerland', The Ombudsman Journal. Univ. of Alberta, Canada, no. 1, 1981, 10–23.

Hogrebe, E.F.M., 'Proposal to introduce data protection and freedom on information articles into Swiss Constitution' in: *Transnational Data Report*, Vol. 1, 1978/79, p. 7.

Huber, M., 'The intercantonal law of Switzerland (Swiss interstate law)', 3 Am. J. Int'l L. 62–98 (1909).

Hughes, C., *The Parliament of Switzerland. Publ. for the Hansard Society*, London: Cassell 1962.

Joachim, A., *The Constitutions of the U.S. and Switzerland. Historically Analysed and Compared*, Fribourg 1936.

Jolles, P., *The Theory of Civil Liberties in Swiss and American Constitutional Law*. Ph. D. Thesis 1947, Harvard University.

Kneubühler, H., 'Housing constructions policies and techniques in Switzerland', *OECD Observer*, no. 18, 19–30 (1965).

Lendi, M., 'Swiss planning law,' in: J.F. Gamer (ed.), *Planning Law in Western Europ*, Amsterdam 1975, pp. 293–320.

Looper, R.B., 'The treaty power in Switzerland', 7 Am. J. Comp.L. 178–194 (1958).

Malinverni, G., 'Democracy and foreign policy: the referendum on treaties in Switzerland', 49 Brit. Yearbook Int'l L. 207–219 (1978).

Mason, J.B., 'Switzerland' in: *Foreign Governments. The Dynamics of Politics Abroad*, New York: Prentice Hall Inc. 1949, pp. 369–392.

Mayer, K., 'Ethnics tensions in Switzerland: the Jura conflict' in: *Nations without a State*, New York 1980, pp. 189–208.

O'Brien, F.W., 'Church and state in Switzerland: A comparative study', 49 Va. L. Rev. 904 (1963).

——, 'Swiss law and subversive groups', 18 NoJre.L.Q. 302 (1967).

——, 'Swiss cantons and anti-communist laws', 1 Ottawa L. Rev. 129 (1966).

——, 'Baker v. Carr (82 Sup.Ct. 961) abroad: the Swiss Federal Tribunal and cantonal elections', 72 Yale L.J. 46 (1962).

Pock, M.A., 'Systems of public responsibility in Switzerland, Germany and Austria.', Univ. of Illinois Law Forum, no. 4, 1023–1062 (1966).

Rappard, W.E., *The Government of Switzerland*, New York: D. Van Nostrand 1936.

Rausch, H., 'Some aspects of Swiss law on prevention of pollution', 6 Int'l Bus. Law. 675–766 (1978).

Rees, I.B., 'Local Government in Switzerland', 47 *Public Administration* 421–450 (1969).

Siegfried, A., *Switzerland: A Democratic Way of Life*, London 1950.

Sallay, T., 'Switzerland Act on assets of victims of national socialism', 12 Am. J. Comp. L. 87–91 (1963).

Spiro, H.J., *Government by Constitution*, New York: Random House 1959.

Stockli, W.A., *Church-State and School in Switzerland and the United States*, Beme: Lang 1970.

Tripp, M.L., *The Swiss and U.S. Federal Constitutional Systems*, Paris: Librairie sociale et économique 1940.

Wassermann, U., 'Switzerland's control of trade in toxic chemicals', 11 J. World Trade Law 288 (1977).

Wildhaber, L., 'Compensation for Expropriation in Swiss Law' in: J.F. Garner, *Compensation for Compulsory Purchase*, London 1975, pp. 220–227

Williams, G., *Relations between the Federal and Cantonal Governments in Switzerland*. Ph.D. Thesis 1883, Columbia Univ., New York.

Zürcher, 'The political system of Switzerland' in: J.T. Shotwell (ed.), *Government of Continental Europe*, New York: The Macmillan Co., 1952. pp. 331–338.

Zeilweger, E., 'The Swiss Federal Court as a constitutional court of justice', 7 J. of the Int'l Commission of Jurists 97–124 (1966).

III. LAW OF PERSONS AND BASIC PRINCIPLES OF PRIVATE LAW

Bolgar, V., 'Abuse of rights in France, Germany and Switzerland: A survey of a recent chapter in legal doctrine', 35 La. L. Rev. 1015–1036 (1975).

Brandon, M., 'Claims against wills and trusts of United Kingdom citizens domiciled in Switzerland', 4 Int'l Leg. Prac. 16–19 (1979).

Dutoit, B., 'Good faith and equity in Swiss Law' in: *Equity in the World's Legal System*, (trans. by R.A. Newman) Brussels 1973, pp. 307–345

Hefti, P., 'Trusts and their treatment in the civil law', 5 Am. J. Comp. L. 553–576 (1956).

Huber, E., 'Trust and 'Treuhand' in Swiss Law', 1 Int'l Comp. L. Q. 64–66 (1952).

International Commission of Jurists, 'The legal protection of privacy: A comparative survey of ten countries by the International Commission of Jurists', 24 Int'l Soc. Sci. Bull. 417–583 (1972).

Meyer, H.H., 'Trust and Swiss Law', 1 Int'l Comp. L. Q. 378–381 (1952).

IV. FAMILY LAW AND LAW OF INHERITANCE

After 1982:

Bücher, A., 'Family Law in Switzerland: Recent Reforms and future Issues – An Overview', 275–296 European J of Law Reform, Vol. 3.

Grossen, J.-M., 'The Contributions of Comparative (or Foreign Law) Studies to Family Law Reform', in: *Droit sans frontières. Essays in Honour of L. Neville Brown*, Birmingham 1991, p. 95.

——, 'Switzerland: Hard Cases, in Annual Survey of Family Law', 26 *Journal of Family Law* 207–211 (1987–1988).

——, 'Switzerland: Further Steps Towards Equality. Annual Survey of Family Law', 25 *Journal of Family Law* 255–259 (1986–1987).

——, 'Switzerland' in: M. Freeman (ed.), *Annual Survey of Family Law 1983–1984*, London 1985, pp. 178–190.

——, 'Agreements Regarding the Financial Aspects of Divorce: How Free? How Binding?' in: J.M. Eckelaar and S.N. Katz (eds.), *The Resolution of Family Conflict–Comparative Legal Perspectives*, Toronto 1984, p. 313.

——, 'Matrimonial Property Law Reform: Choosing a New Legal Regime', *Holdsworth Law Review* (Birmingham) 45 (1983).

Guillod, O., 'Switzerland: Abused Children, HIV-Positive Sexual Partners and Family Reunion', 30 *Journal of Family Law* 417–425 1991–1992).

——, 'Switzerland: Of Personal Freedom and Family Duties', 29 *Journal of Family Law* 441–452 (1990–1991).

——, 'Switzerland: Hints of Things to come', 27 *Journal of Family Law* 305–313 (1988–1989).

——, 'A New Divorce Law for the New Millenium, Switzerland', The International Survey of Family Law, 2000 edn. (ed. by Bainham) 2000, 357 *et seq.*

Hegnauer, C., 'Family Reunions and Modern Medicine under Swiss Law' in: *Swiss Reports Presented at the XIIth International Congress of Comparative Law* (Sydney/Melbourne, 18–27 August 1986), Zurich, pp. 111–123.

Before 1982:

Brandon, M., 'English wills and trusts in Switzerland', Int'l Legal Pract., 35–41 (1977).

Grossen, J.-M., 'Aspects of de facto marriage under Switzerland's privacy law' in: Eckelaar and Katz (eds.), *Marriage and Cohabitation in Contemporary Societies*, Toronto: Butterworths 1980, pp. 258–264.

Hegnauer, C., 'Child Law reform in Switzerland', in: *The Child and the Law*, Vol. 1, Dobbs Ferry, New York: Oceana Publ. 1976, pp. 335–347.

Kellerhals, Perrin and Voneche, 'Switzerland' in: R. Chester (ed.), *Divorce in Europe*, Leyden: Nijhoff 1977, pp. 195–210

Lüthke, H.F., 'Switzerland: Duty of father to support illegitimate child', 1 Am. J. Comp. L. 124–128(1952).

Swiss Family Law, trans. and ed. by J. Russotto and F.E. Samuel Jr., Cambridge, Mass.: Hazen 1965.

V. PROPERTY

Flueler, R. and R. Meroni, 'Acquisition of Real Estate by Foreigners: Switzerland', 11 *Comparative Law Yearbook of International Business* 39–54 (1989).

Köprülü, B., 'Legal Modifications of the Laws Pertaining to Servitudes and Ground Rents in the Swiss Civil Code', Istanbul Universitesi Hukuk Fakültesi Mecmuasi 45–47 (1979) and 421–430 (1981).

VI. CONTRACT AND TORT LAW

After 1982:

Altenburger, P.R. and H.U. Stucki, 'Switzerland' in: *Products Liability*, Vol. 2, London/Rome: Oceana Publ. 1988, p. 63.

Dessemontet, F., 'Switzerland' in: A.H. Kritzer (ed.), *International Contract Manual. Country Handbooks*, Cambridge 1990, pp. 1–14.

Gauch, P. and R. Hurlimann, 'Reform of Medical Malpractice Law: Liability or Insurance? – National Report of Switzerland' in: *Swiss Reports Presented at the XIIIth International Congress of Comparative Law* (Montreal, 19–24 August 1990), Zurich: Schultess 1990, pp. 71–88.

Heiz, C.R., 'Validity of Contracts under the United Nations Convention of Contracts for International Sale of Goods, 11 April 1980, and Swiss Contract Law', 20 *Vanderbilt Journal of Transnational Law* 639–663 (1987).

Honegger, P., 'Product Liability in Switzerland', 7 *Butterworths Journal of International Banking and Financial Law* 421–427 (1992).

Hürlimann, R., 'Subcontracting in Switzerland – National Report' 8 *The International Construction Law Review* 151–169 (1991).

Perrez, F.X., 'Taking consumers seriously: The Swiss regulatory approach to genetically modified food', NYU Envtl. L. J. 585–604 (2000).

Schenker, F., 'Precontractual Liability in Swiss Law', in: *Swiss Reports Presented at the XIIIth International Congreess of Comparative Law* (Montreal, 19–24 August 1990), Zurich: Schultess 1990, pp. 89–101.

Tackaberry, J.A., 'Elementary Economics and the Construction Dispute. An Outsider's Look at the Swiss Law Remedies Available to the Unpaid Contractor', 7 *Journal of International Arbitration*, no. 3, 73–81 (1990).

Tavernier, E. and P.Y. Tschanz, 'Swiss Law of Set-off' in: F.W. Neate (ed.), *Using Set-off as Security*, Dordrecht: Graham and Trotman and London: International Bar Association 1990, pp. 248–263.

Walter, G., 'Mass tort litigation in Germany and Switzerland', Duke J of Comp. and Int'l L. 369–379 (2001).

Before 1982:

Eulau, P.H., 'Inducing breach of contract: a comparison of the laws of the U.S., France, the Federal Republic of Germany and Switzerland.' 2 Boston College Int'l and Comp. L. J. 41–68 (1978).

Formation of Contracts. A study of the common core of legal systems, by P. Bonassies *et al.*, Vols. 1–2, ed. by R.B. Schlesinger, Dobbs Ferry, New York 1968.

Lederer, P.D., 'A comparative survey of products liability law as applied to motor vehicles: Switzerland', 2 Int'l Lawyer 157–161 (1967).

Malawer, S.S., 'Moral damages in wrongful death cases in foreign law', 7 Eastern J. Int'l L. 218–239 (1975); 8 Eastern J. Int'l L. 270–299 (1976).

Pfennigsdorf, W., *Compensation of Auto Accident Victims in Europe. Study of Injury Reparations Systems in France, Great Britain, Germany, Italy, The Netherlands, Sweden and Switzerland*, Chicago 1972.

Reichenbach, F., 'The obligations and liabilities of directors and officers of companies and their protection by insurance (Switzerland)', 9 Int'l Bus. Law. 5–7 (1981).

Reverdin, B.J., 'Swiss law with regard to the form and formation of contracts for the sale of goods', 1965 American Bar Association, Section of Int'l and Comparative Law, Proceedings, 170–173 (1966).

Stucky, H.U. and P.R. Altenburger, *Product liability. A manual of practice in selected Switzerland*, London: Oceana Publ. 1981.

VII. COMMERCIAL LAW AND BUSINESS ASSOCIATIONS

After 1982:

Ackermann, 'Switzerland', in: Powers (ed.), *The Comparative Law Yearbook of International Business*, Special Issue 1993, Deventer/Boston: Kluwer 1994, pp. 463–475.

Altenburger, P.R. and H.U. Stuki, 'Foreign Laws Affecting Franchise Operations, Switzerland' in: *Survey of Foreign Laws and Regulations Affecting International Franchising*, American Bar Association 1982.

Böckli, P., 'Switzerland' in: Pinto and Visentini (eds.), *The Legal Basis of Corporate Governance in Publicly Held Corporations – A Comparative Approach*, Kluwer Law International 1998, pp. 195–218.

Briner, E.K., 'Tax-privileged Corporate Structures in Switzerland', *Intertax* 245–263 (1983).

Daeniker, D., Swiss Securities Regulation: An Introduction to the Regulation of the Swiss Financial Market; with a translation of the Stock Exchange Act of 1995 (SESTA) and implementing ordinances, Zurich 1998.

Druey, J.N., 'Company groups in Swiss Law' in: K.J. Hopt (ed.), *Groups of Companies in European Laws*, Berlin 1982, pp. 131–141.

Forstmoser, P., 'The Duties and Liabilities of Auditors under Swiss Law', 5 *Journal of Comparative Business and Capital Market Law* 305–316 (1983).

Giger, H., 'Legislation and Responsibility with Special Reference to consumer Credit Law' in D.B. King (ed.), *Commercial and Consumer Law from an International Perspective*. Papers from the Conference of the International Academy of Commercial and Consumer Law, Castle Hofen, Austria, 17–24 July 1984, Littleton, Colorado: Rothman & Co., 1986, pp. 27–42.

——, 'The Legal Position of the Consumer in the Planned Reform of the Swiss Consumer Credit Law', 35 *Revista de la Facultad de Derecho de Mexico* 195–213 (1985).

Girod, C.G., *The Close Corporation and the Buyout Right of Minority Shareholders in the United States and in Switzerland*, Masters Work, Harvard University, 1986.

Haenseler and Hohstrasser, *Real Estate in Switzerland*, Basel 1996 (*Swiss Commercial Law Series*, 5).

Jakob–Siebert, T., 'Competition rules in the EEC and Switzerland, a Comparison of Law and Practice', 11 *European Competition Law Review* 255–263 (1990).

Kelley, M., A. Lebrecht, and M. Lanz, 'Exemptions for Institutional Investors or Concepts of Non-Public Offerings: A Comparative Study, Switzerland', U. of Pennsylvania L. of Int'l Bus. 1993, 595–613.

Koenig, B.G., 'Rights and Obligationas of Shareholders and directors in Switzerland' in: Campbell (ed.), *Approaching 2000: The Corporation in Transition*, Deventer: Kluwer 1994, pp. 89–102.

Lachat–Heritier, A., 'Commercial Bribes: The Swiss Answer', 5 *Journal of Comparative Business and Capital Market Law* 79–86 (1983).

March Hunnings, N., 'The Stanley Adams Affair or the Biter Bit', 24 *Common Market Law Review* 65–88 (1987).

Mathys, P., 'Amended Swiss Corporation Law', 27 *International Business Lawyer* 525–534 (1993).

Meier, W., 'Switzerland' in: M.J. Ellis and P.M. Storm (eds.), *Business Law in Europe*, Deventer/Boston: Kluwer 1990, pp. 513–553.

Meiss, F. von, 'Government Procurement in Switzerland', 21 *The George Washington Journal of International Law and Economics* 151–163 (1987).

Nobel, P., 'Switzerland' in: Baums and Wymeersh (eds.), *Shareholders Voting Rights and Practice in Europe and the United States*, Kluwer Law International 1999, pp. 311–330.

Schluep, W.R., 'The Swiss Act on Cartels and the Practice of the Swiss Cartel Commission Concerning Economic Concentration' in: K.J. Hopt (ed.), *European Merger Control*, Vol. 1, New York: W. de Gruyter 1982, pp. 123–151.

Simon, D.B., 'Securities Regulation Investigations: US–Swiss Treaty Attempts to Increase Cooperation in Releasing Names of Swiss-based Account Holders in US Securities & Exchange Commission Investigations', 15 *Georgia Journal of International and Comparative Law* 135–142 (1985).

Stauder, B., 'Warranties and Consumer Protection in Swiss Law', *Arizona Journal of International and Comparative Law* 53–72 (1987).

——, 'Principles of Consumer Protection in Swiss Law' in: D.B. King (ed.), *Commercial and Consumer Law from an International Perspective*. Papers form the Conference of the International Academy of Commercial and Consumer Law, Castle Hofen, Austria, 17–24 July, 1984, Littleton, Colorado (Rothman & Co.), 1986, pp. 389–399.

——, 'Consumer Credit in Swiss Law', 35 *Revista de la Facultad de Derecho de Mexico* 435–448 (1989).

Steiner, H.R., 'Recent Developments in Securities Law: Switzerland', 17 *International Business Lawyer* 138–142 (1989).

Tunik, D.E., 'Switzerland' in: Sorensen (ed.), *Director's Liabilities in Case of Insolvency*, Kluwer Law International 1999, pp. 349–373.

Vogt, N.P., 'Defensive Measures Against Public Offers Under Swiss Law', 4 The Transational Lawyer 53 (1991).

Vogt, N.P. and R. Walter, 'Swiss Joint Ventures' in: J.A. Dobkin and J.A. Burt (eds.), *Joint Ventures in Europe*, London 1991, pp. 199–218

Walter, R., N. Faruque and D.P. Kaenzig, 'An Introduction to the Law Governing the Swiss Joint Stock Corporation', 2 Transational Corporations 495–538 (1993).

Before 1982:

Aeschimann, J.-P., *Essay on the Refusal by a Swiss 'SA' to Give its Approval to a Transfer of Shares*, Cambridge 1963.

Anker, R., *A comparison Between the English Private Company and the Swiss Societe a Responsabilite Limitee with Special Regard to Questions of Liability*, Berne: Staempfli 1956.

Arnold, K., 'Defences to takeovers: Switzerland', 8 Int'l Bus. L. 41–43 (1980).

Bar, T. and M. Karrer, 'Some aspects of Swiss corporate law', 28 Bus. Lawyer 1261–1273 (1973).

Baumgartner, K. and A. Trachsel, 'The stock exchanges of Switzerland' in: D.E. Spray *et al.*: *The Principal Stock Exchanges of the World*, Washington 1964, pp. 93–116.

Bianchi, S., *Business Operations in Switzerland*, Washington 1973.

Briner, R., 'Insider trading in Switzerland', 10 Int'l Bus. Law. 348–351 (1982).

——, 'Switzerland' (on shareholders remedies for corporate misconduct), 9 Int'l Bus. L. 336–338 (1981).

Brunschwig, F., and L. Levy, 'The commercial laws of the World, Switzerland' in: Kohlik (ed.), *Digest of Commercial Laws of the world* 134, Dobbs-Ferry, New York: Oceana Publ. 1981, pp. 1–34.

Commercial Laws of the World, 'Switzerland', Ormond Beach, Florida: Foreign Tax Law Ass. Inc. 1978.

Dagon, R., 'Securities regulation in Switzerland', 6 Vand. J. Trans. L. 511–549 (1973).

Forstmoser, P. and W. Meier, 'Switzerland' in: M.J. Ellis and P.M. Storm, *Business Law in Europe,* Edited under the auspices of the Association europeenne d'etudesjuridiques et fiscales, 1982.

Freimüller, H.-U., 'Anti-trust law in Switzerland: The Swiss Federal Cartel Act of 20 December 1962', 27 Bus. Lawyer 799–802 (1972).

Froriep, A., 'Switzerland' in: S.N. Frommel (ed.), *Company Law in Europe,* Deventer: Kluwer 1975, pp. 509–539.

Galli, B. and V. Galli, 'Switzerland' in: P. Meinhardt, *Company Law in Europe,* Epping, Essex: Gower Press 1975 (looseleaf).

Hirsch, A., 'Company Law in the Common Market from a Swiss viewpoint' in: C.M. Schmitthoff (ed.), *Harmonization of European Company Law,* London 1973, pp. 166–178.

Jagmetti, M.A., 'Switzerland (Letters of Responsibility)', 6 Int'l Bus. Law. 320–328 (1978).

Jenkel, J.H. and B.A.K. Rider, 'Swiss approach to insider dealing', 128 New L. J. 683–684 (1978).

Katzenstein, P.J., 'Capitalism in one country? Switzerland in the international economy', Int'l Org. 507–540, Autumn 1980.

Lalive, J.F., 'Transnational legal practice: Switzerland' in: D. Campbell (ed.), Vol. II, Deventer 1982, pp. 54.

Lang, C.G. and A. Furrer, 'Switzerland' in Basedow (ed.), *Limits and Control of Competition with a View of International Harmonization,* Kluwer Law International 2002, pp. 393–410.

Paschoud, F., 'Formation and operation of foreign subsidiaries and branches, including the extent to which foreign subsidiaries are entitled to special treatment under the law of their incorporation or under international law: Switzerland', 17 Bus. Lawyer 512 (1961).

Price, Waterhouse *et al.* (eds.), *Doing Business in Switzerland,* Chicago 1976.

Reeves, W.H., 'Displaced corporations in war time – Switzerland's answer', 14 Bus. Lawyer 205 (1958).

Reichenbach, F., 'The obligations and liabilities of directors and officers of companies and their protection by insurance (Switzerland)', 9 Int'l Bus. L. 5–7 (1981).

Reverdin, B.J. and E.E. Homburger, 'American close corporation and its Swiss equivalent', 14 Bus. Lawyer 263 (1958).

Reverdin, B.J., 'Selecting a base of operation in Europe: Switzerland, Liechendstein, Benelux' in: Wilson (ed.), *Proceedings of the 1960 Institute on Private Investments Abroad,* New York: Matthew Bender 1960, pp. 311–378.

Schweizerische Kreditanstalt, *Formation and Taxation of Companies in Switzerland. Swiss Credit special publications*, Vol. 38, rev. edn., Zurich: Swiss Credit 1978.

Schmid, R.M., 'Corporate control in Switzerland', 6 Am. J. Comp. L. 27–43 (1957).

Schluep, W.R., 'Introduction to the concept and system of the Swiss Kartellgesetz', 8 Int'l Bus. L. 167–171 (1980).

——, 'Switzerland,' in: *World Law of Competition*, Vol. 6, New York: Matthew Bender 1981.

Schluep, W.R. and C. Baudenbacher, 'Corporation law and the law of intangible property in Swiss Law' (trans. by R. Packham) in: R.A. Newman (ed.), *The Unity of Strict Law*, Vol. 2, Brussels 1978, pp. 355–370.

Speckert, X.M., 'The law relating to restrictive trade practices in Switzerland' in: *U.K. National Committee of Comparative Law, Comparative Aspects of Restrictive Trade Practice*, London 1961, pp. 56–69.

World Trade Information Service, Licensing and Exchange Controls, Switzerland and Lichtenstein, 1962.

Zwonicek, C., 'The Swiss reinsurance market', 29 Int'l Insurance Monitor 6–10 (1975).

VIII. Industrial and Intellectual Property

After 1982:

Brugger, P., 'New Copyright in Switzerland – Model Ideas for the Legislation in Scandinavia?', *Nordiskt Immateriellt Rättsskydd* 147–163 (1990).

Brunner, E., 'A Swiss View of the Role of the Expert in Patent Litigation', 18 *International Review of Industrial Property and Copyright Law* 644–649 (1987).

Dessemontet, F., 'Switzerland' in: Nimmer and Geller (eds.), *International Copyright Law and Practice*, New York: Matthew Bender 1994.

——, 'Letter from Switzerland: The New Copyright Act', 17 *Informatierecht AMI* 183–186 (1993).

——, 'Switzerland' in: A. Bouju (ed.), *Patent Infringement Litigation Costs. A Practical Worldwide Survey*, London 1989, pp. 169–174.

——, 'Inventions in Swiss Universities', 21 *Industrial Property* 338–355 (1982).

——, 'Transfers of Technology under UNCTAD and EEC Draft Cocification: A European View on Choice of Law in Licensing', 12 *Journal of International Law and Economics* 1–55 (1977–1978).

——, *Intellectual Property Law in Switzerland*, The Hague/London/Boston: Kluwer Law International and Berne: Staempli 2000.

Dillenz, W., 'The Copyright Royalty Tribunals in Austria, the Federal Republic of Germany and Switzerland', 34 *Journal of the Copyright Society of the United States of America* 193–200 (1987).

Dutoit, B., 'Unfair Use and Damage to the Reputation of Well-known Trademarks, Names and Indications of Source in Switzerland and France', 17 *International Review of Industrial Property and Copyright Law* 733–745 (1986).

Guyet, J., 'Protection against Trademark Infringement in Swiss Law', 26 *Industrial Property. Monthly Review of the World Intellectual Property Organization* 36–48 (1987).

Liechti, P.P., 'The Collection of Copyright Royalties and the Federal Arbitration Commission in Switzerland', 34 *Journal of the Copyright Society of the United States of America* 214–220 (1987).

Maur, R. auf der, 'Introduction to Swiss Intellectual Property Law', *Swiss Comm. L. Series* 3, Basel 1995.

Pedrazzini, M.M., 'Nullity of Patents in Swiss Law' in: *Swiss Reports Presented at the XIIth International Congress of Comparative Law* (Sydney/Melbourne, 18–27 August 1986), Zurich: Schultess 1987, pp. 125–137.

——, 'Letter from Switzerland', 20 *Copyright* 292–297 (1984).

Schubarth, M., 'Re-establishment of Rights under Articles 47 and 48 of the Swiss Patent Law', 18 *International Review of Industrial Property and Copyright Law* 598–602 (1987).

Troller, A., 'The Hundredth Anniversary of the Berne Convention: the Development of Law in the Copyright Field through the Interaction of the Convention and Swiss Legislation', 22 *Copyright* 208–213 (1986).

Troller, K., 'The Legal Protection of Owners of Industrial Property Rights and of Copyrights in Switzerland against Violation of their Rights', 10 *European Intellectual Property Review* 135–137 (1988).

Walter, H.P., 'The Stay of Infringement or Revocation Proceedings Pending Opposition or Revocation Proceedings before another Court or Authority under Swiss Law', 20 *International Review of Industrial Property and Copyright Law* 281–287(1989).

Before 1982:

Baxter, J.W., *World Patent Law and Practice. Switzerland*. London/New York 1973.

Blum, U.D., 'Selected problems of patent protection for microorganisms under the European Convention and the Swiss Patent Act' in: *Festschrift zum 100 jährigen Bestehen der Firma E. Blum & Co.*, Berne 1978, pp. 89–124.

Bogsch, A., *Design Laws and Treaties of the World. Switzerland: Design statute and regulations, right of priority for designs, provisions in the copyright statute (translation)*, Leyden/Washington 1960 *et seq.* (looseleaf).

Braendli, P., 'The new Swiss patent law', 17 *Industrial Property* 171–177 (1978).

Breitenmoser, J., 'The practice of the Swiss Patent Office', 63 *Trademark Reporter* 197–210 (1973).

Briner, A.E., 'Arbitration on industrial property in Switzerland' in: *Festschrift zum 100 jährigen Bestehen der Firma E. Blum & Co.*, Berne 1978, pp. 169–179.

Briner, R.G., 'Immaterial assets in execution proceedings' in: *Festschrift zum 100 jährigen Bestehen der Firma E. Blum & Co.*, Berne 1978, pp. 203–222.

Dessemontet, F., 'Protection of geographic denominations under Swiss law' in: H. Cohen Jehoram (ed.), *Protection of Geographic Denominations of Goods and Services*, Alphen aan den Rijn/Germantown, MD 1980, pp. 97–134.

Englert, C., 'Turning-point of a holding privilege under trademerk law in Switzerland', 5 Int'l Bus. L. 185–190 (1977).

Gerster, R., 'Switzerland and the revision of the Paris Convention', 15 J. World Trade L. 111–123(1981).

Gevers, J. *et al.*, *Patent Law and Practice of the Major European Countries*, Lausanne 1976.

Greene, A.M., *Patents Throughout the World*, 2nd edn., New York 1978.

——, *Designs and Utility Models Throughout the World*, New York 1983.

Griss, G., 'Licensing and antitrust law in Australia and Switzerland', 77 Patent and Trademark Rev. 8–26 (1979).

Homburger, E., 'Licensing in Switzerland' in: Pollzien and Langen (eds.), *International Licensing Agreement*, 2nd edn., Indianapolis: Bobbs-Merrill 1973, pp. 408–424.

——, 'International trade: Conflict between Swiss trademark law and EEC trade agreement', 21 Harv. Int'l L. J. 756–763 (1980).

Leiss, G.H., 'Practice of the Federal Office for intellectual property in respect of the registrability of trademarks' in: *Festschrift zum 100 jährigen Bestehen der Firma E. Blum & Co.*, Berne 1978, pp. 223–247.

Luchinger, M., 'The influence of third-party trademark infringement actions' in: *Festschrift zum 100 jährigen Bestehen der Firma E. Blum & Co.*, Berne 1978, pp. 249–261.

Maday, D.C., 'Territorial aspect of trademark rights in Switzerland', 50 Trademark Rep. 456 (1960).

——, 'Major provisions of Patent Legislation in selected countries', 13 Ind. Property 211–246 (1974).

Manual for the Handling of Applications for Patents, Designs and Trademarks Throughout the World, Switzerland, Amsterdam: Octrooibureau Los en Stigter BV 1979 (looseleaf), pp. 1–13.

Nimmer, M.B., 'Who is the copyright owner when laws conflict?' (France, U.S., U.S.S.R., Switzerland.) 5 Int'l Rev. Ind. Prop'y & Copyr. Law 62–72 (1974).

——, Patent Law, Article 7 – 'Second Indication.' Information from the Federal Office for Intellectual Property. Int'l Rev. Ind. Prop'y and Copyr. 9: 569–570 (IIC) (1978).

Pedrazzini, M.M., 'Arbitration and the transfer of technology: Note on Swiss Law', 17 *Industrial Property* 262–267 (1978).

Petitpierre, E., 'Letter from Switzerland', 55 *Trademark Reporter* 380–389 (1965).

Preiss, R., 'Publicity employing personalities and characters in Swiss practice' in: *Festschrift zum 100 jährigen Bestehen der Firma E. Blum & Co.*, Berne 1978, pp. 181–201.

Schiff, E., *Industrialization Without National Patents: The Netherlands, 1869–1912; Switzerland, 1850–1907*, Princeton, N.J.: Princeton University Press 1971.

Schonherr, R., 'Slavish imitation in German, Austrian and Swiss case law', 6 Int'l Rev. of Industrial Property and Copyright Law 60–80 (1975).

Tavel, C.H., 'Technology transfer in Switzerland' in: S. Gee (ed.), *Technology Transfer in Industrialized Countries*, Alphen aan den Rijn 1979.

WIPO, *World Intellectual Property Organization. Copyright Law Survey*, Geneva 1979 (looseleaf) (WIPO Publication No. 603(E)).

Ziegler, A. von, 'Product get-up protection in Switzerland' in: *Festschrift zum 100 jährigen Bestehen der Firma E. Blum & Co.*, Berne 1978, pp. 283–302.

Zurrer, E., 'The new European patent system as seen from the viewpoint of a Swiss patent attorney in the chemical industry', 5 A.P.L.A.Q.J. 279–297 (1977).

IX. AIR LAW

Guldimann, W. 'Towards a complete revision of the Swiss Aviation Act' (Lecture at a meeting of Swiss Air Law Society, Basle, Oct. 1980), 6 Air Law 17–22 (1981).

Posefski, A.L. 'Air law – Warsaw Convention and Montreal Agreement – Hijacking victims may recover damages from airline. Hussel v. Swissair' (comment). 5 N.Y.U.J. Int'l L. & Pol. 555–568 (1973).

X. BANKING LAW

Abrams, R.M., 'Tax Evasion and Swiss Banking Secrecy', 24 *Practical Lawyer* 77–83 (1978).

Aubert, M., 'The Limits of Swiss Banking Secrecy under Domestic and international Law', 2 *International Tax and Business Lawyer* 273–297 (1984).

Aubert, M. and D. Cronson, 'Bank Secrecy and Supervision of Swiss Foreign Bank Affiliates', 14 *Comparative Law Yearbook of International Business* 205–223 (1992).

Bar, H.J., *The Banking System of Switzerland* (in collaboration with U. Albrecht), 5th edn. Zurich: Schultess 1975.

Beguin, P.A. *et al.*, 'Managing Money: A Legal Guide to the World's Investment Fund Markets – Switzerland', 9 Suppl. *International Financial Law Review* 77–81 (1990).

Bischoff, J., 'The Factual Significance and Legal Regulation of International Funds Transfers in Switzerland' in: W. Hadding and U.H. Schyneider (eds.), *Legal Issues in International Credit Transfers*, Berlin 1993, pp. 319–344.

Bschorr, P.J. and M.H. Mullin, 'Court-ordered Waivers of Foreign Banking Secrecy Rights: An Evaluation of the American Position' in: R. von Graffenried (ed.), *Beitrage zum schweizerisches Bankenrecht*, Berne: Staempfli 1987, pp. 181–205.

Buzescu, P., 'Foreign Bank Operations in Switzerland: New Regulations and Practical Considerations', 19 *The International Lawyer* 897–913 (1985).

Capitani, W. de, 'Banking Secrecy Today', 10 *University of Pennsylvania Journal of International Business Law* 57–70 (1988).

Collins, M., 'Reviving Thailand's Securities Market' 11 *International Financial Law Review* No. 2, 30–33 (1992).

Daeniker, D., *Swiss Securities Regulation, An Introduction to the Regulation of the Swiss Financial Market*, Zurich 1998.

Dagon, R., 'Swiss Treaty Provision on Disclosure of Professional and Bank Secrets', 29 Bull. for Int'l Fiscal Documentation 417–426 (1975).

Dunant, O. and M. Wassmer, 'Swiss Bank Secrecy: Its Limits under Swiss and International Laws', 20 *Case Western Reserve Journal of International Law* 541–575 (1988).

Giger, H., 'Problems of Bank Guarantee Abuse in Swiss Law', *Arizona Journal of International and Comparative Law*, 1987, 38–47.

Hansen, J.J., 'Insider Trading Laws and Swiss Banks: Recent Hope for Reconciliation', 22 *Columbia Journal of Transnational Law* 303–332 (1983–1984).

Hirsch, A., 'Worldwide Legal Harmonization of Banking Law and Securities Regulation' in: R.M. Buxbaum *et al.* (eds.), *European Business Law*, Berlin/New York 1991, pp. 347–361.

——, '"Dirty Money" and Swiss Banking Regulations', 8 *Journal of Comparative Business and Capital Market Law* 373–380 (1986).

Hoets, P.J. and S.G. Zwart, 'Swiss Bank Secrecy and the Marcos Affair' 9 *New York Law School Journal of International and Comparative Law* 75–105 (1988).

Hurd, S.N., 'Insider Trading and Foreign Bank Secrecy', 24 *American Business Law* 25–49 (1986).

Krauskopf, L., 'Comments on Switzerland's Insider Trading, Money Laundering and Banking Secrecy Law' 9 *International Tax and Business Lawyer* 277–800 (1991–1992).

Lanz, M., 'Switzerland' in: D. Campbell and M. Moore (eds.), *Financial Services in the New Europe*, London/Dordrecht 1993, pp. 265–278.

Levin, J., 'The conflict between Unites States securities laws on insider trading and Swiss Bank Secrecy Law', 7 Northwestern J. of Int'l. L. and Business 318–350 (1985–86).

——, 'Recent Developments in Insider Trading through Swiss Bank Accounts: An End to the "Double Standard"', 5 *Northwestern Journal of International Law and Business* 658–679 (1983).

Malacrida, R. and R. Watter, *Swiss Corporate Finance and Capital Markets – Legal Aspects*, Basle 2001.

Meier–Schatz, C.J. and K.D. Larsen, 'Swiss Securities Regulation and Capital Market Law: A Comprehensive Overview', 18 *Denver Journal of International Law and Policy* 417–464 (1989–1990).

Navickas, J.M., 'Swiss Banks and Insider Trading in the United States', 2 *International Tax and Business Lawyer* 159–191 (1984).

Newton Sipp, N., 'Bank Secrecy Laws in Discovery: Did Minpeco S.A. v. Conticommodity Services, Inc. (116 F.R.D.) adopt an Overly Deferential Approach?', 14 *Brooklyn Journal of International Law* 443–484 (1988).

Nobel, P., *Swiss Finance Law and International Standards*, Kluwer Law International 2002.

Peters, R.G., 'Money Laundering and its Current Status in Switzerland: New Disincentives for Financial Tourism', 11 *Northwestern Journal of International Law and Business* 104–139 (1990–1991).

Raifman, G.R., 'The Effect of the U.S.–Swiss Agreement onecrecy and Insider Trading', 15 *Law and Policy in International Business* 565–611 (1983).

Rapp, J.-M., 'Recent Developments in United States Insider Trading Prohibition and Swiss Secrecy Laws: Towards a Definitive Reconciliation?', 5 *International Tax and Business Lawyer* 1–43 (1987).

Salisbury, W.R., 'International Agreements: Uni Agreements: United States–Switzerland Investigation of Insider Trading through Swiss banks.' 23 *Harvard International Law Journal* 437–443 (1983).

Stauter, R.L., 'Swiss Bank Secrecy Laws and the U.S. Internal Revenue Service', 20 *Case Western Reserve Journal of International Law* 623–641 (1988).

Stultz, E.A., 'Swiss Bank Secrecy and United States Efforts to obtain Information from Swiss Banks', 21 *Vanderbilt Journal of Transnational Law* 63–125 (1988).

Taisch, F. and W. Wyss, 'How to take Advantage of Swiss Private Placements', 11 *International Financial Law Review* No. 2, 28–29 (1992).

Tavernier, E. *et al.*, 'Legislative Developments in Swiss Banking', *International Financial Law Review*, No. 1, 29–32 (1987).

Weber, R.H. and L. Cereghetti, 'International Securities Regulation Switzerland' in: Center for International Legal Studies (ed.), *International Securities Regulation*, The Hague/London/Boston 2002.

Weber, R.H., 'Securities Law–Structuring of a Modern Capital Market: The Swiss Example' in: Norton and Arner (eds.), *International Finance Sector Reform: Standard Setting and Infrastructure Development*, London 2002.

XI. TAX LAW

After 1982:

Boekhorst, P.J., 'Tax Reform at Final Stage – Law of 14 December 1990 on the Federal Direct Tax Law of 14 December 1990 on the Harmonization of the Direct Taxation of Cantons and Municipalities', 31 *European Taxation* 215–221 (1991).

Ehrat, F.R., 'National and International Tax Aspects of Charities and Charitable Contributions: Swiss Report', 43 *Bulletin for International Fiscal Documentation* 570–575 (1989).

Grüninger, H., 'Switzerland: Cross Border Exchange of Information and Administrative Assistance in Tax Matters, in Particular between Germany and Switzerland', 27 *European Taxation* 139–142 (1987).

Grüninger, H. and F.A. Keller, 'International Mutual Assistance through Exchange of Information: Switzerland' in: International Fiscal Association (ed.), *Studies on International Fiscal Law* 499–517 (1990).

Kamber, A., 'Offshore Companies – Anti Avoidance Measures in Switzerland', *International Business Law Journal* 523–528 (1991).

Kelly, G.M., A.E. Lebrecht and M. Lanz, 'Exemptions for Institutional Investors or Concepts of Non-public Offerings: A Comparative Study', 15 *University of Pennsylvania Journal of International Business Law* 595–613 (1993).

Lüthi, D., 'Countering the Abuse of Tax Treaties – A Swiss View', *Intertax* 336–340 (1989).

Müllhaupt, W., 'Seeking Swiss Assistance in Enforcing United States Tax Laws', 4 *International Tax and Business Lawyer* 144–154 (1986).

Oberson, X. and H.R. Hull, *Switzerland in International Taxation*, 2nd edn., Kluwer, 2002.

Before 1982:

Andersen, A. *et al.*, *Tax and Trade Guide: Switzerland*, 3rd edn., Chicago 1977.

Bianchi, S., *The Swiss–Italian Double Taxation Convention*, Basle 1976.

Bird, R. and R. Duss, 'Switzerland tax jungle', 27 *Canadian Tax Journal* 46–47 (1979).

Brassems, E.M., 'Swiss rules for the implementation of relief for foreign taxes on dividends, interests and royalties granted under tax treaties', 19 *European Taxation* 280–290 (1979).

——, 'Switzerland: Swiss measures against the abuse of convention', 19 *European Taxation* 50–60 (1975).

Brassem, E.A., 'Switzerland: Swiss base company: Tax avoidance device for multinationals', 50 *Notre Dame Lawyer* 645–661 (1975).

Braun, W.D., 'The Swiss Base Company: Tax avoidance device for multinationals', 50 *Notre Dame Lawyer* 645–661 (1975).

Briner, E.K., 'Swiss Taxation: New Horizons', 26 *Tax Executive* 243–252 (1974).

'Changes in the anticipatory tax and abolition of the coupon tax', 6 *European Taxation* 34–37 (1966).

Comello, 'The Taxation of Private Investment Income, Switzerland' in: Van Hoorn Jr. and Ullman (eds.), Amsterdam: Int'l Bureau of Fiscal Documentation, 1967 *et seq.*

Diamond, W.H. and D.B. Diamond, *Tax-free Trade Zones of the World*, New York 1979 (looseleaf).

Due, J.-F.: 'Swiss experience and the Canadian wholesale sales tax proposal', 24 *Canadian Tax Journal* 103–110 (1976).

'Federal taxation of corporate mergers in Switzerland', 4 *European Taxation* 207–209 (1964).

Kelly, P.L. and Lagae, J.P.: 'The Belgium–Swiss Income Tax Treaty', *Intertax* 153–163 (1980).

Kronauer, M., 'Information given for tax purposes from Switzerland to foreign countries: especially to the U.S. for the prevention of fraud or the like in relation to certain American taxes', 30 *Tax Law Review* 47–99 (1974).

Loftus, M., 'Taxation and secrecy law relating to bank accounts for non-residents in Switzerland', 7 *Australian Tax Review* 39–43 (1978).

'New Swiss Federal legislation counteracts abuses of tax treaties', 3 *European Taxation* 19–22 (1963).

Oenayer, T., 'Belgium and Switzerland conclude tax Treaty: deviations from the O.C.D.E. model convention of 1977', 19 *European Taxation* 25–29 (1979).

Paulis, E., 'The new tax treaty between Belgium and Switzerland', 9 Int'l Bus. L. 141–142 (1981).

River and Müller, 'Tax status of regional headquarters, Switzerland', 10 Int'l Bus. Lawyer 248–249 (1982).

Ryser, W., 'Aspects of the taxation of foreign permanent establishments in Switzerland' in: *Beiträge aus der Treuhandpraxis*, Berne 1961, pp. 170–185.

Scott, T.W., 'Survey of European wealth taxes', 14 *European Taxation* 374–378 (1974).

'The Swiss tax reform', 16 *European Taxation* 193–199 (1976).

'Taxation of capital gains: Switzerland', 5 *European Taxation* 193–199 (1965).

Sperl, A.R., *The Taxation of Companies in Europe: Switzerland*, Vol. 3, 1975 *et seq.* (looseleaf).

'Some reflections on the unilateral measures taken by Switzerland against the abuse of treaties for the avoidance of double taxation', *Intertax* 60–66 (1975).

'Switzerland. Decision of the Federal Tribunal (17 September 1977). (Spanish–Swiss Treaty of 22 April 1966. Definition of permanent establish-ment)', 18 *European Taxation* 100–102 (1978).

'Taxes on dividends and interests paid by a Swiss corporation to a non-resident', 2 *European Taxation* 187–192 (1962).

'Tax system in Switzerland. Taxes levied by the Confederation, the Cantons and the Municipalities', 26 For. Tax L. Bi-Weekly Bull. 1–11 (1975).

Truog, R., 'Mergers, divisions, transfer of individual assets and their tax consequences', *Intertax* 327–335 (1980).

XII. Labor Law and Social Insurance Law

Arnold, K., 'Worker participation in management: Switzerland', Comp. L. Yb. 143–151 (1980).

Bär, T., 'Swiss work and residence permit regulation', 27 *Business Lawyer* 851–856 (1972).

Berenstein, A., 'Switzerland' in: Blanpain (ed.), *International Encyclopaedia for Labour Law and Industrial Relations*, 1993, pp. 1–188.

Berenstein, A. and P. Mahon, *Labour Law in Switzerland*, Kluwer Law International and Berne: Staempfli 2001.

——, 'Industrial disputes in Switzerland' in: Kahn-Freund, *Labour Relations and the Law*, London, 1965, pp. 220–224.

Bollman, H. and G. Hochstrasser, 'Switzerland' in: C.S. Aronstein (ed.), *International Handbook on Contracts of Employment*, Deventer: Kluwer 1976, pp. 235–242.

Bridel, D., 'The evolution of Swiss social insurance in 1972', 26 Int'l Soc. Sec. Rev., 241–249 (1973).

Dudra, M., 'Swiss system of union security', 10 Lab. L. J. 165 (1959).

Horlick, M., 'Switzerland: Compulsory private pensions', 36 Soc. Sec. Bull., No. 10, 46–47 (1973).

Kolvenbach, W., *Employee Councils in European Companies*, Deventer: Kluwer 1978.

McDermott, T.J. and S. Grosset, 'Labor management cooperation in Switzerland', 14 Lab. L. J. 238–264 (1963).

Siegenthaler, J.K., 'Current problems of trade-union-party relations in Switzerland', 28 Industrial and Labour Relations Rev. 264–281 (1975).

Thalmann–Antenen, H., 'Equal pay: the position in Switzerland', 104 Int'l Labour Rev. 275–388 (1971).

XIII. Private International Law

After 1982:

Arnold, A. and P.A. Karrer, *Switzerland's Private International Law Statute*, Deventer: Kluwer 1987.

Bernet, M. and N.C. Ulmer, 'Recognition and Enforcement of Foreign Civil Judgments in Switzerland', 27 *The International Lawyer* 317–342 (1993).

Blessing, M., 'The New International Arbitration Law in Switzerland: A Significant Step towards Liberalism', 5 *Journal of International Arbitration*, No. 2, 9–88 (1988).

Bond, S.R., 'The New Swiss Law on International Arbitration and the Arbitral Institutions', *International Business Law Journal* 785–792 (1989).

Briner, R., 'Switzerland', 16 *Yearbook Commercial Arbitration* 413–418 (1991).

——, 'Switzerland', 14 *Yearbook Commercial Arbitration* 1–44 (1989).

Bucher, A. and P.Y. Tschanz, *International Arbitration in Switzerland*, Basle/Frankfort-on-Main: Helbing & Lichtenhahn 1988.

Bucher, A., 'Challenge of Awards', *International Business Law Journal* 771–784 (1989).

Egger, W., 'U.S. Jurisdiction in Conflict with Swiss Sovereignty', 12 *International Business Lawyer* 225–228 (1984).

Gaillard, E., 'The Point of View of a Foreign User', *International Business Law Review* 793–801 (1989).

Hoechner, K.M., 'A Swiss Perspective on Conflicts of Jurisdiction,' 50 *Law and Contemporary Problems* 271–282 (1987).

Imhoff-Scheier, A.-C. and P.M. Patocchi, *Torts and Unjust Enrichment in the New Swiss Conflict of Laws*, Zurich 1990.

Karrer, P.A., 'The Relationship between the Arbitral Tribunal, the State Courts and the Arbitral Institutions', *International Business Law Journal* 761–770 (1989).

——, 'The Position of the Arbitration Chapter in Switzerland's Private International Law Codification', 7 *Bulletin of the Swiss Arbitration Association* 13–26 (1989).

——, 'Switzerland's New Law is Modern, Liberal and Pragmatic', 3 *International Arbitration Report*, No. 1, 21–24 (1988).

——, 'Starting International Arbitration: Pitfalls in the Runway' in: *Swiss Essays on International Arbitration*, Zurich: Schultess 1984, pp. 139–145.

Kaufmann, G., 'Court Assistance in International Construction Arbitration in Switzerland', 7 *The International Construction Law Review* 339–357 (1990).

Knoepfler, F. and Ph. Schweizer, 'Making of Awards and Termination of Proceedings' in: P. Sarcevic (ed.), *Essays on International Commercial Arbitration*, London/Dordrecht: Graham and Trotman 1989, pp. 160–176.

Lalive, P., 'Fifth Session' in *Arbitrage Euro-arabe* 111, London/Dordrecht: Graham and Trotman 1991, 218–241.

——, 'The new Law on Arbitration in Switzerland', 55 *Arbitration* 118–120 and 152 (1989).

——, 'On the Conflict Rules Applicable by the International Arbitrator (Note on Art. 187 LDIP and on Art. 4 Rules of the Zurich Chamber of Commerce', 7 *Bulletin of the Swiss Arbitration Association* 27–37 (1989).

——, 'The new Swiss Law on International Arbitration', 4 *Arbitration International* 2–24 (1988).

——, 'Arbitration with Foreign States or State-controlled Entities' in: *Private Investors Abroad*, Albany, N.Y./San Francisco 1988, pp. 1–36.

——, 'On the Neutrality of the Arbitrator and of the Place of Arbitration.' in: *Swiss Essays on International Arbitration*, Zurich: Schultess 1984, pp. 23–33.

Levy, L., 'Dissenting Opinions in International Arbitration in Switzerland', 5 *Arbitration International*, No. 1, 35–42 (1989).

Lüddeke, C.F., 'Arbitration in Switzerland', 55 *Arbitration* 114–117 and 121 (1989).

O'Neill, P.D., 'Has Switzerland solved its Problem as a Site for Arbitration?', 45 *Arbitration Journal*, No. 4, 16–22 (1990).

Poncet, C., 'Switzerland's New Statute on International Arbitration', *World Arbitration and Mediation Report*, Vol. 1, No. 1, 1990, 15–17.

——, 'Switzerland: Federal Statute on Private International Law. Twelfth Chapter: International Arbitration', *Arbitration and the Law* 179–190 (1987–1988).

Reymond, C., 'An Introduction to the New Swiss Law on International Arbitration', *International Business Law Journal* 741–747 (1989).

Samuel, A., 'The New Swiss Private International Law Act', 37 *International and Comparative Law Quarterly* 681–695 (1988).

Sarcevic, P. and T. Burckhardt, 'Conflict of Laws and Public Law: The Swiss Approach' in: *Swiss Reports Presented at the XIIth International Congress of Comparative Law* (Sydney/Melbourne, 18–27 August 1986), Zurich: Schultess 1987, pp. 139–157.

Simmons, G.K. and L.G. Radicati, 'Trustee in Continental Europe: The Experience of the Bank for International Settlements', 30 *Netherlands International Law Review* 330–345 (1983).

Symeonides, S.C., 'The New Swiss Conflicts Codification: An Introduction', 2 *Epitheorese Kypriakou Dikaiou* 4670–4674 (1990).

——, 'The Swiss Conflicts Codification: An Introduction', *American Journal of Comparative Law* 187–246 (1989).

Tschanz, P.Y., 'An introduction to the Revised CCIG Rules', 7 *International Arbitration Report*, No. 3 (1992).

——, 'A Breakthrough in International Arbitration: Switzerland's New Act', 24 *The International Lawyer* 1107–1118 (1990).

——, 'The Agreement to Arbitrate', *International Business Law Journal* 749–759 (1989).

Vogt, N.P., 'Jurisdiction of Swiss Courts in International Cases', 12 *Comparative Law Yearbook of International Business* 161–165 (1990).

Before 1982:

Anderson, R.E., 'Conflicts of jurisdiction: Consideration of the Franco-Swiss Treaty of 1869 in determining the exercise of domestic jurisdiction: Joseph Muller Corp. v. Société Anonyme de Gérance et d'Armement (S.D.N.Y. 1970)' (Casenote), 11 Col. J. Transnat'l L. 477–489 (1972).

Aubert, J.F., 'Renvoi in Swiss Law', 5 Am. J. Comp. L. 478–486 (1956).

Aubert, J.F., 'Switzerland: International jurisdiction', 8 Am. J. Comp. L. 228 (1959).

Council of Europe, *The Practical Guide to the Recognition and Enforcement of Foreign Judicial Decisions in Civil and Commercial Law. Switzerland*, Strasbourg 1975, pp. 146–164.

Jagmetti, M., 'Foreign exchange contracts: The Swiss view', 5 Int'l Bus. L. 30–36 (1977).

McCaffrey, S., 'The Swiss draft conflicts law', 28 Am. J. Comp. L. 235–285 (1980).

Meyer, H.H., 'Obtaining evidence in Switzerland for use in foreign courts', 3 Am. J. Comp. L. 412–418 (1954).

Miller, A.R., 'International cooperation in litigation between the United States and Switzerland: unilateral procedural accomodation in test tube', 49 Minn. L. Rev. 1069 (1965).

Nussbaum, A., *American–Swiss Private International Law*, 2nd edn., New York 1958.

Overbeck, A.E. von, 'American–Swiss succession: The meaning of Article 6 of the 1850 Treaty', 18 Am. J. Comp. L. 595–611 (1970).

Riesenfeld, S.A., 'Domestic effects of foreign liquidation and rehabilitation proceedings in the light of comparative law' in: *Internationales Privatrecht und Rechtsvergleichung im Ausgang des 20. Jahrhunderts. Bewahrung oder Wende? Festschrift für Gerhard Kegel*, Frankfurt a.M. 1977, pp. 433–499.

Schoch, M., 'Conflict of laws in a federal State: the experience of Switzerland', 55 Harv. L. Rev. 738–749 (1942).

Vischer, F., 'Drafting national legislation on conflict of laws: The Swiss experience', 41 Law and Contemporary Problems 131–145 (1977).

XIV. Public International Law

After 1982:

Bourguignon, H.J., 'The Belilos Case: New Light on Reservations to Multilateral Treaties', 29 *Virginia Journal of International Law* 347–386 (1989).

Breitenmoser, S. and L. Wildhaber, 'The Relationship between Customary International Law and Municipal Law in Western European Countries', 48 *Zeitschrift für ausländisches öffentliches Recht und Völkerrecht* 163–207 (1988).

Dubs, J., 'Implementation of International Humanitarian Law at the National Level with Special Reference to Developments of Modern Warfare: Switzerland', 28 *Revue de droit Militaire et de Droit de la Guerre* 287–293 (1989).

Hayman, M., 'Approaching Europe: Swiss Perspectives and Dilemmas', *Legal Issues of European Integration*, No. 1, 71–98 (1992).

Probst, R.R., 'Good Offices' in International Relations in the Light of Swiss Practice and Experience', 201 *Recueil des Cours. Académie de Droit International de la Haye* 211–384 (1988).

Simma, B., 'Termination and Suspension of Treaties', 21 *German Yearbook of International Law* 74–96 (1988).

Wildhaber, L., 'Swiss Neutrality: Legal Base and Historical Background' in: B. Huldt and A. Lejins (eds.), *Neutrals in Europe*, Stockholm: The Swedish Institute of International Affairs 1989, pp. 3–15.

Before 1982:

Aubert, J.-F., 'Switzerland: Foreign Expropriation in Swiss Law', 6 Am. J. Comp. L. 577–587 (1957).

European Economic Community, *Agreement Between the European Economic Community and the Swiss Confederation*, London: Her Majesty's Stationery Office 1972.

Frei, D., 'Switzerland and the EEC: Facts and Trends', 12 J. Common Market Studies 248–264 (1974).

Lalive, J.-F., 'Swiss law and practice in relation to measures of execution against the property of foreign States', 10 Netherl. Yearbook of Int'l L. 153–166 (1979).

Masters, R.D., *Int'l Law in National Courts: A Study of the Enforcement of Int'l Law in German, Swiss, French and Belgian Courts*, Ph.D. Thesis, 1932, Columbia University, New York.

Ralston, J.W., *The Defense of Small States in the Nuclear Age: The case of Sweden and Switzerland*, Geneva 1969.

Switzerland and United Kingdom, 'Treaty on conciliation judicial settlement and arbitration', 4 Int'l Legal Materials 943–956 (1965).

Wildhaber, L., *Treaty-making Power and Constitution. An International and Comparative Study*, Basle/Stuttgart 1971.

——, 'Switzerland, neutrality and the United Nations', 12 Malaya Law Rev. 140–159 (1970).

XV. CIVIL PROCEDURE AND ARBITRATION

After 1982:

Bastard, B. and L. Cardia–Vonèche, 'The Lawyers of Geneva: An Analysis of Change in the Legal Profession' in: R.L. Abel and P.S.C. Lewis (eds.), *Lawyers in Society*, Volume 2: *The Civil Law World*, Berkeley: University of California Press 1988, pp. 295–335.

Berti, S.V. and N.P. Vogt, 'Trial and Court Procedures in Switzerland' in: *Trial and Court Procedures Worldwide*, London: International Bar Association 1991, pp. 172–181.

Berti, S., *Swiss Debt Enforcement and Bankruptcy Law. English translation of the amended Federal statute on Debt Enforcement and Bankruptcy with an introduction to Swiss debt enforcement and bankruptcy law*, Zurich 1997.

Blessing, M., *Introduction to Arbitration*, Basel 1999.

Bucher, A. and P.-Y. Tschanz, *Private International Law and Arbitration*, Basel 1996.

Carr, J., 'The Descreet Charm of the Swiss Lawyer', 5 *International Financial Law Review*, No. 11, 7–10 (1986).

Freimüller, H.-U., 'Attachments and other Interim Court Remedies in Support of Arbitration: Switzerland', 12 *International Business Lawyer* 119–123 (1984).

Habegger, Ph., 'Arbitration and Group of Companies', Eur. Bus. Organization L. Rev. (2002) 517–552.

Habscheid, W.J., 'The Enforcement of Non-money Judgments in Switzerland' in: *Swiss Reports Presented at the XIIth International Congress of Comparative Law* (Sydney/Melbourne, 18–27 August 1986), Zurich: Schultess 1987, pp. 93–109.

Harari, M. and A. Hirsch, 'Swiss Perspective of International Judicial Assistance', 9 *University of Pennsylvania Journal of International Business Law* 519–537 (1987).

Hochstrasser, D., *Commercial Litigation and Enforcement of Foreign Judgments in Switzerland*, Basel 1995.

Imhoos, C., 'The 1992 Geneva Chamber of Commerce and Industry Arbitration Rules under Scrutiny', 9 *Journal of International Arbitration*, No. 4, 121–1339 (1992).

International Arbitration in Switzerland, ed. by S.V. Berti, Kluwer Law International 2000.

Karrer, P.A., 'High tide of private international law codification', L of Business Law 1990, 78–87.

McFadden, J., 'Extraterritoriality: Swiss Supreme Court Refuses United States Request for Information Concerning Insider Trading – Swiss Supreme Court Opinion Concerning Judicial Assistance in the Santa Fe Case, 22 I.L.M. 785 (1983)', 25 *Harvard International Law Journal* 456–463 (1984).

Mirimanoff, J.F., 'Objection to Arbitrators Following the Annulment of a Partial Award: A Potential Jeopardy of Arbitration in Switzerland', *Journal of International Arbitration*, No. 2, 101–105 (1986).

Poudret, J.-F., 'Challenge and Enforcement of Arbitral Awards in Switzerland', 4 *Arbitration International* 278–299 (1988).

Reymond, C., 'Common Law and Civil Law Procedures: Which is the More Inquisitorial?', 55 *Arbitration* 159–164 and 221 (1989).

Schima, H. and H. Hoyer, 'Ordinary Proceedings in First Instance: Central European Countries' in: R. David, H. Engawa *et al.* (eds.), *International Encyclopedia of Comparative Law*, Volume 16: *Civil Procedure*, 1984, pp. 101–140.

Tzchanz, P.-Y., 'A breakthrough in international arbitration: Switzerland's new Arbitration Act', Int'l Law 1107–1118 (1990).

Werner, J., 'Jurisdiction of Arbitrators in Case of Assignment of an Arbitration Clause. On a Recent Decision by the Swiss Supreme Court', 8 *Journal of International Arbitration*, No. 2, 13–22 (1991).

Before 1982:

Bachmann, B., 'The Court of Arbitration of the Zurich Chamber of Commerce' in: Cohn, Domke and Eisemann (eds.), *Handbook of Institutional Arbitration in International Trade*, Amsterdam/New York 1972.

Briner, B., 'Switzerland' (National Report on Arbitration) in: *Yearbook, Commercial Arbitration*, Vol. 3. Deventer: Kluwer 1978.

Guldener, M., 'Switzerland' in: P. Sanders (rapp.), *Arbitrage International Commercial, Union Internationale des Avocats*, Paris: Dalloz et Sirey 1956, pp. 438–467.

Hochstrasser, G., 'A change in the Swiss rules of professional conduct', Int'l Bar J., May 1974 (1974).

Leuenberger, C., 'Swiss Federal Court', 5 Int'l J. of Law Libraries 339–346 (1917).

Morrison, F.L., 'The Swiss Federal Court: Judicial Decision Making and Recruitment' in: J.B. Grossmann and J. Tanenhaus (eds.), *Frontier of Judicial Research*, New York 1969, pp. 133–162.

——, *The Judicial Process in Switzerland: A Study of the Swiss Federal Court*, Princeton 1966.

O'Brien, F.W., 'Jury in Switzerland', 33 Brooklyn L. Rev. 58 (1966).

——, 'Why not appointed counsel in civil cases? The Swiss approach', 28 Ohio State L.J. 1–18 (1967).

Overbeck, A.E. von, 'The role of the judge under the Swiss Civil Code' in: S.J. Stoljar (ed.), *Problems of Codification*, Canberra 1977, pp. 135–150.

Reymond, C., 'The new Swiss Uniform Arbitration Act and international commercial arbitration', Ga. J. Int'l and Comp. L 85–93 (1977).

Rhyne, C.S. (ed.), *Law and Judicial Systems of Nations*, 3rd rev. edn., Washington 1978.

Rice, W.G., 'A glimpse of Swiss intercantonal litigation', 6 Am. J. Comp. L. 235–256(1957).

——, 'Intercantonal public assistance liability in Switzerland', 8 Am. J. Comp. L. 463–484 (1959).

Schindler, D., 'The administration of justice in the Swiss Federal Court in intercantonal disputes' 15 Am. J. Int'l L. 149–188 (1921).

'Swiss Intercantonal Arbitration Convention' in: *Concordat Suisse sur l'arbitrage*, Lausanne: Payot 1974.

Wenner, M.A., 'Swiss judges as arbitrators or as nominators for arbitrators', 35 Arb. J. 22–26 (1980).

Wildhaber, L., 'The Swiss judicial system' in: *Modern Switzerland*, 1978.

Wirth, M.H., 'Attachment of Swiss bank accounts: a remedy for international debt collection', 36 Bus. Lawyer 1029–1040 (1981).

XVI. CRIMINAL LAW AND PROCEDURE

After 1982:

Dijk, J.J.M. van, P. Mayhew and M. Killias, *Experiences of Crime across the World: Key Findings from the 1989 International Crime Survey*, 2nd edn., Deventer/Boston: Kluwer Law and Taxation Publishers 1991.

Imbert, P.-H., 'Reservations to the European Convention on Human Rights before the Strasbourg Commission: The Temeltasch Case', 33 *International and Comparative Law Quarterly* 558–595 (1984).

Killias, M., 'Swiss Research in Victimology in the 1980's: An Overview' in: *Victimes and Criminal Justice*, Volume 1, Freiburg-im-Breisgau: Max-Planck-Insitut für ausländisches und internationales Strafrecht 1991, pp. 55–70.

——, 'Victim-related Alternatives to the Criminal Justice System: Compensation, Restitution and Mediation' in: G. Kaiser and H.-J. Albrecht (eds.), *Crime and Criminal Policy in Europe: Proceedings of the II. Européan Colloquium*, Freiburg-im-Breisgau: Max-Planck-Insitut für ausländisches und internationales Strafrecht 1990, pp. 249–269.

——, 'Recent Trends in Swiss Criminology' in: *Criminological Research in the 80's and beyond*, Freiburg-im-Breisgau: Max-Planck-Insitut für ausländisches und internationales Strafrecht 1988, pp. 75–97.

Pasquier, S.R. and A. von Planta, 'Money Laundering in Switzerland', 18 *International Business Lawyer* 394–397 (1990).

Before 1982:

Bloem, J.H., 'Criminal law – Treaty on mutual assistance in criminal matters between United States and Switzerland', 7 Vanderbilt J. Transnat'l L. 468–479 (1974).

Cohn, S.A., '"Criminal records" – a comparative approach', 4 Georgia J. Int'1 & Comp. Law 116–156 (1974).

Depierre, R., 'Swiss military justice', Mil. L. Rev. 123 (1963).

Kelly, J.T., 'United States foreign policy: efforts to penetrate bank secrecy in Switzerland from 1940 to 1975', 6 Cal. West. Int'l L. J. 211–262 (1976).

Meier, W., 'The organisation of military jurisdiction and the status of judges ad officers of the military justice corps in Switzerland', 11 Rev. Dr. Penal Militaire et Dr. de la Guerre 375–386 (1972).

Pestalozzi–Henggler, A., 'Euthanasia under the Swiss Penal Code', 15 Southwestern L.J. 393 (1961).

Schwartz, B.P., 'The recent Swiss–American treaty to render mutual assistance in criminal law enforcement: An application of the Bank Secrecy Act', 7 New York Univ. J. of Int'l Law and Politics 103–106 (1974).

Veillard–Cybulska, H., 'Modern juvenile codes in Switzerland', 17 Int'l J. Offender Therapy 189–192 (1973).

XVII. TRANSLATION OF OFFICIAL TEXTS

Acquisition of Real Estate in Switzerland by Nonresidents. Swiss Federal Act of 16 December 1983, Zurich: Swiss–American Chamber of Commerce.

Atomic energy 'Draft Federal Order Concerning the Atomic Energy Act', Nuclear L. Bull., No. 20, 45–49 (1977).

Constitutions of the Countries of the World, 'Switzerland', by Flanz and Klein, and Special Supplement, Translation of Draft Constitution, Chronology and Bibliography (by Blaustein, Flanz and Siegenthaler, June 1979), in: Blaustein and Flanz (eds.), *Constitutions of the Countries of the World*, Dobbs Ferry/New York: Oceana Publ. 1982.

'Federal Act of 11 October 1902 concerning the Supervision by the Confederation of the Administration of Forests: Amendments Contained in the Federal Act on Vocational Training, 20 September 1963', 15 *Food and Agricultural Legislation*, No. 2 (1966).

'Federal Act of Patents for Invention of June 25, 1954', 54 Patent and Trade Mark Rev. 279–290, 324–334, 353, 357 (1956).

'Federal Act respecting Work in Industry, Handicraft and Commerce (Labour Act). Dated 13 March 1964', Geneva: International Labor Office, *Legislative Series* No. 3, 1966.

'Federal Act to amend Parts X and X bis of the Code of Obligations (Labour Contracts). Dated 25 June 1971', 1 Int'l Lab. Off. Leg. Ser. Swi. 1–40 (1971).

Federal Constitution of Switzerland (trans. and commentary by Christopher Hughes), Oxford 1954.

'Federal Law of 7 December 1922 Concerning Copyright in Literary and Artistic Works' in: *Copyright Laws and Treaties of the World*, Paris: Unesco 1956.

'Federal Law on Air Navigation of 21 December 1948' in: *U.S. Congress, Senate Committee on Commerce: Air Laws and Treaties of the World*, Washington 1965, pp. 2359–2383.

'Federal Law on Patents for Inventions (of 25 June 1954, as revised on 17 December 1976)',17 Ind. Prop'y June Text 2–001: 001–025; Sept. Text 2–001: 011–012, 023–024 (1978).

'Federal Law Relating to Banks and Savings Banks (of 8 November 1934, as amended by Federal Law of 11 March 1971) including Implementing Ordinance (of 17 May 1972)', (trans. and publ. by the Union Bank of Switzerland), Zurich 1972.

'Federal Law relating to the Procedure of the Federal Assembly and to the Form, Publication and Entry into Force of Legislation, 23 March 1962', 14 *Constitutional and Parliamentary Information* 100–114 (1963).

Instruction Sheet Regarding Current Capital Export Regulations: Swiss National Bank regulations. Issue of 1 March 1990, Zurich: Swiss–American Chamber of Commerce.

'Nuclear protection. Order of the Swiss Federal Department of the Interior on Radiation Protection in Nuclear Research Institutes, of 12 September, 1969', Nuclear L. Bull. No. 4, 31–33 (1969).

Ordinance on Foreign Banks. Ordinance of the Swiss Federal Banking Commission of 22 March 1984, notes, Zurich: Swiss–American Chamber of Commerce.

'Ordinance on Patents for Inventions (Patent Ordinance of 19 October 1977)', 17 Ind. Prop'y, July/Aug. Text 2–002: 001–028 (1978).

Swiss Cartel Law. Synopsis/Official Text of the Swiss Federal Act on Cartels and Similar Organizations of 20 December 1985, Zurich: Swiss–American Chamber of Commerce 1986.

Swiss Civil Code, English version, with Vocabularies and Notes, by Ivy Williams, Oxford 1925; Zurich 1976.

Swiss Civil Code of 10 December 1907 (trans. by R.P. Schick, Annotated by C. Wetherhill, Corrected and Revised by E. Huber, A. Siegwart, G.E. Sherman), Boston 1915.

Swiss Civil Code Articles 641–977 (trans. by W. H. Diggelmann, J.H. Farnum, M. Frey, B.F. Meyer–Hauser, A.E Reber), Zurich 1999.

Swiss Code of Obligations, Volume I: *Contract Law, Articles 1–551*, 3rd edn., Zurich: Swiss–American Chamber of Commerce 1995.

Swiss Code of Obligations, Volume II: *Company Law, Articles 552–964*, Zurich: Swiss–American Chamber of Commerce 1992.

Swiss Contract Law, English translation of selected official texts: Swiss Code of Obligations, Zurich: Amer. Chamber of Commerce 1974.

Swiss Corporation Law, English version of Official texts, Zurich: Amer. Chamber of Commerce 1974.

Swiss Company Law in the European Context (S. Wyler, R. Watter, J. Wyler), St. Gallen 1994.

Swiss Company Law, 2nd edn. (Bruno Becchio, V. Wehinger, A.S. Farha, S. Siegel), Bern 1996.

Swiss Debt Enforcement and Bankruptcy Law (Stephen Berti), Zurich 1997.

Swiss Corporation Law (R. Bosch, D.A. Würsch), Zurich 1992.

Swiss Federal Act on International Private Law. Federal Act of 13 December 1987, Zurich: Swiss–American Chamber of Commerce 1989.

'Swiss Federal Statute on Private International Law of 18 December 1987' (trans by J.C. Cornu *et al.*) 2 *Epitheorese Kypriakou Dikaiou* 4675–4721 (1990).

Swiss Federal Act on International Private Law (F.H. Thomann, B.F. Meyer–Hauser, A. Reber, G.E. Insley), Zurich 1984.

'Swiss Nationality Law. Berne, 29th Sept., 1952', 160 *British and Foreign State Papers* 771–785 (1962).

Swiss Pension Fund Law. Federal Law on the Occupational Old Age, Survivors' and Disability Benefit Plan, Zurich: Swiss–American Chamber of Commerce 1983.

Swiss Securities Law. Parts, Swiss Code of Obligations, Federal Law and Ordinances regarding Investment Funds, Zurich Stock Exchange: Law on Professional Trading of Securities, Listing Regulations, Zurich: Swiss–American Chamber of Commerce 1982.

Swiss Work Permit Regulations. Overview of the Permit System. Federal Council's Ordinance, Types of permits, Qualifying Criteria, Quotas, Zurich: Swiss–American Chamber of Commerce, regular updates.

Switzerland's Private International Law, 2nd edn. (A.P Karrer, Karl W. Arnold, P. Patocchi), Zurich 1994.

Tax Laws of the World: Switzerland, Vol. 1, 2nd rev. edn. Florida: Foreign Tax Law Association 1977 *et seq.* (looseleaf).

'Translation of Legal Texts: Three English Versions of the Swiss Federal Statute on Private International Law' (trans. by W. König). 11 *Michigan Yearbook of International Legal Studies* 1294–1300 (1989–1990).

Index

References are to pages.

Lightning Source UK Ltd.
Milton Keynes UK
UKOW04n1603070414

229446UK00008BA/35/P